The Making of a Black Communist

A VOLUME IN THE SERIES
African American Intellectual History
EDITED BY
Christopher Cameron

The Making of a Black Communist

The Selected Writings of Eugene Gordon

EDITED BY Louis J. Parascandola

University of Massachusetts Press
Amherst and Boston

Copyright © 2025 by University of Massachusetts Press
All rights reserved

ISBN 978-1-62534-868-5 (paper); 869-2 (hardcover)

Designed by Sally Nichols
Set in Miller Text
Printed and bound by Books International, Inc.

Cover design by adam b. bohannon
Cover photo by unknown, *portrait of Eugene Gordon*, c. 1945.
Courtesy of Chiwe Gordon.

Library of Congress Cataloging-in-Publication Data
A catalog record for this book is available from the Library of Congress.

British Library Cataloguing-in-Publication Data
A catalog record for this book is available from the British Library.

This book is dedicated to my grandfather, Eugene Gordon. Thank you for always choosing to do the right thing.

Your lifelong contribution to Black American history shall be noted here for generations to come.

—CHIWE GORDON

Contents

Acknowledgments xi

Introduction 1

A Note on the Selections and the Text 31

Autobiographical Writings   33

"SOUTHERN BOYHOOD NIGHTMARES"
International Literature (APRIL 1934): 49–58   34

EXCERPT "ONCE I WAS AFRAID"
No Date, Unpublished, Eugene Gordon Papers   50

"NEW ORLEANS NEGRO FAMILY"
No Date, Unpublished, Eugene Gordon Papers   68

"KILLER AT LARGE"
No Date, Unpublished, Eugene Gordon Papers   82

"JIM PETERS' BLACK BOY"
No Date, Unpublished, Eugene Gordon Papers   96

"HOW LT. GORDON TOOK HIS SEVEN COLORED HEROES
INTO THE JAWS OF DEATH—AND BACK AGAIN"
Boston Post (Sunday Supplement) (APRIL 20, 1919): 40.   104

Fiction   113

"ROOTBOUND"
Opportunity (SEPTEMBER 1926): 279–83, 299   114

"GAME"
Opportunity (SEPTEMBER 1927): 264–69   128

"COLD-BLOODED"
Saturday Evening Quill (JUNE 1928): 48–51   144

"BUZZARDS"
Opportunity (NOVEMBER 1928): 338–42 154

"SARCOPHAGUS"
Saturday Evening Quill (JUNE 1929): 36–39 166

"THE AGENDA"
Opportunity (DECEMBER 1933): 372–74; (JANUARY 1934): 18–22 . . . 176

"GOOD THING IT WASN'T A COLD NIGHT"
Circa 1943, Unpublished, Eugene Gordon Papers 192

"AND I ASK, *WHY*?"
No Date, Unpublished, Eugene Gordon Papers 200

Nonfiction . . . 205

EXCERPT "THE NEGRO PRESS"
American Mercury (June 1926): 207–15 206

"THE OPPORTUNITY DINNER: An Impression"
Opportunity (JULY 1927): 208–9 218

"THE NEGRO'S INHIBITIONS"
American Mercury (FEBRUARY 1928): 159–64 224

"A WORD IN CLOSING"
Saturday Evening Quill (June 1928): 72 238

EXCERPT "CHRISTIANITY AND THE NEGRO"
The Lantern (MARCH 1929): 14–18 242

"THE NEGRO GROWS UP"
Plain Talk (JULY 1929): 81–86 248

EXCERPT "NEGRO SOCIETY"
Scribner's Magazine (AUGUST 1930): 134–42 258

"THE LEGION TAKES BOSTON"
The Nation (OCTOBER 29, 1930): 469–71 270

"THE NEGRO'S NEW LEADERSHIP"
New Masses (JULY 1931): 14–15 276

CONTENTS

"SCOTTSBORO—AND THE NICE PEOPLE"
Labor Defender (AUGUST 1931): 157 — 284

"NEGRO NOVELISTS AND THE NEGRO MASSES"
New Masses (JULY 1933): 16–20 — 288

"BLACKS TURN RED"
Negro, edited by Nancy Cunard, Wishart & Co., 1934 — 300

EXCERPT "THE BORDEN CASE: *The Struggle for Negro Rights in Boston*"
League of Struggle for Negro Rights (AUGUST 13, 1934) — 312

"THE POSITION OF NEGRO WOMEN"
(Gordon with Cyril Briggs), Workers Library Publishers, 1935 — 318

"FROM 'UNCLE TOM'S CABIN' TO 'STEVEDORE'"
New Theatre (JULY 1935): 21–23 — 332

"HOW PROSTITUTION HAS BEEN FOUGHT AND ALMOST COMPLETELY ELIMINATED IN THE USSR"
Moscow Daily News (APRIL 1937): 6 — 340

"ALABAMA AUTHORITIES IGNORE WHITE GANG'S RAPE OF NEGRO MOTHER"
Daily Worker (NOVEMBER 19, 1944): 10 — 346

"CULT OF THE WHITE WOMAN"
1944, Unpublished, Eugene Gordon Papers — 350

EXCERPT "BLACK WOMEN'S LONG TOUGH COURSE":
From 'Dat Gal' Carline to This Woman Angela," 1972
Unpublished, Eugene Gordon Papers — 362

Notes   369
Index   385

Acknowledgments

I wish to thank those who made this project possible:

My students and colleagues at Long Island University, Brooklyn, where I have taught for over thirty years. I particularly wish to thank one of my former graduate students, Tiani Kennedy. She has been a friend, sounding board, and often unofficial editor.

My editor, Brian Halley, who has patiently guided me through this process and Christopher Cameron, coeditor of the African American Intellectual Series. I would also like to thank Ben Kimball, production editor, Sally Nichols, EDP manager, and the rest of the staff at the University of Massachusetts Press for their help and support. In addition, I thank the anonymous reviewers of the manuscript whose suggestions, and sometimes criticisms, helped make this a better book.

My deepest gratitude goes to Chiwe Gordon, Eugene's granddaughter, for allowing me access to and to publish from the Eugene Gordon Papers at the Schomburg Library, part of the New York Public Library. Chi's encouragement and support were vital to the project.

The staff at the Schomburg Library, particularly in the Archives and the Prints and Photographs collections. The Eugene Gordon Papers are housed in the Schomburg Center for Black Culture, part of the New York Public Library.

From the moment I first reached out to Professors Verner Mitchell and Cynthia Davis, they have given encouragement and advice. Their book *Literary Sisters* has been a guide for me. I also thank Verner for sending me copies of Eugene Gordon's FBI files.

I wish to thank my brother, John, who as usual has been a great source of support and encouragement, reading parts of the manuscript and offering helpful suggestions. The Nero family has also provided comfort and support.

My biggest debt, as always, goes to my wife, Shondel Nero, who continues to be my greatest source of strength. She has patiently read and discussed all things Gordon over the past few years, taking time out from her own valuable research to assist me. Our endless discussion provided not only a helpful ear but also a necessary distraction from work. I look forward to sharing more love and adventures together.

Introduction

A popular communist work song of the 1930s has the line "Negroes ain' black—but RED!"[1] This description aptly applies to Eugene Ferdinand Gordon, an African American writer and activist who became a dedicated communist. Gordon's biographer, Daniel Candee, describes him and his second wife, June Croll, as being Zelig-like[2] characters, "the Communist everyman and everywoman, fleeting representatives of those who lurk in single sentences within more famous radicals' memoirs, in brief acknowledgments of their actions or arrest in newspapers, in FBI files, and in the corners of photographs."[3] However, in many ways, this underestimates Gordon's actual contributions to Black radical politics and literary movements, which were often not merely on the periphery. This type of assessment is unfortunately common when considering Gordon, who not only was everywhere but, in fact, was often an active, sometimes central, figure in what was happening around him.

Born and raised in the South, Gordon was a reporter, editor, fiction writer, and political activist. After moving North, he wrote for the *Boston Post* and became a leading figure in the burgeoning Boston Renaissance movement in the 1920s. Gordon was the founder of the Saturday Night Quill Club, whose members included such luminaries as Dorothy West and Helene Johnson, and editor and contributor to the club's journal, the *Saturday Evening Quill* (or simply the *Quill*). He also was part of the Harlem Renaissance, editing and publishing in two of the most important Black periodicals of the period, *The Messenger* and *Opportunity*. In addition, he was a contributor to numerous leading mainstream journals such as *Scribner's Magazine*, the *American Mercury*, and *The Nation*. Finally, he was a long-standing member of the Communist Party and an author and editor for such leading communist journals as the *New Masses*, the *Moscow Daily News*, and the *Daily Worker*. Furthermore, he was often at the forefront of many of the party's most significant activities between 1930 and 1945, including the Scottsboro Boys incident, the George Borden shooting in Boston, and the Recy Taylor rape case in Alabama.

Why then has he been so unfairly neglected? Perhaps one reason is that it is not easy to place him neatly within a movement, as a somewhat genteel author involved in literary circles in Boston and New York or as a hardcore Marxist, one who held onto his communist beliefs long after many had ended their relationship with the party by the time of the Hitler-Stalin pact of 1939.[4] As a member "in good standing" of the Communist Party, Gordon was under constant FBI surveillance and was forced to resort to using pseudonyms in a desperate attempt to publish his writings.[5] Despite this seeming shift in his political views, it is possible to trace the trajectory of Gordon's transformation into a communist. The seeds were planted in his hardscrabble youth in the Jim Crow South and bloomed in his later migration to Boston and New York. Gordon's passion for social justice and his courageous stand against oppression, traits he learned early from his father, remained a constant thread in his life and work.

To get a real sense of Gordon, and where to place him, one needs to consider him in his totality, to read his autobiographical, literary, and political writings, and to see the ways in which his ideas developed and changed. It is then possible to observe some consistent traits that connect the different genres he worked with as well as the different phases of his life. The necessary rehabilitation of Gordon's reputation has already begun in recent years.[6] However, a fulsome study of him has been hindered by the lack of a collection of his various writings, creating a lacuna that has made it difficult to examine his work in any depth. This anthology intends to fill this gap in the existing literature and, it is hoped, enhance interest and knowledge in this significant, but still understudied, figure, one at the forefront of movements advocating workers' rights, anti-imperialism, and antiracism.

GORDON'S YOUTH IN FLORIDA

Gordon's views largely have come out of his early upbringing in the South, his time in school at Howard University, the years he served in the US Army, his time spent as a reporter, and, finally, his many years as a member of the Communist Party. His life was shaped initially by his parents. His father, Elijah Gordon, was a seminal influence on Eugene. Elijah, a Georgia-born native, was taken to Liberia as a three-year-old boy by several family members in 1871 as part of

INTRODUCTION   3

an early Black nationalist emigration plan. The scheme failed, and by 1881, Elijah was the only one still alive. He was brought back to the United States by his well-off father, Charles Gordon, and once rescued, Elijah would go on to travel throughout Europe and gain a certain sophistication that would inform his encounters with others, particularly whites. Eugene would revere his father, who became a minister, for the remainder of his life, no doubt inspired by his worldliness, his principled behavior, his courage and strength, and his ability to survive the ordeals he endured at such a young age and in his later encounters with American racism. His father's skepticism of Black emigration schemes, such as Marcus Garvey's plan to return to Africa in the 1920s, and his desire to remain in America and be an American, was also indelibly burnt into Eugene's consciousness.[7]

After returning to the United States, Elijah migrated to Oviedo, Florida, and married Lillian Burke in 1888, with Eugene being born on November 23, 1891. Oviedo was first settled by the Timucua, a branch of the Seminole Indian tribe. During and shortly after the Civil War, homesteaders arrived and Oviedo became a village of about eight hundred people, part of the thriving citrus and celery industry in central Florida. Located about eighteen miles from the more urban center of Orlando, the hamlet became important once the Oviedo Depot was built by developer Henry Bradley Plant as part of his railroad system in 1887.[8] The railroad's arrival boded well for the town's prosperity and attracted many African Americans to work the land. However, despite its newfound good fortune, the city was far from a paradise for Blacks, marred by white racism as Black plantation hands increased. As one white Floridian newspaperman stated, "One race or the other must leave and the whites are going to remain."[9] Blacks who chose to stay learned a bitter lesson, as turn-of-the-century Florida had more per capita lynchings than anywhere else in the United States. The state retained that dubious distinction for the next quarter of a century.[10]

NEW ORLEANS

Not surprisingly, this virulent racism, coupled with a series of cold spells that damaged the citrus crop, caused Elijah to pack up his family in about 1895 and move to South Rampart Street in the northernmost part of the French Quarter in New Orleans. "South Rampart Street was the main commercial corridor in 'back o' town,' originally a swampy area at the rear of the city where New Orleans' racial order relegated Black residents in the late 1800s."[11] It soon became a vibrant part of the city. Here, Elijah Gordon opened a small shop where he sold ice, coal, and wood and, when money was tight, occasionally worked as a longshoreman.[12]

Arriving in a city of almost three hundred thousand after having lived his early years in a place with fewer than one thousand inhabitants must have been a shock for young Eugene. Although New Orleans's racial diversity, including Creoles of many shades with all the attendant tensions, was exciting, it must have also taken some adjustment. While Jim Crow segregation was on the rise at the time Gordon's family arrived, the city "remained surprisingly integrated as far as housing for the laboring class was concerned."[13] However, the close proximity between the races may have only heightened white racism. Most whites felt that Blacks were inherently inferior by nature. Henry "Major" Hearsey, a white supremacist journalist, went so far as to advocate for the genocide of Blacks, stating that a race war was inevitable and perhaps even desirable: "Then the negro problem of Louisiana at least will be solved—and that by extermination."[14]

Gordon spoke of the racism he encountered in the city in several writings, including his unpublished autobiography, "Once I Was Afraid."[15] Here he listens as Blacks describe a white man as being "like a snake in the grass." He learns of a white man and his light-complexioned wife being lynched and how Gordon's mother was glad that the woman as well as the man was also killed for "Foolin round with a white man." Nowhere is this animosity between the races more palpably expressed than in the unpublished semiautobiographical piece "Killer at Large." It was the racist attitudes of people like Henry Hearsey that led to the violent shooting spree by an irate Black man, Robert Charles, who was illegally arrested. Charles's pent-up fury at his mistreatment was unleashed in July 1900, which led to him shooting several white policemen, ending with his eventual brutal death at the hands of the police. The white backlash was horrific as twenty-eight people were killed and over fifty wounded; most of the victims were Black. The lesson that Eugene learned from this incident about the simmering effects of racism and the ultimate futility of its consequences would long remain in his psyche.

HAWKINSVILLE, GEORGIA

The Robert Charles episode and its bloody aftermath served as an impetus for Eugene's father to move once more, about 1903, this time back to his own hometown of Hawkinsville, Georgia. Hawkinsville was a return to the rural South. In 1900 the town had 2,103 residents, a total that would increase to 3,420 in 1910.[16] With an economy based on cotton and its placement in transporting people and goods along the Ocmulgee River, Hawkinsville was going through a relative boom period when the Gordons moved there. However, it, like Oviedo and New Orleans, was no panacea for racism. In "Southern Boyhood Nightmares" Gordon recounts several horrific encounters with racism in Hawkinsville. In one, he was almost lynched by a white mob after standing up to a white man who ran Eugene and his vehicle off the road. He was only saved when an elderly white man, an ex-Confederate soldier, who was a friend of Gordon's father and grandfather, spoke up in his defense. This was not enough, however, for Gordon's father, who returned with his pistol, ready to seek justice. Again, it is "the same austere man who, earlier, in the morning, had interceded for me" that restores order. Thus, Gordon learned that some whites were not enemies but allies.

Gordon learned other lessons as well, some not as optimistic. In one incident, Gordon witnessed the burnt remains of a preacher who had been roasted for using a gun to defend himself from a white man.[17] In "Jim Peters' Black Boy," Peters' helper Ad is treated as a slave by his owner. His inner rage, as it had with Robert Charles, wells up and finally leads him to kill Peters, fulfilling Eugene's father's prediction that when the Black boy does wake up, "That will be the day Jim Peters goes to sleep never to wake up."

THE IMPACT OF GORDON'S GROWING UP IN THE SOUTH

Lorraine Elena Roses, citing some passages from Gordon's biographical notes in the Eugene Gordon papers, indicates that the writer's youth in Florida and New Orleans is conjured up as "idyllic" and "a childhood paradise."[18] While Gordon took great comfort in his family life, his unpublished autobiography, telling tales filled with racial discrimination, belies this bucolic notion of his childhood. He tells his autobiography in the straightforward reporter's style he knew so well. He lets the details tell the story, sink in for the reader, offering little commentary of his own; however, Gordon's early years in the South would have an enormous impact on him. It was a time when he saw numerous reactions to the white racism that was all around him. He recalls his mother teaching him "that to be called a 'nigger' was to be outraged, humiliated, degraded. It was a signal for immediate combat. A white man's smile of friendship, she insisted, was like Judas' kiss. My mother taught me that no white man was to be considered seriously as a friend: he was not to be trusted." Eugene's mother was a brave woman who would forcefully defend herself and her children if necessary, but her instinctive behavior was to avoid whites at all costs and to try to have her husband protect the family. Gordon's paternal grandfather, on the other hand, advised Eugene he "must not for a moment 'forget' who and where he is." Avoid whites whenever possible and act deferential when an encounter was unavoidable. This seems to comport with Booker T. Washington's accommodationist strategy: try to fit in with whites and not cause problems. This distrustful if pragmatic advice from his mother and grandfather about dealing with whites contrasted sharply with what he was taught by his father: to resist racism forcefully and stand up for one's rights, but to try to develop relationships with potential white allies if possible. Elijah believed that Blacks should not be fearful of whites; moreover, he taught Eugene that not all whites were the enemy. Elijah's courage and unbending principles would be qualities that would remain with Eugene in adulthood.

Gordon took another lesson from the Robert Charles incident, one reinforcing what he had learned from his father. The young boy had heard tales that some poor whites had expressed muted admiration for the Black man's bold act of defiance. They could identify with his rage since they suffered similarly from poverty and police brutality. The boy was beginning to conceive that working-class whites and racial minorities might be able to unite to fight a common foe. Such an alliance would be the worst nightmare for both racists and capitalists. Despite the rampant racism Gordon had witnessed in the South, he saw the power that could be exerted when whites aligned with Blacks, as was the case with the elderly gentleman in "Southern Boyhood Nightmares." Although there are immediate thoughts of, out of frustration and anger, wanting to inflict pain on all whites, Gordon's time in the South also provided the first steps on his path of wanting to work with allied whites against common oppressive forces. By the time Gordon left his childhood experiences behind, a transformation had begun to take place in him as he relates in "Southern Boyhood Nightmares": "My mind was finally able to evolve out of, shake itself free of, the grotesque 'race' psychology in which the environment of my youth had clothed it." As Daniel Candee states, "Something had changed between Eugene's boyhood nightmares and adult reflections."[19] Although he was not yet a Communist, he had already, even if unknowingly, begun to gravitate toward it as a path to combating racism.

WASHINGTON, DC, AND MARRIAGE

In 1912, Gordon gradually inched his way out of the Deep South, attending Howard University in Washington, DC. Despite his intelligence, Gordon's time in the South had not fully prepared him to attend the most prestigious African American school in the country. As he states in his "Autobiographical Notes," he "was never scholastically or financially prepared to stay at Howard."[20] In fact, he writes that he entered "as a candidate for the high school, or prep, or Academy, department of the University."[21] His limited financial resources were also a challenge. He received little from his family, even his better-off grandfather, who thought Eugene should make it on his own. He worked as a janitor and as a waiter to help with expenses; however, he had to wear well-worn clothes to his classes, which caused him shame.[22] Although he never graduated, the two years Gordon spent at Howard introduced him to the world of the Black intelligentsia, including Alain Locke, one of his teachers, and the English and journalism courses he took would help prepare him for his future career as a journalist.[23]

While in Washington, Gordon met Edythe Mae Chapman (1896–?);

they married on January 10, 1916. In Boston, the two shared a number of households. Chapman had studied at the well-known M Street School from 1912 to 1916 where she may have been taught by writer Jessie Fauset. She went on to attend Boston University, graduating with a bachelor of science degree in religious education and social services in 1934 and a master's degree in social services in 1935.[24] While both Eugene and Edythe had shared interests in writing, their union, for a variety of reasons to be discussed later, was not a happy one.

MILITARY

In 1917, after leaving college, Gordon attempted to join the army, perhaps in the same patriotic spirit encouraged by W. E. B. Du Bois, who, in his editorial "Close Ranks" (*Crisis*, July 1918), urged African Americans to join the armed forces in the hope the country would reward their service upon their return. Regardless, Gordon's initial experience with the military was unsuccessful. He had hoped to become an officer in the highly competitive training at Fort Des Moines but was rejected. Lieutenants W. N. Colson and A. B. Nutt speak about the difficulties for African Americans to succeed in their essay "The Failure of the Ninety-Second Division," a unit that seemed designed "to operate for the purpose of causing the failure of those who might ultimately become officers."[25] Dejected by his failure to become an officer, he returned home but was soon drafted.

Despite his initial rejection, Gordon had a distinguished military career. He received training at Fort Devers near Boston and then at Camp Upton on Long Island before being sent to France and made a Second Lieutenant in the Ninety-Second Division.[26] While in the army, he participated in the bloody battles of the Argonne and Metz.[27] Theodore Roosevelt was chosen honorary president of Gordon's regiment after he gave an address to the soldiers.[28] Gordon wrote of one particularly harrowing war experience in an article for the *Boston Post* (Sunday Supplement) on April 20, 1919, "How Lt. Gordon Took His Seven Colored Heroes into the Jaws of Death— and Back Again." In this encounter Gordon led his men into enemy territory and came back with several captured German soldiers. For this action, he was awarded a World War I Liberty Medal and the

INTRODUCTION 9

French Croix de Guerre. While serving he also founded and edited "the *Bayonet*, the official publication for the 2nd Separate Battalion of the Massachusetts National Guard."[29]

BOSTON

Upon his return from World War I, Gordon moved to Boston, perhaps to avoid the South, with all its lynchings in the deadly Red Summer of 1919. Gordon may have also chosen to live in Boston because he felt that "without doubt Massachusetts remains until now the most liberally disposed state toward Negroes." However, employment was the chief reason for his move.[30] Gordon's article on his military heroics in the *Boston Post* was his entry into the world of journalism. He took a position at the newspaper where he was initially employed as a copy editor. Gordon soon rose in the ranks, editing three columns: the page for women, recipes, and short stories. He became one of the first Black managing editors of a major white newspaper, continuing at the *Post* until 1938. While working at the *Post*, Gordon also took courses in journalism at Boston University.

Blacks have always had a complicated relationship with Boston. It has been the home of such prominent figures as Revolutionary War hero Crispus Attucks, poet Phillis Wheatley, abolitionist Prince Hall, orator Maria Stewart, activist David Walker, school integrationist William C. Nell, and Underground Railroad leaders Lewis and Harriet Hayden among many others. However, while the city is often seen as the cradle of liberty and one of the most progressive places in America, it has not always been welcoming to its Black residents. Slavery had existed in Boston since 1630 and was gradually ended in 1783, not because of an abolitionist spirit but because owners' rights to possess slaves were no longer protected. The New England Anti-Slavery Society was established in 1832, and the city was the birthplace of white abolitionist William Lloyd Garrison's groundbreaking newspaper *The Liberator*. It was where the famed all-Black 54th Massachusetts Regiment that fought valiantly in the Civil War was formed. Unfortunately, however, the many anti-abolitionists in the city "were generally not supportive of drives for social equality."[31]

After the Civil War, the Black population in the city soared as part of the Great Migration from the South, expanding to almost twelve thousand by 1900. Soon Black immigrants from the Caribbean and Africa would come as well.[32] These initial migrants resided largely in the West End on the North Slope of Beacon Hill, derisively called "Nigger Hill" by many white Bostonians.[33] Racism intensified with these shifting demographics, particularly marked by the influx of Irish immigrants who were often in competition for low-paying jobs with African Americans. The first Irish mayor of the city, Hugh O'Brien, took office in 1885. "In capturing city hall, the Irish took the municipal jobs, appointments and patronage that went with it, including control over police, fire, and the Boston Public schools."[34] The Irish continued to control the powerful mayoral position for the next few decades, capped by the election of Democrat James Curley, who served four terms as mayor beginning in 1914. Sensing that the only way to hold even a modicum of power was to concede to the Irish, "a group of local Black political leaders traded power for patronage."[35] The city still retains this generally negative reputation among many African Americans.

This was the challenging environment that Gordon entered when he moved to the city after World War 1 when Blacks made up only 2.2 percent of the total population in the city, most living in Lower Roxbury and the South End areas, which housed the majority of Boston's twenty-one thousand Black citizens.[36] Gordon would be a part of this relatively small group of "Afro-Bostonians," to use Lorraine Elena Roses's term, and soon helped form its "Boston renascence." Regardless of the racial environment, he found success in the city, joining Boston's "Talented Tenth." By 1925, he and Edythe were living in "a gracious neighborhood one-half mile northwest of Harvard."[37] He seemed on his way to the top, but there was the constant fear of white authority he had learned both in his upbringing and in his time in the war.[38]

THE SATURDAY EVENING QUILL CLUB

Once ensconced in Boston, Gordon soon immersed himself in the city's fledgling Black cultural movement, organizing the Saturday Evening Quill Club in 1925; the club would often assemble at Gordon's

Cambridge home, and he edited annual anthologies of the members' work from 1928 to 1930. The purpose of the journal was "originally conceived as an experiment, . . . containing essays, articles, poems, short stories, and plays by Negro writers, and drawings by Negro artists, [all] . . . members of the Club for distribution among themselves and a few interested friends."[39] He also said that the writers did not intend to start "a revolution." There were a range of opinions expressed by the contributors to the journal, but in general it was somewhat conservative both in its politics and in its literary style, unlike more radical literary journals such as Wallace Thurman's *Fire!*. Gordon also stressed an American tone. As editor, and in his own writings, there was no return to Africa, either literally as Marcus Garvey proposed or culturally as advocates like Alain Locke recommended. Instead, Gordon "considered the Afro-American to be as American as apple pie. . . . Gordon realized that black writers had some rich sources unavailable to whites, but he asserted that they must use the 'same method' and 'the same medium,' or language available to white authors."[40] It is also notable that although all of its members were Black, the club was open to other races, which "is significant when one considers that a few years later, Gordon would embrace communism, an ideology that minimized the importance of race and maximized that of class."[41]

The *Quill* was funded by members of the club without any white sponsors. Members in addition to Gordon and his wife included authors Dorothy West, Helene Johnson, Florida Ruffin Ridley, Waring Cuney, Gertrude "Toki" Schalk, theatrical producer Ralf Coleman, and artist Lois Mailou Jones.[42] Gordon collected these disparate talents and was able to meld them into a coherent whole. He mentored several of the younger writers such as West, perhaps influencing the direction of her writings since both of their works tend to be "geographically precise and grounded in a gritty urbanism and a proletarian aesthetic." In addition, their stories often "are bleak depictions of mismatched couples trapped by finances and social pressure."[43] Gordon was a particularly strong advocate for the women, who made up a majority of the members of the club.

Gordon was the driving force behind the *Quill*, and he did an excellent job editing the magazine. He was essentially a one-man show as he did "all the work from selecting the writings to deciding upon the type, the art and the format and reading all proof from first to last."[44] The annual publication received favorable reviews from the *Boston Herald*, the *Amsterdam News*, and *Commonweal*.[45] Gordon also wrote short stories, poems, and essays for the *Quill*. In "Negro Fictionists in America" he complained that African American writers could not get fiction accepted in Black magazines unless it was simple, uplifting, wholesome, formulaic, and above all, focused on Harlem. Authors were often pressured "to 'interpret' Harlem to the satisfaction of those who were willing to pay enormously for the *right* 'interpretation.'"[46] Gordon's fiction in the *Quill* did none of those things. Instead, he wrote pieces with dark humor, irony, and violence, stories that often ended with a twist. "Cold-Blooded" (June 1928), for instance, tells of a reporter who is criticized for not putting enough passion into his articles until he is assigned to cover a fire that takes place in his own home. "Sarcophagus" (June 1929) concerns a white professor of Egyptology who is confronted by a Black man who insists what the professor is teaching is all wrong and that ancient Egyptians and Ethiopians were Black. The meeting ends in tragedy for both men. Although the *Quill* was successful, the annual issues ended after the 1930 edition, in part because Gordon's "interests were far to the left of most of the members."[47]

HARLEM RENAISSANCE

At the same time that Gordon was helping to grow a "Boston Renaissance," he was beginning to venture forth into the larger Harlem Renaissance. He was managing editor of an important Harlem Renaissance magazine, *The Messenger*, during 1927–28. *The Messenger* had begun as the house organ for the Brotherhood of Sleeping Car Porters headed by A. Philip Randolph and Chandler Owen. In its early years the periodical was socialist in its leanings, but by the time of Gordon's tenure, it had toned down its radical politics and was near the end of its run.

Gordon also attended the *Opportunity* dinner in 1927 and developed friendships with such luminaries as Langston Hughes, Richard Wright, and Paul Robeson. He wrote four stories for *Opportunity*, the organ of the National Urban League: "Rootbound," "Game," "Buzzards," and "The Agenda," all winning literary prizes. Despite these awards, and the accolades of his contemporaries, Gordon has, with the notable exceptions of Lorraine Elena Roses, Verner Mitchell, and Cynthia Davis, been virtually ignored as a literary figure. This is perhaps not surprising given that until recent years many literary critics have virtually ignored the influence "of the Marxist-Leninist nation thesis and its focus on black folk culture as the basis for a national, oppositional culture."[48] Although not all of his fiction writing is top tier, Gordon's stories augment the wealth of Black literature in the 1920s and '30s, adding another voice to those such as Langston Hughes, Claude McKay, Richard Wright, and Ralph Ellison who "with varying degrees of enthusiasm, embraced some aspects of the 'black nation' thesis."[49]

Gordon's early fiction writings were all in fairly mainstream Black publications such as the *Quill* and *Opportunity*, not like the overtly radical political ones where Gordon's nonfiction would appear in a few years. However, the stories listed above from *Opportunity*, with themes of violence, colorism, misogyny, and marital discord, perhaps portend the problems in his own relationship with Edythe,[50] his dislike of being defined solely by race, his inner struggles over authoring pieces for establishment Black periodicals, and the beginnings of his radical political beliefs. His self-penned note in *Opportunity* (July 1927) demonstrates his frequently caustic wit: "I was born colored in Oviedo, Florida, and have remained more or less so since. I honestly admit I am not proud of being known everywhere I go and by everything I do as a colored man. I [am] less annoyed in this respect, however, in Massachusetts than [in] Washington, D.C, or Oviedo, or New Orleans."[51] Gordon would author one more story for *Opportunity*, a full-throated paeon to Communism, "The Agenda" (1933–34). It would be his final piece of published fiction and his last significant piece in a non-Marxist venue.

WRITING FOR THE MAINSTREAM PRESS

In the late 1920s and early '30s, Gordon began to publish essays in a wide range of periodicals, including several mainstream ones such as *American Mercury, Plain Talk, Scribner's Magazine*, and *The Nation*. He was one of a handful of Black writers who was able to reach publication outside of African American venues. All of these pieces tend to be satirical and critical of African American and capitalist society. His first major piece with a mainstream journal was "The Negro Press" (*American Mercury*, June 1926). The periodical, edited by the iconoclastic H. L. Mencken, helped gain Gordon a wider, more diverse audience than would generally be the case in African American publications such as *The Messenger* and *Opportunity*. Gordon had already evaluated Black magazines for *Opportunity*, and he selected the month's best editorials for *The Messenger*, often angering editors with his choices. In the *American Mercury* piece, he dismisses the vast majority of Black weeklies as "little more than waste paper" and narrows down to about a dozen those that are reputable. Nevertheless, even these select papers are largely influenced by the white papers. This scathing indictment of the Black press further infuriated many Black editors.[52]

Gordon's sardonic humor is also on display in some of his nonfiction pieces from this period. These articles, often critical of African American behavior, again angered many Blacks as they felt Gordon was holding them up to scrutiny in front of whites. "The Negro's Inhibitions" (*American Mercury*, February 1928), for example, was widely read, and many readers offered their opinions on it, good or bad. Gordon's scrapbook provides over twenty reviews and letters to the editor about the article,[53] many of the Black commenters discussing their fears of conforming to white stereotypes of them:

> He [the Negro] is afraid to be seen eating a pork chop, or even a wing of fried chicken. The sight of a watermelon sets him to blushing. When he sings his spirituals, it is in an affected and "artistic" manner; the old innocent gusto is gone. When he needs a razor he sends a white agent to buy it for him. He is ashamed to be caught drinking gin. He forbids his wife to wear gaudy clothes. He is ashamed of his kinky hair, and tries to get rid of its kinks. He spends many thousands annually on quack decoctions guaranteed to bleach his skin.

In "The Negro Grows Up" in *Plain Talk* (July 1929), there are several indications of his changing views. He praises Blacks for their growing ability to hold themselves up to the mirror:

There are involved at least six factors that tend to prove the truth of my assertion. The first is that the American Negro has become critical of himself and thereby tolerant of outside criticism. Second, he is less credulous of and also somewhat cynical toward what his preachers tell him about heaven and hell. Third, he has fewer inhibitions than formerly. Fourth, he is beginning to chafe under the patronage of paternalistic whites and to show evidence of desiring to propel his own craft. Fifth, he has begun a serious but enthusiastic study of Negro history. And, sixth, he is less distrustful of and bears less prejudice toward whites than was once the case.

Notable among these factors are the increasing distrust of organized religion and the need for working with whites to advance common causes. These would be growing concerns of his. In concluding the article, Gordon speaks about the transformation of Blacks as not being complete: "He will continue to develop for some time, for he has not yet reached full growth." Ironically, this was also the case for Gordon's own development into a communist. In this article, for example, he still extols more conservative-leaning Black thinkers such as George Schuyler, whom he would soon excoriate, and he would praise "excellent" mainstream groups such as the NAACP and the Urban League for having both Black and white members.

Gordon criticized not just Blacks in these articles. He was unafraid to roast whites as well, including ones with power and influence. In "The Legion Takes Boston" (*The Nation*, October 29, 1930), for example, Gordon quotes from speeches on the wholesomeness and patriotism of this quintessential American organization. However, he then goes into a description of the drunken, warmongering, lawless behavior of the revelers at the convention, behavior that is only accepted by the capitalist city merchants and politicians because of the money the largely white legionnaires bring to the city's coffers.[54]

SOCIALISM AND COMMUNISM

Inspired by the Russian Revolution of 1917, many Americans, displeased with the capitalist system, began to consider Marxism more seriously. However, socialist and communist groups initially gained almost no traction among Blacks in the 1920s. The Socialist Party in particular did little to address the concerns of Blacks, positing that the destruction of capitalism would bring an end to racism. As early as 1903, its leader,

Eugene Debs, famously stated, "We have nothing special to offer the Negro, and we cannot make separate appeals to all the races."[55] This was essentially echoed by most socialists including James Oneal, who in his pamphlet *The Next Emancipation* (1922) wrote that there was no racial issue; it was a labor problem.[56] Socialists tended to believe in a system of "evolutionism" in which "societies evolve inexorably through a fixed series of stages, from lower to higher." Such a system, with its hierarchies, was prone to believing in "racial superiority and inferiority."[57] Throughout the 1920s, the party had often been guilty of white chauvinism, particularly in the case of unions. Many Blacks, even if they agreed that racial prejudice was largely based on economics, maintained that special attention needed to be given to address the situation of racial minorities. Du Bois, for example, exclaimed, "The Negro Problem . . . is the great test of the American Socialist."[58] If that is true, then the socialists generally failed with Blacks. Unions often resisted accepting Black members into their ranks, and for the many members of the party who were foreign-born, the problems of African Americans had little relevance.

Initially, the Communist Party of the USA (CPUSA), founded in 1919 and controlled by the Soviet-run Communist International (Comintern), was not much different than the socialists in its views on the Negro Problem, placing little emphasis on race and maintaining that racial prejudice stemmed from capitalism and would be eradicated when the system was overthrown by workers of all races. By the late 1920s, the CPUSA attempted to change this. They formed a specific organization for Black members, the American Negro Labor Congress, to organize workers. However, the group met with mixed results, often encountering resistance from white unions.[59] The Communist International Commission's "1928 Resolution on the Negro Question in the United States" contained several directives that would hold appeal for Gordon such as advocating for the end of racism within the party and for white workers to actively support Black concerns, including "organizing active resistance against lynching, Jim Crowism, segregation and all other forms of oppression of the Negro population."[60] Perhaps most important for Gordon was the proposal to create a separate Black nation within the Black Belt in the South. While Gordon rejected Garvey's idea of repatriation to

Africa, he advocated the concept of a Black nation-state in the United States. Although controversial among many Blacks, Gordon was an ardent supporter of this proposal, continuing to advocate for it even later in life.[61] However, because of reservations about Marxism by many Blacks, in 1929, there were, by some estimates, fewer than fifty Black members in the party.[62]

Several events starting about 1930 helped increase Black membership. First the effects of the 1929 Great Depression roiled the American capitalist system, causing many to seek radical political solutions for the economy. The Depression particularly affected Blacks, who suffered more from unemployment than most whites. Additionally, there were other noneconomic events that stirred Black members to join the party, such as the increasing number of lynchings, which the CPUSA had finally begun to address.[63] The party also began to crack down on white chauvinism. The case of August Yokinen, a Finnish-born member of the party, exemplifies this shift. In December 1930, Yokinen objected when several Blacks entered the Finnish Workers Club in Harlem. Yokinen was expelled from the party for the incident, which drew much public attention, and he was forced to take several actions to prove his repentance before being readmitted to the party.

Other changes within the party took place as well. The party took the lead in organizing strikes to push for change in housing and anti-poverty reform.[64] They advocated for Ethiopia after its invasion by Italy in October 1935. Vigorous attempts to attract African American workers to Communist-led unions also proved successful. In the early 1930s, the CPUSA called for a Popular Front to form an alliance with more mainstream groups to combat fascism. Although Gordon did not completely agree with this shift by the party to attract the liberal left, he remained loyal to the communist cause.[65] In 1935, the National Negro Congress "united union representatives, civil rights workers, and artists across the Left-liberal spectrum in broad support of anti-racist causes."[66] That same year, at the American Writers' Congress, Gordon gave a talk arguing for the need for "a new class, younger black writers and whites friendly to the cause."[67] As a result of these and other efforts, CPUSA membership grew "to seven thousand in 1938."[68]

GORDON'S CHANGING POLITICAL VIEWS

Gordon's turn to communism had not happened overnight. His antiracist, anticapitalist views had been developing since childhood, when he learned from his father that the alliance of Blacks and whites in the struggle against white oppression could be a powerful force. His disillusionment over the lack of change in the treatment of Blacks after their participation in World War I also fueled his dislike for capitalism as did the worldwide economic downturn caused by the Great Depression of 1929. Articles such as "The Negro's Inhibitions" highlight Gordon's hatred of the divisions between Blacks over issues such as colorism, social class, and gender. What particularly irks him is the desire of many middle-class Blacks to attempt to assimilate into the white capitalist world. As Mary Helen Washington observes, the CPUSA with its grassroots appeal to Black workers was an attractive alternative for many to mainstream American politics, especially during the Depression.[69] Gordon was one of those drawn to the party's emphasis on such issues as the fight for civil liberties, economic justice, peace, and fair wages; as a result, he entered the party during its Third Period, from 1928 to 1934.[70] Robin D. G. Kelley reiterates the point about the party's appeal:

> Black working people entered the movement with a rich culture of opposition that sometimes contradicted, sometimes reinforced the Left's vision of class struggle. The Party offered more than a vehicle for social contestation; it offered a framework for understanding the roots of poverty and racism, linked local struggles to world politics, challenged not only the hegemonic ideology of white supremacy but the petit bourgeois racial politics of the black middle class, and created an atmosphere in which ordinary people could analyze, discuss, and criticize the society in which they lived.[71]

"The Negro's New Leadership" marked Gordon's first foray in a Marxist periodical, the *New Masses* (July 1931), closely associated with the CPUSA. In the article, Gordon denounced Black leaders as being "weak, vacillating, hypocritical, ignorant, venal, and self seeking." Organizations such as the National Urban League and particularly the National Association for the Advancement of Colored People (NAACP) are characterized as being inadequate to address the problems of Black people. The NAACP (renamed the "Nicest

Association for the Advantage of Certain Persons" here) is seen as being "ultra-nice, ultra-respectable, and ultra-fastidious." These "dainty" organizations shirk from confrontations with whites while "the Communist Party of America is going to the very stench-hole of American capitalist class hatred and challenging the thugs and lynchers on their own ground." Often, "the Communists have been beaten insensible for defending the Negro workers." After this article, Gordon was well on his way to becoming a leading Black Communist during the 1930s and '40s.

GORDON'S SHIFTING VIEWS ON AMERICAN FICTION WRITERS

Gordon's position on American literature, especially fiction, also changed as his political views shifted. Gordon had gained some experience with literary criticism through his role as fiction editor for the *Boston Post* and the *Saturday Evening Quill*. In "Negro Fictionists in America" (*Saturday Evening Quill*, April 1929), Gordon traces the Black novel from Charles Chesnutt up to 1929. He particularly considers the challenge posed by one white critic: why was it that "so far, this country has not produced one Negro capable of presenting a sincere picture of himself or his people." Gordon does not dispute the charge but feels that Black writers have not been allowed by white editors and readers to present a realistic interpretation of Black life, one presenting the working class as they really are, making the writings seem "inauthentic." Furthermore, middle-class Black readers tended to want only positive images of the race to be presented. Gordon suggests that Black fiction writers have taken some steps to correct this problem, and he praises those such as Jean Toomer and Rudolph Fisher for being able to criticize Blacks on issues like religion and the middle class.

By the time Gordon wrote "Negro Novelists and the Negro Masses" (*New Masses*, July 1933), his views on the purpose of literature had moved much further to the left. Gordon was among numerous Black intellectuals who helped open "two-way channels between radical Harlem and Soviet Moscow, between the New Negro renaissance and proletarian literature."[72] Gordon was among the first critics "to attempt an extensive Marxist analysis of Black literature."[73] Instead of judging literature by its accuracy to Black life, he maintained that the novel should "touch upon the workers' struggle to survive in a capitalist society." In the past, Black fiction had been presented through the lens of a "peculiar national psychosis," creating "a reactionary culture in response to white supremacy." "For Gordon," Anthony Dawahare states, "political and economic oppression bred cultural repression, which resulted in the 'futile protests' of the folk tales, spirituals, hymns, and work songs. And since the national culture is 'psychotic,' modern black writers, whom he characterizes as petty bourgeois, remain trapped in a tradition of futile protest."[74]

By 1931, Gordon had helped form a John Reed Club in Boston, and edited its journal, *Leftward*. The John Reed Clubs brought together radicals of different races to discuss their work. Gordon embraced the club's credo that "Art Is a Class Weapon."[75] He held out the hope that an alliance of working-class Black writers and allied whites would lead the Black masses away from a harmful bourgeois propaganda and toward a more healthy outlook based on their own interests. This is the type of work he tried to emulate in his own short story "The Agenda" published in *Opportunity* (December 1933/January 1934). The story stresses the need for unity between Blacks and whites despite their initial distrust of one another.[76] The story, which won an honorable mention award from the magazine, "was a prototype for the early fiction that would soon make Richard Wright famous."[77] Despite his sometimes narrow perspective, "Gordon's plea for black literature built upon the working-class foundation of African American black life was an important contribution to the quest for an authentic black aesthetic free from the demands of white commercial culture."[78]

BREAKUP OF HIS FIRST MARRIAGE AND REMARRIAGE

Somewhere around 1931, another seismic change occurred in Gordon's life: his marriage was in tatters. He and Edythe had separated in August 1929. According to an article from the *New Journal and Guide* (August 23, 1930), there was "no riff" between them. They were just leading different lives, with her planning to attend college and him devoting more time to his writing: "We simply are taking the intelligent person's prerogative to experiment with life with a view to discovering as many of life's intent possibilities for happiness as we can." Another possible reason for their separation could have been Gordon's shift to radical politics, one that may well not have sat well with the more conservative Edythe.[79] Whatever the reason for the breakup, a divorce was granted over a decade later on September 15, 1941.

During this period, Eugene also met June Croll; the two were drawn together by their common beliefs in labor unions and radical political causes. June, born Sonia Crowl circa 1901 in Odessa, Ukraine (then a part of the Russian Empire), was a Jew who had survived Russian pogroms. She was also known as Sonia Croll and Mrs. Langston Hughes. By the time she came to the United States illegally in about 1913, she had already developed a distaste for capitalism and had begun to work in New York City's needle trades. She quickly became a part of several antihegemonic "institutions [that] ranged from community mutual-aid organizations such as the Landsmanschafto to industrial unions like the International Ladies Garment Workers Union (ILGWU) to organizations explicitly devoted to class war, like the Socialist Party and the Jewish Labor Bund."[80] In the mid-1920s, at the Workers School of New York City she met Karl Marx Reeve, whom she would later marry. Reeve was the son of the prominent communist Ella (Mother) Bloor. While at the school, June also honed her skills in public speaking and on the teachings of communism. As a result of her communist and labor activities, and several arrests for assaulting the police, June was also placed under FBI investigation. One FBI agent even called her "one of the most important key figures in the Communist Party."[81] After the FBI could not find a US birth certificate for June, attempts were made to deport her, but none were successful, and she remained in the country.[82]

When Eugene and June met in 1929–30, they were well on their way to becoming dedicated members of the Communist Party. Both were also in failing marriages, and their paths would cross in New York at labor union and communist rallies. The couple formed a strong relationship that would continue throughout their lives.[83]

FURTHER DEVELOPMENT OF GORDON'S INTEREST IN COMMUNISM

In the early 1930s, as Eugene and June were developing their relationship, membership among Blacks in the CPUSA was increasing, in part because of the party's defense of Angelo Herndon, the Scottsboro Boys, and George Borden. Herndon was charged with allegedly attempting to incite an insurrection while organizing workers in Georgia in 1932. When he was found guilty in January 1935, his situation became a cause célèbre, setting off a five-year legal battle. Gordon was also one of twenty-four Blacks to sign a statement attacking George Schuyler, who had written a column denouncing Herndon. Partly as a result of such pressure, Herndon was eventually declared innocent by the US Supreme Court in 1937.[84]

In 1931, nine Black youths were accused of raping a white woman in Scottsboro, Alabama. The vigorous defense of the Scottsboro Boys was significant in demonstrating that the CPUSA often acted independently from the Comintern, which did not advocate concern for the case. Gordon soon became a member of the National Committee for the Defense of Political Prisoners, founded by American novelist Theodore Dreiser to bring attention to the Scottsboro case and other injustices.[85] He was also a member of the Scottsboro Unity Defense League. Gordon gave a speech defending the Scottsboro Boys in May 1932 and wrote two key articles on their case in the *Labor Defender* (August 1931 and June 1932). The former article is included in his anthology and is discussed in a headnote to the piece. However, the June 1932 article, "A Call to Millions," will be briefly touched on here. The piece was written on the eve of the planned execution of the boys on June 24, 1932. In the article, Gordon makes a spirited call on both Black and white workers to prevent the execution. The fierce resistance to the planned killing by those such as Gordon helped prevent this outcome, although the boys were still not released. In his article, Gordon eschewed race and looked at the young men as poor workers who must be defended: "Let us demonstrate our determination to save our working-class comrades.... It is our job as workers. It is a task *that must be done!*"[86]

Gordon also played an important role in reporting on another miscarriage of justice in the 1930s: the deadly killing of George Borden by a motor vehicles inspector on July 8, 1934. Gordon's writing on the case in the pamphlet "The Borden Case: The Struggle for Negro Rights in Boston" is included in this anthology. This case must have been especially personal for Gordon since the killing took place in his hometown and the incident was reported in a rather matter-of-fact tone in the *Boston Post* ("Man Shot by Inspector," July 9, 1934), where Gordon was still employed. The *Post*, like other Boston papers, indicated that there was no known precedent for a motor vehicles inspector using a gun while making an arrest; however, the paper went along with the police report completed just hours after the incident that the shooting was justified.[87] It was largely the Communist-backed International Labor Defense and the League of Struggle for Negro Rights, headed by Gordon, that protested the killing.

YEARS IN THE SOVIET UNION

In the early 1930s, another major change would occur in Gordon's life. He was one of several Blacks who made the "pilgrimage" to the Soviet Union, particularly during the Depression years.[88] Gordon took a leave from his position at the *Boston Post* and went to Russia from 1935 to 1938, accepting a job at the English-language *Moscow Daily News*. The paper was founded in 1930 by two prominent Marxists, Mikhail Borodin and Anna Louise Strong. Gordon had two reasons for taking the position: first, he felt his views were too extreme for the *Post* and that he could not stay at the paper much longer, and, second, and more importantly, he wished to visit Russia to study "at first hand that country's problem, which corresponds to the race problem in this country."[89] Most of his writings while in Russia, however, were propaganda pieces praising the Soviet Union. There were a number of writings celebrating the advances of working-class heroes, especially within the Soviet food industry, such as the pamphlet "Pancakes and Caviar."

Gordon wished to challenge Western images of Soviet workers as being forced laborers ("Where Workers Learn to Command the Industry," *Moscow Daily News*, June 26, 1936). There were also writings on journeys down the Volga River and one praising the virtual elimination of prostitution in the country. Gordon additionally spoke about the diverse community in Astrakhan (*Moscow Daily News*, August 10, 1937) and met with both local laborers and Soviet officials.[90] Gordon was so enthralled by communism that he ignored all of the signs of Stalin's terrorist state, refusing to see any of its flaws, initially even supporting the deadly purge initiated by the dictator.[91]

Upon his return to his native country, Gordon wrote an unpublished satiric piece lambasting the United States: "It is good to be home again, in a real democracy. I no longer need to look in the glass to be reminded of my race. I have only to take a seat indiscriminately on a Fifth Avenue bus traveling mid-town or wander toward the doors of the Waldorf-Astoria or any other swank hotel."[92] Unlike during his time working at the *Boston Post*, in the Soviet Union Gordon felt he was free to conduct interviews and report on issues that he was unable to do in the United States.[93] Working for the *Post* was no longer tenable, so once back in New York in 1938, he resigned from his position with the paper and become a feature editor of the *Daily Worker*. These actions drew the attention of the FBI, which extensively surveilled Gordon in the 1940s.[94] Agents saw him as an important player in the party and a danger to democracy who "seems to have more power in the Party where Negroes are concerned than even [Black vice-presidential candidate] James Ford."[95]

RECY TAYLOR AND THE CAUSE OF WOMEN

Gordon had long supported equal treatment of women at home and in the workplace. He helped the women in the Saturday Evening Quill Club advance their careers, particularly author Dorothy West. Gordon, as a skilled landscape painter himself, also advised artist Lois Mailou Jones.[96] He wrote several essays on the cause of women and cowrote with Cyril Briggs an important pamphlet, "The Position of Negro Women" (1935), included in this anthology, which set forth the Communist Party's attempts to improve women's salaries and work conditions.

Because of his strong interest in the cause of women, it is not surprising that Gordon became involved in the case of Recy Taylor, a young mother raped in Alabama in 1944. Gordon was the first to write of the incident in a white newspaper, "Alabama Authorities Ignore White Gang's Rape of Negro Mother (*Daily Worker*, November 19, 1944), included in this anthology. He also wrote of it in a second article for the *Daily Worker*, "Alabama Officials Feel People's Pressure in Mrs. Taylor's Case" (December 12, 1944, p. 4). Gordon went to Birmingham and with Alabama activist E. G. Jackson confronted Alabama Governor Chauncey Sparks, pressuring him to agree to launch an investigation.[97]

Gordon returns to the Taylor case in a previously unpublished piece, "Cult of the White Woman." Gordon compares the cases of Taylor and an unnamed white woman who had allegedly been raped in Florida in 1944. In the Taylor case, the Black woman could identify her rapists, yet the white boys were not brought to trial. In the Florida case, all three boys were given a sham trial and executed on October 9, 1944.

LATER LIFE AND PROJECTS

Gordon had several publishing disappointments in the 1940s and '50s. He had been a prolific author in the 1920s and '30s, yet in the anticommunist era of Joseph McCarthy in 1940s and '50s America, getting his material published was very difficult. There was a palpable "red scare" that led to the creation of the House Un-American Committee in 1938 and, eventually, the McCarthy trials of 1953–54. Despite being under FBI surveillance, Gordon was never asked to testify at any trials; however, in such an atmosphere, even Gordon's nonpolitical writings were not generally accepted for publication. Despite this, Gordon stayed true to his communist convictions. He joined the Committee for Democratic Culture in 1943, along with such well-known figures as Clarence Muse, Elizabeth Catlett, Marvel Cooke, and Fredi Washington, who tried to prohibit degrading depictions of Blacks in film.[98]

One venue that published his work was the *National Guardian*, a weekly newspaper founded in 1948 by James Aronson. Its politics leaned to the left, and it was even accused by some of its critics of being associated with the CPUSA. It was sympathetic to suspected spies Alger Hiss and the Rosenbergs and was opposed to the Korean War and the US Cold War with Russia. The paper also opposed militarism and was sympathetic to anticolonial movements. Thus, it is not surprising that Gordon sought employment there. He did manage to publish a few brief pieces in the periodical, including one condemning the FBI and Joseph McCarthy (May 17, 1954), but his major assignment was to cover the Bandung Conference, the first large-scale Afro-Asian conference, in Bandung, Indonesia, April 18–24, 1955. Gordon was among a handful of Black or Asian reporters at the conference.[99] Gordon lamented the lack of a strong African presence at the conference, a point that irked Aronson, who sent Gordon a harsh memo rejecting the piece, saying the article was "unusable both from policy and from journalistic standpoints." Gordon gave a pointed rejoinder to Aronson, but the piece was ultimately never published.

In this tight publishing market, Gordon tried to be innovative, writing a freelance weekly column, *Another Side of the Story*. He intended to write on a specific topic such as "Abuse of the Negro Woman," and "The 'Free World' Myth." If a newspaper accepted an article, it would be sold to the paper for five dollars and only one newspaper in a given area would be allowed to use it. Unfortunately, he did not find many takers.[100]

In addition, Gordon worked for several years attempting to organize Black Southern radical Hosea Hudson's autobiography. Hudson, not formally educated, had compiled a mass of notes that needed to be edited before it could be published. He approached Gordon for help in assembling the manuscript in the 1960s.[101] After not making much progress on it, Gordon was given $100 a month by leading Black communists William Patterson and Henry Winston as an incentive. The book, *Black Worker in the Deep South*, with the aid of Gordon and perhaps June Croll, was finally published in 1972.[102]

He also attempted to send out numerous fictional and autobiographical pieces for publication, perhaps believing that they would be less controversial than many of his nonfiction pieces. Some writings were new, while some were reworkings of ones he had published earlier. He had been writing his autobiography for several years and sent it to Viking Press. Unfortunately, it was rejected.[103] His main literary project was a semi-autobiographical novel, "Picnic at Court Square," on which he had been working since at least 1945. He sent it to Knopf, but it was rejected, despite being "filled with so much thought and event."[104] Ultimately, the reviewer said the manuscript had "the feeling of a sequence of scenes and episodes in an uncorrelated and in some places seemingly unmotivated fashion."[105] Although Gordon wrote copious drafts of the novel, he never attempted to publish the manuscript again. These attempts to publish were done partly out of a desire to issue what he felt were "important" books, but also for a practical reason: to allow him time to do his work "without wondering where the next meal is coming from."[106] He had always made his living through his pen, and it was difficult to do this when publishing opportunities began to dry up. Nevertheless, he continued to scrape by, alternating between odd jobs, including as a carpenter, and, at one point, even going on welfare.

FBI surveillance on Gordon, significant for years, had increased in the early 1950s. Agents even confronted Gordon on January 15, 1954, asking if he would cooperate with the US government in reporting "on minority groups such as negroes and Jews." He angrily answered, "No." Agents then wrote, "No further consideration is being given to GORDON under the TOPLEV Program."[107]

Gordon's writings may have lessened, but they did not altogether cease. "Though he was no longer charged with party responsibilities, the aging communist still regularly attended political events and recorded his impressions. He also took to writing unsolicited letters of advice to the younger generation of Black activists who continued the struggle for racial equality."[108] He also wrote an article recalling "Blacks Turn Red," the piece he had published in Nancy Cunard's groundbreaking anthology *Negro* (1933). In "'Green Hat' Comes to Chambers Street," Gordon speaks of his initial meeting and later encounters with the controversial shipping heiress.[109]

Gordon published sporadically throughout the 1960s, usually for small Black newspapers. He spoke against the Vietnam War and opposed nuclear proliferation as well as US Cold War policies.[110] His unpublished article "Black Women's Long Tough Course: From 'Dat Gal' Carline to This Woman Angela" is a vigorous defense of Angela

Davis, one of a long line of strong Black women that Gordon felt had not received their proper place in history.[111] The piece on Davis is among the most significant pieces he wrote since the 1940s.

Much of Gordon's time in his later years, however, was spent in more relaxing pursuits. He had long been interested in painting, particularly watercolor. His work was on display in various venues including the District 65 Union Hall, the Hudson Guild Gallery, and the AGA Gallery on 57th Street.[112] Unfortunately, we do not know what happened to these paintings and many do not seem to have survived.

His chief enjoyment in his later years was spending time with his beloved wife June in their apartment in Manhattan. By all accounts, their marriage was "a happy and fulfilling relationship based on a shared interest in radical politics."[113] One can feel the palpable loss in his life when she, a chronic smoker, died of a cerebral hemorrhage on January 7, 1967, at St. Vincent's Hospital.[114] In his eulogy to her Eugene wrote about their activities together: "June and I, alone together in the apartment, she in her chair and I opposite her on the couch, near the window, a feeling content and complete, knowing she was, temporarily, at least, safe." He goes on, "We best enjoyed Sundays and holidays, especially if the weather discouraged our going out, so that we'd not have to make excuses for sitting comfortably near each other, silently reading, or listening to the radio or briefly commenting on a bit of news. I look back upon such moments as the happiest."[115] In a letter to the women from the Emma Lazarus Federation of Jewish Women's Clubs, he speaks of how empty the apartment is without her and how he still imagines her with him there.

Life seems to have lost much of its meaning after June's death as he even left a grim note to those who might find his body, asking them to spend as little on his funeral as possible.[116] His own death from pneumonia followed hers by several years on March 16, 1974, in New York City at Misericordia Hospital. In an obituary in the *Daily World* on March 27, 1974, National Chairman of the Communist Party Henry Winston eulogized Gordon, writing, "This Black American, born in racist Florida in 1891, devoted his long lifetime of productive activity to the struggle against racism and for the enrichment of the life of the masses fighting to break the chain of oppression and class exploitation."[117] These are fitting words by which Gordon should be remembered.

In reflecting upon Gordon's possible legacy, one must consider the often unfinished projects contained in his papers. There are also a number of finished essays, stories, scripts, that are there. In particular is a completed, unpublished eight-hundred-page novel, "The Picnic at Court Square." The novel would need extensive editing, but it is hoped that someday someone will examine his writings further to complete the work that this anthology begins in attempting to restore Gordon to his proper place in the fields of Black radical politics and African American literature. His themes of social justice, inclusion, and equity convey a message that still resonates today. Unfortunately, the recent cases of George Floyd and countless others reiterate that the events that Gordon wrote about are not set in the distant past but echo with us today. His writings continue to be timely reminders that we need to be ever on our guard against racism, injustice, and oppression and of the urgency of our actions to combat these forces.

A Note on the Selections and the Text

Choosing the pieces for an anthology is always a challenging task. I have tried to select works from the three genres in which Gordon wrote extensively: autobiography, fiction, and nonfiction. I have also attempted to choose writings that represented his major interests. To get a sense of the development of his ideology over the years, it seemed best to organize the works chronologically. In that way, the reader can see that his becoming a communist was not sudden but came about through a slow but consistent process.

Gordon's works were published in a wide variety of venues, all with their own editing styles. To keep the integrity of Gordon's writing, I have attempted to be faithful to the original sources as much as possible. This includes his sometimes unconventional spelling and punctuation. He often did not use commas where a reader might expect them and omitted the "'s" on possessives such as Peters'.

I have provided end notes (numbered sequentially restarting after each of the three sections in the book) for references that might be unfamiliar to modern readers. Occasionally, material has been omitted, which is marked by three asterisks (* * *).

Autobiographical Writings

"Southern Boyhood Nightmares"
International Literature (APRIL 1934): 49–58

In "Southern Boyhood Nightmares," published in the Soviet political and literary magazine, *International Literature*, Gordon's early years are seen as largely "painful and unhappy."[1] However, his personal experiences are meant to extend to many other working-class families brought up in similarly harsh environs as is evidenced from the subtitle "The Story of an American Childhood." Gordon's memories are taken from Florida, New Orleans, where he lived from about ages seven to twelve, and Hawkinsville, Georgia where the family moved after leaving Louisiana. One memory, to which he will frequently return, is of Robert Charles, a Black man who shot and killed several policemen in New Orleans before being hunted and killed by the police. This incident is touched on here but will be described at more length in "Killer at Large!" Another memory was from Georgia when he was almost lynched after standing up to a white youth recklessly driving a mule team. A third incident took place in Georgia, where a Negro pastor defied a powerful white man leading to the pastor's lynching and burning. From these incidents, Gordon not only learned of the dangers for Black people living in the South. He also learned about how to deal with whites. Whereas his mother and maternal grandfather wished to avoid confronting whites at all costs, his father felt racism had to be stood up to forcefully. He also learned from him that not all whites were enemies and that it was possible to befriend the more ethical ones. That is the path Gordon would choose later in life.

Southern Boyhood Nightmares

I
The Story of an American Childhood

Looking down upon it from the height of years and the comforting remoteness of a New England town, I realize that my whole boyhood in the South was darkened by a lowly lying cloud of subconscious fear of the white man; a subconscious fear that at times burst through to open terror. I do not mean that a fear of immediate physical injury possessed me night and day, haunting my dreams at night and my imagination by day; it was not a fear of that kind. It was instead an accumulation of ideas suggested by countless agencies—my mother, my teachers, the pastor of our church, the children with whom I played in the gutters of New Orleans, the very atmosphere I breathed, my whole environment—the white man was my natural and eternal enemy, regardless of the guises he might assume or of the methods of approach he might take. Some day, I believed, the white man would come swooping upon me, my mother, my father (although I knew they would have a hard time subduing *my* father), my brothers and sisters, and all my black, brown, and yellow playfellows, and would bundle us together and burn us like so much kindling.

At the age of two I was taken by my parents, with a younger brother from my birthplace at Oviedo, Florida, to New Orleans, Louisiana. Here my education with reference to my white compatriots was begun in earnest. My mother, a brave, brown, small and stern-faced woman, taught me that I was "as good" as any other youngster. I often wondered, at first, why she so insisted on this detail. It seemed to me that so patent a truth should be taken as a simple matter of course. At the same time, I was made to feel, by virtue of having learned this credo, that I should be a coward to quail at the insults my small neighbors pricked me with, and should only follow a natural impulse if I itched to punch their grimy faces. However, when I saw a white acquaintance called into his yard and spanked because he had played with a "nigger," I could not reconcile the contradictions in my mother's philosophy. Why, I wished to know did his mother whip him if I was "as good" as he, and why did his mother call me "nigger?"

Mother disliked such questioning. She would bite her lip and pretend not to hear; she would turn her back, and go about her housework. But when I repeated the question until it rang in her ears, she cried: "She does it because she doesn't know any better. She's showing her ignorance." Ignorance of what? I wondered. Why was she ignorant?

My mother taught me that to be called a "nigger" was to be outraged, humiliated, degraded. It was signal for immediate combat. A white man's smile of friendship, she insisted, was like Judas' kiss.[2] My mother taught me that no white man was to be considered seriously as a friend: he was not to be trusted. They were all potential lynchers and abusers of black womanhood. If they appeared at any time to be friendly, it was because they had "an ax to grind." They were disloyal; they would desert one in a crisis, especially if one happened to be a Negro. They never performed a charitable act for, nor spoke a kindly word to, a Negro, out of the pristine goodness of their hearts. They were blackguards, rascals, cutthroats, rapists, and murderers. How they "got this way" was a perpetual puzzle to me. I had gone to Sunday school and had been taught that Christ was a Jew. Weren't Jews white? Then was Christ like that too? Were the Presidents of the United States like that? And the grocer on the corner—he appeared to be a kindly old fellow: was he like that? Yes, Christ had been a white man, but he was above petty hatred. The Presidents were no better than the rest of them. The grocer? Didn't I have sense enough to know why *he* acted in a friendly manner?

I did not see my mother's contacts with the harsher side of life . . . I sometimes wondered whether she was not afraid to eat the food bought of white tradesmen. So, wondering, I grew older.

I must have been between seven and ten years old when something happened in New Orleans to confirm, as far as I cared then to have it confirmed, my mother's repeated charges. It has been many years ago, and since my facts and impressions came from hearsay and juvenile observation, the incidents are now obscured on my memory. But I do remember very clearly going out one morning to play in front of my father's small "ice-coal—and wood" shop, and seeing the streets filled with policemen. We lived in the rear of our store, at the corner of Third and Rampart streets, and it was on Third street that I first glimpsed this awful and romantic spectacle.

Rumors whirled as thick as the dust from the board surface of Rampart street. White men shoved black men from the sidewalks and dared them to protest. And, of all unheard of dreams! most of these husky Negroes submitted meekly and went, hang-dog-like, about their businesses! I had been taught that black men were much braver than whites, in all circumstances. It did not occur to me that the whites were armed, while the blacks were not; nor did I realize that the police, representing the power both of the state and of the white ruling class, were leagued against the blacks,

Policemen went by all day, carrying long, slender rifles on their shoulders. My white playmates, who had played at horses and cowboys with me yesterday, regarded me today with hostility, answering my anxious questions with impatient sneers. They turned their backs and stayed close to their own doorsteps.

Late that afternoon I heard father telling mother the story. A Negro named Robert Charles had shot and killed two policemen last night, they having gone to arrest him for beating his common-law wife. He had eluded the police. Today they circled the block in which the murders had occurred; stood on rooftops, behind fences and walls, atop cisterns, and clung to the branches of trees. That night a mob burned the only Negro high school, and it held the fire department at bay until the building was destroyed. The mob whipped several Negroes who had dared show themselves after dark.

The police advised my father next morning to keep his store closed. They refused to be held responsible in view of the circumstances, if certain "hot-headed members" of the mob wrecked the place. I remember that father clamped his jaws together and said to the policeman, "Let them try it!" He opened the store as usual but nobody bought anything. Later in the day he closed the place up.

In the meantime mother went about her work with tightened lips and hard eyes. She had a horror of seeing father leave the house or go out of her sight. Reports came in of Negro workers being dragged from street cars and beaten to death. Friends of ours were all but murdered on their way to and from work. But father went. I had unbounded faith in his courage. I worshipped the tall, lean, olive-complexioned, curly headed, stern-faced man who was my father . . . He has said that he expected any moment to feel the blade of a knife piercing his back as he pushed his way through the mobs.

One morning we got word that Robert Charles had been found in a house not far from us. Immediately the whole block was surrounded by militia, policemen, and thousands of excitement-seekers. The battle was on. Some stories said that Charles killed more than twenty of his attackers, picking them off one by one. Negro homes in the vicinity were burned as a passtime. The mob poured bullets and buckshot into Charles' hiding place.

I remember most clearly, of all the incidents of that frightful period, the boast of a white youth whom I knew well. He was talking to a group of his kind, all of whom my mother told me, had taken part with the whipping, burning, and murdering mobs.

"We don't want to hurt these gray-haired old devils," he said, "what we're after are those smart young niggers that'll tell a white man to go to hell."

Finally Robert Charles was killed. Some reports said he walked out of his own retreat, his hands above his head, and was instantly shot down. Others tell us that he was shot into bits through the walls behind which he had sought shelter. At any rate all agreed that when every member of the self-appointed posse had fired a shot or two into his body, there was not enough of it left for an undertaker to trouble himself with.

The bolder outlines of this experience were dimmed in the ensuing weeks, but the deeper impression remained. Following those tense days, when hostility between whites and blacks was felt in the very air, I grew to believe more and more in the doctrine that my environment had repeatedly hammered into my consciousness: Trust no white men; even those who pretend to be your friends will lynch you if offered the slightest provocation . . . Robert Charles became the secret hero of the underprivileged black worker; more than that, I heard many a covert word of praise for him among certain whites. I was all confused . . .

II
A Thwarted Friendship

When I was twelve, our family having been increased by two, we removed from New Orleans to Hawkinsville, Georgia. My grandfather, Charles Gordon, a well-to-do farmer, would have been labeled in the Hawkinsville *Dispatch* a "gentleman farmer" if he had been a white man. He was an ex-slave who had accumulated more than a thousand acres of the best farm land of Pulaski county.[3] Some of the tenants on this place had been with him as long as they could remember. He was their "chief," and he possessed among them both influence and power. He was openly disliked by those "poor whites," whose hatred of the Negro is an inheritance from slavery. Among those of the same plane as himself—J. Pope Brown,[4] for example, at one time candidate for Governor of Georgia and one of my grandfather's "friends"—he was "respected" but he was not accepted as a man.

To go as far as my grandfather had gone in the heart of Georgia, with its race proscription, and its subtle psychology of Negro inferiority, a black man must possess both unusual mental equipment and unusual moral stamina. Yet, to my youthful amazement, the philosophy he had built out of the only life any of us knew (except my father, who having lived in Europe, knew something of freedom) was similar in that of the propertyless, submerged Negro farm hand: to avoid the white man except when expediency dictated otherwise; to temper your trust of the white man with skepticism; to accept his "loyalty" as so much bait to draw you into a hidden trap.

I could not readily understand this philosophy at first. I knew he was not a coward. Cowards did not in that place rise to such stature as his. His thin-lipped, tight-fitting mouth, his penetrating eyes, the superb, proud manner with which he carried his almost square head—these, I knew, were the physical aspects of a mental attitude. It was not until much later that I understood fully the magnitude of his tragedy. An intelligent Negro was (and is) like a king in exile. He is treated with a certain deference by those who hold his life in their hands, but he must not err, he must not for a moment "forget" who and where he is. Let him "forget," and he loses in a moment all that it has taken him and others all their lives to accumulate. My grandfather was an intelligent Negro in the heart of Georgia.

After a few years in the backwoods of Georgia we children were as wild, as free from any city influence, as the field rabbits we hunted on Sunday afternoons. Our lands being extensive, we seldom came into contact with our white neighbors' children. But on those rare occasions when we did, I found that these youngsters were as friendly as my earlier playmates in New Orleans had been. I came to realize that as long as these boys and girls remained uninfluenced by their elders, they were human and lovable; that under the fear of punishment for having played with "niggers," they were hostile and insulting.

We went to school in a log hut on the main road about a mile and a half from home, and this change in our status brought us at once into contact with white children. We met them on their way to the "white" school, which was properly located in an opposite direction. I recall vividly that the first time we met we stared at one another noncommittally and curiously. But a few days later we were smiling at one another, and before any of us had really thought about it or knew how it had come to pass, we were talking about our lessons and our teachers, flipping the pages of one another's books, and calling one another Gene and Ann, Ernest and Bobby.

One morning, proudly and chivalrously acceding to the request of the beautiful blonde daughter of a well-to-do neighbor to tell her what I knew about algebra. I looked down the road and saw my grandfather approaching us on horseback. The blonde young woman—she was about ten—paid no more attention to him than we had been giving to the buzzing of spring insects, but I wilted in fright. No one knew better than my brothers and I that I had violated a fundamental law of the clan.

My grandfather reined in his horse. Our new friends looked on uneasily, wondering what would happen. They looked from him to us and from us to him.

Grandfather glared at them with unspeakable contempt. In a moment terror had displaced their mild stares of wonder, and they backed, sidled, slunk away; they hurried about their business, now and then looking back so as not to miss seeing impending tragedy. Alone with us, he said, in a voice that made us cringe:

"Dog bite it! I told you not to talk to any of these white youngones. What do you mean? Do you want to be lynched? Do you want to be burned at the stake? Get on to school! And don't ever let me see that again, or I'll skin you alive."

I admit I was in more immediate horror of being burned by the "crackers"[5] than "skinned alive" by my grandfather. As a matter of fact, my brother and I had a mutual understanding that the old man was very much of a bluff. However, we did not lightly consider the temper and ferocity of the Georgia white men. We resolved to obey grandfather thereafter.

I wondered what my father would say when grandfather told him. I thought of it all day. It was hard to understand why anyone should even object, let alone wish to burn us alive, merely because we had been civil to a group of kids of our own age.

Next morning we were in a pretty mess. Having been ordered to ignore our new friends, we were at a loss how to explain the sudden change of attitude toward them. But we were saved that particular humiliation. The moment we came in sight of one another they hailed us. As on former occasions, it was the girl who spoke for the whites. She went straight to me and, thrusting a small pink finger at my nose, demanded:

"Why did your pa scold you yesterday?"

I stammered, hesitated, floundered; I told her who the old grouch really was and told her what he had said. Her companions seemed to be deeply impressed; much more so, in fact, than she was. Her reply was prompt and emphatic: "I don't believe they'd do that to you. I'd tell 'em you didn't hurt me, nor nothing."

At any rate I thought we had better not be caught being friendly again, and, making the silly excuse that we'd all be late at school if we didn't hurry, I turned and ran, joining my brothers and sister who stood not far away.

I shall never forget the scorn in her eyes and the contempt in her voice, when she called after me, "Coward! My mother says all niggers are cowards!"

Somehow I felt no resentment toward her. The quick, spontaneous retort had revealed as by a flash of lightning the towering and impenetrable wall of hatred that stood between her people and mine. Vaguely I blamed her mother and father, her older brothers and her sisters, her uncles, aunts and cousins, her friends and neighbors, and every man and woman who boasted a white skin, for the wall. It was years later that I saw how unnatural and flimsy it was; that I found out how easily penetrable the wall was; that I saw it was not a wall, but as the illusion of a wall; an illusion created out of the psychologies of blacks and whites for the sole purpose of keeping them apart. But that day at school I felt sure my mother was correct in what she had taught us about "white folks": "all alike," and all to be mistrusted and hated like rattlesnakes.

My father never mentioned the incident to me, even though grandfather surely told him. My father's courage and thoughtfulness were always awesome to me.

III

Georgia Christmas Morning

Christmas in Georgia was looked upon by whites and blacks as the one day of the year when murder was a sport. Nobody feared being annoyed in that day by some nosey sheriff; that is, unless a Negro, for any reason, chanced to kill a white man. Then, of course, the whites would have the pleasure of putting their Christmas fireworks to profitable use. I knew all this as soon as I was old enough to comprehend even the most elementary of the ugly facts of Georgia life.

One Christmas morning they sent me to Hawkinsville to buy some more candies and fireworks. I drove a swift black horse hitched to a red-wheeled top-buggy. My eight-year-old sister begged to go with me. I was fifteen. We were very happy . . .

At Hartford, a scattered patch of buildings, through which we had to pass just before reaching the bridge that crossed the river to Hawkinsville, a lanky white youth, driving a team of mules, cut across my path, causing my horse to rear. I drew up quickly, suddenly mad with anger. Calling to him peremptorily, I asked him what the devil he was trying to do.

Southern Boyhood Nightmares

I was young. I had inherited much of my father's "nerve" and temper (if not his reckless courage). It was Christmas. I was driving a spirited and beautiful horse. Certainly I must have forgotten for a moment who and where I was!

I was soon reminded. Temporarily stricken dumb by a "nigger's" unheard of audacity, the youth drew up his mules so abruptly that they nearly sat on his lap. Jumping to the ground, he stalked toward us, his pale eyes glittering. My horse stood chomping on his bit and pawing the ground. I was uneasy, for groups of loungers who had seen the incident were already approaching casually, coming within hearing distance. Besides, everybody, including my little sister, know of Hartford's reputation as a "mean and lawless hole." The village swarmed with illiterate, tobacco-spitting "hill billies" on a perpetual lookout for "sassy niggers." So seldom were they fortunate enough to find one that I knew they would never let me walk out of this trap of my own making.

In less than five minutes we were surrounded. My sister had begun to cry nervously, which added to my wretchedness. The "offended" youth was spitting brown tobacco juice and detailing between shots his version of what had happened. His version was, of course, the "correct" one. The whole business had been unimaginable, unheard of, a crime deserving of nothing less than death. They were already discussing on the outskirts of the crowd, possible methods of disposing of me. I heard them numbly.

Shaking with terror, but trying desperately to conceal it, I looked for a sympathetic face. I saw none. The number of heads across which I looked had increased; I thought vaguely that there must be thousands. One of the men, a gangling redhaired fellow in green suspenders and a gray cap, went to my horses head. And I cut at him with the buggy-whip.

In a flash the horse was off. Tugging desperately at the reins, I turned him round toward home. Five miles stretched ahead of us, some of the road was none too good. The mob was after us, yelling for blood. They cried, "Stop that nigger!" "Shoot him!" "Don't shoot, take him alive!" "Don't let him get away!" Someone ran into the road and caught the reins. The mob surged upon us, swept on and overwhelmed us like a storm.

I looked pityingly at my sister. She was crouched in a corner of the seat, her great eyes wide and tearless.

"What'd he do?"

"Sassed a white man."

"Did, did he? Who th' 'ell is he, anyway? . . . Say boy, what's yo' name?"

I told him, a plea in my voice.

"Yea, I know. His pa's that sassy yaller nigger that rides round here with his hat on the side of his head, thinkin' he's white. Passes a white man with out speakin'. Boys, we're in luck!"

"What'll we do with 'im? Will we shoot 'im?"

"No, jus' strip 'im an' give 'im damn good whippin' with that buggy whip."

"I'm in favor of shootin' 'im. Ef I don't kill that nigger today I won't be able to sleep fer a month . . ."

An austere elderly man, who had lost an arm in the Confederate army—I dazedly recognized him the moment he drove up behind his span of beautiful bays—questioned my captors sharply, and they answered him with a deference that amazed me. They seemed, however, reluctant to let him in on their fun. He did not question me; merely looked curiously in my direction every once in a while.

I heard him say, in a drawl I loved because his voice was raised in my behalf: "I know his grandad. And his dad, too. His dad's a right smart fellow." I noticed with a thrill of pride that he had not used that offensive epithet in referring to my father. "You men let that boy go on home, you hear me? If he's done anything that's deserving of punishment, I'll see that his dad whales the stuffin' out of him. . . . Go on home, boy."

That was his first statement directly to me. My acknowledgment of it was too hurried to be gracious. I went.

I told my father everything, imitating gestures, mimicking the inflections of different voices. I showed how they had strutted back and forth before us, and I waxed dramatic as I described the tone of his own insulter. My father's tanned, lean face tightened, and his stern gray eyes became mere burning slits. When he called to mother to bring his revolver, his voice lashed but inspired me. Mother hesitated, father strode into the bedroom and got the revolver out of the top bureau drawer. He tossed it upon the buggy seat.

Mother whimpered, "Papa, be careful. Those crackers will kill you, sure."

Father said to me, "Get in." He swung himself in and snatched up the reins. I felt the hard revolver lying on the seat between us.

During that long swift ride he said hardly anything. He asked: "Can you pick out any of them? Did they do or say anything to your sister?"

The wheels of the buggy churned up a cascade of white sand as we carved into the space before a small Hartford general store, in front of which a crowd of laughing hooligans stood. The crowd split in two, dazed with astonishment. Father did not wait for it to recover.

"Who are they?" he asked me, loudly enough for all to hear. Outnumbered ten to one, I felt as secure as if I was surrounded by a regiment of friends. With irrepressible gusto I pointed them out.

They were regaining their wits now. They swayed forward, muttering threats; pressed against the buggy wheels and grasped the horse's reins.

"Pull 'im out o' there!" yelled someone on the outer edge of the crowd.

Like an echo the retort came back:

"You don't have to pull me out," and tossing aside the heavy laprobe, he stood up.

The loaded revolver suddenly glittered in the sun. It glittered into the eyes of the crowd, which wavered, fell back hesitated for want of an aggressive leader. My father was now on the ground.

"I want to give you fellows fair warning," he was saying, "that my boys are not to be trifled with any more. This is not the first time, but it will be the last ... And who was it that passed an insult–"

He was interrupted by the same austere man who, earlier, in the morning, had interceded for me. This man laid his hand on father's arm and called him by name.

"For God's sake, go home and leave these hot-headed young fools alone! They didn't mean anything. They ..."

Father stood up in the buggy. He delivered a brief lecture, in which he relieved himself of an opinion for every man who had molested me. He offered to meet "personally" "the coward" who had insulted him. No one took up the challenge. I wondered why someone in the outskirts of the crowd did not shoot him down. I still wonder, and decided that his reckless audacity appealed to their imaginations.

He sat down, tucked the laprobe about his legs, took the reins from my hands, and drove through the crowd; it fell back on both sides. He drove across the bridge into Hawkinsville, where he bought the candies and fireworks. Shortly afterwards he drove back beside a sullen but silent group in Hartford.

IV

A Negro Man of God

There was a Negro preacher named Stanley. He was unctuous, mild, and inoffensive, often came to dinner at our house and we listened to his gossip of his wife and his boys, of his farm and his church. Was an ordinary sort of man in every way except in appearance. More than six feet tall, he had the features and the "unforgiving" nature traditionally associated with certain Indians.

I once spent a whole day at his house. He was not there; his boys told me he had gone to carry some corn to the mill. We loafed about the field and we talked.

Late that afternoon, after a day of hunting, making partridge traps, and playing all sorts of games, we went in. I was to spend the night there. It was sundown after a little while. Evening noises were coming up from the fields and the branches. A silken misty smoke hung low over the darkling treetops; they were already mysterious with dusk.

Reveren' Stanley had not come and his wife was uneasy. We sat up in the dark, waiting for him. Mrs. Stanley now and then tried to join us in our foolish banter, but made out poorly. In a little while we too ceased to talk. The old wooden house grew silent. We sat in the kitchen around a table on which burned the yellow flame of an oil lamp. The old house sat almost a quarter of a mile from the main road, so that noises of the highway came to us faintly . . . Reveren' Stanley should have been back in two hours . . . Midnight came.

Mrs. Stanley walked the floor; went silently into the soft unfathomable darkness of the yard; sat down on the kitchen steps to cry. We boys walked down the lane in the main road, keeping close together in the darkness; we spoke in whispers. What could be keeping him? We returned, and sauntered around the "lot," where the mules crushed corn and the pigs grunted and squeaked in their sleep. We saw the gray haze of dawn breaking through the black barriers of night. Daylight came. The sun struggled up blood red through the silken veil of smoke.

We heard someone hollering out front. Mrs. Stanley, her two boys, and I rushed around the house to see who was calling. An ashen-faced Negro, a "hand" on the Stanley farm, met us. He kept turning his whitened, glaring stare across his shoulder. He jerked his thumb over his shoulder, and tried to tell us something in his quavering almost shrieking voice. For several minutes he could make no coherent statement. Finally, after many stammering efforts, he blurted out the whole sickening story. He had heard some of it from an eye-witness and some he had seen himself...

About a mile and a half this side of the mill Reveren' Stanley heard the loud chugging and the vociferous tooting of an auto horn. Automobiles were rarities in those days. They were for the rich only. Reveren' Stanley knew, therefore, that one of the richest men in the county, and, doubtless, one of the most arrogant was clamoring for the road. The road here was really a lane, being very narrow and hemmed in by a wire fence on one side and a rail fence on the other. There was room for only one vehicle, and that fact was clear. The horses had never heard such a sound before. They got excited, terrified, almost uncontrollable. Exasperated, Reveren' Stanley reined in and looked back.

"For God's sake," he cried, "stop blowing that tin horn! Haven't you sense enough to see I can't turn out?"

What! That was enough. Another white man had been "sassed" by a "smart nigger."

"Why, I'll be damned," observed the confounded autoist, mildly. "I'll be double damned!"

He turned slightly aside and drove ahead. His car crushed two of the buggy wheels, ripped loose the already wildly frightened horses, and showered grains of corn upon the sandy road. The horses, still fastened side by side, disappeared in a whirling cloud of dust around a bend in the road. The Negro preacher got to his feet and looked through eyes bloodshot with anger, at the remnants of his goods.

The rich man, some yards ahead, had now stopped the car and was coming back on foot, a pistol in his hand. He aimed and fired. "You black son of a bitch! So you'll sass a white man, will you?" He kept repeating it as he continued to shoot.

Reveren' Stanley, struck a couple of times, managed to grasp his own weapon from the seat of the buggy and to tumble to partial cover behind the rail fence.

"So that's the game you play, heh?" he cried, and returned fire.

The rich man keeled over. His wrist was shattered, and he could not fire again. One bullet had punctured his lung. He lay gasping in the sand, among Reveren' Stanley's scattered grains of golden corn.

A passing acquaintance—another wealthy white man—picked him up and rushed him to the nearest doctor. He spread the alarm as he went. But the best surgeon in Hawkinsville couldn't vulcanize[6] a punctured lung. . . .

The mob traced Stanley by the trail of blood. He was found in an old white farmer's hay loft. The white farmer begged the mob to "leave him be," since he was so nearly dead. They called the old farmer a "nigger lover" and shoved him out of their way. A trace chain[7] was looped around Reveren' Stanley's neck, and, according to the Atlanta *Constitution* the next day, "outraged citizens dragged the Negro back to the scene of his crime and burned him at the stake."

When the man had finished his story he offered to conduct us to the place. On our way we gathered a large crowd, whites and blacks. I wondered how many of the whites had been members of the mob.

We found a blackened, charred, undraped trunk of a man chained to an iron stake beside the main road. The earth for yards around had been churned, cuffed, and ploughed by a thousand broganed[8] feet. All the hair had been burned from the victim's head. His face was merely a blackened skin, drawn taut over the cheek bones; it was like the head of a drum. Great empty holes had displaced the eyes: they looked to me like torn and stretched button-holes. His feet and hands were gone.

Mrs. Stanley dropped just as I had seen a hog drop when struck on the head with an axe. I thought she was dead, and I remember feeling relieved, because she wouldn't have to dream of it for years.

Two men laid her on the side of the road, where presently, I heard her groaning and calling her husband's name. We pulled the stake from the ground and thus removed the chain which held the torso. Some men spread on the ground a large piece of bagging, such as is used for bailing cotton, and they laid the remains upon it. Grasping its corners, we trudged with it to the house. One of the men supported Mrs. Stanley on his arm. She was moaning, and mumbling her husband's name . . .

When I reached my own home that afternoon I found my mother almost insane from fear. She had heard the news and, although she knew that Reveren' Stanley alone had been lynched, she was nearly out of her mind because I had been close to the place where it had happened.

I told the family of what I had seen. I could neither eat nor sleep. Every post in the ground held, for my charged imagination, the blackened, crisped, faceless, handless and legless body of a man who had often laughed and talked with us. Mother later surprised me with the statement that, "after all, there are *some* decent white men left in the world; now, that old man who let Reveren' Stanley hide in his hay loft . . ."

But it was too late then to attempt undoing what had been so assiduously done through the most plastic years of my life. Mother had instilled in me, first, the fear of white men; later, when I was old enough to judge for myself, this fear had given place to hatred. Hatred was intensified by what I saw white men do. It was many years later, while going to school in the North, that my mind was able finally to evolve out of, shake itself free of, the grotesque "race" psychology in which the environment of my youth had clothed it. But those Southern boyhood nightmares have now become such memories as aid me in bringing the historical background of that section to the class conscious workers who are making such nightmares impossible.

Excerpt "Once I Was Afraid"
No Date, Unpublished Eugene Gordon Paper[9]

"Once I Was Afraid" is an autobiographical sketch, well over one hundred pages.[10] In a letter to Elliott W. Schryver at Viking Press, October 3, 1940, Gordon lays out his plan to publish it as a book (Eugene Gordon Papers, Box 5, Folder 4). Gordon explains "that the book I will be writing will indeed be a different kind of autobiography and a real contribution to our literature by and about the different peoples of the United States." He states a fundamental belief of his: "Racial and national antagonisms are *not* inborn, *not* inherited, *not* inescapable; that they are forced upon the young by their elders, either directly (family influence, etc.) or indirectly (general environment), and that if the young were allowed to follow *their* inclinations all would be quite well."

The plan is to divide the book into four parts. The first two deal with his youth in the South. At the end of this period, he is convinced like his mother and grandfather that whites and Blacks must be separated. This is the period where he is "afraid," essentially, of the power of the white race. The excerpt here is from the first two sections. The remaining two books will discuss his education and how eventually he learns that whites and Blacks must learn to live and work together. Unfortunately, Viking never accepted the manuscript, and Gordon never published it as a whole, although he did attempt to publish it in sections.

Once I Was Afraid

I Learn Distrust

When papa opened the door two tall black men came in. Wind blew rain almost to the center of the floor, and for a moment I thought the lamplight was going out. The men had on wet blue overalls, wet blue jumpers and wet black boots. Papa told mamma the men's names and told them she was his wife, and they took off their tall, broad-brimmed dripping hats and nodded at her. They looked down at buddy and me on our hands and knees, then they sat by the table with papa, over against the wall between the two windows. Papa said, "Well, well" and laughed, and they all began to talk.

After a while buddy[11] and I again started to crawl round on the floor—under the tables, behind the stove, under chairs, and around mamma's legs. Mamma was a tree.

"They done et up most all my chickens," one of the men said.

Papa and the men were talking about hunting wildcats. Buddy and I now became hungry old wildcats.

Mamma was mixing biscuit dough in the big dishpan; she was working the dough up and down and round and round, using both hands.

Every once in a while wind blew a sheet of rain against the house; the thick, heavy branches of the old oak scraped the sides of the house and the roof. I thought somebody with big boots on was sliding over the floor upstairs. Booming, cracking thunder sounded like papa's double-barreled gun when he stood in the kitchen door and shot at rabbits in the garden.

One of the men said God must be angry tonight. I stopped being a wildcat and sat behind the man's chair. Why did he think God was angry? Who made him angry? Was he so angry he was crying and the rain was water from his eyes?

The shutters were closed and fastened, but they strained and flapped and knocked. The other man said it put him in mind of some big fellow trying to tear the window open with his hands. Then whistle they both laughed, as if what they had said were funny. The wind all the while whistled and sighed and groaned in the tree, and the chains on the tree clinkled like little bells.

Papa was telling the men about the snake I had seen in the room upstairs.

"Musta come out that tree," one of the men said.

Papa said yes.

I sat behind the man's chair and listened.

With Spanish moss trailing from it like an old man's gray whiskers, the old swamp oak in front of the house was a spreading and tangled forest in itself. Buddy and I knew that bats, owls, tigers, wildcats, panthas, lions and snakes sneaked and crawled somewhere out of sight among the foggy, gloomy, thick and dark-green leaves and branches all tangled with moss. Screech owls sometimes woke us in the night, and to hear that sound above your roof, mamma said, meant death in your house. She said it made her think of a child lost in the night crying for its mother.

Three or four pieces of heavy chain hung from one of the longer and thicker of the low outflung branches. Buddy and I had tried several times to untangle and remove the chains but couldn't, for they had grown into the tree. Mamma said their jangling in the wind made her flesh creep.

Other limbs of the tree spread out over the house, curving downward, mamma said, like the twisted head of a giant making as if he were going to clutch us up. I had heard them say that the sun never shone at the foot of the oak, no matter how bright the sun shone; and no matter how brilliant the sun and how hot the day, you would shiver they said, if you stayed a little while under that tree.

Papa told the men that in Africa some snakes lived in trees.[12]

Buddy came and sat beside me and we listened.

One of the men said he bet that in Africa they didn't hang black men to trees; he said trees were all right for snakes to hang in but God never meant them for men to hang in ... What was he talking about?

Papa was telling the men how mamma tried to kill the snake I had seen.

I wanted to tell them. I wished children were allowed to talk *with* grown people, but . . .

The whole upstairs room late one afternoon was red from the setting sun. By that red light buddy and I were looking at some pictures in a book. We lay flat on our bellies, with our heads partly under the bed. My eyes were on the pictures, and I was making up stories to go with them. A long shadow moving against the wall under the bed distracted me. I looked—and screamed. An ugly, beady-eyed snake! Holding up its flat little head and darting out its forked little tongue, sharp as needles, it was slithering toward the corner.

I grabbed buddy's hand, and, yelling for mamma, dragged him downstairs.

For a moment mamma ran round in a ring, almost crying.

"I wish papa was here," she said.

She took the kettle of water off the stove. She told me to get the ax. She set the kettle down and put buddy on the kitchen table and told him to stay right there. Mamma and I tiptoed upstairs as if to keep from scaring the snake.

Mamma pulled the bed out and looked behind it; looked behind and under the washstand and the dresser. She stood back and struck at the clothes hanging on the wall. I watched for the snake to *plump*! in a nasty mess on the floor. I got near the door; inched toward mamma again, because I couldn't run and leave her here. She, standing off, jerked out the dresser and washstand drawers. I jumped. She peered over the side of the drawers; then, with the ax handle, she poked at the things in them. She began beating the quilt of the bed with the ax.

She screamed.

"There it is! Run, Eugene!"

I started for the stairs. But she wasn't coming so I went back.

Suddenly she grabbed the kettle and poured scalding water on the long curling ridge that had just come in under the quilt. It didn't move.

"Is it dead, mamma?"

She was peeling off the upper covers. She peeled off the quilt and the sheet, shaking each of them away from her. There was nothing—except a wet spot on the mattress.

I never went into that room that I didn't think of snakes . . . .

One of the men said a snake was like a white man; the other said no; he said a white man was like a snake in the grass. I wondered whether that was because the snake bit you before you saw it; and I thought of a white man lying in the grass to bite your foot when you passed. The same man who had said a snake was like a white man now said that hearing all that noise out there made you feel like going and looking, to see whether somebody were chained and groaning and trying to break loose, even though you knew what the noise really was.

Shivers of delightful excitement ran over my body. It was nice to go on playing, even though all those scary sounds were everywhere outside. I felt secure and at peace when I looked across the room and saw mamma cooking or crawled under papa's chair and knew that he and mamma and these men were not scared of *anything*. I wasn't scared, either. And buddy wasn't scared; he was again growling and spitting and saying: "I'ma ol' wildcat! I'ma hungry ol' wildcat!"

God must be angry tonight . . . Did God sound like the wind and the rain when he was angry? Was he angry at these two men? Why? Was he angry at a snake in the grass, that might bite a little boy's foot? He wasn't angry at us, because we hadn't done anything to him. Why was he angry at anybody? . . . Momma had once groaned like that, when we lived with grandmamma and grandpapa Burke behind the orange grove. Somebody had gone and brought back an old woman to see what was the matter with mamma. The old woman had stayed a long time, with the door to mamma's room shut and nobody allowed to come in except grandmamma.

When the old woman had gone away, she had left a baby crying with mamma. And mamma was looking sick but she wasn't crying.

"Where did the baby come from, mamma?"

"Aunt Riney brought you a little brother."

"Where *she* get him from, mamma?"

"God made him."

"Did God make me, too?"

"Yes. God made everybody."

"He made you and papa, too? And grandmamma and grandpapa? And Uncle Felix and Aunt—"

"Yes, Eugene. He made *everybody*."

"Leave your mamma alone, Eugene, and go play," grandmamma had said.

"Mamma, did God give her the baby to bring here? Did God tell her to bring . . ."

"Eugene! Didn't you hear me tell you to . . ."

I now bounded across the floor toward the wildcat. I was a pantha. "I'ma pantha now," I said to buddy. "I'ma hungry ol' pantha now."

The pantha and the wildcat snarled and fought, rolling over then through the thick brushes and the grass, knowing there must be snakes in the grass but not being afraid of them. The beasts raised such a racket that mamma hollered at them to quit it, for she couldn't hear her own ears. But how could she hear her own ears, anyhow? How could anybody hear his own ears? Or anybody else's? Your ears didn't make any noise, so how could you hear them? For a moment I set thinking about it. Perhaps there was some sense in it, but I couldn't get it. Presently, I decided to be a wildcat again.

A long, shuddering moan outside rose higher than the noises of the shutters and of the *shee-ee-ee-eeing* of the rain. I forgot I was a wildcat and stood up, remembering something. I was full of wonder.

"Sound like mamma when she was sick and Aunt Riney brought buddy."

Mamma turned and looked at me. I knew by the way she looked that I shouldn't have said it. But she didn't speak. The look was enough.

Then one of the men said the noise outside was like a dying soul. They and papa looked at one another. Papa listened, holding his head tilted slightly to one side, smiling just a little. The lamplight made his brownish mustache shiny on one side of his mouth. I heard thunder start away over on one side of the sky and come bumbling-jumbling over to the other side. I listened for it to burst open where it had stopped over our heads. It sounded like big, heavy barrels being rolled round upstairs. I backed away from the foot of the stairs, so as to be out of the ways when a big barrel came tumbling down; gaped upward to see what the person would look like who ran down after it; wondered what was in it . . .

One of the men was talking. He said to papa and mamma that he thought they ought to . . . Then he stopped and looked at buddy and me. I stared into the man's mouth; and for the first time I noticed the broadness of his nose, the blackness of his face, and the thickness of his lips. I saw also the hurtedness of his eyes. Papa and the other man were looking at him, too. I looked to see what mamma was doing and saw her standing with a pan of brown biscuits, holding it with a corner of her red-checkered apron—red-checkered like the tablecloth.

Well, what did he think mamma and papa ought to know? I went and stood by papa's chair, still staring at the man. Papa put his hand on my head.

"One time," the man said, "they hung a fellow on that tree out there."

"Yes," the other man said. "Lynched him."

Mamma sat down, still holding the pan of biscuits, and her eyes were so big that a lot of white showed. Was mamma *scared*? Papa was looking in the man's face and not saying a word. *Papa wasn't scared*! The other man moved in a little closer, glanced at the door, and folded his big black hands on the table. I thought *he* was scared.

Realizing that grown people were scared of something made me unhappy. *But papa was not scared*! I got almost on knees; and we listened to the story of the big black man who once lived *in this very house* with his yeller wife. . . .

He came home one day and found her and a white man in bed together.

"Right upstairs there in that very room where this child seen that snake."

I recalled what they had said about a white man's being a snake in the grass.

"Sleepin' like [a] pair [of] innocent babies," the other man said.

"So this here fellow, he kill' dum."

"He kill' dum both?"

"Kill' dum both. Sho did."

Mamma stood up and set the biscuits down. She started putting things on the table where papa and the men were sitting.

"Well, the white folks—the mob—they got after this here fellow an' they runned him all up and down the swamp there, a-shootin' an' a-hollerin' and a-cussin', an' the woods an' fields just a-swarmin' with blood hounds. Well, they ketched 'im and they bring 'im back here an' they hung 'im on that big ol' tree out there . . ."

But he was so heavy—was a big fellow, weighing nearly three hundred pounds—that they had to get trade chains to swing him with. The chains grew into the tree and became a part of it; the man's spirit lived in the tree and haunted it. Some people said his spirit haunted the house, too, and all the woods and fields for miles around—wherever he used to go. Before we moved into this house, the man said, folks passing along the road at night or on a cloudy day used to hear the white man and the yeller woman screaming upstairs there, while her husband hacked them into pieces with an ax . . .

Standing in front of papa, I watched the stairway. I could not understand *why* the man had killed them.

"I'm glad he killed her, too," mamma said. "Fooling 'round with a white man."

How had the woman *fooled* round with a white man? Was it bad to fool round with a white man?

One of the men muttered something about the black man's being headed off by *God Almighty hisself,* if the black man wanted to go one way, and headed off by the white man, if he wanted to go another way; and I thought of the pigs in the lane when we lived at Oviedo and of grandmamma and grandpapa trying to drive them into a pen, while the pigs wanted to go a different way. Between God and the white man, one of the men said, heaven and earth was "all divided up."

"And all that's left for the poor black man is hell," mamma said, laughing.

But I knew she didn't laugh because she thought it was funny.

I listened and I heard everything but I didn't understand anything.

Mamma said supper was ready. She poured some water into the wash pan, so buddy and I could wash our hands and faces.

"You panthas and wildcats come on. Wash your dirty paws," she said.

At the table papa and the two men talked about Africa.

"I bet they don't hang no black men on no trees in Africa," one of the men said. "In Africa a man's a man, aint he, Brother Gordon."

We didn't stay there long after that, and the next thing I knew we were on our way to New Orleans. Back through the swamps of cypresses and live oaks draped with Spanish moss stood the old house at Indian River; miles and miles back through fields and weeds and around crooked lanes and dirt roads there was a great old tree on which a black man had been lynched—right in our front yard! Papa said there wouldn't be anything like that in New Orleans... Were we going all the way in this wagon? No, mamma said. After a while we'd all get on a steamer. But first we'd ride on a train!

"If mamma and papa wasn't still here in Florida," mamma said, "I'd never want to come back again."

The long, long train we were on was going round a long, long curve, and the cars when I looked out the window, seemed to be leaning far over on their sides as the train circled round. Far below there was a thick wilderness of green, green trees. And when I put my head back in the car papa and mamma were looking at the trees and talking about the one on which the man had been lynched in our front yard.

I thought of big black men hanging like oranges on great oak trees; big black men all curled up in big black balls hanging by chains round their necks.

We were on a steamer at last and the steamer, papa said, was on the Gulf of Mexico. We talked about New Orleans almost all the time. We had a good stateroom, papa said, and he said it over and over again, as if bragging and as if he hadn't thought we would have a good stateroom. He said he had been unable in the beginning to get a good stateroom—when he had gone to buy passage. But on the boat one of the ship's officers noticed papa's Masonic pin and pretty soon they were talking with each other.

Papa told the steamship officer about traveling in Africa and Europe. This man, papa said, had also traveled in Europe. So they shook hands; and the white man told papa that if he wanted anything he had only to ask for it. But I didn't see anything so fine about the stateroom. I noticed that the deck was covered with sawdust where seasick passengers had vomited. Mamma said she was sick as a dog but papa, buddy and I were not sick. I ate everything they brought to our stateroom.

Papa said they brought our food to the stateroom because, although he had a right to eat in the dining room, with this nice stateroom we had, yet we couldn't eat there, because we were colored. So they brought our food on a tray. I thought it was nice, eating in the stateroom.

Papa kept talking to mamma about the business of his own he would have in New Orleans. He said he wanted to work for himself; he didn't want to work for any boss, he said—especially for any white boss.

"I'm a young man, and if I start now, we'll be well off by the time the children are grown up."

He said he didn't want his children to work for white people, either.

Mamma said, "Uh-huh" and called for the bucket so she could throw up again.

In New Orleans papa rented the third floor of an old three-story brick house in the warehouse district of Tehoupitoulas street,[13] one in a long row of similar houses squatting flush with the *banquette*[14] and overlooking grimy warehouses across the way. Each story had a wide gallery, front and rear, both covered. The front gallery was trimmed with lacelike ironwork round the eaves and up and down the posts. The banisters were made wholly of lacey ironwork. From our gallery we could see across the row of black old salt warehouses with roofs shaped like the teeth of a saw. Beyond the warehouses lay the Mississippi River, with its levees and wharves, with river boats and ocean-going steamers, barges, tugs, and sailboats. In the blue haze and beyond the river lay the flat sprawling town of Algiers.[15]

Papa stood on the gallery with us and pointed out these things to us and told us about them. He said he had lived in New Orleans before he had gone to Florida and met and married mamma.

Papa went to work on the levee, which he called also the wharf and the waterfront (and just the front). Buddy and I were small but we noticed that when papa came home in the evening he would hold on to the banisters and pull himself up each step. Mamma said papa wasn't used to hard work like this; and at night she would rub his back with Sloan's liniment until he hollered for her to stop, because he would rather have aching muscles than blisters from burning.

Papa would say sometimes that his spine felt as if it were broken; and mamma would wish she could get some work to do. She asked papa whether she should take in washing, or go out and work by the day, because, if she didn't do something, we couldn't afford to pay the rent for this place.

"No, Girl," papa said. "Just have patience."

"It aint patience I need—I got plenty patience," mamma said. "These children can't eat patience. I can't make them no dresses outa patience. And I can't buy nothing at the grocery store with it, either," she said.

Papa said there was no need of being so cross about it; and, anyway, he said, just wait. He was trying to get more money, and, if he did, he might start a little business.

I sometimes heard papa telling mamma about the way the foreman on the levee cursed at the men and, if they talked back, discharged them. Papa said he had to watch his temper all the time.

"You know *you* can't stand no foolishness from white people," mamma said.

Papa grunted. This foreman, he said, wasn't white; he was colored.

"I should've knowed as much," mamma said. "When some Negroes get a chance to boss, they wors'n white people."

"Did they forget they were Negroes, just because they had a little old job bossing other Negroes?"

"No; that's just it," papa said. "They don't forget they're Negroes; they remember it. They remember that if they don't please the white man they won't have a job themselves."

When papa had saved enough money he opened a boarding house, in our big dining room, for roustabouts (as he and mamma called the longshoremen). Papa said a place like that would pay, because many of the men didn't like to bother with carrying lunch buckets. Many of them would eat supper with us, too, if it didn't cost too much. Papa said he hoped someday to open a real business and sell things.

All our boarders were Negroes. Buddy and I would stand inside the kitchen door, the heat of the big range blasting behind us, and stare google-eyed at the double row of roustabouts facing each other, eating, down the long table. The whole room smelled of rank sweat, boiled cabbage, and beer. Momma hated beer, but they brought it with them, buying it in a saloon at the corner.

In their blue overalls and jumpers, each with his cotton hook stuck point down in a little loop behind, the men sprawled over the table and laughed and talked loudly while they ate and drank. They joked constantly with one another, sometimes forgetting where they were and saying things they had to apologize for.

"Excuse me, lady," a roustabout would say to mamma or the women who helped her. "I was thinking I was out on the levee."

"That's the only place you fit to be," another would say, pretending to scold. "You aint used to eating with folks, you done et with your mule so much."

Mamma, small, quick on her feet, and sour-faced, wouldn't say anything. I felt she didn't say anything because she didn't want to give the men cause to get fresh. She couldn't stand rough talk. She would make us go where she thought we couldn't hear it. When she heard us using "bad words" we had picked up in the dining room, she would holler at us or whip us.

One of the men was Jim Dandy, whom they liked to tease because, they said, he was so nasty nice. He wore a clean white handkerchief round his neck all the time and had his hair parted in the middle. He would laugh and make out he didn't care, and I thought he was scared to tell them to let him alone.

One day when they had cornbread for dinner one of the men said it put him in mind of the time the dog turned up his nose at Jim Dandy's lunch. He asked how many had known about it. Nobody had.

"Well, Jim Dandy, here, he took a big hoecake[16] out his lunch bucket and just as he was fixin' to eat it, he seen that ol' starvin' yellow dog that used to hang round all the time. So Jim Dandy—he's a tenderhearted cuss—he breaks off a piece of the hoecake and hands it to the dog. Well, this old starvin' kiyoodle lays the bread down, sniffs it, and looks it over. He's just fixin' to eat it when he takes another look and sees the shape of Jim Dandy's wife's hand on it."

The men laughed.

"An' the dog wouldn't eat it?" somebody asked.

"Sho wouldn't. Looks at Jim Dandy as much as to say, 'How I know your old woman's hands was clean?' an' turns up his nose and walks off."

Mamma was in the kitchen. She laughed. But Jim Dandy this time didn't laugh. He called the man a liar. He said it was all right for them to joke with him but to leave his wife out of it. And mamma stopped laughing and said, "That's right!"

Our next door neighbor on one side of us was an Italian family. High plank fences enclosed our big backyard. The fence between us and the Italian family had several good-sized cracks. In the fence on the other side of our yard the cracks were all covered by our neighbor the day we moved in. We saw him doing it. These people too were white, as were the families on the first and second floors of our house.

We colored children were the only kind in our house. Mamma said it felt funny living with white people. I didn't think so, though. I felt all right. Even mamma would talk to the other people in the house. She would borrow flour or an onion or some pepper from them and they would borrow from her.

The man next door was also an artist, we found out from glimpses of some of the things he did. The privy used by the families in his house and by the families in ours was half on his side the fence and half on our side. From our side I could peep through a little crack just above the seat and, if I kept very quiet, could see everything the people over there did. That was how I happened to see him one day painting pictures of red and yellow and green fruits on a large sheet of glass. I could see also, by turning my head sidewise and pressing the right side of my face against the privy seat, that the upper part of the door of their privy was of glass, with a large painting of watermelons, canteloupes, [*sic*] and bananas on it.

One day while watching him I made a noise, and he jumped up, looking angry. His long bushy hair stood straight out all over his head and his dark eyes flashed. He glared round his place, trying to see whether anybody was spying on him. Not seeing anybody, he snatched up his paints and brushes and hurried out, slamming the door in my right eye.

Mamma said the artist's wife must not have liked his messing up the house with his stuff, so made him do his painting in the privy. I thought mamma didn't like him because he was white—and because he didn't like us.

Theresa was the smallest daughter in the Italian family. She had a big sister named Marguerita. Theresa was friendly. Mamma said she was womanish and fresh. I got introduced to Theresa through a crack in the fence, away down close to the ground. Squatting, she invited me to tell whether I saw any difference between the way she was made and the way I was made.

I looked. I made a fascinating discovery! Then I looked long and critically. Yes, there was a difference! I looked some more, while Theresa obligingly—and encouragingly—squatted. Then she said that that was enough and ordered me to climb up on the fence. She did likewise, and we met face to face. Thus I made a second discovery: Theresa had glossy black eyes, which sparkled, and glossy black lashes, which drooped and curled, and glossy black hair, which hung in black ringlets.

"H'lo," she said.

"H'lo."

"Didja see that bad little girl, when you peeped through the crack in the fence?"

I laughed at her, shaking my head.

"You can't fool me. That was *you*."

Her big eyes widened in surprise and her lips puckered.

"Why—why, it *wasn't* me, neither! That was a *bad* little girl you saw."

I felt vaguely that I understood why she would want me to think it had been somebody else. Vaguely also I understood why she said she was a bad little girl.

"Oh, yes, it was," I said. "I know you."

We kept it up for a few minutes. She let me have the last word. She stared for a long time, then looked me over frankly, as if trying to make up her mind about me.

"What's your name?"

"Eugene. What's yourn?"

"Mine's Theresa."

I knew that, because I had heard mamma talking about her to the woman who helped wait on the roustabouts. I didn't know how or when mamma had learned about Theresa. But here she was, now, yelling at me.

"Eugene, get down off that fence and come in here! Come on! Right this minute!"

She was waiting for me at the top of the stairs. A vigorous slap from behind sent me skidding across the floor.

"You stay down off that fence, you hear me? And stay away from that dirty Italian kid, or I'll give you a good whipping."

I sulked.

"You stay from them dirty little white kids anyhow—all of them. Do you hear me?"

"Yes ma'am."

I went on sulking. Theresa wasn't dirty. I was certain that she wasn't dirty. Anyway, it wasn't the kind of dirt you washed off with soap and water. I suspected that this other was the kind of dirt mamma was talking about. Theresa's mother hadn't made her stop talking to me, so why should mamma make me stop talking to her?

Besides, I had seen and heard mamma talking, from our front gallery, to Theresa's mother on their front gallery. Theresa's mother, a fat little woman of about papa's color, with thick, loose black hair coiled at the back of her head and half-moon gold earrings, always smiled at me and she always said good morning or good evening to mamma. Mamma had even borrowed an onion from her, and she had once given mamma some garlic.

Mamma wouldn't use it. She said Italians smelled like garlic. (I couldn't remember whether Theresa smelled like garlic. As far as I would remember, she had smelled like everybody else. If I got near her again I'd smell her, just to find out.) Mamma told papa she didn't trust *any* white people, because all they wanted was a chance to stab you in the back.

I was not sure whether mamma meant they would stab you with real knives, although I had heard a boy say Italian men carried long, sharp knives. Papa told mamma that these foreigners were not so bad to Negroes as other white people. He said the Italians and the French and the Spanish treated Negroes nice.

"I don't trust none of them," mamma said. "The average white person is just a snake in the grass. I don't trust none of them."

Well, that didn't mean for *me* not to trust them, did it? Anyway, until mamma or papa told me not to trust any of them, I would play with them—when I got a chance. Mamma had already told me, of course, to stay away from all white children, but she didn't really mean that, did she? Because most of the children round here were white, and some of them were nice, too. The thing to do would be not to let her see me playing with them.

On a dull and cloudy morning I got away and went outside the backyard. I heard children playing there and from the back window had seen Theresa leaving her yard.

Mamma and her helper were cooking dinner.

Theresa and another girl of about seven were a short distance away with a number of boys of my age and a little older. I knew most of them, for I saw them regularly from our gallery and they played on the *banquette* and in the street. Knowing them as a lot of little hoodlums, as mamma called them, I wondered why they stood so still and silent here, facing the back wall of an old brick warehouse. As I came closer I saw that their eyes were shut.

Theresa saw me and came and took my hand. She whispered "Sh-h-h-h!" Out here she seemed older than I; she seemed somewhat taller, too. She led me as if I were a baby to a place at the end of the line of boys. Before I could ask her what they were doing, she ordered me to shut my eyes.

"What you playing, Theresa?"

"Shut your mouth, too," she ordered, sharply.

I shut my eyes and my mouth. I listened.

"Now, you're next, Alexander," she said. "Come on. Keep your eyes shut or I'll not let you play."

I could see her leading Alexander away. I peeped. She led him to a corner of the old warehouse.

"Stop peeping and shut your eyes!" the other girl whispered loudly. She came and shook me. "I'll tell Theresa and she'll not let you play."

This girl must have been watching for Theresa. What kind of game *was* this.

Some of the boys whispered, sniggling. They seemed to be almost bursting.

"Keep *quiet*! the watcher pleaded. "Salvatore!"

"Yes, madam."

They could no longer hold their laughter. They quieted down. Wanting very much to play, I kept my eyes closed.

Theresa came back with Alexander. The other girl whispered for Salvatore to come along. Theresa, remaining to watch, said my turn was next.

And here it was!

"Keep your eyes shut, now," she warned me.

She pulled me along by the hand.

"What we go' do, Theresa?"

"Never mind. Just keep your eyes shut and do what I tell you."

"All right, Theresa,"

I pretended to shut my eyes tight, but my very effort at pretense gave me away. She slapped my face angrily.

"Now I won't let you play. You can go right home."

To make sure I reached my own gate, she shoved me all the way there.

"I'll *never* play with *you* again. You looked."

"But I didn't see nothing."

How my face burned where she had slapped me!

"I told you not to and you looked," she said.

"What was we go' do, Theresa?"

"Never mind. If you hadn't looked when I told you not to you'da found out. Now I'll *never* play with you again."

When we did play the game, I wondered whether it had been something like this mamma had been thinking about when she called Theresa dirty. Well, anyway, she *wasn't* dirty. She was nice! I dreamed about Theresa.

Standing on our third-floor gallery and looking across the sawtooth roof of the salt warehouse, I saw roustabouts loading steamboats and ships with boxes and crates and barrels and bales of cotton. I would stare at the men, tiny in the haze of distance, and try to pick out papa among them. Sometimes my eye would pick out a man as papa and follow him everywhere he went for an hour or more.

There would be steamers, one behind another, along the wharf. Each of the steamers and river steamboats had forests of masts and poles and derricks and cranes strung with wires or ropes. The derricks and cranes were on the forward decks and were used for lifting the heaviest things. The creaking of pulleys and songs of workmen seemed to harmonize well, but the shouts of foremen, coming distinctly across the levee and the roofs, were not pleasant. The tooting of boat whistles out on the river, and the rattling and clattering and rumbling of drays and floats and horsecars and wagons, and the sound of freight cars being coupled and uncoupled, and of steel horseshoes on cobblestones—these sounds made a kind of mad music when they mingled with the *puff! puff! puff-puff-puff!* and the *toot-toot!* And the *dang-glang!* Of freight locomotives all along the waterfront.

To stand and look upon all these things as they happened, while black smoke and gray and white vapor from the boats and the locomotives hung over the river on a cloudy day, was to have a feeling of being afloat above a rushing, swirling, clangorous, giddy world, which at the same time was beautiful because it was gentle and peaceful. It was *my* world.

"New Orleans Negro Family"
No Date, Unpublished, Eugene Gordon Papers[17]

This piece is included in the Gordon papers as a separate article, but it is from "Once I Was Afraid." Again, the poverty of the family is emphasized through the unsanitary conditions and the poor health care as well as the rampant racism they experience. His parents' love for their children and for one another is also on display as well as the different goals of the parents: his father wants to be independent and to earn an income, while his mother wants to provide a "civilized," safe place to raise the family. This connection makes the children feel safe and allows their imaginations to comfort them despite the harsh conditions. This bond is shaken when, in a powerful scene describing death from a child's perspective, Eugene's younger sister Gussie passes. The parents also cannot spare the family from the ravages of nature as an apocalyptic storm combines with the breaking of the levees that had been keeping out the flood waters.

New Orleans Negro Family

I now was nine years old.

We had just moved to 2533 South Rampart street, corner of Third. Our home was a one-story cottage-like house covered with reddish-brown paint. There were green slatted blinds on the Third street side. The peaked roof of the house and the shed over the *banquette* on the Rampart street side were covered with slate. The front room on the Rampart street side was a shop.

The house squatted flat on the ground and flush with the *banquette*. We could smell the damp musty earth under the floor, could touch the ground under the floor with a long pencil through a crack.

In the small backyard, paved with bricks, the big cistern and the big four-hole privy and a shed were jammed all together.

"The smells you get round here," mamma said, "is nough to make you puke."

She sure dreaded thinking how it would be in rainy weather, she said. The shed was boarded up all round and had a door opening into the yard. Mamma said it would be a good place to wash clothes in and to store old things. She said she had never got used to drinking water washed from the roof of the house by way of the gutters into those enormous barrels people called cisterns; but here, with things the way they were, she would be sick at the stomach every time she thought of taking a drink. Where we had lived in Florida, she said, people drank from a well or a spring . . .

A gate opened into Third street.

"I don't know what they call it a street for," mamma said. "All them wagon ruts, and them holes deep enough to bury a mule in. Old country road, that's all it is."

Rampart street, in front of the house, wasn't so bad, papa said. We couldn't have everything, he told mamma. What if there wasn't any asphalt—or even cobblestones? The plank covering of Rampart street was better than plain dirt. We had started our own business, anyway, and that was something to be proud of.

"Nothing like being your own boss," papa said.

A single cartrack ran down the middle of Rampart street. One end of the planks covering the street touched the cartrack, and the other end came out to the gutter. The gutter was a deep ditch almost filled with slow-running water covered with green slime, dust and trash.

Oh, this was going to be a wonderful place to live!

During the first day there buddy and I saw boys with nets and buckets catching minnows and crawfish from the gutter. One boy caught two squirming things we thought were eels. The boys said they were leeches and that if they got on our hands they would stick so hard that we would have to have them cut off at the hospital. The boys said they sold the leeches to doctors.

You could also sail boats in the gutter, and maybe go swimming, too—if you could find a place where there weren't any crawfish or leeches.

When wagons, floats, or drays[18] ran over the planks of Rampart street we heard a thunderous rumbling, and the dried manure and the dust boiled up like smoke, making it look like the street was on fire.

Mamma said she was glad we were not the only colored family in this neighborhood, as it had been when we lived on Felicity street. There were plenty of children here, too: white and colored—French and Creole and Italian, next door and round the corner and across the street. That was one reason I liked it so much here. Mamma said the girls round here were the most beautiful she had ever seen. Well, I had never seen as many children in the streets all the time, day and night. The main reason I liked it here was that we had our own store. I had made up my mind that I was going to eat all the candy and fruit I wanted, without having to pay for it, either. People would have to ask *us* for *lagniapp*[19] now!

Our parlor was just behind the shop; the bedroom was next beyond that; and beyond the bedroom was the kitchen, opening into the backyard. Right beside the kitchen door stood the cistern, and on the other side of the cistern was the privy. Then came the shed.

Papa brought home all sorts of secondhand mahogany furniture for our home. One was a four-posted bed with a roof over it like a house. Papa called this roof a *teaster*.[20] It was of mahogany and lined with fluted red silk that ran together to a fluffy little red ball in the center. Papa said that if this *teaster* fell on you while you slept it would be the same as if the roof of the house had fallen, because you would wake up in another world, anyway.

He bought a mahogany center table with a heavy white marble top, and a mahogany *armoire* that was so high it scraped the ceiling. Each post of the bed was as large almost as a telegraph pole—larger at the bottom than at the top. Papa had to get two men to help him set up the bed.

He said he got this old mahogany stuff because someday it would be worth plenty of money.

A mosquito bar[21] was fastened just inside the *teaster* of the big bed. At night when the mosquito bar was down, the bed, papa said, looked like a desert tent. The beds we children slept in didn't have *teasters* but they had mosquito bars. They had to or we couldn't have slept.

We lay imagining we were in tents in the jungle. Mosquitoes and moths were hungry eagles and screech owls trying to get at us to carry us off to their nests away up in the mountains. We lay comfortable and safe and happy, because papa and mamma were near. We lay whispering and giggling until mamma blew out the light and the tents vanished in the dark.

Mamma said that mosquitoes were worse here than she had ever seen them anywhere except at Indian River.[22] That was because this part of the city was built on low, swampy land, papa said, and because in front of us was the Mississippi River and behind us Lake Pontchartrain, both higher above our heads than the roofs of the houses. Only the levees held the river and the lake in check, he said.

"What would happen if the river and the lake broke loose?" mamma asked one night.

"We'd be drowned like so many puppies in a crate."

Papa bought a horse and a wagon, and I felt sure that every kid for blocks in all directions wished *his* father had a horse and a wagon. Bet Bobby and Dicky Arnold wished *their* father had a horse. He was a doctor but he didn't have a horse. Pride swelled in me when I saw the two boys standing on their porch across the street looking toward our place.

"Bobby! Dicky! C'm'ere. I wanna tell you somp'n."

"No, I can't. My ma won't let me."

"Why?"

I could hear their mother's voice inside their house:

"Bob-*bie*! Dick-*ie*! Don't you all *dare* go cross that street!"

"No'm. We're not going any place, ma."

Their mother the other day had slapped and jerked them into their own yard and slammed the gate because they had been playing with us in the gutter. The other boys said she did it because she didn't want them to play with "niggers."

I told mamma.

"That old white woman cross the street, that old Mrs. Arnold, she whipped them two little brats of hers today for playing with Eugene and Ernest," mamma told papa that night.

Papa didn't stop looking at the paper, but his face and the back of his neck got red. Papa had an olive complexion and reddish-brown hair and was sometimes mistaken for an Italian.

"So next time I catch Eugene and Ernest even talking to them Arnold kids," mamma said, "I'll give *them* a good whipping, too."

"How you know 'twas because they played with our children?"

"Because she don't like them to play with no colored children. One of them white boys they was playing with told Eugene she didn't want Bobby and Dicky to play with 'niggers.'"

By the way papa rattled the paper he was reading I knew he was angry.

"Funny way for a doctor's wife to act," he said. "They must aim to make a living round here, don't they? Or they wouldn't be living here."

"Hunh!" mamma said. "Catch *me* going to *him* for anything! I wouldn't call 'im in if I was dying. Sure wouldn't! If their younguns too good for round here, why don't they move over to St. Charles avenue?"[23]

"They will, all right," papa said, "soon's they make enough off the 'niggers' they despise so. But we, you and I, we'll have to stay right on."

"Eugene and Ernest," mamma said, "is just as good as her little old brats. What they want is for all the colored people to kiss their dirty, stinking feet, like that Simple Simon they got slaving for them."

Simon was a Negro hunchback. People said that all the Arnolds gave him for slaving for them was some old pants, a shirt and a pair of Dr. Arnold's wornout shoes, with a few scraps to eat and a corner of the shed in the backyard to sleep in. That's what they said; I didn't know. I liked

Simon, because he told us stories and rode us on his hump. We played that he was a camel. His hands were as big as a shovel and so strong he could lift nine-year-old Bobby high off the ground with one finger.

Yes, I bet the Arnolds were mad because we had a horse and a wagon.

Now that the business was on its feet, papa said, he could work some days on the waterfront. He rented out the horse and the wagon when he wasn't using them. Once in a while he wouldn't go to work on the waterfront but would drive up before the shop, ready to go to the French Market to buy things. He would tell me I could go with him if I wanted to.

I loved the strong, pungent horse-odor. I loved the smell of the livery stable and the harness. I loved the feeling of going somewhere and of seeing the crowded downtown streets with their tall buildings and listening to the sweet, exciting city sounds from a wagon seat. I sat there making stories around everything I saw and wondering about things I had seen but had not understood.

Was it true Dr. Newman and his wife, who lived in the narrow, three-story house catty-cornered across the street from us, didn't like their daughter's husband, Dr. Turner, because he was short and black and drank too much? She could pass for white, people said, so why didn't she? Why didn't all colored people who could pass for white not pass for white? Dr. Newman and his wife and daughter could, mamma said, but they didn't.

I had heard old Mrs. Marshall tell mamma that God made people the way they were: he had made white people white and black people black, Mrs. Marshall said, because *he* wanted them like that. That was why colored people and white people ought to stay to themselves, separately. But if God made white people white and colored people colored, and if he wanted them to stay like that, why were Dr. and Mrs. Newman so white that you couldn't tell the difference?

Papa had asked Mrs. Marshall that. She said that, oh, you could tell the difference, all right. When papa asked her how she could tell, if she didn't *know*, already, she said that, well, anyway, God could tell and that if colored people went round fooling white people like that, God would punish them ... I just *couldn't* understand!

After a hard rain we could see water through the cracks of our floor—could even touch it with the finger, if the crack was large enough.

And that was fun. Buddy and I would play that the house was a great, big ship crossing the Mississippi River. But mamma and papa didn't like to have water under the house. Mamma said it was no wonder so many people died of malaria. She wished we had an upstairs house, she said.

"I trust nobody in this house won't catch malaria," mamma would say.

"Or anything else," papa would say.

Then they would start talking about sister Gussie. She was five.

She sat, most of the time, just watching the rest of us play. She wouldn't smile and she wouldn't speak. She would only sit in a corner of the front door, her head resting against the jamb, and watch us. Her boney legs were so bent inward at the knees that she rocked from side to side when she walked. She sat in a corner of the front door of the shop watching us play on the *banquette*; and sometimes she started crying, all at once, and calling for mamma, because she wet herself.

"Poor little darling! It's *so* hard for you to get up and walk, aint it, honey?"

But it made me angry to see mamma treat sister Gussie like that. I thought mamma should spank her. She was just dirty, I thought, to wet herself, as big a girl as she was. And mamma never even scolded her.

One day she had a fever and couldn't get out of bed.

Malaria? Malaria! Sister Gussie's got malaria!

I thought she didn't have malaria. She only wanted to be petted. Of course she was sick almost all the time, so mamma and papa had spoiled her. Was she sure enough too sick now to get out of bed? I myself had often tried to fool mamma when I wanted to be petted and wanted people to feel sorry for me.

No, she aint got no malaria.

Dr. Rossi said she didn't have malaria. She was sick, though, he said.

I was sorry I had thought she was just pretending.

She wouldn't eat. The doctor said mamma must make her eat. I wondered whether sister Gussie wasn't just trying to show how pettish she could be. Mamma or papa would hold her up in bed and force the spoon between her teeth. She would bite the spoon. Mamma would slap her to make her open her mouth and cry, so some food could be slipped in. Sister Gussie wouldn't cry. She would look surprised; then she would look hurt; and she would primp her mouth and shake with sobs, but she would hold her jaws close together.

I knew then that she was very sick, because none of us ever fooled like that with mamma and papa, unless he wanted to be whipped. Sister Gussie didn't seem to care whether they whipped her or not. Yes, she was sick, all right.

"Give her liquids," the doctor said. "She's *got* to eat."

The doctor was white. He was oldish, with scant brown hair and pale eyes that looked worried through silver-rimmed glasses, and his thin face was full of up-and-down lines.

Sister Gussie said she was hungry! Mamma gave her soup and soft grits with milk and mashed bananas. She ate everything. And I *knew* she wasn't sick.

"Has she had a movement?" the doctor asked.

"No. We're worried about that."

The doctor gave her some medicine, but it didn't work. However, she ate everything. Papa and mamma said they wondered whether they ought to keep stuffing victuals into her. She lay a long time with closed eyes; she lay open-eyed and quiet, making no move.

"Gussie, want to get up? Want to sit on the chamber pot?"

"No ma'am."

"Honey, your stomach hurt?"

"Yessir."

Papa touched her stomach with his finger. She winced.

"Mamma," papa said.

He was excited when he called her mamma, for he always said Girl.

"Mamma, come here!"

She came running.

"What's the matter?"

"Feel her stomach. Careful!"

Mamma felt of sister Gussie's stomach.

"God, have mercy! Papa . . ."

They turned back sister Gussie's nightgown. Her stomach was round and tight—like a small round melon.

"My poor baby! It hurt much, honey."

"Yesm'am."

They felt it carefully all over.

I moved nearer.

"Mamma, can I feel it?"

Papa looked down at me.

"But be careful. Sister Gussie's mighty sick."

I touched her. I thought of a stone with a skin stretched over it. I thought of the Cuban and Porto Rican children's pictures in the papers when the war with Spain was going on last year.

"My! It's *hard*!"

I ran and told buddy and sister Stella.

"We better give her an enema," mamma said. "Don't you think so, papa?"

"I reckon so. You go 'head. I'm going to get Dr. Rossi."

The enema wouldn't work.

She began to cry, softly, with eyes wide open, staring at mamma.

"Sister Gussi got m'lary?" sister Stella asked.

"No," mamma said. "Sister Gussie's constipated."

We looked on, curiously and full of wonder.

"Y'oughter just feel her stomach," I said. "I *felt* it. Just like a rock was in there."

Buddy and sister Stella looked at mamma, but her face was enough to keep them from asking.

Dr. Rossi hurried in. He did again what mamma and papa had done. He also asked her to swallow some medicine. Give her nothing but liquids, he said. And the next day he did the same thing; and the next day, too. Liquids were poured into her; *everything went in but nothing came out!*

"If she don't do something soon," the doctor said, "she'll burst."

Mamma tried the enema again. Maybe it was too large. Papa bought another ... The doctor said:

"One of the best children's doctors in New Orleans is this Dr. Turner, that colored doctor, right across the street, here. Dr. Newman's son-in-law. I'm going to call him in."

Mamma and papa looked at each other.

"You know him?" mamma asked. "They say—"

"People say he's drunk all the time. Well, maybe. Maybe not. Anyhow, he can come look at her. I know he's a good doctor."

Dr. Turner came. He was a short little black man with sleeked, straight black hair and a small mustache that looked like a corkscrew on each upper lip. I thought he didn't seem drunk. We stood close about sister Gussie's bed. We watched the white doctor and the colored doctor.

I looked at Dr. Turner's short black fingers as he felt gently, keeping his eyes on siter Gussie's face. She lay watching, seeming only half awake.

Dr. Rossi too was watching Dr. Turner.

Dr. Turner stepped back from the bed.

"Strange case. Strangest case I've ever seen." He sighed. "I'm afraid it's too late. She's in a coma."

Mamma stared at him for a moment; then she scooped up her apron and buried her face in it, and she ran from the room, sobbing. Buddy, sister Stella and I were shocked at mamma's crying. Sister Gussie must be dying... Papa was talking quietly with the doctors. We children stood staring and listening, now and then looking at the bed where sister Gussie lay still. If she was dead, then she wouldn't ever get up again. They would bury her in the ground. She wouldn't be here any more...

Mamma and papa stayed up all night with her. Maybe she wouldn't die. Next morning she lay just as she had lain yesterday, seemingly almost but not quite asleep. She looked at us but did not seem to see us.

Mamma was crying and papa's eyes were swollen and red. It was awful to see grown people crying!...

Then sister Gussie moved her head, so she could look straight up—moving it with a jerk, so that her neck was a little crooked but so that she could look straight up. Papa put his hand on her heart.

"When will the doctor be here?" mamma asked, sniffling.

"Directly."

Papa was feeling her heart. He snatched his hand away and put his ear against her heart. He straightened up with a deep sigh that burst into a bellowing sob, startling us and making sister Stella whimper.

I looked at sister Gussie. Only the whites of her eyes were showing.

Papa smoothed her eyelids down with his fingers.

"Your sister Gussie's dead," he said to us.

We stood staring at her in silence, full of wonder and full of strange questions...

Our shop was closed. White crepe was hanging on our front door. I walked through the shop and the parlor and the bedroom—tiptoeing softly where people sat saying nothing—and out through the kitchen and the yard.

I went out into Third street and walked round to the front of the shop to look at the closed windows and the closed door and the crepe. Crepe was on *our* house this time. This time somebody was dead in *our* house. It was sister Gussie. I stood trying to imagine all it meant now and would mean thereafter. Sister Gussie was dead! She would be put in a hole in the cemetery. We would have a funeral. *We—we* would have a funeral! We wouldn't see her anymore after that. It would be as if she were gone away for good. . . .

The weather was cloudy—was misty, damp, and cold. We had a fire in the grate in the parlor. Third street was a great gutter running with black mud.

People from our church came—Mr. and Mrs. Martin, Mr. and Mrs. Watson, Mr. and Mrs. Lewis. Old Mrs. Marshall came, too, and plenty of people I did not know. Some of them went to the cemetery. We had two carriages. Papa and buddy and I had a piece of white crepe round one arm. Men along the *banquette* faced us and took off their hats, and I had a funny feeling all over my body. I had seen people doing that many times when funerals passed, and now they were doing it for *us*. It was hard to believe that *we* were in a funeral. Just think! Sister Gussie was the cause of all this, and she so little, too . . .

It was raining. Mudholes and puddles of water were everywhere. The horses hitched to our carriage made sorrowful sounds with their feet. A gray, dull mist was around the old tombstones and vaults, and we rode through the puddles and past the tombstones and vaults and came to a place where we got out and saw a hole in the ground with fresh earth around it. We stood in the mud.

Elder Marks prayed above the coffin. It seemed awfully little out here. He said *Dust unto dust* and papa and some of the other people picked up handfuls of mud from the pile that had been dug out of the grave and they threw it on the coffin down at the bottom. I looked down and I saw water coming slowly over the coffin. And for the first time, now, I knew what death meant. Sister Gussie was in that terrible hole in a box with muddy water all over her face and all over her body. *And she couldn't get out!* . . .

Gradually, after many days, I could think of her without shuddering with terror. It was better, however, not to think of her, for to think hurt too much. But when Elder Marks or any other Christian now spoke of heaven and judgment day and of people's rising from the dead, I thought about sister Gussie and wondered how she could come up through the water and mud and dirt, and through the lid of the coffin, when Gabriel blew his trumpet. She would come up, I knew, but *how*?

And now that she would be whiter than snow[24]—whiter than white people—how would it feel to meet her, we being still colored? I was curious about that.

It was spring again and in the air there was a feeling something like the end of the world was coming. That was what I heard people saying. I hadn't noticed it before they spoke about it, but I too could feel it now. Papa read from the papers that men were working day and night building the levees higher. The river in front of us and the lake behind us were about to break through! They had already broken through at some places. People in their homes had been washed away. Their houses had been crushed in on them while they slept.

"It's dangerous to go to sleep," people said. "The floods might come."If it come, 'twon't make no difference if you sleep or wake. It'll get you."

Men in front of our shop joked about the flood. They were scared, though. We could tell by their jokes that they were scared.

The weather got warmer.

Cakes of ice bigger than a house were floating down the river. Big cakes of ice jammed the middle of the stream, piling up, papa said.

"Just wait till all that ice melts," people said. "Then you'll *see* something."

"I'm afraid this warm weather'll make the river overflow," papa said.

He said the flood might spare us, because we were about midway between the river and the lake. Besides, the lake didn't look as if it was going to break through right now. It was the river that had to be watched, because it was the river that was bringing all that ice from up north.

Not only was it warmer now but cloudy, too.

"Worst thing could happen would be for it to rain," a customer in the shop said.

It was already raining! A wind came up from behind us, from across the backyards, and it shook great sheets of rain up and down and across the streets and it slapped them against the houses. The sky reddened as if the city were on fire. But no fire could burn in *this* rain storm, unless . . .

Maybe the end of the world! . . . People said fire and brimstone on judgment day would burn the world up—maybe even the rain couldn't put out *that* fire! I stood under the shed in front of the shop, looking at the reddened sky and watching and listening for Gabriel's horn.

But the glow faded and, suddenly, darkness came. Lights show through windows up and down Rampart street. Rain on the shed sounded like bed ticking being ripped into long strips. The gutter was level with the *banquette* and the street. Lightning split the sky into ragged pieces and thunder cracked through them and rattled the windowpanes. It was as if something had knocked the bottom out of the cistern, for the rain didn't come in drops after that. It poured down in a stream. I was scared our roof would give way.

"Eugene," mamma called. "Run out to the shed and get the washtub. Quick!"

Water was coming through the bedroom ceiling!

I dashed through the yard to the shed, up to my knees in water. Water was rolling over the upper edge of the cistern.

"Oh, mamma! The cistern's running over. Water's just *pouring* out!"

"All right. Put that tub down there. See if the ceiling's leaking anywhere else."

"Mamma! Look!" sister Stella called. "Water coming up out the floor!"

The flood had come! The river had overflowed! Would we be drowned like puppies in a crate?

Mamma jerked sister Stella away. A corner of the kitchen already was under a layer of muddy water edged with white foam. Water was creeping toward the center of the floor.

Buddy, sister Stella and I looked through the crack where we had often seen water gleaming beneath the floor. It was coming through!

Mamma got a broom. She opened the kitchen door. She was going to sweep the water into the yard. But water in the yard was already to the top of the doorsill. Mamma shut the door and put the broom away. We stood watching the water spread over the kitchen floor.

I ran into the bedroom to see whether any more had come through the crack. It had not. But if I jumped up and down on the spot the water would squirt up through the floor.

"Eugene! Stop that jumping in there! You crazy?"

There was hardly any leaking from the ceiling. The crashing sound of rain on the roof had stopped. There was a faraway rumbling of thunder. Water on the kitchen floor was not rising any higher, but it was not going down, either. When we walked heavily we heard water sloshing beneath us.

It had gone down in the backyard, but the cistern was still spilling over. Water ran down its side all around in one continuous sheet.

In the privy it was almost to the level of the floor.

My! Suppose *that* overflowed!

The whole *banquette* and all Rampart street were like a river. I wondered where we could get a boat, for certainly we'd need one.

Men stood under our shed in front of the shop and watched women raise their dresses to their waists as they crossed the street. Some women—and men, too—took off their shoes and stockings. Mamma said the women were just glad of a chance to show off themselves in front of the men. Whenever a woman raised her skirt so that the tops of her stockings showed, the men under the shed whispered and snickered behind their hands.

Rain stopped and the sun came out.

Papa told us that night that down near the river people were using row boats in the streets. First floors of houses and the water was creeping farther and farther into the middle of the city. Thousands of men were working like slaves to pile up sandbags on the levee. The soldiers were out....

"Th' wont be much sleeping in New Orleans tonight," papa said.

"I wouldn't dare shut my eyes tonight," a man passing our shop said.

We waited and watched, but the flood did not come. The gutter went down. The privy went down. Papa said if we didn't draw some water from the cistern it might burst. Crawfish and crabs crawled about the backyard and the *banquette*.

Now for more malaria and more deaths, mamma said. And they stuffed us with medicines.

After church on Sunday the whole family went down to the river. Papa said he wanted to show us ships floating over our heads. None of us knew exactly what he was talking about, but as we got near the river we could see that the levee looked like a mountain. We stood away off at the foot of it and stared up its slanting side. Then it was plain that we hadn't come *down* to the river, for if we were to see the old Mississippi at all we would have to do some climbing. The river was high, high up there over our heads. And up there, tied to the wharf, we could see the masts and riggings of ships swaying and rocking. Like ships on top of a mountain!

"Killer at Large!,"
No Date, Unpublished, Eugene Gordon Papers[25]

It was the rampant racism in New Orleans that led to the violent shooting spree by Robert Charles in July 1900. Like many such incidents, it started over what seemed like a harmless encounter. Charles and another Black man were reported to police as "two suspicious looking negroes." Charles made what to the police officer was "a menacing gesture," and the officer grabbed him. When Charles attempted to break free, the officer fired a shot, whereupon Charles returned fire, shooting but not killing two of the officers.[26] A police manhunt of enormous proportions was the immediate response, and before Charles was gunned down, he killed a number of the police and wounded several others.[27] "At least twenty African Americans" according to Daniel Candee "were killed by rampaging mobs."[28]

This gunfight, which occurred only a few blocks from where Eugene lived, and the backlash, made an indelible impression on the nine-year-old boy. In the semiautobiographical piece "Killer at Large," Gordon relates the aftermath of Charles's rampage. The lesson that Eugene takes as he thinks to himself is *I want to be like Robert Charles, . . . Die with my boots on!* But after he has had some time to think about it, he checks his anger and hails two white friends from across the street. The two boys answer him in a friendly manner, but "their mother yelled at them from inside the house not to dare speak to those niggers." The boy's instinct is to try to look at whites as potential friends and allies, even after such a horrific incident, but the racist system makes it nearly impossible for any such bonding to occur, a lesson that is taught to children at an early age.

Killer at Large!

I pushed open the gate of our yard and went out into Third street early one July Monday morning and I caught my heart in my mouth to find myself standing right behind a big policeman. Another was directly across the street, and still another on this side [of] the street, at the corner of Rampart, near the front of our shop. Not since we had come to live in New Orleans had I seen so many policemen, and I stood gaping up and down Third street, counting the blue uniforms. But I gave it up, because there were too many. Each of them had a long, slender rifle in his hand.

The policeman in front of me turned round.

"What th' hell you want here, nigger boy?"

"Nothin'!"

I backed into the yard, fastened the gate, and, my heart bumping painfully against my chest, ran and told mamma.

I led the way through the house to the shop. Mamma opened the broad, deep window into Rampart street. It was here we displayed our fruits and vegetables on step-like shelves. We could see policemen from here, too; and from this window we could see them for a block and a half out Third street in the direction of the river. Their backs were toward us and they all held their rifles as if about to shoot. Mamma pointed out some on roofs and cisterns and in trees.

She went and opened the door of the shop. There was a slight frown of worry about her mouth and eyes as, standing just a little inside the door, she peered up and down Rampart street. I wished papa were here, and I knew mamma wished it, too, but he had gone to work before we had got up and he wouldn't be home until night.

Mamma stepped outside the shop upon the *banquette* and she stood looking up and down Rampart street. She glanced at the back of the policeman who stood just on the other side of the gutter in front of the shop, but she was too timid to ask him what it all meant, although I could see she wanted to do so.

She stepped back inside.

"Funny th'aint no colored people nowhere in sight."

There were no women in sight, either—no colored women and no white women. White men and boys were everywhere. They were standing and talking in little knots, now and then pointing with sticks or clubs. They all seemed to be friendly with the policemen.

"Something's up," Mamma said, "and it's no Sunday school picnic, either."

Buddy, sister Stella and baby Reginald had crowded into the shop. Mamma made them all go back to the kitchen. She told me to stay with her. We began to carry the crates and boxes of fruits and vegetables outside and to arrange them on the step-like shelves under the window.

"Bet it's some poor fool of a colored man's done something," mamma said, in that hopeless tone.

"Why, mamma?"

"Why! Because you don't see nothin' but white men round here, that's why. Where's all the colored people we see hangin' round here every mornin'?"

"Maybe it's too early..."

That sounded foolish and I knew it. Mamma paid no attention to what I had said. When she finished, she again looked up and down the street, watching, I knew, for somebody who could tell her what had happened.

"Watch for the ice wagon," mamma said, coming inside again. "We got to get a hundred pounds today."

She went back to the kitchen.

Sunshine began to glint on the slate roofs and to fall goldenly down the length of the street. It made the policeman's rifle barrels look like silver. Everything was frighteningly quiet. I got up on a box inside the broad, deep window and began to watch for the iceman. It was as if nobody lived in the city except policemen. When a streetcar passed it seemed to be unusually noisy but there were few passengers.

Catty-cornered across the street from our shop I watched a policeman stealing up behind another, jokingly, turning now and then to make signs to the one standing in front of our shop. When the funmaker grabbed the other policeman's gun, he almost got his face knocked in with the butt of it, for the policeman wheeled round, yelling, and struck him with all his might with his rifle.

"You goddam fool!" he yelled. "I oughter turned round shootin'!"

The policeman in the street in front of our shop was laughing. He called across the street:

"You thought the nigger had got you, didn't you, Tony?"

"The bastard!" Tony yelled, and I wondered whether he meant the funmaker or "the nigger."

Anyway, mamma had guessed right. It *was* some poor colored man they were after.

A group of young white fellows stopped in front of the open window, and they looked me up and down with such insolence and hatred that I backed down off the box, ready to shout for papa. I would call papa, I thought, though he wasn't there. That might frighten them. Then I wondered whether policemen in the street before the shop would arrest them if they tried to hurt me.

As I watched them, determined not to be outwitted and trying to guess what they intended to do, the policeman looked round. My heart leaped with joy, and I raised my hand to attract his attention. He saw me and he saw them, and as I was about to cry out that these men wanted to hurt me, something hard struck me above the bridge of the nose between the eyes and I thought my head had been smashed open.

Someone yelled "Perfect hit!" and I heard loud laughter and shouts of "nigger," and when I could see again I noticed that the policeman's back was toward me. The young fellows were now away over in the middle of Third street talking with another policeman.

I climbed upon the box again, feeling vague pains through the dizziness in my head. My nose was bleeding.

I heard loud, rough laughter coming toward me. Another crowd! I got down off the box, for I didn't want to be too tempting a target a second time. It seemed that this crowd of white fellows and I saw Frankie at the same moment. Frankie was a boy I knew, a Negro boy, and at that moment he was running as fast as he could along the *banquette* on the other side of Rampart street.

One of the fellows picked up a potato off our stand and hurled it at Frankie. It nearly hit a policeman, who wheeled about with his hand on his revolver. When he saw who had thrown it and at whom it had been thrown, and heard Frankie's shriek of terror, he bent double in laughter and he slapped his knee and yelled:

"Watch me shoot that rabbit!"

He didn't shoot, although he held up his revolver and twirled it in his hand, so that the gun glinted wickedly on it. I thought somehow of the darting, forked tongue of a snake.

Two Negro men, dressed in overalls and jumpers, were coming up Rampart street toward Third. They were walking side by side but were silent, it seemed; were slowing up as they came, watching all about them, as if uncertain whether to come on or go back.

Across the street I saw Dr. Arnold and his wife on their porch with Bobby and Dicky. They were talking with the policeman who had frightened the Negro boy. I did not see Simon, the hunchback Negro who worked for them and who had a place to sleep in their backyard shed. Dr. Arnold was nodding in the direction of our shop, while the policeman turned and stared. I imagined the doctor and his wife were telling the policeman they didn't like papa....

Just then the two Negro men reached a point directly in front of the shop window, and some half-grown white boys met them and stopped in front of them and blocked their way.

The men said nothing. They tried to go round the boys. And before I could guess what would happen next, one of the boys struck one of the Negro men across the face with a stick and another tripped him, and they shoved him into the deep gutter. He struck the water *plopf!* and floundered about on the edge of the *banquette*. But they tramped on his hands and kicked them loose. Two of the boys jumped on his head and pushed him into the water and held him there.

"Papa! Papa!" I shouted. "Bring your pistol, quick! They killin' a man."

The other man broke loose and ran round the corner into Third street. He was crying out to the policeman to stop the boys. The policeman who had been standing in front of our shop was gone. The Negro man was running back and forth, trying to cross the street toward Dr. Arnold's house. Mrs. Arnold, seeing him getting nearer, screamed and pushed her husband aside and ran inside. The policeman turned and met the man.

"For God's sake, don't let 'em kill me!" the man was yelling.

The white boys had all gone now.

The policeman grabbed the Negro man's collar and shook him.

"Shut up your goddam gibbering, you," he hollered, "and tell me what's the matter with you."

The man tried to tell.

"All right." The policeman shoved him and he stumbled to his knees. "Get on with you," the policeman ordered, "before I lock you up."

But the Negro was pointing toward the place where the attack had been made on him. The policeman came near the spot. He stopped and stood gawking into the gutter. He straddled the gutter, then reached down and caught the other man by the shoulders and dragged him out and tossed him on the *banquette*. The man lay crumpled up, his head bent under his left shoulder.

"He's dead!" I said aloud, stepping down from the box in the window.

I was surprised to find mamma, buddy, sister Stella and baby Reginald beside me. Mamma and buddy had seen it all.

An ambulance came and got the man.

Mamma was silent and her face was hard. She went and stood in the door.

"The dirty, filthy white scum!" she screamed.

The policeman, half way across the street, turned round and looked at her.

"Yes, I said it!" mamma cried. "You cowardly white beasts!"

The policeman started toward us.

"Mamma!" I yelled in terror.

"Hey, there!" Dr. Arnold called.

The policeman looked toward Dr. Arnold; stopped, and stared from Dr. Arnold to us.

"Come here a minute," the doctor called, beckoning with his finger.

The policeman went back. During the few minutes they were talking, the policeman turned twice and glared at mamma. She did not move. She stood with her hands on her hips and her head up. I hoped he wouldn't come back, for I felt sure mamma would get papa's pistol and shoot him.

He didn't come back.

"He'll have it in for us now, all right," mamma said, going back into the shop.

She asked me whether we had had any customers. There had not been one. She went back to the kitchen.

Papa came home earlier than usual that evening. Mamma fell upon him, crying. She clung to him, kissing his cheeks and caressing his hair.

"I thought you would never, *never* come!" she said.

Papa laughed quietly and patted mamma's shoulder. He pushed her gently from him.

"Hell's loose all round here tonight," he said. "Beating up Negroes right and left. Men, women and children. Dragging them off the cars and even going into their homes after them."

"What's happened, anyhow?" mamma asked. "I know it's some poor Negro, though. Did some Negro kill a white man? I been wantin' to ask somebody all day but I aint seen a soul to ask."

She went on getting supper.

"I'll tell you all about it," papa said.

He went into the parlor. We could hear somebody running along the Third street side of our house. We heard shouts and yells coming nearer. Something crashed against the house—a brickbat or stone. Now a crowd was running by, hollering. We heard the word "nigger." Now it was quiet again outside.

Papa came from the parlor with the pile of Bishop Turner's[29] magazine, the "Voice of Missions." His face was tight, his jaws set, and his eyes cold and hard. He waited for mamma to clean the top of the stove, then he removed the lids and, twisting two or three papers together, he laid them on the fire.

Mamma's head was bent over her work. She asked no questions, but we children stood in gaping wonder. Mr. Robert Charles had given papa those magazines and papa had liked them. Now he was burning them . . . We saw papa get his revolver from the dresser drawer, examine it, and lay it on top of the dresser beside a box of cartridges.

"Anybody been here looking for me today?" papa asked, coming back into the kitchen and sitting at the table.

Mamma was putting the food on.

"No. Why?"

"Oh, anybody. Civilian? Policeman?"

A strange thought struck me. I gazed big-eyed at papa, my mouth wide open. He was looking at the newspaper, "Killer at Large!" the headline said.

"No. Nobody's been here."

"Not in the store, either? Looking round, maybe, or asking questions?"

"Why, no."

Mamma dropped on the chair near papa and stared at him, trying to see his eyes. Papa was looking at the newspaper.

"Why? What happened, papa?"

Papa glanced at us. We sat at our places at the table, watching, listening and not eating. Papa glanced at the window. We children did, too. He looked at mamma.

"I thought Robert Charles might've come here," papa said, frowning to himself. He spoke in a low voice. "Being I'm one man he knows he can trust." Papa stroked his mustache, thinking, "On second thought, though, I reckon I'm mistaken about that—about him coming here. He's man enough to stand on his own feet. I don't think he'd do nothing to compromise his friends."

Mamma sat staring at papa's eyes. We children sat staring and listening. We heard fire engines rushing by. Somebody hollered. We sat staring.

"You all eat your supper!" papa said to us.

We began to eat, still staring at him.

What's happened, papa?" mamma asked again, quietly. "Is he mixed up in this trouble?"

Papa read through a piece on the first page of the newspaper. He laid the paper down and started to eat.

"They're after Robert Charles for killing two policemen," papa said.

"Oh!"

Mamma, holding her hand on her heart, looked at papa.

It happened last night, Sunday night. Papers were full of it. But you couldn't believe the papers, papa said. They called him a fiend, a black brute, a degenerate, a rapist, "and everything else," papa said, "'cept a child of God." It was all lies, he said. He knew they were lies, because he knew Robert Charles. Charles was no degenerate and he was no rapist; he was interested in only one thing, papa said, and that was becoming a Moses of his people. So if he killed one policeman or two policemen or any number of policemen, papa said, he did it because he was driven to it and he thought because there was nothing else he could do.

"You reckon they'll search this place here?" mamma said.

"They will, all right. Wonder they aint been here already."

We began to listen for the policemen's coming.

"The mayor's offering a big reward for him, dead or alive," papa said, "so he'll try to find a place to hide where he can trust the people. He knows he can trust me."

He looked at mamma. They stared at each other, and they looked at us.

"Hurry up and finish your supper and get to bed," mamma said.

"Would you take him in, with the children here?" mamma asked. "Do you reckon . . ."

Papa looked worried.

"You reckon," mamma asked, "they found out he knows you?"

Papa laughed shortly.

"If they did they'd been here, all right. They're beating up and murdering everybody they think ever had anything to do with him. They call him an anarchist. They say he wanted to destroy the white race."

Papa laughed again, shortly. Mamma said "Hunh!"

"For years and years," papa said, "the white man kicks you around and treats you like a yellow dog. 'Don't go there.' Or 'You come here!', they say to the Negro. They make him kiss their feet and they lynch and burn him if he don't. Then when he stands up like a man and says he's tired of being treated like a cur and sick and tired being lynched and burned, they're *so* surprised! Why, the dirty anarchist! To dare talk to white men like that!"

Papa got up and walked round the floor. He sat down again.

"You better be careful, papa," Mamma said. "You better be careful how you talk. And I don't want you to go down on the waterfront tomorrow."

Papa was a longshoreman.

Mamma told him about the murder in front of our shop. She told him about her run-in with the policeman.

Papa's laugh this time was just a grunt.

"You tell *me* to be careful and watch *my* tongue; you better take your own advice." He looked at mamma hard for a moment, then he patted her hand. Don't give 'em any excuses. That's what they looking for."

Next morning—Tuesday—the streets were filled with white men and boys with guns and revolvers. Papa said they were deputies. He told mamma to notice that there were no Negro deputies and he said he reckoned she knew what *that* meant.

"*They* call 'em deputies but *I* call 'em mobs," papa said.

He said the newspapers talked about riots but that there were no riots.

"'S big difference between a mob and a riot. Maybe a little rioting wouldn't hurt so much."

Papa put his pistol in his belt under his coat and went down to the levee.

When he came home he told mamma he had made friends with the policeman in front of the shop and had got him to promise to look after us.

"Hunh!" mamma said. "*I* don't trust 'em."

"I don't, either," papa said. "But it's better to have them with you than against you. A five-dollar bill helped," he laughed.

"I don't trust none of 'em," mamma said. "An' think of all the things we need that we could buy with five dollars."

"Well, maybe we bought a little safety for you and the children."

We kept the shop closed all day Wednesday. Wednesday night papa said that maybe a hundred colored people had been beaten up and no less than ten killed. They were beating everybody they thought had ever known Robert Charles. Papa said he thought he ought to stay home tomorrow, because they might come. While papa was talking, the policeman to whom papa had given the money came in and asked if he and his friend could go to the back yard.

I noticed that they took off their hats and spoke politely. Papa was polite with them, too. He opened the back door and showed them where the privy was. Mamma didn't even look at them. When they had gone back to the street mamma said:

"You smell the whiskey on their breath? They didn't want to go to no privy."

Papa laughed.

"Certainly not. But what of it? We can feel just a little more safe when they're round. They'll at least keep any mobs from collecting in front of the place.

Thursday night, when papa came home from a walk round the neighborhood, he said they had taken away the policeman who had been stationed in front of our shop. A new one was there. Papa said that when he came in this new policeman turned and watched him. Mamma asked papa whether he thought it meant anything, especially, and papa said it might. Mamma and papa made us got to bed early but they were still up when I went to sleep.

Next morning papa read that the Negro high school had been burned. Firemen had been held at bay by the mob. No arrests had been made. A streetcar had been stopped and all its passengers ordered off—all except a lone Negro. The mob had made him stay aboard and they had set the car afire.

Papa read:

"The car was reduced to ashes, with the shrieking Negro fighting desperately but futilely to escape. The mob of young white men and youths just laughed at his pleas to be allowed to live. Someone shouted back at him that Robert Charles hadn't allowed Sergeant of Police Aucoin and Patrolman Cantrelle to live. Police arrived on the scene shortly after the mob had satisfied its lust for revenge and dispersed."

Papa laughed bitterly.

"Revenge! As if the white man needed revenge! If anybody needs revenge, it's people like us. The brave, superior white man!"

Papa read that police were now making [a] systematic search of all houses in the vicinity of Dryades, Sixth, Rampart, and Saratoga streets. They were arresting Negroes who had copies of the "anarchistic" "Voice of Missions," "a particularly vicious magazine which incites Negroes to violence against whites" and that which was published "by a Negro bishop in Atlanta." This magazine, papa read, had been distributed by Robert Charles and his black accomplices "in their plot to exterminate the whites."

Papa laid the paper down and looked at mamma.

"Just what I thought they'd do," he said. "The bloodhounds are on the trail, and it don't make any difference if the scent is false."

"I don't know what would be worse," mamma said. "To have Robert

Charles come here to hide or mobs to come here to kill us and burn us out."

Papa was just about to speak, but loud knocking at the front door stopped him. He waited a moment, listening. We listened, watching papa. The knocking came again, louder. Buddy whispered, "That Robert Charles?" Nobody said anything to him. Papa got up and went and took his pistol and slipped it into the side pocket of his pants. Mamma trailed after papa, holding her heart, and we children trailed mamma. We went through the bedroom and the parlor to the shop door.

"Who's there?"

"It's all right. Police. Mind if we come in and look round?"

Papa opened the door. Two, big, tall policemen came in. They had on long, black raincoats, glistening wet, and high dome-shaped hats with beads of water on them. Their hands were under their raincoats, but their clubs dangled outside.

"What can we do for you?" papa said.

They smiled briefly and looked round the shop. They glanced round the parlor; but in the bedroom they went and opened the armoire and looked in it, punching the clothes with their clubs. They looked under the four-poster bed. They went on through the kitchen to the backyard and they looked in the shed. When they came back their hands were out and they held revolvers.

They smiled again.

"Sorry to bother you all, but it's our duty. Just trying to protect you, you know."

Papa smiled back and nodded. He locked the door after them.

"Hunh!" mamma said. "Protect us! Like a cat protects a mouse."

Papa sat down at the table and picked up the newspaper again.

"I thought that was Robert Charles," buddy said.

Papa looked round at us as if surprised.

"Why aren't they in bed?" he asked, crossly. "You all go on to bed," he ordered.

Papa was out most of Friday. Mamma was scared they would kill him, but, she said, maybe they thought he [was] white. There were so many dark-skinned white people in New Orleans, she said, that a mulatto might pass.

Friday night I was awakened by shooting. It sounded like a war. I sat up in bed, listening. It was quiet in the house. Why didn't papa and mamma say something.

"Mamma."

"What you want?"

She came in from the shop.

"I was scared. I didn't know where you was. Papa gone out?"

"Yes. You better go on back to sleep," mamma told me. I lay listening. I sat up again, later, when I heard papa talking. I must have fallen asleep and his coming in wakened me.

"Well, they got him," papa said, in a sad, tired voice.

I held my breath, listening. Mamma and papa came from the shop into the parlor, next to the bedroom.

"Before they got him, though, he got most a hundred of them," papa said. He laughed shortly. "Talk about dying with your boots on!"

The way he said it made it sound nice to die with your boots on.

"Reckon they'll stop beatin' an' killin' Negroes now," mamma said.

"It's time the dirty yellow dogs let up," papa said.

I could hear him walking round the floor in the parlor. I could hear him walking.

"You know what them stinking mobs've done?" papa hollered. "You know what they've done? Oh, how I'd like to lead a mob of blacks against them."

"Sh-h-h!" mamma whispered. "You better be careful, papa!" Then: "What they done? Killed somebody we knowed? Papa did they—?"

"They're *so* brave!" papa said. "They're—You know what they did. Killed that hunchback! Simon. Simple Simon, of all people! Now, what could *he* do to them? What did *he* have to do with Robert Charles? Beat that poor hunchback's head to such a pulpy mess—I *seen* it, with my own eyes! it looked like a—looked like a dog I seen once that the street car run over . . . ."

I hadn't known papa cared so much about this hunchback, Simon. We children liked him because he let us ride on his hump. White children and colored children. We played he was a camel. But mamma and papa always called him Simple Simon and said he kissed the Arnolds' feet . . . .

All at once I heard papa laughing . . . It sounded like laughter and it sounded liked crying. He stopped and neither mamma nor he said anything.

"The children sleep?" papa asked quietly.

"Yes. Poor things! I'm glad they aint old enough to know—"

"Thank God for that," papa said. "But they'll meet it soon enough."

I thought of Dr. and Mrs. Arnold's boys, Bobby and Dicky, and whether now that Robert Charles was dead and the white people had stopped killing colored people we could talk about it tomorrow. I wondered what they would say about Simon. Would they be *awful sorry?* . . .

"If I ever catch these children playing with them Arnold kids, or any other little old white kids round here," mamma said, "I'll whip them so they can't sit down. I just dare–"

"I never felt so much like killing in all my life," papa said quietly. "Never felt so much like killing white men. I'd just like to take . . ."

I was worried about what mamma had said. Well, she needn't know . . . I wondered whether Robert Charles had had any children and how they felt now, and I wondered whether the men the mobs had killed and the men Robert Charles had killed had had any boys ten years old, like Bobby and me and some other boys I knew and how these boys felt now. All these children must feel like fighting and killing one another now, all right. I bet they did!

I want to be like Robert Charles, I thought. *Die with my boots on*!

Next day, Saturday, the policemen were gone and the colored people were on the *banquettes* and in the streets again. I saw Bobby and Dicky on their porch, and I called them. They answered me, but their mother yelled at them from inside the house not to dare speak to those niggers.

"Jim Peters' Black Boy"
No Date, Unpublished, Eugene Gordon Papers[30]

This autobiographical essay may have originally been intended for "Once I Was Afraid." However, it works well independently. The piece speaks about the psychology of racism and its damaging effects. Jim Peters treats Ad similarly to the way the Arnolds treated their servant Simple Simon in "New Orleans Negro Family," worse than enslaved people would have been treated. Young Eugene, instead of sympathizing with Ad, cannot comprehend how he could stand being treated as he is. Eugene even adds on to the insults by not acknowledging his name, just as others have denied him an identity other than being a piece of property. This piece shows again the process of how a naïve boy gradually gains a sense of the unfairness of life. As Gordon's father predicts, eventually Ad will explode, which is what occurs. As in "Killer at Large!" people can only be oppressed for so long before violence happens. Violence and oppression are inexorably linked. And when the explosion occurs, whites as well as Blacks will suffer, demonstrating why both races need to try to prevent the root causes of oppression.

Jim Peters' Black Boy

Ad was Jim Peters' black boy, people said. Ad *was* a black boy. Ad belonged to Peters as truly as African slaves in the South used to belong to certain wealthy whites. The Peters farm was next to ours, and we kids used to see Ad often. None of us knew anything about him—where he came from, how old he was, whether he had any kinfolks, whether he got any fun out of life. We in the midst of our families thought Ad must be awfully lonesome, but that was no reason why we should worry about him. We never saw him with boys or girls.

We saw him in the Peters field when we got up in the morning—that is, when we thought to look over that way, across the road; and we saw him feeding the mules and the hogs, milking the cows and chopping wood just before it got too dark across the field to see anything. We thought Ad must be lonesome because he was always by himself; yet we thought he must also have lots of fun. I often used to think that Ad must be happy.

The reason why I thought he was happy and life was so full of fun for him—in spite of everything I knew was pretty bad with the way he had to live—was that his eyes softened and watered like those of a gentle housedog whenever he saw us, and his face, as glisteningly black as mamma's new patent leather belt, would break into the soft folding curves of his smile. His eyes and teeth were as white as his body was black. It was nice to see his smile. Its indefinite beauty, as I now recall it, gave me a fleeting but distinct feeling of pleasure.

Although Ad's smile made us feel good, we saw it seldom for we saw him only a long way off. He was disgraced in our sight; he was an outcast; he was Jim Peters' slave. I don't know exactly how or when we began to avoid him as if he carried some repulsive disease, or to tolerate him when we could not escape temporary contact, as one tolerates a homeless old dog in a moment of pity. I cannot recall that my father had anything to do with it, but mamma, it seems used to order us to "keep away from that dirty, ignorant Ad." We got the impression from the older people's attitude that nice children, or the children of nice people, fouled themselves if they so much as spoke to Jim Peters' black boy.

I didn't try, of course, to understand why Ad's smile had that effect on us. In fact, I didn't think about it; none of us children did. It simply seemed to happen that whenever it was possible we put ourselves where we could see Ad and he could see us—always keeping a respectable distance between us. We would be standing there looking into the road through the wide cracks of the gate. We would see Ad coming along the road with his ax on his shoulder and his old yellow dog jogging in his footsteps. Buddy or I, or even Sister Stella, would say softly (so mamma or papa back at the house couldn't hear us); "Hello, Jim Peters' black boy," or "Hello, sundown in Africa," and laugh so hard at our wit and daring that we rolled in the weeds fringing the field.

Ad would stop and observe us, balancing the ax on his shoulder. His eyes and teeth would scintillate for a moment—less than a second—and he would say, "'Lo, Jeems. I always corrected him, "My name's not Jeems; it's Eugene." But it made no difference. He would say, "Awright, Jeems," and go on toward Peters' gate farther along the road, his long, lithe body under his ragged overalls and shirt moving with the sinewy rhythm of a great black cat's, his big bare feet making on the sandy road shapes as delighted our eager imaginations.

Sometimes we would be playing near the big gate on a Sunday morning. Mamma and papa would be away at church. We could hear the faraway sound of a Negro fieldhand's "hollering" a work song (and this was a terrible sin on a Sunday), the malady falling in patterns as clear and distinct as the separate sounds made by little stones dropped in a well and yet as harmoniously together as the successive ripples that followed. A mockingbird singing in the orchard back at the house would, ever so often, spring into the air with a graceful ruffle of white and blue feathers.

Then there would be three sharp cracks of a whip; there would be an agonized wail: "O Lord, have mercy! O Lord, have mercy! O Lord, have mercy! O, Lord, have mer . . ." We kids would stop playing and stare at one another. We would stare with open mouths toward the sounds. We would hear the lash still . . . Swash! . . . Swash! . . . Swash . . . Swash! . . . "O please, Mr. Jim! O please, Mr. Jim! O please, Mr. Jim . . .

O Lord, have mercy! O Lord, ha . . ." There would then arise another sound: "Ow-w-w-w-w! Ow-w-w-w-! Ow-w-w-w-w-w!"

That was Ad's dog howling.

There would be silence. Sister Stella in fluffy starched Sunday dress and her hair plaited in pigtails would look as if all the terrors of the Georgia countryside had been caught in her big brown eyes. She would pucker her mouth and whimper.

"Keep quiet!" buddy or I would scold, pretending that we weren't scared. "What're you crying for? It's only old Jim Peters whipping Ad. Keep quiet."

We would go back stealthily to play close to the door of our house. Later on, one of us would whisper: "Did you hear how that old dog howled?" and the other would say: "Yes. I guess Ad's glad to have something love him." There wouldn't be any fun left in all the rest of that day.

When papa and mamma came from church early that evening, I would watch for a chance to tell him what we had heard. Papa would look very angry, as if we hadn't had any business hearing what we had. But he would lay his hand on my head and tell us not to be scared. I wasn't afraid, with a father like that, but I used to tremble when I thought what might happen to us if papa died. We knew that Jim Peters would like to grab our land and that he and papa had quarreled more than once over the boundary line. We knew that he used to make holes in the fence between his place and ours, so his hogs could get into our pasture among our hogs, or ours go over into his place. We felt sure that later he would come over and swear that we had stolen his hogs. We had seen things like that done—or had heard about them so much that we thought we had actually seen them.

Besides, even we kids knew that Jim Peters was a deputy sheriff. He was the law, and he could do as he pleased.

Sister Stella and buddy had told mamma about the whipping. She and papa talked about it.

"When will that spineless jellyfish wake up!" Mamma said, angry.

"When he does wake up," papa said, "that will be the day Jim Peters goes to sleep never to wake up."

There were lots of questions I wanted to ask. Why didn't Ad run away where old Jim Peters couldn't find him? If he went to the city he could get paid for working. Peters didn't give him anything but some dirty rags to wear, scraps from the table to eat and an old yellow dog to hunt rabbits with. I couldn't understand it, because I had seen Ad sitting on Jim Peters' lap driving in to town with another white man. He must have liked the black boy to allow him to sit on his lap. Maybe old Peters whipped Ad as papa sometimes whipped me, "because I love you, my son." But if that was true, why wasn't Ad given clothes, food, and a bed to sleep in—and a gun to hunt with?

Buddy and I had a gun. Ad had to sleep in the cotton house, either on a pile of old rags and cotton, winter and summer. In the winter he had to go looking for pine knots in the fields to keep a fire in the kitchen stove. For that Mrs. Peters would let him sit in the corner behind the stove and warm himself. Of course I knew why Jim Peters wouldn't let Ad have a gun—or thought I knew. He himself carried a pistol all the time. He made Ad go hunting with a dog. But the black boy was a swift runner. People used to say that he could outrun his dog and catch the rabbit they both were chasing. Both the boy and the dog were hungry all the time, it seemed, so Ad must have thought that unless he got the rabbit himself the dog would eat it. He carried an ax when he went hunting, so that if the rabbit ran into a hollow in a tree and hid he could chop it out.

Fall came and went. We ground our cane and killed some hogs. The branch in the low ground had a thin sheet of ice over it. Christmas was only a little way off.

"I think one of old Peters' hogs is in the pasture, papa," mamma said one night. She had thought she saw the hog when she went to milk that evening. It didn't have any mark in its ears and she thought old Peters was up to one of his tricks. Papa told us to go down in the morning and drive the hog back where it came from and to fix the fence where it had come through.

I found the hog and chased it back through a hole in the rail fence. The weather was chilly. The fields had been harvested long ago and many farmers had turned their hogs and cows from the smaller pastures into the open fields. Here the hogs sometimes rooted up enough lost corn or potatoes to fatten them for killing and the cows found tender grass enough to save piles of hay or fodder.

I stuck some chunks of wood in the hole and climbed on the fence to look at the world beyond. There was Ad coming out of the woods nearby. He had his ax but I did not see the dog and was surprised.

Ad's long supple body seemed to be shrinking from the cold. I wore heavy shoes, a cap, woolen mittens, heavy underwear beneath my overalls and shirt; he had on only two pieces. His old pants were thin and the patches were dropping apart. His shirt was so full of patches it looked like a crazyquilt. He was barefooted, just as he had been when we had last seen him on the road one Sunday in summer. The last time I had seen him the sun on his skin made it glisten like well-polished black leather. Today his body did not glisten; his face was ashy gray.

"Ad is frozen white," I said.

Every incidental detail of that encounter returns clearly as I write ... He came up from the woods on the Peters side of the fence with his ax on his shoulder. I thought of the title of a story I had read in a farm paper we took, "A Yellow Dog's Love for a Negro." But the question which followed recollection of the title was Where's Ad's Dog? For the dog was not following him, and I had never known that before. I didn't believe anybody else had. Even when Ad rose in the wagon the old yellow dog followed, jogging along wither under the middle of the old mule or under the middle of the wagon. Maybe something had happened to the dog and that was why Ad looked so terribly sad ....

Sad or not I was thinking of some flippant greeting for him. I had been going over in my mind for some time an epithet I had never used before (because it had been a long time since I had seen him so near) and here was a chance to spring it on him. I was going to say, "Hello, midnight in a coal mine." At the same time I was trying to figure out why Ad let us do things like that to him. Why didn't he knock our heads off?

But there wasn't time to think much about that now. I had time only to reassure myself that he deserved my contempt. He was years younger than Peters but just as large and strong. Yet he let the white man tie his wrists and ankles together and flail him with a rawhide whip. "That big simpleton wouldn't kill a fly," mamma had once retorted to papa's prediction that "this dull-witted worm will turn someday." Mamma had added: "A worm can't turn if all the stuffing's been stomped out of it."

The worm, I thought. He's just a big black worm and he deserves all the names I call him.

Standing with my feet between the rails of the fence and holding on to the top rail, I swayed back and forth in rhythm to the words I chanted under my breath, "Ad is a worm." In another minute I'd be closer to him than ever before and so far from my home that nobody could hear me if I screamed at the top of my voice. Yet I was not afraid to taunt him. I couldn't imagine myself screaming because of Ad. But as he came opposite where I stood I thought for a frantic moment that this man was not, *could not be,* Ad: the face was an ashen gray mask and his body trembled like an old man's with palsy.

He stopped in front of me with the ax on his shoulder. He looked at me sadly. I had never before seen Ad drunk. "He's drunk," I said, and was scared. I was scared of his eyes because he did not smile. His face was gray and tight and his eyes were dull and fixed. I was terrified because his eyes were dull and worried. Then his features gradually relaxed. He looked back toward the woods and I thought of the yellow dog. If I mentioned the dog and Ad answered me I'd no longer be scared. We'd talk and I'd feel as if we were neighbors, and I would not then want to run. Think of wanting to run from Ad!

"Lo, Jeems," he said, and smiled.

I laughed, happy because he was the same old Ad. When I thought of how I'd insult him to his face I laughed again. I said flippantly: "Hello, midnight in a coal mine. How's the slave tod—"

His face was tight and gray again.

"My name's Ad, from now on, Jeems. You know my name. My name's Ad . . . " I stepped backward, down from the fence, ready to fly. This was not the same old Ad. "I's sickn tiahd bein' kicked around. I don't make no funner you, do I? I'm sick . . ."

It was the word "sick" that made me notice the red whelps across his neck and shoulders and the blood on his ragged shirt. I ran, springing through the woods of the pasture. I looked back once. Ad was running too . . .

"Well, the worm turned," papa said quietly that night. "He killed old Peters this morning. Chopped off his head with that ax."

Mamma went on about her work as if she had been expecting to hear something like that, although we all knew that she had not been. She just said, "God help that poor black boy now," and it sounded almost like a prayer.

Papa said, "Hunh!" and sat biting the end of his mustache and looking angry. He didn't look worried; he looked angry—as if he'd like to fight. Then he said: "I hope the Lord will forgive me, but I don't believe He gives a damn about that 'poor black boy.' . . . To be white in this man's country is to be God's elect . . ."

Papa himself was a black man of God. A Baptist preacher. Papa said:

"Didn't you hear the bloodhounds and the shooting? I don't believe they've got him yet, though." He spoke softly, because we never could tell at night whether somebody might not be lying low outside, spying.

I whispered to papa: "What did Ad do with the old yellow dog?" and told what I had seen.

"Killed it to keep it from following him. Had to kill the only friend he had in the world, so its love for him wouldn't betray him."

Since they hadn't caught Ad yet, papa said, getting out his pistol and loading it, we'd better be prepared.

Mamma blew out the lamplight and told us to go to sleep. Papa and mamma sat up in the dark, just as they had done in New Orleans one time, and talked. Softly. It seemed very homey and cozy with everybody here close together and we feeling safe because papa was at home and he was not afraid of anything.

I lay thinking of the New Orleans mob that had overflowed South Rampart Street, where we lived at the corner of Third, as the ugly Mississippi in Spring used to overflow the riverfront. The mob was looking for Robert Charles, who had shot some policemen, but they beat up and shot every other Negro they came across in their hunt. So we kids lay whispering under the covers; tingling with the sense of terrors in the woods outside and whispering recollections of Ad.

Deep in the night I heard the hounds' baying and the vengeful, angry cracks of guns.

Papa got up and mamma asked him terrifiedly where he was going. He said nothing but opened the door quietly and went on the back piazza to listen. When he opened the door we could hear the dogs and the guns clearly. He came in and sat down again. He started telling mamma about a lynching he had seen when I was a baby, away down on Indian River, in Florida. Then there was silence among us in the dark.

"O God," I prayed in my inner consciousness, "don't let them lynch Ad. Don't let the mob catch him."

But God either didn't hear me or, as papa said, He just didn't give a damn . . .

"How Lt. Gordon Took His Seven Colored Heroes into the Jaws of Death— and Back Again"

Boston Post (Sunday Supplement) (APRIL 20, 1919): 40

After returning from World War I, Gordon moved to Boston. He hoped to find a job in newspapers and went into the hiring office of the *Boston Post*, a white-owned newspaper, wearing his uniform, including a gold bar indicating his rank and a buffalo insignia. He was hired and worked as an editor at the paper until 1938. Gordon wrote of a harrowing war experience in this article for the *Post* on April 20, 1919. In this encounter Gordon, a second lieutenant, led his men, an all-Black regiment, into enemy territory and came back with several captured German soldiers. He has to overcome numerous obstacles along the way, not only from the Germans but keeping the loyalty of his own men as well. His quick thinking, his bravery in battle, and his ability to command are all on display in the essay. He would demonstrate these same qualities throughout his life. A fictionalized version of the incident, titled "Playing Hide and Seek with Jerry," is in the Eugene Gordon Papers, Box 2, File 23.

How Lt. Gordon Took His Seven Colored Heroes into the Jaws of Death—and Back Again

It was the 6th of November at 11 o'clock in the morning. I received the following memorandum:

Head.1st Bn., 367 Inf.

Memorandum:

Lieutenant Gordon with 8 men, 2 automatic rifles, and 4 riflemen with hand grenades will proceed at once as a reconnaissance patrol to reconnoiter the Ferme de Mulon.

The patrol will move out by way of the trench Remise and will take cover there if attacked by the enemy.

Our machine guns will be on the alert to cover the patrol in case of necessity.

The patrol will return to our lines before dark.

The section of the trench occupied by my platoon dipping down hill and into No Man's Land. From the crest of this hill can be seen the Mulon farm, about three quarters of a kilometre distant, and slightly to the right of our front. The position it occupied made it more a part of the enemy's possession than a part of No Man's Land. For it stood only about a quarter of a kilometre this side of Pagny, which was an enemy stronghold.

With my eight men I followed my trench round to the end, where it made a sudden dip into No Man's Land. Then, while the men kept under cover of our trench, I looked for the trench Remise. But I did not find it, because it was not there. Its only existence was on an obsolete map. So I decided to rely entirely on my own judgment.

The day was generally fair and there were fitful bursts of sunshine. All about us lay hills and wooded ridges, but directly before us lay a level valley, stretching away to and beyond Pagny. Three-quarters of a kilometre distant lay the Mulon farm.

It is a group of ancient stone buildings clustered at one end of a stone enclosure.

I found that my patrol, immediately on coming out of our trench, was exposed in broad light of day to every surrounding hill, to every suspicious clump of brush for kilometres around. Straight ahead of us, about 300 yards, was a stretch of cottonwood trees, running parallel to the farm and at right angles to the highroad. I signalled to lie down.

Lying flat in the weeds, they were well hidden. I ordered by signal the man on the extreme right of the skirmish line, formed when we lay down, to run forward and drop. Then, to the man on the left I gave the same signal. When the whole line had advanced in this way for about 50 yards I varied tactics by having them crawl a few yards, then lie still, while I signalled them to rush forward individually again, until finally the cottonwood trees were reached.

SCOUTED WAY TO COVER

These were neatly arranged trees in perfectly arranged rows, and not too dense to prevent on seeing in every direction. The rows of trees formed vistas to the high-road. I now sent out scouts, three men with 10-pace intervals, 25 yards ahead. We advanced slowly and cautiously. On the right was a little hut well covered with branches. The scouts investigated while the patrol lay motionless in the weeds. Then, finding all clear, they signalled forward. On the left was another little hut, and the same tactics were repeated. We reached the end of the wood.

There was no covering here. I looked across the valley and could see the ridge along the top of which we ran our lines. It seemed very far away. Then I looked in the other direction and beheld the high smokestacks on Pagny's big brasserie, standing like sentinels. I looked to where the wood had ended and saw a small stream, a prolongation of our cottonwood stretch, with willows on its bank. And the men lay in the grass, wonderment in their faces, their eyes on me. I signalled forward.

There was another stretch of cottonwood trees about 200 yards straight ahead, joining at right angles to the stream. Bur just this side of it ran a wire entanglement. I could plainly see that from my distant position. So I signalled the scouts to go along the woods on the outside of the wire, up toward the left, until they should find an opening in the wire. We followed slowly. Suddenly the scouts halted and signalled forward. The opening had been located and we went on.

Then a man close behind me, I was at the head of the column of files, whispered: "Lieutenant, I think we ought to go back. This is farther than anyone else has ever come, even at night. You're getting ready to get us killed out here."

And I turned round and looked into his ashen face.

I signalled the scouts in. Then I said quietly to this man: "You go out as a scout, and if you even appear to hesitate, I will kill you."

And he went, while the others followed me without a murmur.

HEARD CRY "AMERICAN"

When the scout reached the newly found opening, I signalled halt and down. We advanced to him, proceeded through the opening and entered the woods. The trees here, too, were arranged in orderly rows, and for a long distance. Far away, at the end, was a mill, often designated as an enemy outpost, standing on a creek. It stood in plain view down a vista of cottonwoods. We went through several rows. There were dugouts interspersed here and there ahead of us, and I know that we were no longer in No Man's Land, but in German territory.

The realization of this fact gave new significance to the whole situation. My very blood danced, my spirits were militant.

I signalled down.

The men lay still and quiet, while I stood looking and listening.

Far away to the left a machine gun barked. An artillery shell whined as it flew over and burst in the direction of our lines.

Then all was still.

I looked back for a glimpse of our lines. They were gone.

A man whispered my name, and. I looked down. He was pointing off toward the left, and he said, "I see a man!"

I looked, but saw nothing.

Then suddenly, even as I looked, I heard voices coming from that direction Moderate at first, they presently rose to shouts: "Americans! Americans! American soldiers!"

Meanwhile I swallowed, something that had suddenly risen in my throat and cautioned the men to be still and not fire until they got the command. Then I attempted to ascertain the strength of the enemy. From the noise made, I judged them to be about a company. I doubted that they knew our strength and was determined to keep the men concealed so as to make counting difficult.

I suddenly realized they were advancing. I said, "Steady men. Don't fire until I order. Then all will fire together. It may not be necessary to fire at all; we'll see . . . . Load!"

"Clickety-click! Click! Click! Click!" went the rifle bolts, while the automatic men settled down hard for business, and "Kamerad! Kamerad! We surrender" (or words of like import) cried the Germans.

"Oh hell!" I cried, "This is too easy. Lie there men."

And with cocked pistol I sprang through the screen of trees and weeds and received the procession as they came, a sergeant holding above his head a dirty white handkerchief, and six privates, all praying to be allowed to live.

I called the patrol out and had the Germans surrounded. We marched them boldly back over No Man's Land without being fired upon. And we had not fired a shot.

PREPARED FOR DANGEROUS TRIP

Although prisoners had been taken our mission had not been accomplished, for we had not reached the Mulon Farm. And what did those dugouts hold in the way of souvenirs? And as we marched the prisoners back I decided on a plan. I would steal out early the next morning and explore the dugouts. I would go and return before a patrol order was issued.

At 10 o'clock on the morning of the 7th (the next morning) the sergeant had eight picked men ready before my P.C. [Poste de Commande]. We started out at 10:30, but I had sent one man back when we reached the place where our trench dipped into No Man's Land. He had suddenly become aware that he was suffering from an "awful stomach ache."

We followed the same route as the day before, reaching the dugouts quickly and without incident. We found them to be bare. Someone had been there.

Disappointed, I stood for several moments in the door, while the men lay concealed in the weeds, covering with their arms any possible route of approach. Then a happy idea occurred to me. Why not go to the Mulon farm? It was only a quarter of a kilometre away, and, besides, I could complete my mission of yesterday. I signalled the patrol to rise and reform.

We set out down the neatly arranged rows of cottonwoods, now and then lying flat but never crawling. Every man followed loyally, looking toward me with confidence in his eyes. Finally we reached a strip of woods about 50 yards from the farm and running parallel to it. It extended to the high road on which the upper end of the farm rested.

When the patrol had lain down we found ourselves facing a long stone wall. On the right, near the road, stood a group of gloomy, gray buildings, heavy iron rods shielding their shattered windows, jagged shell holes in their roofs. They loomed silent, gloomy as a prison fortress. I wondered what those heavy, gray, forbidding walls concealed. I would soon see.

I lay there and mentally disposed of autorifles, riflemen and hand bombers. Then I called two men in whose courage I had some confidence and gave them their instructions. They were to take two men each and station themselves at the openings in the wall. When they had posted themselves, I followed the seventh man, crept through a shell hole close to the ground in the wall of one the old buildings.

MEETING THE FIRST ENEMY

We were at a large, bare barnlike structure with a dirt floor. An old grist mill with a pile of straw before it stood in the centre. I looked about cautiously, carefully. I listened intently. No one was to be seen or heard.

But outside could be heard the report of a big gun back of the hills—back a little distance in German territory. I turned to Private Bolden, who, with bayonet fixed and rifle at high point, walked to the left of me.

"Walk behind me," I ordered, and we passed through the barn into the garden beyond.

There were footprints here, freshly made, too, footprints of someone who wore hobnailed[31] shoes. There was no mistaking the evidence. The enemy was here and had probably just gathered some vegetables for his dinner. It was interesting.

We walked stealthily, following the ancient wall on the right of us. A wooden gate hung open from a gap in the wall. I peered through and discovered a courtyard of considerable size. Turning to Bolden, I whispered "Follow, close. When we enter here we shall be entirely separated from the other men. We may have to fight our way out."

"Yes, sir," he answered.

We crept through.

The four walls to this courtyard were three buildings on three sides and a high stone fence on the fourth. A gateway opened onto the high road through this fence. The great place was silent.

I advanced a few paces and halted, looking cautiously about. Again we crept a short distance. I stopped dead. On my right a wooden door hung open. A German soldier, perfectly oblivious to any impending danger, sat. He held in his hands a sheet of the Berliner Tageblatt[32] (I observed the name instantly), but his gaze was on the ceiling.

I gestured Bolden to look, and we amused ourselves for several seconds in observing him. Then I noiselessly thrust my pistol through the door toward his head, while he turned a white, expressionless face toward us, his lips muttering what his voice would not convey.

"Hands up!" I ordered. He obeyed, rising at the same time, his hands fumbling, his eyes dilated, but full of supplication. I then motioned him out and searched him, turning him over, at the completion, to Bolden.

"Who are in the buildings?" I asked in my very bad German.

"Soldiers," he answered, also, of course, in German.

"How many?"

"Five."

"Anybody else?"

"An officer."

An officer! If I could but get him—

"Are they armed?" I demanded.

"Yes," and as an afterthought: "There is a sentry outside that gate," pointing to the gate opposite. "I advise you to go back the way you came."

"Very good," I said, referring, of course, to the information.

We rushed him across the yard to the gate. I said to Bolden: "Can you hold him in here while I slip around and try to peep into some of these windows?" There were windows, doors, and cellar exits opening into the courtyard.

"Certainly, sir," was his emphatic reply.

"Good," I answered, turning away.

THE OFFICER APPROACHES

I was immediately arrested in my tracks. I heard footsteps approaching in the cellar, drawing toward the exit near which we stood. I ran quickly to the right of the cellar exit, placed my back hard against the wall, trained my pistol on the steps and awaited the unknown's approach.

He came carelessly, jauntily, his cigarette in his lips. He stopped short, staring at Bolden and the prisoner. He seemed for a moment stuck in his tracks. The cigarette dropped from his lips, his careless, jaunty manner fell from him like a cloak. And he stared.

Suddenly he awoke. It dawned upon him that perhaps other black soldiers were about (Bolden is very black). He turned quickly and saw me. The pistol was in his face, he turned as though on a pivot and bounded down the steps. Neither my command to halt nor the bullet which went crashing after him checked his flight. And I heard his footsteps dashing over the cellar floor even after the door had been slammed behind him.

I thought quickly after that. It was necessary. The pistol report had sounded the alarm. We were isolated from the rest of the patrol. And the five armed Germans were somewhere within. I looked up at the buildings about me—tall, gray, sombre; ugly black rafters and beams gaping through shell holes in the roof like the discolored teeth in a death's head. The windows and doorways stared black and forbidding.

"Through the gate!" I ordered Bolden. But the prisoner protested. The sentry! The man on post!

"Bother that!" I cried. "Follow me, and keep a sharp lookout. Watch the prisoner!" and I stepped through the gate onto the road, Bolden following with the Boche.[33]

I looked straight up the road and saw clearly the whole situation. About 25 yards ahead the road was blocked by a high wooden fence. A sentry, standing on a wooden platform, was looking through his [field] glasses toward our lines. Evidently he had heard nothing. His rifle, bayonet fixed, leaned against the barricade within reach of his right hand, his pistol was in the holster on his hip. And like a good soldier, like a wideawake, alert sentry, was looking diligently for the enemy.

Well, the enemy had come.

With cocked pistol aimed at his head I ran with all my might toward him. He heard and jerked himself round as though worked by a spring. Surprise, consternation, alarm, fear played like lightning over his bearded face as he kicked down his rifle, tore off the pistol belt from the platform with his hands above his head.

There was no time for parley. I pointed the way toward the left of the barricade and doubletimed back of them to where our comrades waited at the wall.

No member of my patrol had fired a shot. No man was struck for enemy casualty; we reached our lines without a casualty. I looked at my watch: it was 12 o'clock, noon.

I reported the prisoners to the major and stood attendance while he gave me the devil for going a.w.o.l. to get them.

Fiction

"Rootbound,"
Opportunity (SEPTEMBER 1926): 279–83, 299.

"Rootbound" is Gordon's first published story, a haunting tale of marital infidelity, perhaps a mirror of what was occurring in his own life. Its dark themes may have been disconcerting to many readers of the somewhat staid *Opportunity* magazine, although the story was awarded fourth prize in the periodical's 1927 fiction contest. The protagonist, Cassius Johnson, takes a "high yaller" prostitute from the appropriately named Redlyte Street and, almost like a sociological experiment, marries her in an attempt to reform her. He is drawn to her beauty, her whiteness, "as white as any Nordic beauty's, full youthful breasts—all the charms which had attracted men since her early girlhood." But it is her very beauty that causes "trouble" as he discovers her one day back on Redlyte Street, going off with a white man, likely for money. He agonizes over what to do, and the tension is raised as Cassius interrogates his wife. When his worst fears are realized, he physically assaults her, leading her to call him "a filthy black brute" and a "nigger." Although he threatens to leave, in the end he is still torn by his love for her and his lack of self-worth, rooted to the spot.

Rootbound

At the junction of Pleasant and Redlyte Streets, Cassius Johnson was suddenly stunned by what he saw. Chaotically he recalled his favorite sally[1] that his sable complexion alone, as flawlessly black as polished lacquer, prevented his blushing or blanching. But this was no moment for recalling witticisms. . . .

Skyscrapers were toy blocks on a string which unseen fingers twirled about his head.

As street lights flare without warning, so did judgment through the murk of his brain. Red mist dissolved from his eyes, and he squinted in focusing them again on the cause of his agitation.

Some distance ahead, having turned from Redlyte Street into Pleasant, and swinging with the nonchalant stride of a school girl through the late afternoon throng, went Markia, his wife. Her arm was linked with a white man's. She was laughing, occasionally casting coquettish glances at her companion's profile.

"If that was *me* she was with people would be staring like we were a pair o' freaks. And I'm her husband, too! They don't even look at *him* . . . with another man's wife! Just because she's a damn high yaller. They think she's white. . . . Fools!"

Johnson stood in the middle of the sidewalk, head lowered, eyes following, with a murderous glare, the progress of Markia and the white man toward the subway. Home-going crowds jostled him with maddening unconcern.

"Headed for home—now. But where's she been? That's what I want to know. Yes, I do know, too. . . . My God, on Redlyte Street—again! After all her promises; after all I've slaved and given up for her! And I suppose this isn't the first time either. She seems to know. . . ."

Home-goers bumped him. Dazedly he heard the ugly throaty oath of a man who had to step into the street to pass. Johnson started after his wife. . . .

Home-loving man that he was, he felt self-pity over-awing him. Memories in one great wave washed over him; left him floundering.

He remembered the intimacies of his small apartment; talking machine,[2] books, easy chair near the back window; davenport with old green cover, table spread with bright-colored magazines; familiar pictures on the walls; fences, trees, piles of refuse in backyards as seen from the kitchen window.

These memories were woven into the pattern of his existence. They were [the] background of his life. Loving them, he wished never to leave the objects and surroundings inspiring them. As he often said to Markia (calling her Birdie at such times), "I'm a great oak with roots running down, down deep into the solid rock of earth. I'm bound by love to you and these things around us. I'm rootbound. I'm the oak, and love for you and these is the roots. Dig me up and set me out elsewhere, and I would die."

Markia often recited this to their friends. Markia was intelligent and sensitive to beauty, with all her faults. She called him her poet. To their friends, lounging comfortably about the small living room and smoking cigarettes, Johnson would say, his face burning (they could not see the blush!): "I'm a primitive man with a civilization complex." He would wink at Markia and chuckle at their friends' grimaces, adding parenthetically: "Took extension work in psychoanalysis last year. . . . As I was saying, it's funny a husky, iron-muscled son of Ham like me should hold an effete post office job and find his greatest comfort lazing around home with a book or magazine. But peace is so *sweet*. How I hate to be disturbed!"

Peace at last was spent. What a revolutionary idea! . . . Tomorrow he would sell everything. By this time tomorrow he would have left Markia. Had promised her to be home early to go to the movies, yet, look at her! . . . He winced. The end of everything!

"No woman can play me for a sucker and get away with it. What did I marry her for, in the first place? No man black as I am's got any business with a woman that can pass for white. That was the first bull. Second place, why did I go to Redlyte Street for a wife? Could've married the best! Reform her! Take her out of the gutter and clothe her in decency. . . . Rot ! Bunk! . . . Listened to her prattle. Little Miss Innocence led astray by wicked men. . . . More rot! More bunk!"

In the background of his consciousness hummed the music of quiet and eternal repose: silent city streets; distance clock sounding like chimes at midnight; deep, regular snoring of a man next door. . . . These memories *must not* interfere with his resolve. . . .

"I'll leave her! Swore she'd be true. All she wanted was a chance. A chance! Like hell! Chance to run wild with white men while I slave my head off. Pardon me!"

Blood-shot eyes in a harried black face looked levelly into calculating gray eyes set deep in white skin. A timid blonde woman dangled from the tall white man's arm. The white man's mouth was a red mark on a grim white mask. Johnson's heavy lips, folded back, revealed strong teeth of a snarling beast's. The white man gripped Johnson's right arm.

"Let him go, dear!"

The woman's terrified eyes beseeched the white man. Johnson, restraining himself, said nothing; glared from one to the other; squinted red eyes, bit the corner of his lower lip. Passersby turned in astonishment; lingered, craning necks.

"Let him go, dear. Don't you see he's drunk? Let him go!" Her voice had become nervously imperative. She stamped a foot.

"Damn fool!" Johnson jerked his arm free. "You're a couple of damn fools!"

Before [the] white man or crowd could collect his wits Johnson had hurled himself through a subway entrance and bounded down stairs.

An express was disappearing into blackness, its red lights making less and less glow in the recess of the tunnel. He had missed them. Those fools up there. . . .

Leaving the subway train he hastened upstairs into cool night air. Once more he was thinking rationally. He had settled it. There was nothing to do but go away. He would even be magnanimous in his treatment of Markia: "I'll divide with her what little money I've saved and let her stay there. I'll go, martyr to a woman's unfaithfulness. . . . I'll be hanged if I do!"

If anyone went it would be she. Everything in the flat was his; had owned most of it before he'd ever seen her. Why make further sacrifices for her? He's already sacrificed honor, self-respect, old friends. After five years of making a fool of him, *her* sacrifice would begin tonight. He go?

"Hanged if I do! Oh, I don't know. Why be vindictive? I'll let her stay. I'll take what I need; to hell with the rest. She can do what she dang pleases with it. I'll go. I'd rather roast in hell a thousand years than spend another night near that . . . that woman. I'll go; but God! how I hate the thought of giving up—everything! To uproot the old oak at last! It can't stand it. It just can't."

From the sidewalk before the two-family house he could see a light upstairs. Its yellow glow shone between drawn shades and window facings. A tumultuous flood of regret made him gasp as he mounted the stoop. All the beauty of marriage, all the contentment that accompanies a successful livelihood, banished in a moment. This morning he had left home with the sensation of her unfolding arms still twinkling in his blood. Since then what a tragedy! Another probably had felt those same arms. He himself would never again feel them, because this night. . . .

On the second landing stood Markia. She was posturing daintily in the frame of the doorway, gaslight a yellow haze behind her. She was a pretty pink and white doll, eyes innocently blue, shingled hair scintillating gold. Again, slender body inclined forward, small feet close together, arms extended backwards, tiny pink fingers grasping the two ends of her apron strings, she was a poised butterfly.

"Hello, Cassie! Rather late, aren't you? Dinner's been waiting for ages and ages. Almost went to sleep waiting for you. Aren't we going to the movies? Changed your mind? What kept you so late? What's the matter, Cassie?"

Instead of his usual impulsive act of drawing her to him, Johnson had passed into the room, glancing with hasty suspicion around the cramped apartment. In the kitchen the table was set; wisps of vapor floated above hot dishes.

"Says she's been waiting. Couldn't have. She's just put that stuff on the table."

He tossed his hat on the table covered with bright colored magazines, and threw his overcoat upon the davenport. He approached Markia, who now stood erect. Her round face was crimson.

"The movies?" he asked, trying to be casual. He did not realize that casualness had been dissipated with his unusual behavior on entering. "The movies? Surely you don't wont [sic] to go right out again! Have a nice time?"

Her large eyes, larger and bluer than ordinarily, were fixed on his face in a fascinated stare. The crimson stain was gone. She closed the door and backed against it, never removing her eyes from his.

"I asked if you had a nice time down in the old haunts. What's the matter? Didn't lose your tongue down there too?" Folding his arms with the gesture of a relentless inquisitor, he backed against the mantel.

He wondered whether her look of puzzlement was genuine or assumed. How could it be anything than assumed?

"What you talking about, Cassie?" What's the idea of starting that sort of talk as soon as you get home? Aren't you well?"

His blunt laugh was mirthless. It made her start. Her eyes were still too large. "You're awfully funny," she said, in a tone that belied her statement. "You're laughable."

Her husband grunted, "Really? Glad *you* think so. Got a fine sense of humor tonight, haven't you? Why don't you laugh, then?"

He was thinking: "Why do things like this have to happen? Why do suspicion and distrust always come between people when they're happy?" He appraised her. She was the most desirable woman he had ever known.

"There's no man living who wouldn't want her. God, how can I give her up? To some other man!"

She was watching him, eyes sullen now. One small foot beat a tattoo. Her rounded cheeks had regained their natural color.

"Well?" he bellowed, so suddenly that she started. "I'm waiting. I think I've been rather patient, don't you?"

Hands on straight hips, eyes narrowed, chin elevated, slender body erect, Markia assumed the offensive. "Cassius Johnson, what's wrong with you? If it was July instead of March I'd think the heat had affected you. What you driving at?"

It was his turn to start. A new thought was glimmering faintly. . . . She went on: "If you've heard anything about me that's made you suspicious I wish you'd kindly tell *me* about it. I think I've a right to know, don't you? Oh, Cassie," with an outward thrust of the arms, an involuntary move toward her husband, "What's wrong?"

He was disarmed; whipped. Odds and ends of emotion beat upon his heart, and he was happy without knowing why. Husbands often made mistakes. "If only I've made a mistake, dear God! If only I've. . . ."

"Sit down, Cassie. You're tired, that's what's the matter. You're tired...." Her voice was like the deep rich tones of a violin. He sank upon the davenport, his senses unsteady. Vaguely he suspected trickery. He wanted to spring up and cry out in protest; to take this golden and white woman in his arms and beg her to tell him everything; to hear her deny all insinuations he had made and all charges he would make.

She was kneeling before him, her round, smooth face, serious with concern, upturned to his. His pulse throbbed hotly and he thrilled with the joy of possession; he saw her long curved throat, as white as any Nordic beauty's, full youthful breasts—all the charms which had attracted men since her early girlhood. Attracted men! That was the trouble now. Gently he laid his rough hands on her shoulders. He noticed the contrast between his hands and her throat and neck....

"Tell me truly, Birdie, dear: where did you go this afternoon, and who was that man with you? I'm your husband, you know ... and your pal."

She started to speak, hesitated. He saw the flash of pain across her eyes. Her head dropped. He stiffened; caught his breath. His fingers involuntarily clutched her shoulders. He felt her flinch.

He waited. The gaslight burned with a whirring noise. The old mantel clock ticked. Every sound was ominous.... He waited, his grip on her shoulder growing tenser. She squirmed, blanch-faced; wriggled free; stroke first one shoulder then the other. Her eyes avoided his. He was losing patience.

"What you acting like that for? Aren't you going to tell me?" He saw her with a new suspicion.

"Yes."

He started; gulped; licked his lips.

"Well?" His voice was choked.

"I went out...."

"Of course," impatiently. "Certainly. I saw you."

"Where?" They were examining each other's face. He thought of a cat at bay. With mad intensity he watched her, holding his breath.

"I saw you coming out Redlyte Street...." Was that a movement of surprise? He wondered ... Silence.

"I'm still waiting to hear where you'd been. And who was that man?"

He swallowed quickly; again licked his lips. He was saying to himself: "I want the truth, but I don't want it. I'm afraid. . . ." He waited.

Her face was averted. Dropping to a sitting position on the floor, she leaned back against the table. With an unsteady pink forefinger she traced patterns in the carpet.

"I'm still wait—"

"So you want to know where I went and who I went with. Well, I admit I went out, so you don't need to puzzle about *that* any more."

Bent low, her head was a ball of polished gold under the gaslight.

"The gentleman you saw me with is an old friend. Knew him before I ever saw you. I used to see him when I lived with Mayme on Redlyte Street. Oh," hastily with a swift glance at her husband, "he was never more than a good friend. Just like brother and sister we were. He used to come to see Mayme. . . . Remember her? No, he wasn't anything to me except . . ." He intercepted another swift glance. She dropped her eyes. He sneered: "Oh, of course not! Just brother and sister—"

"Well, I'm being square with you," she cut in hotly, meeting his eyes defiantly. Again averting her face, flaming, she continued: "After you'd married me I kept my promise and didn't see any of the old crowd. I'd just about forgotten Jack—"

"Oh, Jack, eh? You *did* know him *very* well, didn't you?"

"—had for a fact about forgotten Jack ever lived. Then I met him on the street one day. Said he was glad to see me; asked me how I was getting along; congratulated me on having such a fine husband; told me Mayme had been asking about me."

"Do you mean to sit there and tell me this fellow still hangs around that girl? Isn't he married? Does she still live down there?"

"Yes, he hangs around her. He's married her. . . . Just like you did me. He's crazy about her, too."

Johnson began to feel a strange joy singing in his head. He said almost eagerly: "So he took you down to see his wife. How is she? . . . Funny he's still living there after getting married."

"She's sick. Been sick quite a while. As I was saying, I met Jack—then, Mr. Nash, if you don't like 'Jack'; we met on the street one day—"

"By appointment?"

"Certainly not! Please don't be nasty. It was accidental. He said Mayme was sick, and asked when I could go to see her. I told him today. He said he's meet me in the subway, which he did, and we went together. When you saw us we were coming back."

"Uh huh . . . So he escorted you back?"

"Why, yes . . ."

"I see . . . What's the matter with Mayme? Find out?"

She did not reply immediately. After a hurried glance at his face she resumed her aimless pattern making, face averted. Then, hesitatingly:

"Well, she thinks it's her lungs. . . . Coughs awfully. . . ." She shot him a sidelong look. His eyes were on her. "Even while I was there someone phoned for a doctor, she coughed so."

"Someone 'phoned. . . . The doctor came?"

"Certainly!" she directed at him a quick questioning glance.

"What's *his* name ? The doctor's, I mean."

"How should *I* know? . . . Say, you are cross-examining me, aren't you? You don't believe me, do you?"

Her look this time was direct and unwavering. Their eyes met squarely.

"Honestly, I do not," shaking his head. "I did at first, but . . . If you don't mind I'll call Mayme and ask how she's feeling." He ignored Markia's startled gasp, going on: "I know she'll be glad to hear a word of cheer from her old teammate's husband. . . . What's her number?"

He rose and moved toward the telephone on a small table in a corner. He could not see the ashen pallor of her face.

"Listen. Cassie, I—"

"What's the number? I mean phone number. I remember the house number. 'Twas twelve. If she's living there yet it's still that." He tarried, phone upraised.

"It's not in her name. You ought to have sense enough to know that." She wriggled around to face hm. "I don't know whether her husband spells his name with a K, a G, or an N."

"He placed the receiver to his ear. "Information, please. . . . Information, what's the 'phone at 12 Redlyte Street? Party's name's Nash. . . . No 'phone there? You sure? . . . That's funny! Oh, all right."

He set the instrument down and turned to Markia. She still sat on the floor, but inert, slumped, like a rag doll emptied of sawdust. He had never before seen her look so ill. His judgment told him she was frightened.

"Deliberately and maliciously lied," he shouted in his inner consciousness. "If she lied about this, she's lied about everything else."

For the second time that day he felt hot blood dazing him. He felt, all at once, a maniacal desire to grasp her curving white throat in his big rough hands and squeeze out her breath. But not yet. Let her further incriminate herself. . . . She was standing before him, hands on her shoulders. She moved backward at sight of his face. He cought [*sic*] her wrists and jerked her forward. He was saying to himself:

"I won't lose my head. I won't hurt her. I'll give her enough rope to hang herself, then walk out and leave her. . . . forever." Again he felt unconsolably sorry for himself. To her he said:

"You've told me all I want to know. Five years ago I took you out of the gutter and gave you a decent home. I knew what you were, so that's one against *me*. But I thought that you had a spark of decency in you. . . . Decency! Huh! I might have known what you'd do, given a chance. Running the streets with a white man! In spite of what I knew, I had to play the fool . . . Why will black men be such damn fools about yellow women? I . . ."

She was struggling to free her arm. Her face was mottled with crimson rage. He was suddenly afraid to release her. A woman so angry might do anything. They wrestled; blundered about the cramped room; sprawled together over the upset table. She sprang away from him, first up. They stood panting, snarling across the wreckage of furniture and magazines.

"We've been married for five years, yes." Her voice was no longer like a violin, but metallic, hard and grating. It shot out on gasped puffs of breath. "You admit you knew what I was, don't you? You admit your eyes were wide open. Didn't I tell you when you married me you took a chance? And what did you say? You said: 'I don't care, Birdie, dear.' You said: 'Life itself's a chance.' I said many times, I said: 'They say it's hard for a woman to make a complete turn after living like this so long.' Remember? And you said: 'Birdie, you're educated and beautiful. 'Birdie,' she mocked, lispingly: You said: 'Birdie, all you need's a chance; that's all you need—"

"A chance!" interrupted the enraged husband. "My God! Haven't I given you a chance? Didn't I take you out the gut—"

"Oh, Lord," she groaned, backing wearily against the wall, "do I have to listen to all that rot again?" Thrown off his guard, he sputtered:

"I intend to have the truth if it takes all—"

"You may have it, and it needn't take all night, either."

"Where'd you been with that man?"

"I thought we'd settled that." She sighed.

"You mean—you mean . . . Then my guess was right, wasn't it?"

"My dear, I don't know what your guess was, but I'll give you the benefit of the doubt. You were right."

"Who was he?"

"Friend."

"A friend! What's his name?"

"Doesn't matter. You wouldn't know him, anyway."

"Then it's not Jack Nash?"

"No."

"Was he white?"

"I suppose so, He's never said he wasn't. . . ."

With two long strides, circumventing the overturned table, the man was beside her. Desire to murder had never been so strong. Snarling, he seized her shoulders; forced his nails into her flesh; hammered her against the wall. The house shook under each impact. The chandelier rattled. Whimpering, cowering to remind him of a whipped puppy, she was a child in his hands. Without warning, she struck him across the face with her clinched fist. She recoiled sharply, crying in a startled voice when blood trickled from his nose:

"Dear, dear Cassie! I'm *so* sorry! Come let me wash it off . . ."

He shoved her roughly. "Get away from me, you street walker. Never mind washing it off. You'll have plenty to wash off *your* silly mug in a minute."

The woman quailed as his big hands, hook-like, clutched her throat, squeezing until the blue of her eyes disappeared. Then, panic possessing him, he released her quickly. Her head lolled forward. She dropped like an old skirt from a hook in the wall. She lay still; presently, strength returning, she dragged herself up. He thought he had never before seen hatred so unmistakably expressed in a woman's eyes. Even while this impression touched his brain he tried to justify his actions. "She admits running with a white man. She admits . . ."

Her hysterical voice cut upon his chaotic meandering. It was now his chief concern to prevent neighbors' hearing. These walls were none too thick; a man's snoring on the other side . . .

"... You brute! You dirty, filthy black brute! Fine specimen of manhood you are. How can a nigger so black be so yellow? You damn ..." Her voice broke; she wept.

Transfixed with amazed hurt, he stood open-mouthed. . . . She had never before shrieked like that nor said such things to him. "So, to her, I'm just a black nigger . . . since she's been associating with white men. Only needed something to bring it out. . . . How could I stay here now, even if I wanted to?"

She was leaning against the wall, weeping; spasmodic, long drawn sobs that jerked the body. She checked herself; regarded her husband. Her eyes were reddened, face streaked and smeared. She said, as if expecting immediate and positive agreement: "Of course you'll leave me now?" Her tone implied weariness; it was without vigor or color. Arms dangling, she continued to regard him. Mouth atremble, eyes tear glazed, she said again: "Cassie, when do you leave me?"

He bit his lips. Strangely, his only passion now was overwhelming pity. He was wishing for only the semblance of an excuse to seize her in his arms; kiss her trembling mouth; stroke her golden head. Then he remembered the epithet. He said to himself: "She called me a nigger. She called me yellow. A woman can't love a man and say things like that . . ." To her:

"Yes, I'm leaving you. What do you expect? You flaunt your misbehavior in my face, then lie, and abuse me? I leave tonight. . . ." He felt a catch in his throat; paused, stared at the floor. "You can stay here till you find something to do—and another place. I'll give you half of what I've got in the bank . . ." He looked furtively toward her. He expected to see her head rise disdainfully, her lips sag in a sneer. She still held her attitude of dejection, however.

"You're very kind," she said faintly. "Thank you for . . . for helping. . . . Where you going tonight?" She looked at the mantel clock. "It's awfully late. Where do you expect to go?"

He bit his lip. Strangely, his only passion now was pity. Keener than before was his sorrow for his own plight. Martyr to a woman's unfaithfulness. . . .

"Never mind about me. I'll make out."

He passed her, entering the bedroom. Returning, he laid open on the floor his worn suitcase and a miscellany of clothing. He avoided looking directly at his wife, but, moving around with great rapidity, presented an appearance of eager haste. Observing from the corner of an eye, he saw her making her way, somewhat totteringly into the bedroom. He heard the door close.

For many minutes he knelt beside his open suitcase, looking about like a man awakening in a strange room. Rising, he righted the overturned table, replacing the magazines. Then, after a moment's uncertainty, he forced his agitated body into his beloved easy chair. In the bedroom his wife was crying again, spasmodically; such gusts of sobs as shake the body. Now she was sniffling into her pillow. After a while the sobbing was hushed. Quiet was on everything. The man sat still. The mantel clock ticked above other sounds. The gas burned with a whirring noise. Across rooftops, muffled by distance and darkness, tolled the hour of midnight. He felt more at ease now; more like his old self.

"In a few minutes I'll get up, get my things, and get out. No woman, least of all a high yaller, 's going to make a monkey out o' me."

Drowsiness settled on him. . . . This was how he liked always to feel. The quiet neighborhood; papers, magazines and books inviting him; Markia asleep nearby; gaslight purring like a contented cat; old clock ticking from the mantel. . . .

He roused himself. No time for peaceful contemplation. The time to go was now, before he fell under the spell of slothful ease. Let Markia rise tomorrow and find herself alone. . . . . He slouched deeper into the velvety softness of his chair. Through the wall which separated his apartment from his neighbor's came deep rumbling of a tired man's snoring. It was the diapason[3] of a magnificent organ; ripple of running water through deep glades in summer; crooning of a mother's voice over a sleeping infant. . . .

Johnson straightened; rubbed his eyes. There lay the old and familiar surroundings. He must get a move on.

He pulled himself from the chair and went into the bedroom. Markia was sleeping restlessly. On the floor beside the bed lay her clothes just as she had stepped from them. She had not even turned down the gas; it showed up pitilessly her swollen features. She lay with her knees drawn slightly upward under the covers, one white arm, blotched with bruises, across her gold head. The other hand pressed a small handkerchief against her lips. It was spotted red.

A hurricane of memories rushed over the man; nights of love-making; days of thinking on other nights to come; her tender commiseration; her eagerness always to make him happy; her unburdened laughter; her gaiety that had enlivened his prosaic life; his books, papers, talking-machine work; his orderly, care-free, routine existence; peace and comfort; home....

Then another man had come. Oh, hell! How did he *know* that? Merely seeing her on the street with a stranger proved nothing. But it *did*. She had brazenly confessed—by implication, at any rate....

The distant clock struck once. A tomb could hardly be more peaceful than the house now was. It seemed that all the world had lain down to serene sleep. Johnson could hear the sonorous breathing of the man next door. It suggested contentment, restfulness, luxurious repose in bed; sleep and romantic dreams, a life of routine plodding; an oak with massive roots extending through eternal centuries to the earth's very center; such a tree as would die if its place of habitation or its manner of growing were disturbed.

Like a sleepwalker he went toward the kitchen. He paused at sight of his dinner on the table. Picking up a cold asparagus stalk, he bit into it reflectively. He turned out the light, then slunk into the bedroom, turning out the living room light as he passed through....

He stumbled over his open suitcase; butted into the door jamb; was temporarily shaken from stupor. With the finality of doom it again enveloped him. He went on as in a trance, unbuttoning his coat, his vest, his shirt, his trousers. Dropping instinctively upon a chair, he loosened his shoe laces, then, using ultimately one great toe then the other, removed his shoes.

Presently he was stretching himself in his nightshirt. Mechanically he turned out the light and pushed up the window. A sea of cool-air overflowed the room.

How soothing the bed to a wearied body! Markia moved restlessly in her sleep; stretched out her arms and drew him to her. Drowsily, like one on the frontier between the lands of reality and dreams, he listened to his wife's deep even breathing; slept....

"Game,"
Opportunity (SEPTEMBER 1927): 264–69

"Game," like the earlier "Rootbound," is filled with violence, revenge, suspense, and marital tension, although it is even darker in tone, with a tinge of the gothic and Edgar Allan Poe. In the story, Sam Desmond works in a meat market, is henpecked by his wife Rita, and is jealous of the family cat, who is pampered by Rita. When the beleaguered husband can no longer stand being harangued to bring home game for his wife, he brings it but not the kind she is expecting.

Sam, like Cassius in "Rootbound," is riddled with self-esteem issues. He sees himself as "An ugly little runt" who was "lucky" to have a "pretty," "yaller" woman. Even her cat was "yaller." Rita names the cat Mussolini because she wants to deceive herself that "there's a real man round the house." The story may be a projection of Gordon's own discontent and anger with his marriage. Sam, in fact, lives in Cambridge, where Gordon resided at the time. Unlike the protagonist in "Rootbound," who is enraged at his wife but paralyzed into a state of inaction, Sam vents his fury, indicating his inability to control his emotions and perhaps manifesting Gordon's own secret desires. The story was awarded half of a first prize in the 1927 *Opportunity* fiction contest. Gordon later attempted to publish a slightly different version of the story under the pseudonym Egor Don.[4]

Game

As Sam Desmond, porter of the Greater Boston Meat Market, entered that concern's front door, he noticed the deliveryman Roberts returning the telephone to its accustomed place. He noticed also that a mirthful grin was playing havoc with the deliveryman's countenance, breaking its black surface into numberless shining facets. He knew that a message had come for him, and, in the light of many experiences, suspected that it was not a pleasant one. Roberts grinned like that only when there was a possibility of making his colleague uncomfortable.

Sam shuffled the length of the sawdusty aisle of chop-blocks and display cases of a variety of meats to a rear room of the store, where, removing his overcoat and hat, he put on a soiled white jacket, and a skull cap made from the upper portion of a woman's stocking. He knew that Roberts' unconscious love for the dramatic would never permit him to deliver the message before it was asked for, and as he returned to the shop he was resolved to have it out.

"Well, Black Boy," he began, "what's nibblin' at *your* funnybone?"

Roberts carried a basket of meats to the delivery truck at the curb and returned before he had decided to satisfy Sam's curiosity.

"Matter with me, little Snow White? Why, th' ain't nothing the matter with *me*. Is it, Mr. Bamberger?" Mr. Bamberger was president of the Greater Boston Meat Market, and occasionally revealed his democratic nature by joking and laughing with his colored employees. Now he merely smiled discretely and continued taking turns about the floor.

"That telephone call," Roberts announced, "came from your better three-quarters, Sam. She want you should tell her how long it take you to eat your lunch. Say ever time she call you up you jus' gone to lunch or jus' gettin' back. Say don't she feed you 'nough? She say—"

Sam held up his hand. "Never mind no more Miller and Lyles,[5] Black Boy. What she wants? That's what I want you to tell me."

Roberts was moving from one clerk to another picking up parcels, and, reading the addresses scribbled on them, arranging them in a basket he carried. He stopped in the midst of this occupation and said impressively.

"What she say, Snow White? She say you better bring her home some game, that's what she say. She say she want a rabbit or a squirrel or a ven'son steak, or somp'n like that; she don't care what, jus' so long's it's game." He delivered his parcels to the truck and, returning, "She say and don't forget somp'n nice for Mussolini," he called, his voice shattering into loud laughter.

The six clerks, Miss Schulte (the cashier) and Mr. Bamberger all laughed at this.

"Damn Mussolini!" Sam was busy now at the big refrigerator, attending to the long-deferred task of top-to-bottom cleansing. "I wish that lousy yaller devil 'ud die or something," he muttered.

"Yeah, damn the cat!" Roberts retorted with gleeful scorn. "Damn Mussolini all you want to, but be mighty particler you don't do it to home. Ef Marguerita ever hear you talk like that 'bout her cat you be lookin' for another place to hang out at."

"Is that so!" Sam threw the scrub brush down, the better to use his hands for gesticulating. "Is *that* so!" He approached the deliveryman, who lolled against a showcase watching a clerk quarter a small pig. "Well, let me tell *you* something, Black Boy. You say she better not catch me cussin' round the house. All right! You watch what I say. She's gonna catch me doin' more than that yet. I'm getting' sicken tired of bein' bossed round by a woman and a dirty yaller cat. And when I get sicken tired anything I put my foot down and stop it. That aint no hot air; I mean it. You jus' watch, Black Boy, I'm tellin' you."

For a moment he glowered, his runted gnarled little black figure tense and purposeful under the heat of his synthetic anger. Roberts alone laughed, a jeering guffaw that was weighted with scorn and skepticism. "What you think, Mr. Bamberger," he called, pausing on his way to the truck. "When Sam's better three-quarters start naggin' at him old Mussolini join in and spit on Sam. Gee, but that make little Snow White mad." Mr. Bamberger and the clerks immediately donned sober faces. Probably the memory of a tale Roberts occasionally repeated of Sam's running wild with a cleaver at the Roxbury

Market, from which place he had come to Bamberger's, sobered them. They probably thought it wiser—and perhaps safer—to enjoy Sam's discomfiture with straight faces. They had never seen Sam's wife, about whom Roberts had built for their amusement a tradition of pugnacious determination. Roberts admitted that Marguerita had been engaged to him before Sam came along, but insisted that he passed her up because he thought it foolish in a man so black marrying a yaller woman like Rita. They would attract embarrassing attention on the street. Sam said Roberts was a wall-eyed[6] liar.

When he finally heard the spasmodic back-spitting of the delivery truck and saw Roberts scoot with it across the soiled front of the plate glass window. Sam sidled up to Mr. Bamberger, who was talking to Miss Schulte at the cashier's cage. The porter's tone was deeply confidential.

"Mr. Bamberger, I want to get a rabbit or a squ'rrel or a ven'son steak, or some sort of game, to take home to my wife. She's jus' crazy about game, you know, and she called up an' said—"

"Yes, I know, Sam," interrupted the rotund head of the Greater Boston Meat Market. "I heard Roberts telling you about it. And I said then to myself, I said, 'it's too bad we didn't know sooner,' I said to myself, 'because,' I said, 'I'd like to accommodate Sam.' But there aint any more in the shop, Sam." The small gray eyes were sympathetic. "If you'd just been about a half hour earlier," he appended in a regretful voice. "As it is, Sam, Roberts got the last order of game now delivering it in Brookline. Sorry, Sam. Save you a rabbit tomorrow, if you want me to."

Sam declared that this would be satisfactory, and requested that Mr. Bamberger charge it. "But Mr. Bamberger, you can give me something for that lousy yaller cat, though, can't you?"

"Sure thing, Sam! Just tell Mike over there . . . 'O Mike! Fix up some liver or something for Mussolini, will you?' . . . 'Charge that to Sam, Miss Schulte.' And tomorrow, Sam, you'll have the game for your wife. We're getting in a fresh supply in the morning, see? . . . Got the refrigerator all cleaned out, eh? Well, finish that up before you go tonight, Sam." He turned and resumed his tete-a-tete with the cashier.

II

Through six years of diligent service to the Greater Boston Meat Market Sam had attained the full confidence of the management and certain prized prerogatives. One of these was the privilege of remaining until every one had gone every night and closing the store. It had been a long time since Mr. Bamberger or Miss Schulte or Mike had locked up. Even when he had an engagement to go out with Marguerite, Sam preferred to exercise his prerogative. Being black offered few enough prerogatives, God knew, and he would be a fool not to grab those proffered. him. At home a mere cipher, he felt like a man of some consequence when he was allowed the staggering responsibility of putting out the lights (all except the one over the cash register) and closing and locking the front door. It must have impressed people who passed along Tremont street and saw him. They must have thought him a partner in the concern.

As usual Sam put out the lights, except the one over the cash register, looked about proprietarily to see that everything was all right, and then went out into the cold January night and locked the door. The liver for Mussolini was concealed in an outer wrapper made of a sheet of the *Boston Transcript*, left in the store by a Back Bay customer, and Sam carried it pressed under his arm. Turning north on Tremont Street, he boarded at Northampton a car for Cambridge.[7]

As always when going home he was painfully aware of every step he took from the door of the shop to the car stop, and of each revolution of the wheels of the car from Tremont and Northampton streets to his stop in Cambridge. He was going home after a hard day's work; taking fresh meat to a lousy yaller cat that spit at him to show its contempt; thinking up a presentable lie for a lazy yaller woman. What had he married her for, anyway? Because she was pretty? Well, she was pretty, all right, and no getting away from that. She was a little broad acrosswise and rather heavy on her slippered, slip-slap feet about the small apartment; but pretty, just the same. An ugly little runt like him was lucky to have a woman like Marguerita.... Lucky? Well, he didn't know so much about that. After all, why was *he* lucky? Why wasn't *she* the lucky one? Of course he had a good looking high yaller woman for a wife, but what didn't *she* have? She had a little runt of a black man who would slave for her; somebody who would show up her handsomeness by contrast; somebody who was just crazy about her, and she knew it; somebody she could boss around; somebody who'd continue to slave like a fool the rest of his life for her. That's what she had. And in spite of all this she seemed to love the lousy yaller cat better than she loved him. "What you call him Mussolini for?" he once asked her. "Because," she had responded, so promptly she must have been thinking about it, "I want to kid myself there's a real man round the house." Of course she loved the cat better than she loved him.

Straight down the middle of his meandering thoughts the car rumbled across the Harvard Bridge, then rattled down Massachusetts Avenue past Technology, and, at Sam's signal, came to a hissing, wheezing, grumbling stop at Lafayette Square. Sam observed the window display of ornate furniture in the store before him as a crazy fantasy. He could feel the complete petering out of his earlier incipient spirit of rebellion. Oh, what was the use, anyway? Straight down Massachusetts Avenue, about two blocks away, lay Central Square. If he had any money... He shrugged, then cut across Lafayette Square into Columbia street.

The second-floor-rear window was alight, an indication that Marguerita was in the kitchen. Now what would he say? The truth? Yes, but suppose she wanted to know why he had not gone elsewhere? Bamberger's wasn't the only market on earth, he very well knew. What was the matter with the Manhattan right there in Cambridge? But she knew that he had no penny above his scant allowance.

He removed his hat and overcoat at the top of the stairs. From the kitchen a triangle of yellowish gaslight cut into the darkness of the hallway. There came also the sound of frying meat hissing above that of Marguerita's padded footfalls, and an odor of hot porkchops floating on a haze of gray smoke. He wondered whether she had heard him enter; was certain that she had not, since she had not called for the game. He stood still, trying to decide what to do. Mussolini came out the kitchen door, resembling in his sleek-sided massive bulk a lion cub, and stopped to look Sam over. Then the cat advanced down the hallway toward his mistress' lesser portion, his yellow back arched, his stiff tail standing up like a malignant finger, accusingly. Mussolini rubbed against Sam's legs, almost unbalancing him; sniffed curiously at the parcel of liver, uttering deep throaty supplications.

Sam's reason warned him to observe restraint, yet he disobeyed, and shoved the cat with his foot. It was not a kick, but merely a vigorous push, that made Mussolini sprawl on his side. Immediately the hallway was filled with a yowl of angry protest. Marguerita came hastening from the kitchen, wiping her hands on her soiled apron, slip-slapping glidingly, and peering into the twilight haziness of the hallway. Mussolini ran to meet her, casting backward at his mistress' husband baleful and reproachful glances.

"Wassa matter, Mussolini, darlin.' What's happened to Mother's 'ittle darlin'? What—"

Sam stepped briskly forward, as though he had but that moment entered the hallway. His wife was glaring.

"Sam Desmond, what you—"

"Dark out here," he said, rather hurriedly. "Stumbled over him. Guess he smelt his meat. I—"

"I thought 'twas you. Slinkin' round here worse'n Mussolini. What you up to now? I know it's something you ashamed of. I bet you didn't get my game." She waited for him either to confirm or abrogate her suspicion. He was silent, which indicated confirmation. She went on: "That's it, now, ain't it? You didn't get my game. You didn't get my game. I knew it. Give me that meat. I knew you wouldn't."

She left him standing miserable in the semi-dark hallway. Mussolini stalked ahead of her into the kitchen. For a moment Sam listened. . . .

"I knew you wouldn't. You never do . . . Come on, Mussolini, and get your dinner, pet. You're the only real male around here . . ." Sam could easily distinguish the part of her address meant for him: "Some day you're going to find yourself looking for another woman . . ." Yes, that was his. He had memorized it years since. He stood motionless, waiting for the rest of it. There it was: "I'm sicken tired of your carelessness. You don't think about doin' nothin' to please me once in a while . . ." Every time he heard this accusation he resented it anew. He felt that it was maliciously untrue. He renounced it with a surging burning resentment. She interrupted his smoldering meditation: "I ask you to bring me—"

"But they didn't *have* any, Rita! You might know they must not have had any if—"

"Oh, that's no excuse! Suppose they *didn't* have any. Is old Bamberger's the only meat market in town? What's the matter with the Manhattan right here at Central Square? No, that aint the reason. You just didn't—"

"But you know I haven't got no account at the Manhattan, Rita. An' I didn't have a pen—"

"Account! Account! Don't make me choke myself laughin'. You haven't got any charge account anywhere, if that's what you mean. Old Bamberger only takes pity on you and lets you have things because he knows you're too dumb to walk out on him and look for a decent job . . ." He could hear the loud frying of something freshly laid in the skillet. The hissing momentarily blanketed her voice. Presently, however, it broke through: "Account! Account! No, you *aint* got any account. And you aint any account either."

Making a gesture of resignation to the smoke-filled odor-laden dusk of the hallway, Sam shuffled toward the bathroom. His narrow shoulders drooped lower than usual, and he was angry with himself because he could think of none of the fine set-speeches he often rehearsed on the car going home. He closed the bathroom door and lighted the gas. Above the sound of running water he could hear Marguerita's baby talk addressed to Mussolini: "Come on, oo po' 'ittle hungry kittsy cat, an' get its supper. Come on, dear!"

Mussolini! The lousy yaller beast! Oh, if he could only do something with that cat! Perhaps then his wife would transfer some of these generous affections to her husband. But he did not pursue the notion. It was a will-o'-the-wisp, and not worth pursuit. Mussolini was already twelve years old; he was wiser than most cats of greater age, and as truly an institution of the Desmond household as Marguerita herself. There existed about as much likelihood of his getting rid of that husky feline as there was of his making up to resemble Valentino.[8] Mussolini! The lousy yaller . . . Sam buried his face in the cold water, holding his breath; removed his face and rubbed it with a towel until it glistened in the mirror above the wash basin like polished patent leather. He preferred cold water for his face even in winter, he said, for it soothed his nerves. He studied himself for a moment in the glass, then grimaced.

"So she wishes I wasn't so black, does she? He muttered, recalling the oft-told tale. "Oh, well, I should worry! I sure don't look like nobody's little Snow-Flake, 'spite what Roberts calls me."

"Sam, come out that bathroom and get your dinner—if you want any. You must think I'm gonna stay in the kitchen all night."

Sam chuckled grimly as he shambled toward the kitchen. "What a difference when she speaks to me'n when she speaks to that lousy yaller beast."

There being no dining room, they ate in the kitchen, utilizing a folding camp-table which was kept in the kitchen closet between meals. As Sam took his place he watched his wife's face covertly, hoping to determine the extent of her displeasure. She slip-slapped about, jolting the table when her soft ample person made contact with it; filled his plate with bony fried fish, his cup with inky black coffee, and his soul with leaping, shrieking passion for revenge on Mussolini. Why should *he* have to eat fish? He hated it, and Marguerita knew he hated it. He noticed that *her* plate held two browned pork-chops, and suspected that punishment was being visited upon his appetite and stomach for his failure to bring her game. And this angered him, for he had bought those chops with the natural and logical intention of eating one of them himself. He felt resentment swelling, bubbling, in his breast; rising to his throat, and clogging it; to his eyes, making the tears burn beneath his lids; making him blink his eyes rapidly and lower his head as if looking for something under the table.

Marguerita took her place opposite him, scanning him from squinting eyes. Her full fleshy jaw was set, and as she struck back from her moist cheek the vagrant lock of black straight hair, Sam knew that she not only was prepared for a quarrel but would welcome one. He was still reluctant to give her cause, provided she did not think she had cause enough already. There was so far no sound reason for his exploding. If he did, of course, it would be just *too bad*. Yes, he would hold his temper inside. She merely sought an excuse to jump on him; he knew that, and swore that he would give her nothing that even resembled a cue. So he began slowly to thread the fish, picking out with his fingers the innumerable needle-like bones.

The cat sat to one side, regarding them from slitted yellow eyes. Glimpsing what he considered Mussolini's contemptuous regard of the master of the house, Sam sensed a sudden desire to injure it. There

Mussolini sat, its great sleek yellow back hunched, its massive head, like a wise old man's, tilted to one side, and a diabolical smirk on its too human features. He wanted to see it squirm in pain, to hear it yowl and spit defiance to no avail. He did not doubt that but for the lousy yaller beast Marguerita would be a better wife.

"You make me sick, Sam Desmond! Here I am all day workin' my head off to make a home for you, an' you can't even do me a little favor."

Sam munched distastefully his fried fish and boiled potato, dropping his eyes from the angry gaze of his wife's; then he looked across at the kingly usurper on the floor. Mussolini, with long, slithering strides, came forward as if once more to demonstrate his priority rights. Crouching slightly, he sprang upon his mistress' lap and thrust his yellow head into her plate. He sniffed about for a moment but, presumably finding nothing to his taste, he sat back with lazy and smug complaisance, almond eyes indifferently fixed on the man opposite.

Then, as if to show further the extent of *his* prerogatives, he lifted a soiled white paw and did what Sam in delirious lapses dreamed of doing but which in sane moments haunted him only sub-consciously: Mussolini slapped Marguerita's face. With a petulant shove she sent him to the floor. "Get down, Mussolini. I don't feel like playing tonight. I'm mad."

The cat stretched, curled over on the crescent of his back to wash himself, then stalked around the table and sprang upon Sam's lap. For an instant the man shrank in confounded amazement. Why, the damn, lousy, yaller! ... Why, he'd never dared to do that before! It was downright defiance, that was it; defiance in the presence of his—of *their*—mistress. With a quick, vicious gesture he hurled the cat to the floor. Mussolini made no sound but stood lashing his tail and looking from the man to the woman; seeming in his attitude to demand the woman's intervention.

The next moment Marguerita had bounded from her seat, nearly upsetting the light table, and had planked Mussolini in Sam's plate. "There, Mussolini," she cried. "And you," she snarled, "Mr. Nice-Nasty, you just touch that cat again if you dare! Just lay your black hands on him again—just go ahead and do it ... I'm sicken tired of you goin' round here actin' like you was just too disgusted to live under the same roof with me and my cat ... That's right Mussolini, eat! ... If you're so disgusted why don't you find somewhere else to stay? You make me ..." She resumed her seat and glared at him.

With an impatient quirk of the body Sam sent the table skidding against the set tubs. There was a clatter of broken crockery on the floor, the scurrying of heavy footfalls of a frenzied yellow cat, the wide-eyed incredulity of an over-sized yellow woman.

Sam left the scene in silent triumph. It has occurred to him so suddenly, so instantaneously, that he was confused as to how it had happened. Certainly he had done nothing so radical before in all his married life. Marguerite [*sic*] said nothing. In silence too she took down the folding table and put it into the closet. Then she began to wash the dishes ... Sam did not often exhibit such temper.

Sam was now in the front room with the radio. He had the earphones on and did not hear his wife's calling until she screeched near his head. He felt that the first round of this fight was his; every detail of her present demeanor seemed to proclaim it. Clearly she was upset. He removed the earphones with methodical slowness and frowned at her, thrilling at the experience.

He heard her say: "Well, why don't you do something? Didn't you hear me? He's chokin'!"

She had already turned and slip-slapped quickly back to the kitchen. Muttering, Sam followed. "*He's* chokin'? *Who's* chokin'? What you talkin' 'bout?" He disliked having to admit that her seeming discomfiture at his sudden exhibition of temper was due to something else.

In the kitchen Sam saw Marguerita on her knees with the coughing Mussolini squeezed to her pillowy breast. Tears were on Marguerita's cheek, and she was rocking from side to side as through trying to sooth a fretful child.

"O Sam, Mussolini's got a fish bone in his throat! See if you can get it out. I've tried everything I know," she whined, "an' nothin' don't seem to work. Oh, he's chokin' to death! Oh! Oh!"

Sam straightened his frail shoulders. "Then let the yaller lousy beast choke to death! He can die and go to heaven for all I care." Sam returned to the radio.

For a while he stood holding the earphones in his hands, listening to Mussolini's coughing and Marguerita's baby talk. Then there was silence. Presently he heard his wife coming back, and he hastened to put the phones over his ears and sink into the cushioned armchair. One glimpse of her face told him that she was contrite. He did not like to see her angry or upset. She sat beside him, on the arm of his chair, and pulled his head down against her breast.

He tried to think of Mussolini's recently lying there, but her caresses dulled his senses and exhilarated him. "Naughty boy," she scolded playfully. "Naughty boy, not to bring mama what she wanted. And mama was mad too; yes, she was. Mama just as mad as she could be." She fondled his head running her soft fingers through his tight hair. In spite of himself his soothing rebellion cooled under her ministration. It always did. "Naughty boy! If you had brought mama's rabbit Mussolini wouldn't't've got a bone in his little pink throat, 'cause' you've had the chops then, an' . . ."

Sam shook himself free.

"Oh, you still angry with mama, is you, naughty boy? Why you still angry with your mama?"

"You like that lousy yaller cat better than you do me! I'm getting' sicken—"

"Oh, that's it, is it? Naughty boy jealous of Mussolini!" Her soft deft fingers stroked his cheeks, his throat, his eyelids. He lay back, half listening to the dance music from the Copley Plaza, half hypnotized by the woman's caresses. Resentment was all burned out. He lay back, feeling the throb of her heart beneath the warm soft breast.

"You won't forget tomorrow, will you, Sammy boy? And you won't be nasty to Mussolini any more, will you?"

His senses were dissolved and merged. "No, never . . . You got the bone out all right? That's good . . . Tomorrow I'm gonna bring you the nicest, biggest, fattest . . . Les go to bed. I'm all in."

III

The ever-recurrent flare of resentment at Mussolini's presence in the bed flickered for an instant, then glowed angrily thru the rest of Sam's waking hours. The beast lay between him and Marguerita, its warm furry body wedged close. Sam could hear its throaty purr at intervals, like the distant whirr of an aeroplane. Thus was husband separ[a]ted from wife. He knew that if he moved nearer her Mussolini would challenge him with spitting and scratches; yet, if he lifted the lousy yaller beast by the scruff of the neck and dropped it to the floor, he would suffer verbal attack from Marguerita. His thought became an irrational patchwork; he wondered whether she permitted the cat to sleep between them solely to keep him away; speculated dully on ways and means of banishing it forever; listened to his wife's deep regular breathing...

Rabbits, squ'rrels, ven'son steak—game; a big yaller cat caressed by a big yaller woman.... He slept...

His wife, sitting up in bed, was shaking him and calling his name loudly. Through the murk of drowsiness he heard her saying: "That fish bone's still in his throat, Sam! *Please* see if you can't get it out. If we don't do something he'll die! Don't you guess you could call up some doctor now? Mr. Williams downstairs would let you use his telephone. Oh, listen to the poor little darlin'! He's just gaspin' for breath... Sam Desmond, would you lay up there an' let a poor innocent dumb animal suffer"... Well, you're even worsen I thought you was. Don't you ever speak to me again, so there!"

She was out of the bed, the cat pressed to her bosom, pulling down the shades, lowering the window, fumbling for matches and the gas jet. There was in her actions all the intense, compact suffering of the mother whose babe lies dangerously ill. Finding it impossible to sleep longer Sam sat up, scratching and rubbing his eyes. The cat was coughing and clawing at its throat. Sam felt suddenly an overwhelming sense of compunction, but before it could move him to action Marguerita had dragged him, cover and all, to the floor.

"What's the matter with you, Sam Desmond? You crazy? I told you to call up a doctor! D you want Mussolini to die?" She tossed her husband his old bathrobe from the foot of the bed. "Put that on and go downstairs and call up a doctor."

But Sam caught up the old garment and hurled it at the choking feline, who, momentarily terrified, wriggled from Marguerita's arms and scampered under the bed. It's [*sic*] coughing had ceased. Sam stood glaring down at it for a moment, then turned to his wife.

"Damn that cat! I'm getting' awfully tired of so much foolishness, d'you understand? I mean it, Marguerita! I'm sicken tired of playin' butler and chambermaid to that lousy yaller cat. First thing you know you'll wake up some morning and find you aint got no cat nor husband neither. An' another thing," he cut in, raising his hand to check Marguerita's impending retort. "I'm sick of sleepin' in bed with a cat. I'm tired of that nasty beast layin' up between us. I didn't marry no cat, an' I aint goin' to sleep with none no more. I mean that, believe me! I think it's about time I put my foot down roun' here."

He scowled at her for a moment, but she stood in stupefied silence, her eyes fixed on his. Then he crawled into bed, dragging the covers with him, and turned his back to her. After a little while he sensed that she had turned out the light. He heard her push up the window and run up the window shade, then get heavily into bed. A flood of exultation overswept him as he realized more fully the prodigious extent of his victory—a victory without bowls [sic]. For a long while both lay silent. Presently he heard Mussolini's pat-pat-pat, noted the abrupt cessation of the footfalls, then, before he could speculate on the cat's intention, Mussolini was walking across Sam's head seeking its place between the man and his wife.

With a muttered "damn!" the man sprang up, dragging the covers with him and, seizing the animal, tossed it across the room. It uttered a howling wail of protest, an imprecation, Sam thought, and spit at him. Sam wondered whether in its defiance it would spring at him in the dark. But Marguerita was out of the bed again; pulling down the window and the shade; making a light. Sam hastened to return to the covers. He lay silent and disturbed, his face to the wall. Without a word to her husband Marguerita picked up the cat, crooning brokenly over it; then kissing it noisily, she placed it again in the bed. Sam wondered how much resentment a man's breast would hold before it exploded like an overfilled gas bag....

IV

In the morning Sam heard his wife slip-slapping, slipper-shod as usual, in the kitchen. He rose and went into the bathroom. Above the noise of running water he heard her calling to him: "The cat's still got that fish bone in his throat. I want you to take him to the animal hospital in the Fenway on your way to work. You won't have time to eat no breakfast, but I got you a cup of coffee ready."

Sam found Mussolini caged in an old basket. Marguerita had packed it with clean cloths and covered it with old window screening. Grumbling, his shoulders hopelessly drooped, Sam gulped his coffee, then picked up the basket and left the house. At the hospital examination disclosed nothing more than an inflamed throat. There probably *had* been a bone, it was explained, but certainly there was none now. Sam proceeded to his work, arriving half an hour late.

Roberts observed to the clerical force sometime during the afternoon that "maybe you folks don't know Sam here's Mussolini's nurse maid." "Yeah," he called loudly, from the rear of the store, "Sam nursin' Mussolini now. 'S'wife make him take the cat out to walk when he come to work in the mornin', then walk home with it at night. See that basket Sam bring in here this mornin'? Well, Mussolini's in that. Jus' as nice an' comfy. Aint he, Sam?"

The porter listened in pretended good humor.

The telephone rang, Mr. Bamberger answering it. "Why, yes, Mrs. Desmond, your husband's right here. No, no trouble at all. Just a minute."

Sam was laconic to the point of gruffness. "What's that? Yup! ... Oh, the cat? Well, it's ... dead! I said he's dead! Yup, dead. D-E-A-D. Finee! Compree? Expired. Passed out.... Yup, at the hospital ..." He hung up the receiver and turned to the questioning stares of the house. To the proprietor he said: "Never mind the rabbit, Mr. Bamberger. She don't want it now. Lost her appetite, I guess."

Sam swept the floor. He sprinkled fresh sawdust all round, cleaned out the back room, and washed the rear and front windows, inside and out, despite the biting cold! Coincidentally, it was a busy afternoon for the others, too, being Saturday; for which Sam was thankful. He didn't feel like a lot of cheap talk....

It was nearly closing time. Roberts came in from the rear, calling loudly and somewhat excitedly: "Say, Snow White, what's the big idea? Mussolini aint no more dead'n I is. Why—?"

"If he aint no more dead'n you, then he's all ready for the embalmin' fluid—an' don't know it. That cat's dead, I'm tellin' you ..."

Sam closed the shop as usual that night, leaving fully an hour later than the others. He carried no basket, but, instead, a parcel in butcher's wrapping paper, which, in turn, was wrapped within a newspaper; a parcel which may have contained a dressed rabbit or a squirrel or a venison steak. As he waited for a car at Tremont and Northampton streets he grinned into the frigid semi-darkness; then, holding the parcel aloft before his face:

"Why don't you yowl for your mama, you lousy yaller rascal?" he apostrophized, in a low tense voice. "Why don't you spit on me? ... So she wants game, does she? Well, she'll *get* game!"

"Cold-Blooded"
Saturday Evening Quill (JUNE 1928): 48–51

If Poe was the literary model for "Game," O. Henry, master of the surprise ending, would be the model for "Cold-Blooded," published in the first issue of the *Quill*. Joseph Mahoney works as a reporter for the Boston *Morning Bulletin*. His editor keeps lamenting that Mahoney's stories lack any human angle. Mahoney is assigned to cover a story about a fire in his neighborhood. He is finally able to please the editor with a story that is "thrilling in its very starkness." Then the editor learns why the story is so personal for Mahoney.

Cold-Blooded

Charley Bream, city editor of the Boston *Morning Bulletin*, thrust Mahoney's story back at him. "For God's sake," he cried fretfully, "put a little warm blood into it, won't you!" He scowled at the middle-aged, fish-eyed, gum-chewing reporter in the shiny blue serge. Mahoney shoved his yellowed straw hat further toward the rear of his half-bald head, but he neither spoke nor blinked. "I'd give it to Jim here to rewrite," Bream complained, "if I didn't know you so well. But I know you *can* do it every damn bit as well as Jim."

Mahoney, standing beside the city editor's desk in the corner, glanced with apparent disinterest at the solemn rewrite man designated as Jim. Then he returned to a perusal of his story. He glanced at his chief. "Oh, I see," he said at length. "You want sob stuff in an ordinary thug story." Voice and shrug combined in conveying contempt. He sauntered toward his desk against the left-hand wall midway the long room.

Mr. Bream's face and hairless head reddened. He whacked the desk with his fist. "Never mind the flippancy, Mahoney! *I'm* the city editor, and you'll write as I want you to . . . or you'll get through."

Mahoney plucked his yellowed straw from the back of his head and tossed it behind his typewriter; then, having draped his shiny blue coat over the back of his chair, he seated himself. He read through the story rapidly, muttering something under his breath. Glancing sidewise toward the street-end of the room where the editors sat; he shrugged then inserted in the typewriter a blank sheet of paper.

He leaned back and chewed with unconscious vigor. On the wall behind his typewriter was pasted a photograph clipped from a newspaper: a woman in filmy white propped up in bed and holding on each breast a very young infant. The caption above the picture read: "Wife of Bulletin Reporter Mother of Husky Twins" and underneath: "Mrs. Joseph Mahoney, wife of Joe Mahoney, of the *Bulletin* reportorial staff, with the two youngest Mahoneys, born at Roxbury Lying-in Hospital yesterday."[9] The picture was more yellowed than Mahoney's old hat.

The reporter contemplated the pictured group for several minutes, his jaws working rhythmically. Then he contemplated the blank sheet in the typewriter, his forehead unwrinkled, his eyes more fishlike than ever. Finally he began to write, striking with full-armed force.

At the end of the room overlooking the street the re-write man was typing interminably; the assistant city editor, the high back of whose desk abutted the city editor's, was glancing through the afternoon papers; the city editor in his corner was writing with a pen; and the office boy, a copy of "Sherlock Holmes" pressed close under his arm, was sorting some mail and placing it in the reporters' boxes. These occupied wall space just at Mr. Bream's left.

Under the augmented bedlam of Mahoney's old machine, Tom Malloy, assistant city editor, rose and leaned forward across his desk. "Whassa matter with 'im, Boss?" he whispered, jerking a stubby thumb toward the reporter. "Not falling down on the job, is he?"

Mr. Bream glared at his assistant. "Who do you mean? he asked bluntly.

"Frog Mahoney. I noticed you sent 'im' back to rewrite his story. Usually he's pretty good, you know. I was just wondering."

The city editor was writing again. "Oh, Mahoney," he said, and paused, He narrowed his smallish gray eyes at his assistant, an eager-to-please, conscientious little "Yes-Boss" man with a beautifully polished skull. "The story's all right," declared the boss. "All right *as* a story, good English, 'n everything; but it's too damn dead. Dead!" His voice mounted, and his round, puffy face and hairless head crimsoned under the slight exertion. The assistant city editor nodded understandingly. The rewrite man, facetiously called, "Jim the Sphinx" because of his silent solemnity, stopped pounding and listened deferentially, and the office boy halted his leisurely movements and stood at attention.

"You mean he didn't put in any human interest?" Molloy queried mildly.

"Sure. That's what I mean. Anybody almost can get stark facts, but anybody can't put flesh and blood and breath into a story, and make the people live. Get what I mean?" He laid down his fountain pen and leaned his shirted, overstuffed body forward. "Now, here's this burglary out here in the Back Bay, see. The mother's alone in the house with her baby, and the baby's crying in another room. In come the burglars where the baby's crying, see, and when the mother wants to get to the child, the thugs drive her back. See the possibilities."

"Yep. Sure, Boss!" The assistant city editor was enthusiastic.

"Sure, I can see that, all right," intoned Jim the Sphinx.

The office boy grimaced.

Mr. Bream continued: "Well, the district man out there is right on the job, see, and he covers it perfectly."

"Jacobs would, of course, he's a damn good newspaper man. But I send Mahoney here out there to get a slant on the human interest angle, see,—the horror-stricken mother separated from her child by these thugs, and all that sort of thing." The city editor paused and stared out the window. "And he brings back a tabulation of cold facts that have as much life in 'em as I've got sex appeal."

If his peroration was intended to provoke mirth it failed of its purpose. The city editor seldom made so long a speech; his opinions were usually posted on the bulletin board; but when he did speak, it was with the tacit understanding that those close at hand were to sit or stand at attention until he had finished, then react to the speech as they suspected he desired. They listened now rather solemnly and ill at ease, for Mahoney stood beside the desk with the revised story. And they knew that he had heard much of what the Boss had said. If there was anything less funny than the idea of the over-stuffed, bloated-faced, suspendered, hairless city editor's having sex appeal, it was to have the cold, uncanny "Frog" listening in on a speech he wasn't supposed to hear.

The city editor noticed the silence, and turned, to scowl at Mahoney. The assistant city editor was suddenly busy at countless details; directing the movements of photographers, answering his desk 'phone, marking clippings from rival sheets. Jim the Sphinx worked like an automaton. The office boy was everywhere at once,

"Sherlock Homes" pressed open under his arm. Having read the story through, the city editor tossed it into the wire basket on his desk. The reporter chewed absently; stared absently before him; ambled absently back toward his typewriter. He seemed unaffected by what he had heard. He removed the gum from his mouth and stuck it underneath his typewriter desk. From a pocket of the shiny blue coat draped on the back of his chair he removed a pipe and scraped out its odoriferous bowl with a penknife. Then he stuffed it with fresh tobacco from the watch-pocket of his trousers, lighted it, sat down and placed his feet on his desk, and leaned back once more to contemplate his family. As he gazed, his eyes were human eyes, no longer those of dead fish. He was like a man who sees pleasant things in his sleep.

The fire signal sounded above the head of the rewrite man. It continued to sound at brief intervals for many moments. No one seemingly heeded it. Mahoney, his face now cast in a beatific smile, regarded the wife and twins through the blueish haze from his pipe. The office boy occasionally answered the telephone and shouted a message, the assistant city editor conferred with the chief of the photograph department, the solemn rewrite man, hammered flesh and blood upon the skeleton of some district man's telephoned story, and the city editor opened the glass door of the bulletin board and hung up a newly written memorandum. Reporters, drifting in and lounging aimlessly, sauntered over to the bulletin board.

In the street three stories below fire sirens were screeching. The telephones in the four booths, toward the center wall at the right of the room, jangled almost incessantly. Reporters had to go to the assistance of the office boy. Fire engines in the street roared above creaking brakes and squawks of frightened automobiles. Reporters and photographers were being dispatched to cover the fire.

Mahoney removed his feet from his desk, stood up, locked his typewriter in, and went over to read the newest memorandum:

> Reporters on this paper are expected to use their brains in writing stories, but not to the exclusion of their hearts. Get the

facts, but also get some of the little human details that change stark facts into living things. Use your imagination as well as your eyes.

"Lotta bunk," Mahoney muttered, and turned when the office boy, pushing open the telephone booth, yelled to the city editor: "Mr. Bream, it's Gallagher. He says it's important." Gallagher was the Charlestown district man.

Mahoney leaned against the glass-encased bulletin board and stared at the man in the booth. Engines roared by below. The rewrite man was looking out the window. The assistant city editor pushed back his chair and looked into the street. Reporters from the other end of the room sauntered forward and tried to peer over the shoulders of those ahead, tried to see down into the street. A heavy, slowly-moving mass of black smoke had smeared itself above the roofs of the tall buildings.

Mr. Bream emerged from the telephone booth, head and face flushed.

"Some fire," he soliloquized, resuming his seat. "General alarm."

Tom Molloy sat down and waved the reporters lack to their places. "Get t' hell away from over my desk, you fellers!"

Mahoney reclined against the bulletin board, his pipe cold, his deadened eyes on the sour-faced rewrite man at the typewriter. He removed his pipe and hammered the contents of its bowl into his palm, shook his palm over the metal waste container, and returned to his place. He dropped the pipe into a pocket of the old coat on the chair, fumbled beneath the desk a moment with his fingers, transferred his gum to his mouth, and began to chew. He tilted back his chair, crossed his ankles on the desk top, and smiled at the wife and twins.

"Must be pretty good-sized by now, Frog." Mahoney looked up at Jacobs, the district manager from the Back Bay.

"You mean the kids? Yeh. Two years old day after tomorrow. Great trio. Great kids . . . You married, Jake?"

"Sure. Got a kid two years old myself."

"Great institution, family, Jake."

"Greatest in the world, Frog."

Typewriters were thumping over all the room now. Fire engines still roared at intervals. From where he sat Mahoney could see the sleazy, shapeless form of smoke, like a blot of ink, on the sky. Jacobs dropped upon the chair beside him, observing:

"Must be *some* fire over in Charlestown. Rather glad I don't live over there."

Mahoney stopped chewing and squinted at Jacobs. "That's funny. Charlie Bream hasn't."

"Mahoney!"

He stood up. It was the Boss' voice. Mahoney trudged slowly toward Charley Bream's desk. Red and harassed of face, the city editor glared up at him.

"Good Lord, Mahoney, do you think you're going to a funeral?"

The reporter stared, saying nothing.

"I'd like to see you really concerned about something once in your life. Here, hustle over to Charlestown. Right away. Better take a taxi. Help cover that fire. And get some life into it! I started not to send you, but—Imagine you got a personal interest, see? That's all. Get!"

When Mahoney had "got," the city editor raised his troubled features to his assistant across the desk and made a gesture indicating extreme fatigue. "Whoever nicknamed that bird "Frog," he groaned, "certainly knew *his* onions." He dashed the point of a blue pencil viciously through a new reporter's copy.

The dour-faced rewrite man let up on his clatter and said portentiously [*sic*]: "Well, I bet he gets some life into his story *this* time, all right."

"Why?" asked the assistant editor.

"Because he lives right in that section."

Mr. Bream was interested. "That so? I didn't know that. I thought Mahoney lived in East Cambridge."

"Not in East Cambridge, Boss," contradicted the assistant city editor, apologetically, "and not in the section where the fire is, either." He turned to the rewrite man. "You're wrong, Jim. Frog *was* to move to Charlestown, but he ain't done it yet."

The thudding of typewriters mingled with the roar and blare

of traffic below, and the frequent blasts of auto horns, the nerve-cutting scrape of faulty auto breaks, the rumble of an occasional wagon, the yelling of newsboys, the murmur of voices at the other end of the room, the ringing of telephones, the scratch of pens on paper,—all this combined to change the city room into a crazy bedlam.

"Here, Johnnie, run down and get a coupla extras. Quick!" The assistant city editor tossed the office boy a nickel. When the papers were brought, one of them was handed to the city editor: the assistant spread out one on his own desk.

"Great Scott," he said, "seven dead!"

"Any names given?" asked the rewrite man.

"All unidentified, so far. Here's the names of some injured."

He ran through the list, reading them aloud.

"Nobody any of us knows, is there?"

"No."

... The photographers came in, talking loudly and excitedly. The assistant city editor consigned them "to [get the] hell outa here with that damn racket." Mahoney came in, fishy eyes more fishy, his shoulders slumped, his yellowed straw hat barely retaining contact with the back of his head. As usual, he said no word to anybody. He removed his glistening coat, and draped it over the back of the chair, tossed his yellowed hat to its place behind the typewriter; then, sitting down, he unlocked his desk. He inserted a clean sheet of paper in the typewriter, and sat staring before him. He turned presently and looked around.

"Say, George," he called to the man at a desk behind him, "got any mucilage?"[10]

"Sure, Frog." George passed it over.

Mahoney picked up a clean sheet of paper, dabbed mucilage on each of its four corners, and, leaning forward, stuck it over the typewriter clipping of his family.

Now he began to write, and he continued steadily for an hour. His story completed, he took it to the city editor.

"This is good," the Boss said, skimming through it hastily. "This is good, Mahoney! Thrilling in its very starkness! You omit no detail: paint a perfect, living picture; yet there isn't a bit of gush or sob-stuff in it." He tossed the copy into a wire basket, and, leaning back, studied the reporter. "Now, that's the kind of writing I've been after you to do." He smiled benignly, as if to cause forgetfulness of all past harsh words. But Mahoney was not looking at him; his mind seemed remotely distant, his eyes were almost opaque in their gray dullness, and his jaws moved incessantly upon the chewing gum. The assistant city editor, the rewrite man, and the few reporters who chanced to be near, all smiled in sympathy. "Frog" was a queer bird. Nothing could even touch him, let alone move him. Here he was receiving all this acclaim and acting as if he didn't so much as hear.

"That all, Boss?"

"All? Whaddyer mean, 'all'? Whaddyer want now, a leave of absence?"

"Yes."

The city editor whacked his desk with his fist; his harassed face and hairless head reddened. "Whaddyer trying to hand me, Mahoney, a good time? I can't say a pleasant word to you fellows but what you want to take advantage of it. What—"

"Then I guess you didn't read my story, after all," muttered Mahoney, turning away. A moment later they saw him staggering out.

The city editor grunted.

The assistant city editor laughed contemptuously. "Run into summa that white mule hootch[11] over there in Charlestown, that's what he done. That's why he wrote that story so well, Boss."

Jim the Sphinx suspended typing. "But Frog never drinks that stuff," he assured them, gloomily.

"Well, what makes him act so?"

"He said the Boss didn't read his story." The rewrite man was mildly belligerent.

The city editor reached over, picked up the copy, and began to read slowly. Suddenly his big hands fell heavily to the desk, and his puffy face and hairless head went white. The assistant editor and the rewrite man stared.

"It says here, 'The known dead are Mrs. Margaret Mahoney and her two children, Joseph and James, aged one year, eleven months . . .'"

The city editor was rumbling heavily down three flights of stairs, crying, "Mahoney! Mahoney! I didn't know! . . . For God's sake. . . ."

"Buzzards"
Opportunity (NOVEMBER 1928): 338–42

This story is almost identical to an earlier story called "Alien" in the June 1928 issue of the *Saturday Evening Quill*. "Buzzards" revisits some of Gordon's favorite themes: violence, revenge, marital discord, issues of race/color, a surprise ending. However, he does it differently here. First, the story is told through the eyes of a white schoolteacher, Mary Spence, transplanted from Massachusetts to a Georgia plantation when she accepts a marriage proposal from a man she had just met in a lonely hearts magazine. She is warned by her husband to avoid contact with one Negro in particular, "Fried Face," horribly disfigured after being hit with a kettle of boiling lard. While alone on the plantation one day, Mary questions what she, a proper Boston lady, is doing in Georgia surrounded by a bunch of "darkies." All of her worst racist fears now play out, including fear of the subconscious sexual encounter with a Black man. She inevitably encounters and kills Fried Face when he either trips or lunges at her. All of this seems almost preordained, and it is where a less-skilled writer might have ended the story. However, it is the last section of the story when she begins to consider what she has done that is perhaps the most compelling and contains the biggest surprises.

Buzzards

Sensing it to be nearly noon, the woman hastened preparation of her husband's dinner ... In her native Massachusetts it would be called luncheon. This Georgia idiom irritated and perplexed her.

"Georgia barbarity! I'd never get used to it if I lived here a hundred years.... There you go, Mary Spence,—Mary Spence! Mary Spence Lankster, you mean—there you go talking to yourself again. You'd better stop it, or you'll find yourself in a Georgia madhouse before long."

She had seen Georgia and her husband for the first time just a week ago. He had answered her letter in *Love's Messenger*, and she had succumbed to his laboriously pictured "extensive green acres" and the enchantment she would there find as his wife. Mary Spence, school teacher, of Boston, had been married to John Lankster, farmer, of Whitingsville, thirty minutes after she had descended at the Whitingsville station. Since then she had felt like an expatriate bound to a queer foreigner in a strange land.

Going to the woodpile outside the picket fence, she gathered a basket of dry pine chips. With these she built a quick hot fire. The resin-soaked wood burned like gasoline, and even before she could replace both lids the stove was hot.

As always since her coming here, she was beset with vague and unaccountable terrors. The mid-summer heat oppressed, and she wondered dizzily how the corn and cotton crops retained their freshness. She wondered why she had come; wished forlornly for her classroom of New England youngsters; thought uneasily of laughing, coal-black Negroes whose big feet, unshod, caressed the burning earth.

She began to whimper, casting quick frightened glances about the barn-like kitchen. Vigorously she beat a mixture of corn meal, egg, and milk, trying to drown other and familiar noises with the clatter of spoon on tinware.

She thought again of her classroom, counting each separate face: there is Micky, and there is Solomon, and there is Joe, the little black-eyed Italian ... and George Collins, the little colored boy. John says I mustn't speak to the Negroes here. They might misunderstand. Didn't misunderstand in Boston.... "But this is *not* Boston. Mary, dear ... Oh, I've *got* to go for that water. Wonder if milk wouldn't do. Don't see why it shouldn't. For heaven's sake, why isn't there a well here in the yard? More Southern efficiency."

She ceased beating the mixture and fetched a pan of milk from a shelf in the corner. With the tip of her finger she touched some to her tongue: grimaced.

"Sour! I might've known that, with no ice anywhere within a thousand miles. And I don't know anything about making sour-milk bread."

To delay the inevitable trek to the spring she began again to beat the mixture. With quick nervous quirks of the head, her eye starting, she looked about at each unfamiliar sound. She thought of the man she had wed and gritted her teeth in sudden resentment against him.

Day after day these sounds and these thoughts had harassed and haunted her. She remembered weeks spent with other women in the Maine woods, but could not recollect one instance of fright. The noises there, she explained to herself, were intimately friendly, not hostilely sinister. Then there were not slinking around perpetually a host of odorous, barefooted, grinning Negroes.... John had warned her not to trust any of the blacks, 'ceptin' them as lives on th' place. Some of these darkies, he had assured her, hearing that a Northern white woman was in their midst, might try to take advantage of her ignorance of Southern custom. This custom required that the blacks stand uncovered in her presence, that they address her always in most respectful accents, and that she bear toward them a dignified and superior attitude. She wondered why the blacks of the plantation differed so radically from those of Boston's South End; was glad John had instructed her in firing the double barrelled shot gun.

Day after day these thoughts, impressions, fears, and, misgivings recurred. Day after day she was sent rushing frantically from the barnlike kitchen to the securer shelter of the sleeping quarters by a pig's squeak, or by the shrilly, wailing cry of a sparrow hawk, or by the sleepy growl of the yellow hound dozing under the edge of the house, or by the flutter of frilled newspaper on the kitchen shelves when the wind blew through, or even by the crackle of fire in the kitchen stove. These unrelated, indeterminate noises drove her almost to madness. Shrieking suddenly, she would rush from the kitchen and across the twenty feet of shaded yard, dashing into the one-room sleeping quarters. Chickens fluttered crackling [sic] from her path. The dozing hound lifted his aged head and regarded her contemptuously. Inside the sleeping quarters, she would close and bar the heavy board door, then stand silently behind it, awaiting with thudding heart the terror's approach. But nothing so far had happened. Presently she would return, her thin pale face slightly flushed, her near-sighted gray eyes, peering apprehensively through gold rimmed glasses her long lean fingers gripping her flat chest. She would proceed to the kitchen she had just left and occupy her hands with repeatedly neglected chores.

So far, today, she had not run. She had vowed yesterday that she would never again be so foolish. Breaking another egg into the pan, she stirred with all the energy of her thin arms. She beat upon the side of the pan with the spoon, purposely raising as loud a din as possible. Now she paused, exhausted, and listened.

Hens were clucking in the cotton. An auto horn sounded from the highway a quarter of a mile distant. A heavy persistent drone of summer insects wove a background for all other noises. The kitchen fire had ceased crackling, and the woman removed the lids and laid on more chips. The kitchen fire roared.

II

She looked into the wooden water bucket on the shelf outside the kitchen door. Even as she had feared, it was all but empty. Some dead flies floated in the warm water which remained.

Descending the steps, she hastened across the white, shaded yard to the door of the sleeping quarters. She mounted the steps and peered at the mantel clock above the fire place; surprised at the lateness. She ran back to the kitchen muttering:

"I must get over this foolishness. What's the matter with me anyway?" Her voice rising to a plaintive wail, she said: "Oh, why did I ever do such a crazy thing? A man I'd never set eyes on.... Why didn't I stay up there in Boston?"

She removed the water bucket from the shelf, hung the tin dipper on a nearby nail, and, with a long, outward sweep of her thin arms, emptied the water into the yard. It showered in a semi-circular fringe upon an old hen, and her brood; and the biddies fluttered their downy, featherless wings, cheeping loudly. The woman stood watching them for a long time, disquietude for the moment forgotten.

Now she started toward the gate in the side of the fence—the one which lay nearest the corn patch and the woods—with the bucket in her hand. She paused and stared about, her heart leaping painfully at the unexpected squawk of a jay bird in the oak overhead. Her eyes were large with apprehension as she stared toward the grove where lay the only water supply. She hung the bucket on a picket of the fence and ran into the house. Presently she returned, balancing a double barrelled breech loader[12] in her right hand. Removing the bucket from the fence, she started toward the gate.

Bringing herself to an abrupt halt, she gazed fearfull [*sic*] at the firearm; laughed jerkily, cutting off her voice sharply, as though startled at its sound. Then she began to whimper, turning round and round as though expecting attack from every side. She stared at the open door of the sleeping quarters as if in anticipation of someone's springing out, then turned her scrutiny upon the door of the kitchen. Stooping, she searched the far reaches beneath the house. A short distance toward the front, and somewhat to the right, of the house, huddled a miscellany of outhouses—barn, corral, cotton house, and corn crib. She stood, wondering whether some day someone would conceal himself in one of those buildings and watch her; possibly slink out and assault her.

She thought again of "Fried Face," the Negro whose face had been turned into a hideous scar when, in a fight a few years before, he had been knocked into a kettle of boiling lard. She realized that it was principally of him, whom she had not yet seen, that her husband had warned her.

"He's th' trickiest nigger you ever clap your eyes on, Mary, an' you got to be keerful. If you ever git caught away from th' house, an' you have your gun, an' he meets you an' looks like he wants to be too friendly, why, just don't wonder what to do. Shoot, that's all. Shoot quicker n'hell, 'cause ef you don't t'll be too late."

"But how shall I *know* him?? Mary had asked, deeply concerned.

He spat a brown rivulet. "Oh, you'll know him, all right 'nough. Ugliest black devil you ever clap your eyes on. An' always grinnin', which makes 'im look uglier 'n hell."

It must be a hundred in the shade, she thought, plucking from her body the sticky clothing. Heat waves wriggled in broken horizontal and perpendicular lines across the top of the corn. The air was tuneful with droning, lazy summer sounds. Above, so high as to resemble swallows, two turkey buzzards circled and swirled. The sun shining upon them turned the repulsive scavengers into birds of glittering silver: the rusty black feathers, naked necks and heads wattled with red and black warts, the disgusting odor of carrion which was a part of them—these characteristics of the creatures she could not know.

She wished she could reach such heights, above the featherduster tops of the pines, above the sinister influences that hedged her. She thought of the buzzards as aviators flying cross country. She wished this were so, and that, losing their bearing, the flyers had to descend in the cotton patch to seek information as to reaching Boston. She stood gazing upward, her mouth open.

A red-headed woodpecker on the roof of the corn crib beat a ruffles,[13] as on a drum. With a breathless shriek, the woman raised the gun, her starting eyes appraising this new terror. She lowered the weapon, resting its butt beside her foot on the ground.

"Mary," she scolded, "you've got to get over your silly fright. Shame on you! You're worse than a child, you are." She seemed suddenly aware of the breech-loader beside her. "Take that gun right back where it belongs."

Setting the bucket on the ground, she obeyed, returning empty handed. Pausing midway, [in] the yard, she gazed slowly about her. She felt fairly secure within the enclosure of the yard, buttressed as she was by the kitchen and the sleeping quarters. But before her, across acres of corn drooping in the heat, lay her asylum of horrors, the dense wood of oak, pine and sweet gum trees, all intertwined with a rank growth of vines sheathed in impassable undergrowth. The memory of eerie jungle sounds arising thence day and night drove her to the verge of frenzy whenever the time came to go for water. She would ask her husband *today* to have a well dug in the yard.

Her roving eyes alighted on the yellow hound under the edge of the house, and she tried to whistle to him. He opened the bleary eye nearer her and observed her gloomily.

"Come, doggie, come!" She stooped and snapped her fingers; emitted the thin imitation of a whistle. "Come on—like a nice doggie. Come!"

But the dog stretched his yellow boney hide and, with a long groan of comfort, turned over, resuming his interrupted siesta.

Stung with rage, the woman began with her eyes on a search of the sand-swept yard. She grabbed up a stone, about the size of an egg, and drawing her skinny arm far back, heaved the missile with all her strength. It struck the house, but, with a yelp of mingled fright and indignation, the hound scampered up and loped across the yard, his tail between his legs. She saw him circling crazily in the shade of a cotton stalk, and, after a moment, lie down.

She was contrite. "What's the matter with me?" she whimpered. "I never used to be like this. Even the dogs hate me. I must be going crazy."

She looked into the clear cloudless sky where the sun blazed, a disc of greenish red. Far to the north, so distant as to resemble butterflies, circled and swirled a flock of turkey buzzards. They were surfaced with glittering silver sheen. She thought of lost aviators. . . . The clock struck once.

Panic assailed her anew. That *must* be twelve-thirty; yet, to save her, she could not recollect having heard twelve. The bread was not yet made nor the bacon fried. Potatoes had not been washed. The table was still to be set.

"Here I am failing as a housewife already. That will never do, as much as I hate everything." She went hurriedly and peered at the clock, then, returning, groaned.

"The bell should've been rung a half hour ago. What *is* the matter with me?"

The bell was affixed to the end of a wooden "arm" fastened to the farther side of the kitchen. Her emotions were a strange mixture of self-reproach, self-pity, bewilderment, anger, and unaccountable fear. She hastened now through the kitchen and out the rear door. Grasping the worn rope in both hands, she swayed the bell to and fro. . . . School bells in Boston; carillon[14] in the tower of the Christian Science temple; noonday services at King's Chapel; the sonorous peals of theatre organs. She rang on, enthralled by memories aroused in the tones of the bell. The old hound slunk around the corner of the house and, lifting its mangy yellow head, howled in her face. She ceased in consternation.

"Dear me! I must have rung that bell ten minutes. Takes me right back to Boston. What will John think?" She laughed pointlessly; recalled uneasily what her husband had said just this morning: "Try to ring th' bell right on time; I don't want no trouble with any of these niggers." "Fried Face," he explained, was doing a little hoeing for him this week; the other darkies were all right, but this one . . . "Don't forget th' bell, Mary."

She wandered into the kitchen; stood gazing bewilderedly at the cooling stove. She sat on an upturned box and tried to marshal her scattered and distracted wits into some sort of orderly array. Her head had begun to ache about the eyes.... Bread to be made, meat to be fried, potatoes to be washed and peeled, blackberries to be picked over, water to be brought from the spring.... "No, not fried meat and potatoes today."

"I forgot!" She clasped her head and rocked from side to side on the box. "I forgot all about it—John wanted cabbage and boiled potatoes.... What *is* wrong with me?"

She rose wearily and went into the sleeping quarters. When she emerged she again had the gun. Walking rapidly, as if her mind were definitely settled, she crossed the yard, picked up the bucket from the ground and plunged into the simmering oven of the corn.

III

As she drew nearer the spring the house she had left seemed to recede into unfathomable distance. She remembered without effort dreams in which similar phenomena had predominated: a starting from a certain spot and a subsequent vain effort to return. Gradually a deadening fatalism gripped her. She felt that she would never go back, for her strength would leave her. She thought of the present as a horribly torturing nightmare. She longed to awaken in bed in her room at the Franklin Square House.[15]

She began to slacken her pace; to place each foot ahead of the other on the clearest and softest spots. She picked out tufts of grass to step upon, because these gave back no scrunching sound. The rattle of the staves in the water bucket, made loose by standing in the sun, was as the rat-tat-tat of a machine gun to her taut nerves. She stopped, knelt, and set the bucket beside her. Then, lifting the butt of the shot gun to her stomach, she pressed back both triggers. Rising, she picked up the bucket and continued toward the spring. She craved a backward glance, just as she had craved it yesterday and the day before, but, as on previous days, she felt that if she so much as turned her face, a long black arm would stretch from the tangled and sinister wilderness and draw her in. She must look this unseen Terror in the eyes.

Each chirp and lilt of bird was devilish music to enchant and befuddle her; each rustle of grass was a crawling, slinking Negro with lust in blood-shot eyes; each twit of cricket, each whirr of grasshopper, each burr of locust, each crack of twig, each sough[16] of breeze in the foliage, each bay of distant hound; the drone of insects; the dance of heat waves before her eyes—each, all were flails to a harassed spirit.

Finally the spring lay before her. It bubbled silently straight up from a rock-encircled hollow. Rising like a verdant wall, towered the tangled underbrush, vines and trees. Long, green grass spread along the woodside. A tall pine, killed by lightning, probably, stood some distance from the woods. A red-headed woodpecker was beating a ruffles on the hollow trunk. She laid the gun in the grass beside her and dipped the bucket deep into the clear water. Water splashed over her broad-toed tan shoes when she withdrew the vessel. Water poured through the cracks made by the shrinkage of the staves. With a departing moan she sat down. In a moment the bucket was empty.

More nightmare stuff, like barely escaping the clutches of a determined enemy and suddenly finding the door inadequate to close him out. Yet, so far, nothing had happened to her. Nor had anything happened yesterday or the day previously. "But sometime something *must* happen; something *had* to happen, else she would become a shrieking maniac. Once it happened the spell would be broken and she would be her old self."

She pushed the bucket with her foot, and it sank into the water. Now, out of the medley of midsummer sounds, there arose another unlike any of the rest. It was the sound of a man's snoring. She could not see him; she could only judge by the direction from which the sound came as to where the sleeper lay. She thought of "Fried Face," and, with a quick movement, she rose, jerking the gun from the ground. Somehow she knew that it *was* "Fried Face." She was sure it could be nobody else. Wild, maddening desire to fly, to soar above the corn tops, weakened her. To escape before he awoke! . . .

She stood fast, listening. The snoring had ceased. The medley of sounds was unbroken save by the persistent barking of distant dogs. She turned swiftly, but a low chuckle arrested her. Jerking herself about, she saw him. He was bare-headed and, save where the burn on the right cheek had left a livid mass, coal black. The scar was like pounded beefsteak, rare. He was sitting in the grass, half reclining on his left elbow, appraising her. He stared at the sun, and she thought his eyes narrowed; ran his sullen gaze over her, from head to foot. Then he grinned, revealing a twisted toothless cavity.

"You Mr. Lankster's wife, Ah guess, ain't you?"

She resented his lazy familiarity, but nodded in spite of this. She was thinking: "He knows I'm scared stiff; that's why he treats me like this . . . not even standing. But he wouldn't act like that if I was a Southern woman. Not much like the good plantation darkies I've heard of. That repulsive face!" . . .

"Ah thought so." He chuckled, nodding. He rose. "You f'om up No'th, aint you?" he had made an almost imperceptible move forward.

She thought of the protection of the gun, and resentment shot hot blood to her cheeks. She resolved to use such tactics as she was sure he was accustomed to.

"What's that to you, you filthy nigger?" As she noted the rapid change of expression in his face: "I suppose you'll have to be taught your place," she added grimly. She thought: "He's afraid. He's afraid. I've got him cowed. . . . Lord, if I can only keep him so."

The man stared, round-eyed; shifted from one foot to the other.

"But, lady, Ah wa'nt doin' nothin' to nobody. Ah jes ast you ef you was Mis Lankster. Ah don't never bother nobody ceptin' dey bothers me fus'. Ah'm a peace-lovin' man, das whut Ah is, an' Ah don't bother. . . ."

Reassured now, she felt all fears leaving her. She felt cool; the vast woods were merely woods, no more formidable in their mysteries than the shrubbery of Boston's parks. She experienced difficulty in restraining a shriek of laughter. How John would stare when she told him. But she did not even smile. She held the shotgun steadily, balanced in her right hand, both its triggers ready, looking the image of undaunted ruthlessness.

"And let me tell you another thing, Fried Face, or whatever your name is. I've heard you're a holy terror around here. Well, I'm known as just that myself where I come from. If you behave yourself and stay in your place you needn't fear me, but if you don't. . . ." A daring suggestion clipped her brain. She went on recklessly: "Ask my husband if I wasn't the champion woman sharpshooter of Boston. As I said, if you behave yourself and stay in your place you needn't fear any harm, but if you don't—well, I've warned you. . . . You may go, now." She lifted the gun meaningly, saying to herself: Georgia isn't so bad, after all. I'm going to like it.

"But, Missie, Ah—"

"You may go now, I said!"

He gulped; hitched up first one, then the other, of the straps of his blue denim overalls; shuffled his feet. She again noticed that, with barely perceptible movements, he was approaching her. She was panicky. Suddenly the man leaped, or stumbled, toward her. In moments of calm, after, she was as much baffled as now in her efforts to determine what he had done; whether his motion toward her had been intentional or accidental. At any rate, she knew that the gun was at her shoulder, that it boomed twice in lightening succession [*sic*], and that the man, first, falling, rose, turned, and, screaming fled.

She saw a shower of blood raining about his shoulders; saw him stagger, fall, and lie motionless in the short grass beneath the dead pine. Sunshine and flies enveloped him.

IV

Her heart pounded against her hard chest and horror seeped up through her. Still, she was calmer and less afraid than at any time previously since her coming South. She kept thinking of herself as a murderer, and then renouncing the idea. She drew out the bucket, filled and dripping. It was no longer leaking. Balancing the gun in her left hand, she hastened to the house.

"It was self defense . . . purely self defense. He was trying to attack me. I'm *not* a murderer. If I hadn't killed him he'd have killed me. It was self defense. . . . Purely self. . . ."

She set the bucket on the shelf, put the gun in its accustomed place, and remade the kitchen fire. She was somewhat surprised that her husband had not yet come, but did not think long on the matter. She completed the breadmaking, prepared and cooked the cabbage and potatoes, then made some crust for the blackberry pie.

"It was certainly self defense, if there ever was such a thing. A woman has a right to defend her . . . honor!" She stopped sweeping the floor, fanned at a persistent fly, now stunned by the significance of her discovery. Her *honor!* She sat down heavily on a chair beside the table, as though the weight of this idea was too great to bear standing.

"I hadn't thought of that. In the South no white woman is ever convicted for defending her honor, even if she kills a white man. How in the world could they think of convicting her for killing? . . ."

She sprang up, trembling. She had been defending her honor, that was it. She had been defending her honor. . . . Bees droned and flies buzzed through the hot humid air, a blue jay cried from the branches of the tree in the yard, a woodpecker beat a ruffles on the dead pine at the edge of the woods. She was indifferent. Her heart still pounding, she walked several times from the kitchen to the sleeping quarters, to the outhouses, and around the fence outside the yard. Once she walked as far as the highway. She stood for a while gazing toward the spot where she knew the body lay. She was all this time wondering at her calm detachment, amazed that she was neither remorseful nor afraid.

"I'm a good Georgian at last . . . How John will laugh. I've even acquired the Georgian's psychology." She laughed loudly.

The clock struck five just as she seated herself in a rocker on the front piazza. It occurred to her all at once that John was five hours late. She rose, and, going to the rear of the kitchen, looked down the long, grass-grown roadway which separated the corn patch from the cotton field. Her husband had gone down that way. . . .

There were voices toward the front. The hound was baying spasmodically. Trembling with an incomprehensible fear, she hastened through the yard and around the kitchen and the sleeping quarters to the front piazza. A group of men, none of whom she had ever seen before, in their shirts and with sleeves rolled to their elbows, were in the act of coming from the house. They carried rifles in their hands, and revolvers bulged from their hip pockets. Long-eared dogs panted in the heat. One man, squat, red-faced, with soiled handkerchief around his neck, held a coil of rope. They looked at her queerly, she thought, and she wondered incoherently what had become of boasted Georgia chivalry.

"You Miz Lankster?" asked the man with the rope.

"Ye—yes . . . I . . ."

"Mighty sorry to have to do it, Miz Lankster, but—"

A fleeting shadow crossed the piazza, swept the yard toward the corn and on the woods. A big black turkey buzzard, following the shadow, thrust out its ugly talons and perched, rocking clumsily, on the branch of the dead pine. The woman, watching screamed; clapped her hands over her mouth; waited for the man to continue.

"We jus' fetched the body in—your husband's, I mean. Got in 'n argument with a nigger 'bout what time to stop for dinner, an' th' nigger cut 'is throat. We're looking fer 'im now. You ain't set eyes on 'im, I guess, have you? Name's Cruthers, but they call 'im 'Fried Face,' cause he's . . ."

They were staring open-mouthed at the woman, for, instead of listening, she was shrieking with laughter.

"Sarcophagus"
Saturday Evening Quill (JUNE 1929): 36–39

This is a story that Gordon seems to have thought about a great deal. There is a peice with a similar motif with a very different plotline called "Hidden Place" in his papers. "Sarcophagus," is, again, a story of violence, revenge, suspense, and racial conflicts; however, Gordon does break some new ground. The story revolves around a white professor named Niles giving a lecture on Egyptology at Boston University to sixty white graduate students when a Black man, Hezekiah Thompson, interrupts the lecture, stating that he is a former professor of history from a small college in Georgia. Thompson goes on to say that the white professor is incorrect in stating that Egyptians were not Africans. Niles, angry and embarrassed, tries to dismiss Johnson, telling him to go examine a sarcophagus at the museum. Johnson is told that if he looks deep down in the sarcophagus, he will see the evidence that proves Niles's point. This is when the murders begin.

"Sarcophagus" is an intriguing story, one that Lorraine Elena Roses calls one of Gordon's "strongest short stories"[17] The discovery of King Tut's tomb in 1922 brought a frenzy of "Tutmania" and raised questions about the race of the ancient Egyptians. It is a debate that continues until today. In the story, Gordon seems to come down on the side of those who believe they were Black. However, Roses is correct when she states, "The text is open to extensive interpretation, but on its face it indicates not only the arrogance of white men high in the academic hierarchy but that madness that can be an outcome of continuous racial oppression."[18]

Sarcophagus

"My name, professor," apologetically declaimed the bald, nose-spectacled, goateed black man, rising in the rear of the room, "is Hezekiah Thompson. You have probably heard of me: I'm professor of history at the Star of Zion Baptist College, in Macon . . . Macon's in Georgia." He paused, and there was a noticeable twitching of the left side of his neck and face. Meeting only with cold silence, he went on defensively: "I came up here to Boston University just to take this wonderful course of lectures in Egyptian and Ethiopian History at the Summer Session. I notice every day you ask if anybody'd like to make a comment or ask a question on your lecture, and nobody ever says anything. Today *I'd* like to ask a question."

The class of sixty white graduate students turned and stared as the speaker paused a second time. Then they turned and looked at the wizened, grayish, sharp-featured Professor of Egyptian and Ethiopian History. He sat behind a small table at the front of the room, frowning, and frequently glancing at the clock above the door on his left.

"Well?" he prompted bluntly.

The man from the Star of Zion smiled. "I'd like to make a brief statement first," he said, addressing the students rather than the lecturer. Self-consciously he fingered his black-and-white striped tie; felt of the flaring wings of his high collar; stroked the wide black ribbon which festooned gracefully from the glasses on his aquiline nose. He went on, the muscles of his neck and face twisting spasmodically: "My statement is this: The white professors of history, as well as the white so-called historians, are in league to ignore the black man's contribution to civilization. For instance, all our lives we've been taught that Ethiopians were just ordinary Negroes; why, the Bible itself says so. But as soon as it is found out that the Ethiopians were a people of great importance—"

The professor rose and picked up his green cloth bag. "Mr. Thompson, the class period is ended," he said shortly. "I'm sorry. You'll—."

"So am I, professor, but—"

The professor, his face red with anger, struck his palm upon the table. "That's enough from you, sir! If you care to stay and see me after the others are dismissed, all right; but I refuse to listen to you further—under the circumstances." He took out his watch, glanced at it, replaced it, then made a gesture of dismissal to the students.

"That's all," he said.

Immediately the room was abuzz with voices. The professor stood tapping the table nervously with his knuckles as the men and women passed out; as some of them lingered, sitting on the broad arms of their chairs; as they whispered excitedly behind their hands, staring from the angry white face of the professor to the twitching face of the black man. Thompson now sat forward, silently, on the edge of his chair, his eyes glittering.

Presumably convinced that many had no intention of quitting the room, the professor peremptorily ordered them to leave.

"Our friend evidently has some deep-seated grievance against white folk in general and against me in particular," he said, with forced jocularity.

When the last had departed, closing the door after them, the professor said abruptly: "Now, then, Mr. Thompson, what is your trouble?"

The black man picked up his rusty brief case and his straw hat and moved to the front of the room. Laying his belongings in a chair beside him, he sat down directly in front of the professor and crossed his long, thin legs. His lower lip was quivering now, and his head was making short, spasmodic jerks. His eyes were glitteringly bright.

The professor backed round until the table stood squarely between them; glanced toward the door, gripping the edge of the table firmly as if to give his nerves stability.

"Well," he said impatiently, "begin."

"Yes, sir. I will. I wish you'd sit down, though, I'd feel more at ease. You make me feel like yelling when you stand there like that." The man laughed mirthlessly; stared round the room. "As you can see for yourself, I'm somewhat nervous, professor. It doesn't take much to get me all wrought up. What are you looking at me like that for? Do you think I'm crazy?" He seemed about to rise, but the professor,

Sarcophagus

laughing as if to conceal a fear, signalled him to remain as he was. He himself sat down, somewhat off from the table. He glanced at the clock at the door, then looked at the man before him.

"Crazy? Nonsense! Why should I think that? . . . You are nervous, though, are you not?"

"I am, professor. Very. Sometimes I'm frightened at myself. I . . ." His deep-set black eyes seemed alternately to dilate and contrast. They wandered round the room. "I'm very much affected that way when anybody crosses me. When I get excited or lose my temper I—"

"We'll not discuss any unpleasant subjects, Mr. Thompson. You say you are a professor of history?"

"Yes, sir. . . . Well, no. That is, I was. It's rather amusing: you'll laugh. My college sent me up here—that is, the trustees told me I ought to come—to take this course. But yesterday—" He laughed, picked up his brief case from the chair beside him, fumbled in it, and withdrew a letter. "Yesterday I got this." He half rose and passed the envelope across the table. "Just read that, will you, professor?"

The professor drew out the folded typewritten sheet, opened it, and read. He replaced it in the envelope and passed it back without comment.

"Don't you think that's rather queer, professor?" demanded the black man. He pursed his rather thin lips and glared round the room. His neck and face began to twitch. He said loudly: "Well, *I* do, whether *you* think so or not. Get me up here, then send me a request for my resignation." He frowned and stared at the door.

The professor began tentatively: "Then you're interested in Egyptian and Ethiopian history. How did your interest in this subject come to be aroused?"

Thompson stared, puckering his forehead; beat his head and tapped it with his knuckles. He looked up quickly.

"How? I'll tell you how, professor. Why is it that colored people— Negroes if you please—are being denied credit for their contribution to civilization? Take—

"But they're not, are they? Don't you think your premise is unsound?"

"No, I don't. My premise is perfectly sound . . . perfectly sound. As sound as I am." He smiled across the table. "Not very sound, then,

I suppose you say. But never mind that. They'll never get me inside a strait-jacket again.... The grass was green round there. Plenty of fine old shade trees. Do you know, professor, there's something about fine old shade trees that just . . . that just. . . ." He bent his head and tapped it with his knuckles. "Say, professor," he cried, snapping his fingers, "ever read Joyce Kilmer's poem about trees?[19] It goes—"

The professor's face was a white, taut mask, moistened at the forehead with clammy sweat. In one hand he clutched his old Panama hat, and in the other his bag. He stared at the door.

"I annoy you, I see. I tire you with my random chatter." The man from Macon leaned forward and shook a long black finger at the professor. "If you had tried to leave me alone here, something would happen to you.... But I tremble, and I am sorry. To the point. *Revenons a nos moutons!*[20] So now. Take this recent discovery of Tutankhamen's tomb.[21] He was a black man until it was found he had carried remnants of a dazzling civilization into his tomb. Then he became a white man. Even Ethiopians, that we've always been taught were pure African Negroes, are 'white folks' now. Can you beat it? as the boys say. In other words, everything that's any good is white. Now, isn't that so, professor?"

The professor had been watching and listening with evident interest. He shook his head. "I shouldn't say so. You are obviously laboring under a very strange hallucination. You . . ." He halted himself as if suddenly reminded that he had said too much, peered apprehensively at the man before him.

But the listener was calm now. The twitching was scarcely visible, and the eyes were no longer dilated. He appeared to be the professor of history whose title he had but recently held.

The lecturer smiled, rose, and placed his old Panama on his head.

"I'm glad to have been of service to you, Mr. Thompson," he said, moving toward the door rather hurriedly. He stopped. "If ever I can—"

"But you're not leaving yet, sir," cried the black man, jumping up. "Why, you haven't answered my question." He picked up the brief case and fumbled in it, pulling out a book. The professor, half way to the door, stood looking at him, his forehead knotted in a frown, his thin pinkish lips opening and closing as though tasting something unpalatable.

"Here . . ." The man turned the pages, moistening his thumb on

Sarcophagus   171

his tongue. "Here, professor. Here is a passage in a book you wrote yourself, 'The Glory of Cheops.' On page 191 you say this; listen, professor, to what you say yourself. You say:

'The inhabitants of both Abyssinia and Ethiopia were mixed races. In Abyssinia southern Semites immigrants from the Arabian Yemen on the other side of the Red Sea, were the dominant race; and in Ethiopia Hamitic Lybyans from the western desert were the ruling class, while the mass of the people were probably racially Hamites if not actually of Lybyan origin. The whole region involved was inhabited in antiquity, as it is today, by dark-colored races in which brown prevails. But they are not,' you say here, professor, 'they are not, and were not, African negroes, although many individuals in the same region show a mixture of black blood, many of them being blacks of the slave class.'"

He closed the book with a vicious snap, and narrowing his eyes, leaned forward and thrust a quivering finger under the professor's nose. He asked angrily: "Why do you all delight so in labelling a whole race, professor?"

The professor made a gesture of weariness. "What need is there of my telling you that you are wrong? You don't seem to be able to concentrate on anything save the one delusion of your grievance. Let us have done with this nonsense," he said sharply. "If you doubt that these people were not Negroes, go to the art museum—ever been there?"

"I've spent a part of every day, recently, in the Egyptian and Ethiopian room."

"Well, I am curator of that department. I want you to go there and look at the skulls of those mummies in the glass cases. Many of them have become unwrapped. Examine the skulls closely. If you see any resemblance between them and a Negroid skull, I'll be glad to make a note of your discovery when I revise my book. By the way," he said, as if with sudden inspiration, "here's something you might do. Have you seen that great nineteen-ton granite sarcophagus—the one with the lid back against the wall?"

The man stared at him, his neck and face beginning to twitch, his eyes to dilate and glitter. The professor backed toward the door; the black man followed.

The professor made an arresting gesture. "Wait a moment. I want you to go in the art museum—tell them I sent you, if you wish. Tell them Dr. Niles sent you to do a little research work for him. Go to the Egyptian-Ethiopian room and explore that biggest granite sarcophagus. Get down inside of it, and later report your findings to me. "

The smile about his lips as he turned away seemed more grim than salutary.

Thompson stared after him, his neck and face twitching, his eyes dilated and glittering. Then he ran forward very swiftly, and just as the old man reached the brink of the staircase well, shoved him. The body shot out, shrieking, sprawling, whirling, descending, the green bag dropping away from it. The bag landed far below with a smart thud. A moment later there came the sound of a heavier, more compact object striking the hardwood floor. There followed no other sound, save that of the ancient elevator creaking on its cables in the nearby shaft.

Thompson returned to the room, put on his hat, and picked up his brief case. He went out and rang for the elevator. He seemed singularly composed and detached. His eyes were but slightly brighter than normally, and even had the aged elevator man not been near-sighted, he could not have detected the verist tremor of nervousness in his passenger. But the operator paid no heed, and as soon as Thompson had stepped out, the elevator man lowered the car to the basement.

Thompson detoured widely round the right of the stairs. The man had fallen on the left. At the front door he looked back. He saw protruding from the shadow beneath the stairs the gray head of the professor on the floor.

Once in the street he alternately walked and ran. He ran only when no one was near him. Looking continuously over his shoulder, he muttered: "They'll get me yet. What chance has a poor beast of a black man, anyway? They'll track me down as sure as fate."

Persons meeting him strained their ears to pick up fragments of his soliloquy: stopped and looked after him. When he noticed this he silenced himself, increased his pace until he reached a corner, then turned swiftly from view.

When he arrived at the art museum there was an hour until closing time. He mounted the flight of white marble stairs, turned to the left down a long vaulted corridor with a series of doors opening into each side of it, and came at length to the entrance of the Egyptian-Ethiopian department. It was built to represent an ancient Egyptian tomb, and had the appearance of being carved into the solid rock of a mountain. Beside the door, in a chair tilted back against the wall, there sat a uniformed guard, asleep, his cap pulled over his eyes.

Thompson walked in and looked about. He was like a man standing alone in the center of a musty tomb. Through a crevice of a window, high up, a yellowish blade of daylight cut the eternal gloom. Other light came dimly from concealed bulbs round the border of the low and rugged ceiling. The walls bore protuberances of glass shelves weighted with objects from the country of the Nile: statuettes, fragments of alabaster vessels inscribed with the names of forgotten dynasties, and samples of pottery from the burnt rooms of the western Defufa;[22] mud sealed impressions from the same source, brass bowls, glass jars and decorated pottery from the Meroitic[23] cemetery; scarabs and golden crocodiles from the Great Cemetery of the Hyksos[24] Period; busts of black granite of a King of the Twelfth Dynasty,[25] and so on, interminably.

"No wonder they want to claim the Egyptians and Ethiopians for the white race," he muttered, "when you look at all these things." He had been here countless times before, and on each occasion he had made the self-same observation.

Leaning against the walls, underneath the shelves, were a dozen mummy cases in cubic figurines and fantastic coloring; mummies of men and women dead two and three thousand years, in glass cases. Some of the wrappings had fallen off, exposing powdering bones. The man bent close over these and studied the shapes of the skulls.

There were a few wooden sarcophagi, but these were empty. Against the wall in a corner stood a great granite sarcophagus weighing, with its upturned lid, nineteen tons. A small card with this information printed on it hung from the wall. About this monster trunk-like casket there seemed to lurk centuries of shadows. Thompson stooped and examined the figures in relief on the surface of the granite hulk. There were pictured here a procession of slender Negroid figures, some with staffs in their hands, and others with what resembled pails and bags and tools. Then came figures of jackals, serpents, and hawks. There were others which he could not identify.

But he had no doubt that these figures represented Negro men. He ran his finger over them and smiled.

There was a sound of footsteps on the flagstones of the corridor. Thompson dropped to his knees at the end of the nineteen-ton sarcophagus. The legs of the guard's chair clicked as they dropped to the floor, and someone was talking to him—an indeterminate rumble of men's voices that conveyed no meaning. Then one of the men said loudly: "But I would swear I saw him come this way! They said he did. They said . . ."

Thompson's neck and face began to twitch and his glistening eyes to seek the dimensions of every corner. He looked upward and, with a quick gasp, grabbed his brief case. Then, clutching it in his fingers, he seized the broad ledge of the sarcophagus and drew himself up its seven-foot wall. Throwing his leg over, he scrambled down, as into a pit.

The lid was quivering at the disturbance. It had left the wall and stood like a malignant thing of reason, pondering whether to seal the captive in. The man was now struggling madly up the steep smooth side, scuffing it impotently with the toes of his shoes, trying to get out. The lid veered. It smothered shrieks in a muffled roar of thunder. A statuette toppled, shattering itself on the flagstones. Mummies two and three thousand years old shivered in glass cases. Echoes spent themselves in the vault-like chamber.

Reverberations died in distant corridors; then silence, save for the five o'clock gong.

Without, the guard's chair had come down again with a click. The man rubbed his sleepy eyes as he stood in the doorway. In the vault-like room beyond, a yellow blade of sunlight cut the thickening gloom. A thin cloud of dust particles dance in it. Corners were already dark. Objects in corners against the walls were already indistinguishable. . . . Ah! The sarcophagus lid was down. So that was the cause of the big noise, was it?

The guard stretched, yawning.

"All out!" he called; simply a routine detail. "All out!"

When the guard got downstairs the director was locking the office door. The guard said:

"Mr. Hawley, did you locate the superintendent? George came round to the Egyptian department looking for him, but—"

"Yes, we found him." The director slipped his key into his pocket, set his straw hat at a more jaunty angle, twirled his cane, and started toward the street. "He has just left."

The guard said suddenly: "Oh, by the way, Mr. Hawley." The director paused half turning. "That big sarcophagus lid fell just now. It—"

"Oh, did it? Well, I'm not surprised. Dr. Niles warned me of it yesterday. Said the slightest vibration would cause it to fall. So I intended to have it lowered anyway . . . when we got round to it. Don't have to bother now, though, do we? . . . Good night."

He went on into the expanse of the evening, twirling his cane.

"The Agenda"
Opportunity (DECEMBER 1933): 372–74;
(JANUARY 1934): 18–22

"The Agenda" is the best example of what Gordon would consider proletarian fiction. It in many ways anticipated the work of writers such as Richard Wright, particularly in a story such as "Bright and Morning Star" (1940). "The Agenda" itself seems to be the type of story Wright had in mind in his "Blueprint for Negro Writing" (*New Challenge*, 1937). It also seems to anticipate some of the material in Granville Hicks's anthology *Proletarian Literature in the United States* (International Publishers, 1935). The story, published in two installments, concerns the unlikely pairing of a Black and a white communist who are assigned to infiltrate a Klan meeting and uncover their plans to prevent the formation of a union. The two decide to disrupt the meeting and go back to warn the union members of the plans. A problem occurs when it is discovered that Johnson, the Black man, cannot command the getaway car because he doesn't know how to drive, so they will have to steal a Klansman's robe (a "nightie") for Johnson, and he will have to infiltrate the meeting. Johnson struggles to believe that a white man will risk his life in the cause of Blacks, and he realizes that his own life depends on this tenuous faith. In the end the white man proves himself and the two men ride off in triumph to the union meeting. The story won an honorable mention in the *Opportunity* fiction contest. This would be Gordon's last published fiction, although he continued writing stories and an autobiographical novel.

The Agenda

When he got off the train at Atlanta the Negro Communist Party representative speculated again on what Snell would be like. He had never met a southern white comrade in his natural haunts, and in spite of all reason to the contrary he had some misgivings. He had been told that he would find Snell up one dingy and smelly flight in a cubbyhole of an office, probably alone. The prophesy turned out true. Pregnant with heat, a rusty coal stove stood bulging in the center of the floor. The room was misty with smoke, but he got a massed picture of low walls plastered with frayed and tattered newspaper clippings, mimeographed sheets, and multicolored lithographs from the Soviet Union. It was a stuffy room and very warm, for neither of the two soiled windows was raised. Snell, in a ragged red sweater and a greasy gray cap, hunched over a desk in the corner. The district organizer looked up and the two men regarded each other.

"I'm—"

"You're Cass Johnson,"[26] Snell said shortly. "Been expectin' you. Set daown."

"Georgia cracker gone Communist," Johnson marvelled. He threw his old topcoat across the back of a chair near the heater and sat down. Looking at the white man, he sat listening abstractly to the noises in the street. Johnson thought.... Things've certainly changed in the South, all right. Georgia cracker a Communist! How long've I been away from this state? Let's see.... He reckoned quickly.... Nineteen years.... No Negro would trust a white man two feet in those days, he recalled, and looked at Snell again. Nordic type, according to anthropologists of the Lothrop Stoddard school:[27] whitish blonde even to the stubble on the skin.

The district organizer rose and came round the desk. He was so tall and skinny that Johnson thought he would break in two. He thrust out his hand to the black man and Johnson stood to shake it. They looked self-consciously at each other. To cover the momentary embarrassment, the white man said: "Busy's hell daown here. How's everything in Noo Yawk?"

Johnson sat down feeling somewhat better. He said to Snell: "Thing's pretty lively in New York. How's the movement down here?"

"Not so bad it couldn't be worse. Havin' a little excitement right now, as you know. Negro sharecroppers wantin' to organize an' the Klan terrorizin' 'em." With his hands in his trousers pockets he stalked round the small room. "Not makin' much headway 'mongst the Negroes raoun' here, but if we can git them sharecroppers organized....." His back to Johnson, he stood gazing through the window across the roofs of two-story frame houses opposite. Johnson heard soft easy laughter trailing after Negro workers passing by. He heard the sudden squawk of jubilant Negro laughter. He smiled and crossed his legs.

He said: "You know why I'm here, I suppose. I mean, the specific task?"

"Sho. Certainly. That Cane Valley rumpus." Snell turned from the window to his desk.

Johnson nodded. "That's it, all right, You all alone here?"

"Sho. I'm the only paid worker. Other comrades come in raoun' sundaown. What say we git daown to business."

"Good idea...."

Snell got up and went to the door leading to the stairs and listened a moment. He locked the door and returned to his desk, motioning Johnson to draw his chair closer. The district organizer pulled out a drawer and withdrew a creased road map. He pointed with a long soiled finger, his long body forming a question mark. He picked up a half-emptied package of cigarettes from the sheets of mimeographed and typed paper and newspaper clippings on his desk, and held it toward Johnson, who helped himself. Sticking a cigarette between his own lips, Snell offered Johnson a light and then lighted his own.

"This is the main road," he said, shoving his finger along the wavering black line of the map. "An' right over here is what they call Cane Valley."

"Raise plenty cane over there, I guess?" Johnson hazarded. Snell looked at him speculatively. The black man laughed shortly and wholly without mirth. He thought.... Gee, this is a solemn son-of-a-gun.... "No attempt to be funny at all, comrade," he said. "Only wondered why they called it Cane Valley."

Snell spat on the floor, "Low rich country," he explained soberly. "Jest fit fer cane growin'. Sho raise plenty *hell* over there. More hell than cane. That's why *we're* interested. . . . As I was sayin' right 'bout here is Cane Valley, an' just 'bout here is where the fellas been meetin'."

Johnson questioned Snell about the distance of this meeting place from the nearest sharecropper's house; the distance from the nearest home of a white sharecropper. Yes, the district organizer informed him, the white sharecroppers were beginning to show some interest. The reason they hadn't come over and joined the Negroes was that there was no organization. There was no doubt that they'd all soon be united under the banner of the Party. Of course the Klan knew that. That was why it was so mad. Snell and Johnson contemplated the map in silence, both men sucking on their cigarettes.

"That place is some distance from here—from Atlanta—isn't it?" Johnson measured the distance with a pencil. "Yes; I would say about ten miles."

"About eight miles," Snell told him, adding: "We can make it in a car in little or no time. You got a car?"

The Negro laughed. "Comrade, I'm a Communist. Where'd I get a car from? My rich uncle isn't dead yet—but it won't be long, now."

The district organizer looked interested. "You got a rich uncle, eh? Invalid, or something?

"Yes, Uncle Sam. Very rich and very sick."

Snell smiled fleetly. "'Sho, of course," he grunted. Listen, I tell you what we'll do—"

"Rent a taxi from one of these Negro independents round here, why don't we?" Johnson went to the window and looked into the street. "Here's one turning the corner now. One of them brought me up there from the station."

"Oh, yaas, they's plenty of 'em raoun', but we don't have to do that. I got it all figgered out. I figgered you wouldn't have no car, so I doped it all out like this. The Klan's holding a big pow-pow tonight"—he bent over the map again and Johnson came and looked over his shoulder—"right about here." His finger rested on a point beside another road directly east of the Cane Valley location.

Johnson sat down and crossed his legs. "They planning some new deviltry on these sharecroppers tonight?"

"Reckon so. That's one of the things on our agenda—to find out."

The men stared into each other's eyes. "How?" Johnson asked.

"Well—one of us, that is—'ll have to git into the konklave an' find out."

Simultaneous laughter shattered the tension. "*One* of us, you say. You mean *you will*." The Negro stretched out his strong black hands. "Look at that. How in the world do you expect *me* to get into any Klan meeting?"

"I ain't *expectin'* you to do nothin'. This here ain't a one-man job, comrade. We got to work it together. This the way I figure it. You drive the car an' I go in, Then you wait some place on the road with the engine runnin'. When I come out—*if* I do—you be ready to git off to a flyin' start an'—"

"But wait a minute!" Snell broke off and stared at him. "I'm sorry to seem to be objecting," Johnson apologized, "but I don't drive. I can't drive. I have never driven."

Snell squinted at him contemplatively. He removed the cigarette butt and ground it under his toe. "Hell!" he said, and scratched his head.

"Do they go to these meetings dressed in their nighties and pillow-slips?" Johnson asked.

The district organizer nodded, staring blankly at the tattered wall. "Sometimes they do, an' sometimes they don't. Why?"

"Well, I thought if they did I might get in, somehow—if I can get an outfit and you . . . you drive, don't you?"

"Yaar. Sho, I drive."

Johnson uncrossed his legs and bought his feet down to the floor. "Say," he cried, and at a warning glance from Snell he lowered his voice. "Say, I've got it! If you can fix me up, I'll get in, while you drive the car. How's that?"

The district organizer considered. He rose and went to the door: opened it and peered down the dingy flight to the street; returned to his chair and sat down. "That's an idea," he said at length. "Damn if that ain't an idea!"

Johnson sat staring at him. He was thinking. . . . Can I carry off this thing? Do they go to these meetings in costume? Will they do it tonight? Suppose they don't—what then? . . . "Do you know anything about these Klan shindigs, Snell—that is, what the ritual is, and everything? Could you give me any hints, or—"

"Don't you worry about that, boy. I know plenty." His laugh was barely a grunt. "I uster be a big s . . . . in the Klan."

Johnson was conscious of clamping his jaw to prevent any show of amazement. He said, with studied calmness: "That so? Tell us about it. How'd you come to get out?"

"Don't want me to be a damn fool all my life, do you?"

"Well, after all," Johnson argued, "the Klan *is* a long jump from the C.P. That's true, isn't it?"

"You goddam right it is, buddy. . . . Say comrade, you don't need to have no doubts about me. I been all over this thousands of times deeper'n you ever will."

Johnson laughed. "Cigarette." Snell tossed the package and a box of matches to him. "You say you used to be in the Klan. You left to join the Party?"

"No, by god. Left because I seen it wasna't no place for no decent white—decent human bein' to be at. I was marked for death long befo' I ever heard tell of the Party?"

"That so? Gee. . . . Then you have some of this regalia, I guess."

"Nope. Not a rag nor a stitch of it. Burnt it all up on the public lot."

He added regretfully: "Wish I hadn't, now."

"Then, how—"

"But I know how to git all we need. I'll tend to that later on. Right now let's settle this. Here's our agenda. " He planted both feet on the floor under his desk, a pencil grasped in his fingers. Scratching on a pad, he said: "1. Go to Angell's from here and borrow regalia and a car. 2. Put on regalia and drive to Klavern. 3. While I stay in car with engine runnin', you git in—"

"If possible," Johnson interrupted, blowing cigarette rings and chuckling.

"Damn the 'if possible,' comrade! Yo git in an' learn what these b. . . . are plannin' fer tonight. Then you hotfoot it back to the car. 4. We set out for Cane Valley." He looked up and they regarded each other.

"What shall we do when we get there? You haven't said yet—"

"We'll make up the agenda on the way out. It's correct to plan, as you know, comrade, but the planning mustn't be too comprehensive."

He bent again over the scratchpad. Johnson studied him. He glanced at his wristwatch.

"What time is it?" Snell asked.

"Quarter past five. What time's the meeting in Cane Valley?"

"Oh, not till late. Th'ave to meet in the dark, you know. We better be leavin' here soon." He gave Johnson's clothes a cursory inspection. "You better leave that overcoat here." He stuffed the pad into his hip pocket, folded the road map, and switched on a bulb above his desk. Someone was rapping on the door, and Snell sprang over and opened it. "Hello, Jim," he said. "Jim, this is Comrade Cass Johnson, from Noo Yawk, Comrade Jim McCarthy."

Johnson shook hands with McCarthy, a short and solid young fellow with Irish features, and a bared red head.

"Knew you the minute I saw you," he told Johnson. "Where you goin', Snell?"

"Over to Angell's, now, then out to that Klan meet. From there out to the Valley."

"What you going to Angell's for? To get a nightie?"

"Yep, and a car. There won't be any way for you to git in touch with us ef we don't turn up. Just set tight."

"O.K., Snell. So long."

It was cool in the dirty street with its flickering dim lights. Shadows were already piling up in the corners.

"How tall are you anyway?" Johnson asked, glancing towards Snell's thin sharp profile. They were cutting across a vacant lot, and the black man recalled what his companion had said about burning his regalia.

"Six-foot-four," Snell said a little pridefully, and grinned, "You ain't no runt yo'self."

"Jus six feet, even.... Say, aren't you cold, with nothing heavier than that sweater?"

"Naw!" he glanced down at Johnson's hands. "Better be sho to keep them gloves on. Lucky for you it's cold enough for gloves."

"Don't the gentlemen of the Klan wear gloves, as a rule?"

"No. Now, listen, comrade. This fella Angell is a Klansman, see? I pick him out to borrow from because he's a klexter—outer guard. He don't have to git 'way down inside. You see, ef you act like you're him you might git away with it."

"And if I don't act enough like him—what then?"

"It ain't hard to do. You jus' do what I tell you, see? Another reason I picked out this guy is because he lives 'way back from the street. Lots of trees and shrubbery round his house. See?"

"No, I don't, but I guess it's all right. Do you suppose he'll be alone?"

"I reckon so. They ain't nobody but him and his wife, and she's away. They ain't no servants or nothin' on the place." While he was talking Snell was looking up and down the street along which they hastened apparently observing passing automobiles. Now he hailed a taxi driven by a Negro, and they got in. "Rear of Peachtree an' Grady," he instructed the taxi man. "Now, listen, comrade," he whispered to Johnson. "Listen. You go up to the house an' git in conversation with Angell. You're intelligent. I don't need to tell *you* what to say. Say anything. I'll be outside gittin' the car ready. Soon's I git it out I'll come an' we'll gag this bird, or something; truss 'im up somewheres, an' borrow a coupla nighties."

"I see."

Snell tapped on the window in front of him. "Right here, big boy." They got out. Snell paid the driver and stood watching until the cab was out of sight. Then he and Johnson cut across the broad street diagonally toward the rear of a great solid house silhouetted within a grove of oaks against a late autumn sky.

"These kluxers certainly live in style, don't they?" Johnson said.

"Sho do, the bastards. . . . Now there's the garage over yonder," pointing off to the left. "Over that away is the side piazza. That's where you go in. Everything O.K., comrade?"

Johnson nodded and headed toward the side of the mansion, hung about with veils of shadow that appeared to swing from the trees. There was a slight crunching sound as he walked, and he wondered how soon a dog would bark, or someone would challenge him from the house. Then suddenly there flashed into full and blazing intensity of outline all the hazy doubts that had troubled him for the past hour or so. Was this man Snell really to be trusted? . . . Is it possible I picked the wrong man? . . . What kind of a trap was this he was sticking his head into? He halted sharply and looked back toward the garage. But it was hidden from view in the dusk around the vague corner of the mansion. There was a light ahead in the room off the side piazza. He shrugged and went on. As suddenly as doubt had besieged him, reason besieged him now. There were a hundred good reasons why Snell would be no one but the man he was sent to work with. He began to recount the reasons. . . .

He was on the piazza, and even while he hesitated, wondering what he was going to say, a man called through the partly opened door: "Who's there? What do you want?" He was in his shirtsleeves, and was in the act of rubbing his face and neck with a hand towel. He was a tall man, but inclined to bulge midway,—as tall as Johnson,— and he looked to weigh about as much as Johnson did, around 180.

"I'm looking for a Mr. Angell," Johnson wondered what he was to say next, and was angry at his slow-wittedness.

"I'm Mr. Angell. Who're you?" The man beyond the door was obviously suspicious. He made no effort to let the intruder in, and he appeared to be content to remain inside.

"I came up here to . . . I'm—"

The intent stare in Angell's eyes at something behind Johnson impelled the black man to wheel; then he stood frozen in indecision, his heart hammering against his breastbone. A tall man in Klan regalia stood there, his arms crossed on his breast, his eyes fixed on the Negro Communist. Johnson wondered frantically whether this man could be Snell; decided emphatically that it could not be. Snell had no uniform. The man inside, undeniably puzzled, nevertheless quirked[28] his lips in a strange smile—a smile of amusement and contempt. He motioned the Negro aside and rushed the door open. But the Klansman shoved Johnson from behind, urging him through the door and into the dining room. The black man rallied his wits and calculated quickly. He thought: How far will I be able to get, if I try to do up both these birds? Or should I try to *do* 'em up, instead of getting away to report to Snell? Or is this . . . He tried to penetrate the man's identity through hood and gown. He wondered how many hooded devils skulked in the shadows of the great lawn. Scheming for advantage, he backed against the wall, watching.

He saw the uniformed Klansman extend his hand to Angell; saw the other silently take it. . . . There was no coherence in what he saw immediately thereafter, for the action was too swift. He was aware of the man in shirtsleeves hurling through the air and landing on his side under the dining room table; of the Klansman's beckoning for an assisting hand; of his aiding in blindfolding and gagging Angell; of their turning him face down and binding his hands behind his back, of leaving him there while he followed the Klansman into the other room.

The Klansman lifted his hood and revealed the grinning face of Comrade Snell, who put his finger to his lips and, turning, proceeded into a bedroom. He opened a closet and rummaged there a moment. He withdrew with a Klan costume, extending it toward Johnson. "Quick! Put it on." Johnson silently put it on and went to the dresser to look at himself in the mirror. He laughed aloud.

"Shhh!" Snell cautioned. "All right, now," he said. "We'll go through the dining room and make sho our brother is well fixed, then we'll get outer here and fly like hell. Wait a minute."

He twirled up the skirt of his gown and plunged his hand into his hip-pocket. He brought out a great jack-knife, which flicked open by pressure on a spring. He led the way out, and Johnson saw him stop beside the telephone to snip the wires. Angell was lying as he had been left, but making strange sounds of protest. Snell paused beside him a moment, then looked at Johnson.

"Better tie his legs," Johnson suggested.

His companion nodded, his eyes searching the room. He trod across the dining room to the kitchen, returning a moment later with a length of clothes-line. Binding their host's legs, they tested the gag, put out the light, and ran across the lawn to the car.

"How far to their meeting place?" Johnson asked, when the coupe was out on the road.

"Not far." Snell was gurgling. "You'd ought to see yo' face when I came up in the back o' you."

"You don't know how near I came to killing a comrade," Johnson said seriously. "Where'd you get that rig?"

"Right here in this here car. Looks like they were out last night."

"You mean Cane Valley?"

"Uh. They been whippin' them Negroes two 'n' three times a week." Johnson said briefly, "I know it."

For a while there was no sound except the engine's hum. Being in a closed car, they were rather safe from detection. Johnson wondered whether it would have made any difference if they could have been seen.

"Is it all settled what you're to do?" Snell asked, as they finally entered upon a stretch of open country road. Dark woods lay on each side of them. Traffic was fairly brisk, approaching headlights making great yellow globules in the crisp night.

"I don't mind going over it again. . . . Let's see. I'm to be the outer guard,—the klexter. That's correct? All right. I guess I'd better not do much talking; listening is what I'd better do."

"Correct again," Snell said.

"My purpose is to find out what's on their agenda for tonight's hellishness in Cane Valley. Correct?" Snell nodded. His tall peaked hood was bent back against the roof of the car. "Suppose I'm challenged. What shall I say? Suppose someone—"

Snell interrupted. "I fergot to tell you this, an' it's damn important, too. Good thing you mentioned it."

"Oh, what a thoughtful little comrade *you* are!" Johnson said sarcastically. "What did you forget to tell me?"

"The password at the outer door. "It's *White*."

"You mean it's the word 'white'?"

"Uh. The password at the inner door is *Supremacy*."

Johnson grunted as the significance of the two words manifested itself.

"You might be asked if you know Mr. Kotop," Snell told him, watching the small mirror above their eyes.

"That so? Who the hell is he?"

"Nobody. If they do ask you, you say, 'No, but I know Mr. Potok.'"

"Say, what's the idea of all this hokus pokus [*sic*]?" Johnson demanded, laughing somewhat nervously. The import of this venture was beginning to impress him.

"You better remember what I tell you," Snell warned earnestly. "*Potok* is *Kotop* spelled backward."

They both laughed. Johnson said: "And what or who is Kotop, may I ask?"

"Kotop is the letters k-o-t-o-p, and they're initials of the words 'Klans observe their oaths persistently.'"

Johnson considered the matter in silence. "I see," he said at length.

They went over the formula again, then Johnson repeated it aloud, alone. He was repeating it the second time, when Snell interrupted. "Here's the place."

He drove the car into the low underbrush still thick with leaves, and lowered the glass in the door. The sounds rushed in upon them like a stream. They sat for a moment in silence, listening to the noise of cars around them; listening to the hum of indistinct voices suspended among the branches of stark trees. It was dark. There was a sound of crunching underbrush and of breaking twigs. The air was tense, as if with anticipation.

"How do you feel?" Snell whispered.

"Rather eerie, but otherwise all right. Like I did the night I had to go into No Man's Land[29] the first time. It was a night just like this—snappy, a little windy, dark. And November."

"An' you stand jest as much chance gittin' back," Comrade Snell whispered encouragingly. He sought Johnson's left hand. "This is the Klan handshake," he explained. "Jest an ordinary handshake, 'ceptin' you use the left hand. If they challenge you when shakin' hands, you turn the other party's hand toward yo' lef'. If you challenge him, he'll turn his'n toward his lef'. Clear?"

"Sure." They put out the lights and got to the ground.

"I'm stayin' here, now. Better orient yo'self, so you can find the car. Lots depends on a clear head, remember." Johnson nodded, studying the location with a view to orienting himself. He started off down the gloomy dirt road. He looked back and saw Snell standing tall and ghostly beside the car. When he looked the second time there was only the vague shadow of the coupe, for Snell had disappeared.

Once more misgivings assailed him. Was he the dumbest fool that ever walked on two hind legs? Wasn't he the damnedest fool for coming out there with someone he had met for the first time today! Suppose the Ku Klux Klan in some way had got hold of the Party's communications and planned all this just for him. For an awful, insane moment he was determined to turn back; yet, he reasoned, the Klan meeting was *here*. There was no doubt about *that*. Klansmen were trailing all around him in the opaque darkness, making white grotesques against the ragged blackness of the trees. And ever so often a revealing headlight on a car swept scores of gowned figures into view. A tingle ran through him when he realized, all at once, that he, to an onlooker, was just as mysterious as these fools. Not only were they here, he pursued the thought, but they were intent upon some business very serious to them. . . . And undoubtedly just as serious to those sharecroppers at Cane Valley. Trick or not, my place is here. . . . He thought suddenly that it would be funny if his costume were marked somewhere behind, as a sort of identification to the Klansmen. Once he stopped and pretended to fasten his shoe. No one, apparently, gave him special attention.

When he got to the place where they were turning off the road into a narrow footpath barely discernible in the dark, he too turned off, wondering how far it should proceed before halting to take his stand as the klexter. He did not have long to speculate, however. He saw before him an open grove lighted by a small wood blaze, the light from which could not reach far, on account of the crowd massed around it. He glanced briefly into the twilit area, then turned his back on it and took up his post at the entrance. Klansmen tramped by him, singly and in groups, and twice he distinctly heard a voice greet him as Angell. He thought it safer to say nothing, but it worried him whether he was behaving as Angell usually did.

He estimated that he had been there for half an hour when a man in street clothes approached. He was big and bulky in the milky darkness, and he paused uncertainly when he saw Johnson. The heart of the Communist once more hammered against his chest and rose into his throat, clogging it. He knew, even here among the trees, that this man was Angell. He knew it before he was aware of the pistol in the Klansman's hand. And for the first time he had the disquieting awareness of being unarmed. He stood rigid, his arms folded across his breast. That was the way Snell had stood—it must be orthodox. No one had passed through for a long time, and he presumed the meeting must be well under way. Thus far he had been unable to hear anything from the grove. He hoped, however, that he would be able to steal in, when Angell got by, and lose himself among the others. Thus he would be able perhaps to pick up useful information.

Angell, scrutinizing the outer guard closely, stopped eye to eye and toe to toe with him. Johnson dreaded the necessity for speech, but there was no way out. "Who're you?" he growled in his chest. "Stand back, there," he ordered.

The man continued to stare. He glanced swiftly at Johnson's gloved hands, and it occurred to the Communist that this maddened fool might grab off the concealing hood. Johnson took a deep breath; braced himself. Then, lifting his right foot, he shot it down upon that of his enemy, at the same time grasping the hand which held the pistol. With a quick upward movement of his left elbow, he rammed the man's chin, wrenching the pistol from his grasp. Taken by surprise, the Klansman grunted painfully and fell over into the bushes. Immediately, however, he was on his feet again, terror in his eyes and his mouth wide for shouting.

"Yell, and I'll kill you," Johnson whispered sharply. "Out of here! This is a Klan meeting."

"I'm a Klansman, you damned fool." He was panting. "I'm—"

"Where's your—your regalia?" He wondered, suddenly panic-stricken, whether he had used the right word. "Where's your hood? What's the pass-word—both of 'em? You a Klansman? Like hell, you are!"

All this time the Klansman was trying to speak. "But I tell you a nigger—"

"Yah! I reckon you're going to tell me some nigger stole your outfit from you."

"You fool! That's exactly what happened. Say, if you're a Klansman, why don't you know who I am? Who am I?"

Johnson was aware that the man awaited a chance to grab the mask, despite the pistol at his belly. The Communist shoved the weapon into the fleshy midsection. "Move on. And keep going." He hunched the intruder along backward, with his knee. "What the hell you think this is, a game, that I should tell you who *you are*? If you're a Klansman, aren't you supposed to know the laws of the organization? And isn't one of the unwritten laws that nobody's to get into an argument with a suspected spy? You a Klansman, and don't know what we do with spies? Get your hands up, you son of a yellow...."

The man lifted his hands, blubbering but saying no word. Johnson pressed the pistol harder against the prisoner's belly with the left hand; reaching up with the right, he untied the four-in-hand necktie[30] and removed it. "This is going to be rather awkward," he acknowledged, "but if you make a crooked move it's going to be taps for you." The Klansman was saying, in a wheedling voice: "You wouldn't kill me, would you, Klansman? 'White' is the password, if you want it. 'White.' That's the password for the outer door. The other password—"

"Shut up, you bastard idiot!" Johnson touched the man's mouth with the pistol. "Open your damned mouth." He crammed the tie in until the Klansman gagged. "Now lie down here—face down ... No. Get up. Take off your clothes."

There was an unintelligible gurgle of protest.

'Take 'em off, and be damned quick about it. Keep your dirty paw away from your mouth, or, by God, I'll plug you! Hurry up. Take 'em off...." He himself helped, pausing now and then to listen. The meeting in the grove had become riotous. That enthusiasm would indicate an interest too keen to stray even for a moment. Being midway [between] the grove and the highway, and hidden from both, Johnson felt secure. When the original and genuine klexter stood in all his potbellied nudity, Johnson picked up the clothes and searched them. There were odds and ends of stuff, all of which he returned to the pockets; however, he transferred to his own pockets two handfuls of cartridges. Then taking the suspenders, he ordered the Klansman again to lie down. He knelt and tied the man's hands behind his back. He tore a sleeve from the shirt and with it he reinforced the necktie gag.

"I know it's a little cool out here," he told the klexter. "And it's starting to rain, too. But you'll be found before you freeze. At the worst, you'll only be a little uncomfortable." Johnson tied the man's legs together with the other sleeve. He stood up, contemplating his handiwork. So the password is—"

There was shouting within the grove. There was the crack of a rifle. The man on the ground floundered like a huge whitish fish. Johnson thrust the pistol under his robe, straining eyes and ears toward the woods.

"Let's go, fellers! All aboard for Cane Valley!" A shriller and more youthful voice shrieked: "All off to the barbeque! We want nigger meat! Does anybody down here like dark meat?" Johnson moved out toward the highway, half running. A shout pursued him! "Yeh. I like darkey meat!"

There were five quick reports of a pistol. Johnson darted into the woods. He gathered up his robe and ran faster toward the spot where he remembered leaving Snell and the car. There was a volley of rifle shots; there was that mad medley of voices peculiar to whites of the South when they start out in the night to plunder and kill. Johnson had never before heard it, but he sensed its import as one who has never before lived near the sea senses all the subtle and mysterious moods and sounds and vibrations of the sea and surf. It meant, here, rapine. It meant death without mercy. It meant torture to black women and their daughters. . . . Johnson ran on, the shouts of triumph following like a mockery. Suddenly there was *no* sound behind him. The very woods seemed to have suspended its breath; the night hung murmurless and moody; the night hung cunning and deceitful. Here was the car; he opened the door. He clutched at his throat, wholly an automatic gesture. There was no sign of Snell. He looked frantically for some note, running his hands over the floor of the car and the cushions. There was no message. There was nothing.

He thought madly. . . . I'll *have* to drive. I'll *have* to learn. I'll *have* to get out of here. Oh, where the hell is Cane Valley? Where the hell is that goddam Georgia . . ."

Rain upon the roof of the car was like a thousand fingertips caressing a drum. He fumbled in the dark for the light on the dashboard. Behind him in the scattered area of the woods he heard the insane shouts and curses of frustrated men. He did not know why they were prostrated, but he knew that cry. Shooting was more frequent now. Bullets pinged across the top of the car. There was a sound of running footsteps and he thrust desperately for his pistol. Even while he pulled it out, tearing off his glove the better to get his finger upon the trigger, a hooded face appeared at the window, and a voice commanded, "Wait!"

Johnson knew that voice. This was not the place to temporize. Yet he dared not betray his identity. That was Snell's voice—perhaps. Perhaps it was the voice of a man he had never seen before. "It's me—Snell, comrade," the man whispered into the car. He was in beside Johnson; he was at the wheel. The engine buzzed; hummed; sang. The car throbbed; it shot through the underbrush like a bullet. It found the main road and enveloped the cries behind it in the purr of its motor as it sped at 40-60-70 miles an hour toward Cane Valley. The cooling rain pelted through the windows.

Johnson said, "Where the hell were you?"

Snell laughed softly. "Rippin' tires. Musta ripped a thousand. Every durned car in half a mile got a gutted tire. If they git to Cane Valley tonight they'll have to walk it, the sons of—"

"What's our agenda, when we get there?" Johnson asked, the Klan already forgotten and the problems of the Negro and white sharecroppers of Cane Valley obsessing his mind.

"Yes," said Snell, jerking off the white hood, "the agenda. Say, you better take off that damn nightie and nightcap, ef you don't want one o' them sharecroppers to make hamburger outer you with a shotgun. . . . . Now the agenda. . . . ."

"Good Thing It Wasn't a Cold Night," Circa 1943
Unpublished, Eugene Gordon Papers[31]

"Good Thing It Wasn't a Cold Night" deals with a Black youth, Jimmy, rushing home to Harlem late at night because of a curfew. The story was probably written in 1943 after a white police officer shot and killed a Black soldier in Harlem. When rioting occurred, Mayor Fiorello LaGuardia imposed a curfew for Harlem on August 1, 1943.

The young man in this story encounters a sick white woman and is unsure what to do. His instinct is to help her, but he knows he could be in trouble if the police see him outside Harlem. The woman tells him where she lives, but he does not know if he should risk taking her there. He meets a white man who says the woman is drunk and tells the boy to leave, which he does. The police see him and question what he is doing out. Jimmy tells them he was helping a friend. The police verify Jimmy's story and tell him to go home. As he returns to Harlem, he sees that the woman is still in the same location, "like a discarded old dress." He feels an "agonized pity" for her and then sees the police are trailing him, making sure he returns to Harlem.

"Good Thing It Wasn't a Cold Night" is a simple story, but it poignantly portrays the inhumanity of many people toward those who are suffering. Most just think the worst of people in need and do not want to be bothered with their problems. The story also reflects the unfeeling nature of the police and their frequent need to control Blacks at all costs. There is a similar story in the Gordon papers entitled "The Crime Wave."

Good Thing It Wasn't a Cold Night

The old newsstand on the southwest corner of Twelfth Street off Third Avenue was dark, but the boy coming toward it across the avenue was uncomfortably certain that he saw a woman beside it. As if he had been expecting or looking for her—which, as a matter of fact, was true. He wondered whether she had wanted to hide or to be seen when she leaned herself in that corner. He thought as he came nearer that she had got there because it was a good place to lean in.

He felt panicky. Funny to find somebody he'd hoped never to see, though he'd been looking for her more than a week. He hadn't been looking because he'd wanted to find her. He'd been looking because he hadn't been able to help himself. He hadn't wanted to find her. Newspaper headlines and stories—such as those in that evening's Journal American—had started him on the crazy hunt. The headline had shrieked that there would be a "2 AM CURFEW IN WAR ON CRIME." The story, listing the latest muggings, had said that anybody caught at 2 a.m. away from his own part of the city would be questioned by police.

Well, he was a long way from Harlem. And it must be nearly 3 a.m. now. This, in other words, was *it*. The big tower at Fourteenth Street and Fourth Avenue was already striking three. This was it, all right, for, slowing up though he did, he couldn't escape her. She was calling to him, in a loud, husky whisper, to come to him. She looked as if she might be sick; he wouldn't know. What he did know was that the woman was white. Propped in the corner between the newsstand and brick building, she looked as if she would topple over at any minute.

He should be running, he thought, instead of stopping to see whether she was—well, drunk, or really sick. He teetered on the curbstone a few feet from her, staring and trying to figure it out. Suppose he ran and she screamed. That would be bad for him. Headlines tomorrow would say, "MUGGER ESCAPES!" Or—and he was scared of this one—"MUGGER SHOT TRYING TO ESCAPE."

Nobody else was near at the moment, though scores were passing back and forth two blocks away on Fourteenth Street. Somebody would be bound to pass this corner before long. Maybe a police car.

A man and a woman came rapidly toward him down Twelfth Street. They too were white. Everybody around was white—but him. The couple glanced first at him, then at the woman in the shadowy corner. They hesitated as if about to stop, and then, with a glare at him that made him wish he had never paused, they went on across Third Avenue.

"I think she's sick, Ann," he heard the man say.

He heard Ann say: "No doubt about it. Sick from too much liquor."

He knew that the next remark was about him, though he could not hear it. He was uneasy.

He stared after them as they passed under the elevated tracks to the other side of Third Avenue and blended with the shadows in the middle of the block.

The woman by the newsstand was moaning for help. Why, she wasn't drunk! His mother sounded like that when she was sick. His mother was no drinking woman. He took a step nearer and saw that she was about his mother's age or older.

"Please, son, I'm sick. Help me."

Scared, he looked up and down both streets.

"What's the matter, ma'am?" he whispered.

She closed her eyes, wagged her head from side to side and groaned without speaking.

"Where d'you live, ma'am?"

"Seventh Street. Seventh Street near First Avenue. Please help me, son."

He slithered his tongue over his lips.

"Well, I—I . . ."

A man was coming along Third Avenue from the direction of Fourteenth Street. Seeing that the man was white, the boy again remembered that this was not Harlem and that it was past 3 a.m.. Should he tell this man what had happened? Maybe together they could do something for the woman. She was human, even if she was white. Some people thought Negroes were not human because they were black. Well, a sick woman was a sick woman. He wouldn't want anybody to pass up his mother sick on the street at 3 a.m.

The white man, stopping short, eyed the boy and the woman. "What's going on here?"

He didn't act like one of those detectives the papers said were roaming the city. He seemed to be just curious. He was a big fellow and had an easygoing manner.

"Mister, I think this woman is sick. I was passing and she groaned. She asked me to help her."

The man continued to stare at both the boy and the woman. She has slumped almost to the ground. Her head drooped and her eyes were closed. The man touched her shoulder gingerly. That was enough to send her completely to the ground. She sat, moaning.

"She tell you where she lives?" he asked the boy.

"She said Seventh Street near First Avenue." "Where do you live?"

"Me. I live up on 155th Street."

The man looked the boy up and down.

"You're a long way from home, boy. If I was you, I'd go back there and mind my own business."

The boy thought that wasn't bad advice. He had hoped, as a matter of fact, that things would take just this turn. It let him out, at the same time taking care of this woman. All he had to do now was make a run for it. He'd mind his own business hereafter, all right, and nobody'd have to remind him. He wanted to make sure of only one thing before he ran.

"Will you see she gets home all right? Because I believe she's sick. Good thing it isn't a cold night."

The woman was holding her side and muttering. Saliva trickled from the corners of her mouth. The man, bending over her, scrutinized her closely. He avoided touching her.

"What's the matter, lady?" he shouted, as if to a deaf mute. "Are you sick? Too much to drink?"

He listened for her answer. She mumbled. He straightened up. Shrugging, he turned to the boy.

"Drunk. Rotten drunk. Better get away from her but fast, boy. Before she starts crying."

The boy, doubtful, uneasy, moved off to the opposite side of Twelfth Street. He stopped and looked back. The man was disappearing among Third Avenue's elevated pillars. The woman was crumpled on the sidewalk.

"I think she's sick and I've a good mind to go back," the boy argued with himself. "No matter what happens."

He stood on the curbstone contemplating the woman on the ground across the street. It was the approaching police car that jolted him to reality. His heart raced and hammered but he resolved to control his legs. He sauntered in the direction from which the police car was coming.

It drew over and stopped beside him.

"What's the matter, boy? What are you doing down here?"

"I had some business to tend to and was on my way home."

"Business, huh? What kinda business? Monkey business?"

"No, sir. I went to see a fellow—I went to look at a radio."

"Where'd you get the radio?"

The boy, bewildered, shook his head.

"What radio?" he asked.

"The one you went to see this fellow about, dummy! What'd you do with it?"

"I fixed it. I left it there."

"Fixed it and left it where? Where's this fellow live?"

"He lives over on Avenue A. He asked me to come over—"

"Where'd you learn how to fix radios?"

"Learned it at home. I—"

"Lemme see your draft card, boy."

His heart having calmed down somewhat, began to race again. He emptied one pocket after another into his hands, but his draft card was not there. He made a gesture of despair.

"I must have left it in my other clothes."

"Must have left it in your other clothes, huh? Too bad you didn't bring 'em with you, because you'll need 'em before you get out. Come on, boy. You better get in this car. Where'd you say this fellow lives? What's his name?

The boy, shoved down between the driver—who had not yet said anything—and the other cop, recalled stories about the third degree. Once in the movies, a man put between two others in a car like this had been tossed out dead. But these men were police. They were tough but they didn't kill you like that. Didn't have to. All they had to do was beat you up. They'd probably beat him if he didn't give them the story they wanted. That would be as bad as being killed, because he would feel the beating longer. He had always hated being beaten. He couldn't stand being struck when he couldn't hit back.

He was pinned in between the two like a stick of wood in a vise.

"What's this fellow's name, boy? Say what's the matter with you? Can't you speak?"

"His name's Cohen. Larry Cohen. He lives over on Avenue A. Three-sixty-one, Avenue A."

"Three-sixty-one Avenue A," the driver repeated, steering against a red light across Third Avenue.

The car kept on across First to Avenue A.

"Why you niggers don't stay in Harlem..."

The driver interrupted himself to say: "Three-sixty-one's on this side, Bill. Along here somewhere."

"That is, if he didn't make it up," the first officer said.

"I didn't make it up. There it is. Right up the street there, on the right. Where that bakery sign is."

The first cop opened the door and stepped to the street. The boy, about to follow, was shoved roughly back into his seat.

"Keep your eye on him, Martin," Bill said to the driver. "If he tries any more monkey business, let him have it."

"OK, Bill. I got him covered."

The boy and Martin watched as Bill flashed his light over the names in the vestibule letter boxes. The street was dark and deserted. A young fellow, passing on the sidewalk, slowed down to stare at the cop with the flashlight and at the police car.

"What th' hell you gawkin' at? Get a move on!"

Shouting it, the driver made a move as if about to get out of the car.

The young fellow ran, darting round the next corner.

The boy, realizing that neither cop laughed, cringed in his seat. He thought they would take it as a good joke. Instead, they seemed to look on it as an ordinary incident. Tough babies. He began to tremble as Bill returned to the car.

"Repeat that fellow's name, boy," the cop said, flashing his light into the blinking brown eyes.

"Cohen. Larry Cohen."

"You sure? You sure he lives here?"

"I was with him here just a little while ago."

"Says you. Does he always take his name outta the bell before he goes to bed? Ever strike you as funny how he does that?"

The boy, not knowing what to say, suggested that he himself go and ring the bell. Neither policeman answered, and the boy waited, half rising.

"All right. What you waiting for? Come on show me the name."

The boy, shrinking from the hard muzzle of the pistol at his spine, walked ahead of the policeman into the vestibule. He found and pressed a bell over against the entrance to the hallway. The policeman's flashlight revealed only a blurred name penciled on a bit of dirty pasteboard. The name was not Cohen. The boy kept on pressing. Far away they could hear the bell ringing.

The cop tried the door. It opened.

"What floor is it on, boy?"

"Top floor. Fourth floor, front."

His foot inside the door, the cop reached back and grabbed the boy's shoulder.

"Get in there ahead of me . . ." He stopped abruptly, listening.

"Somebody's calling out the window," the boy said.

They returned to the sidewalk.

"Who is it?" a woman yelled from a top-floor window. "What you ringing my bell for? What you want?"

"Family lives here named Cohen?" the cop yelled back.

"Cohen? Cohen, you say. That's a common name. Lots of Cohens live round here. But there don't live no Cohen in this flat."

The policeman looked at the boy, who was staring, wide-mouthed, at the woman.

"You're police, yes?" she called. "What you want?"

"Listen, lady. We got a colored fellow down here says he was visiting a Larry Cohen in your apartment. What about it?"

The woman screamed.

"Oh, yes. Larry's my son. My first husband's name was Cohen. But that was eighteen, nineteen years ago and"—her voice rising—"Jimmy! Jimmy? That you down there, Jimmy? What happened, Jimmy? What they arrest you for?"

A youth's head appeared suddenly beside hers in the window.

"Larry! Larry!" the boy shouted. "Tell them where I was most of the night. They don't believe me."

"Wait a minute," Larry called.

He ducked back into the room. In another minute he was on the sidewalk. He threw his arm protectively around Jimmy's shoulder.

"What happened? What they arrest you for?"

"Said I should've staid in Harlem.'

"Say, officer," Larry protested. "Jimmy here's one of the best radio engineers in New York. If he was a white boy—"

"That's enough from you, young fellow. Read the papers and see what's happening. We got orders to keep Harlem where it belongs after a certain hour and I don't care—"

"Say, what is this?" the driver cried, getting out of the car. "Why don't you folks up there mind your own business and go back to bed?"

Somebody was in practically every window on both sides the street for a block.

"Get on back upstairs before I run the both of you in," the cop said to Larry.

Larry, belligerent, shut his mouth and turned away.

"Say, you, boy," the cop ordered Jimmy. "Get the hell out of here. Get up to Harlem where you belong. And stay there. Go on, now!"

Jimmy started off at a trot, following the same route he had taken nearly two hours earlier. He was still a long way from Harlem, he thought, and anything could happen if these policemen decided to follow him.

As he neared Third Avenue he remembered the woman. He stopped short, peering into the shadows surrounding the old newsstand. Yes. There she lay, like a discarded old dress. A wave of agonized pity swept up through him and flooded his eyes with tears. He looked back. The police car was just turning into Twelfth Street from Second Avenue, trailing him.

Jimmy, staying close in against the buildings, began to sob aloud as he ran.

"And I Ask, *Why*?"
No Date, Unpublished, Eugene Gordon Papers[32]

"And I Ask, *Why*?" is a very short, seemingly very simple, story that leaves much unspoken. Two young friends, one white and one Black, plan a fishing trip. They have been friends for several years, and their friendship has withstood challenges from those who do not like it. However, on this day, the Black boy asks the white boy why his mother is cleaning clothes for the white boy's family. This puzzles him since each family is from the same working-class background. It is likely not the first time the Black boy has had this thought about the differences between him and his friend, but it is the first time he asks why this situation exists. The white boy, sensing that his mother (and perhaps himself and what he perceives is the natural order) is under assault, takes offense. The Black boy retreats, his question unanswered, and they resume their walk to the fishing pond.

Gordon uses this coming-of-age tale to chronicle the innocence of children and how this innocence can be challenged by society as the children get older. Gordon is someone who feels that racism is not something innate but is learned and that this education by society begins at an early age. In this incident the boys' friendship remains intact because the Black boy did not pursue it; however, there will likely be more tests of their friendship ahead, and it is not clear whether they (particularly the white boy) will be up to those challenges.

And I Ask, *Why*?

Timmy McCall sat on the frayed edge of Jimmy Ward's rickety front porch, waiting. Jimmy shouted from inside:
"Say, Ma, ask him if he got up before breakfus."
Jimmy's mother, washing clothes in a galvanized tub on a box near the pump, asked Timmy whether he had et. He said, "Yesm." He said he'd hardly been able to sleep all night—that he'd kept turning his flashlight on that old clock—on account of thinking about going fishing today.
"Firs time you be going fishin' this season, aint it, Timmy?"
"Yesm."
"You sho do love fishin an swimmin an things like that, don't you?"
"Yesm'. I sure do. Jimmy does, too, don't he?"
"He sho does." Jimmy's mother laughed softly. "You an Jimmy, y'all been friens ever since I can remember. Recollec that time the p'lice 'rested y'all because you took Jimmy in that ol Municipal Swimmin Pool."
"I sure do. I won't never forget that."
"You was nine and Jimmy was eight. *My, My*! Seven years ago! That ol judge, he made Miz McCall whup you an' he made me whup Jimmy. He thought that gonh break up y'all's friendship."
"It didn't, though. Take moren that to smash up our friendship. Aw, for Pete's sake, Jimmy! Come on outta there, willya?"
Jimmy came out, still chewing. He stopped beside his mother at the washtub under the chinaberry tree.
"You don't have to buy nothing for supper tonight, Mama. Just wait till I come home with this big ol basket *fulla* fish."
Jimmy's mother perennially laughed at that perennial joke. But over her tub, hands resting on the slanting washboard, she proudly observed the boys out of sight.
"Say, Timmy, I been thinking."
"What with? I mean *what*?"
Lanky black boy and lanky white companion moved with graceful

ease in blue denim trousers and hip rubber boots. Each carried a wicker basket and fishing tackle. Timmy's dog Gippy followed close. Jimmy said, as if he'd been concerned with the question a long time:

"I been thinking how my ma washes for your ma—doing it ever since I was little. It's a funny thing—you know?—how all of a sudden you start to thinking about something y'aint never thought about before."

Timmy McCall and Jimmy Ward understood each other. Timmy refrained from kidding or saying "What?" again. He strode on beside his Negro friend in the violet and orange sunlight of this May Georgia morning. Jimmy would say what was in his mind when he'd shaped it up enough to let it out in words.

"Well, my ma, she washes for your ma, but she—I mean *your* ma—she aint a rich lady, is she? Don't she work over in the mills?"

Timmy looked at him sharply. "Sure, she aint rich! What you talking about? Do I look like my family's any damn millionaires?"

"But, just the same, Mama washes clothes for her."

"Well, don't she get paid for it? Doesn't my mother pay her? She don't wash 'em for nothing, does she?"

"Wait a minute, Timmy. You don't get the point. What I mean is suppose my mother works over in the mills, see, and your mother, she does housework and takes in washing—"

"Why, *my mother* don't even do her own washing, let alone—'"

"That's what I *know*. That's what I'm *talking* about. Why don't she do her own washing? I mean my mother washes her own clothes."

"Sure she does! Say, what the hella you talking about, Jimmy? Sure, your mother washes her own clothes. And she washes my mother's, too."

"And I ask, *Why*? What's the reason your mother's got to have my mother wash youall's clothes. Your mother wouldn't wash our clothes."

"She sure wouldn't! She don't even—Say! What's eatin you all of a sudden? Hunh?"

"Nothing. Listen Timmy. I *know* your mother don't even—What I'm asking is *why don't* your mother wash her own clothes? Don't she have time? Or is she too tired? Or is it she thinks she's better—"

Timmy McCall stepped in front of Jimmy Ward in the middle of the weed-bordered path. Clear gray eyes were hardened to a squint.

Jimmy squinted clear dark eyes. Black boy and white boy were ready to fight each other. Gippy squatted in the path on his haunches and, head on one side, observed. Timmy said loudly:

"Say! You're talking about my mother, now, see? We may pal around, and things like that, but you're talking about my mother now. I don't go in for no talking about my mother, see."

"I don't either. But I been thinking—Oh, forget it, tough guy! He shoved past Timmy. "Come on. Let's go."

Gippy rose from his haunches and followed close behind.

Nonfiction

Excerpt "The Negro Press"
American Mercury (JUNE 1926): 207–15

"The Negro Press," published in the prestigious *American Mercury*, was Gordon's first exposure in a mainstream publication, affording him a wider audience than he had received in Black publications such as *The Messenger*. Edited by H. L. Mencken and drama critic George Jean Nathan, it was one of the few white-owned journals to publish Black authors. Gordon was one of only a handful of Black writers to be published in such journals in the 1920s, giving him prominence during the years of the Harlem Renaissance.

In this article, Gordon speaks of the history of the Black press, from its beginnings in the nineteenth century to the 1920s, when some 220 Black journals existed. However, Gordon feels only about a dozen should be taken seriously, the rest simply being "wastepaper." As was often the case, Gordon's unsparing criticism of those who he did not feel were up to the task caused him to make some powerful enemies. However, as at least one critic (signed J. A. R.—most likely veteran Black journalist Joel Augustus Rogers) stated, Gordon "is doing splendid work by these criticisms in helping the Negro press to know itself, which is the first step for real progress in the individual, the race, or the business concern." The article was later reprinted in *The Annals of the American Academy of Political and Social Science* (November 1928): 248–56.

The Negro Press

It was on March 30, 1827, about 38 years before Lee welcomed Grant to Richmond, that New York gave the country its first example of Negro journalism. Called *Freedom's Journal*,[1] this paper had, like all of its immediate successors, but one reason for existing: to preach the black serf's liberation. If, a hundred years hence, there should exist no records of that period save a file of such papers, the historian might still sense the temper of the time from the very names they bore: *Rights for All*[2] (published at New York), the *National Reformer*[3] (bearing a Philadelphia dateline), the *Paladium [sic] of Liberty*[4] (from Columbus, Ohio), and the *Herald of Freedom*[5] (also from Ohio). But when Lincoln put his signature to the Emancipation Proclamation, in 1862, all save two of the twenty-odd Negro papers of the pre-war years had ceased publication. Today but one of them serves: the *Christian Recorder*,[6] established in 1848 as the *Christian Herald*.

Mustering 220 journals, more or less, published in thirty-six States and the District of Columbia and read by 5,000,000 people weekly, the Negro press as we know it today is a recent growth. Yellowness[7] marks it, and is flaunted as a badge of progress. In a letter to *Opportunity: A Journal of Negro Life*, Robert S. Abbott, editor and publisher of the Chicago *Defender*, says proudly, "We were the first [Negro] paper to use large headlines. Nearly all the other papers called our paper the 'yellow journal' when we first began using these up-to-date practices and methods." But not now. Yellowness has become nearly universal. At the start it was adopted simply because it brought increased circulation. But now there is an additional reason: the Negro press is thus given a retaliatory weapon against the white press, and it is used assiduously and effectively.

There are few American dailies which do not occasionally play up the story of a spectacular offense by a Negro, and always, in such stories, the projecting fact is that the evildoer is black. In the headlines, as a matter of course, his race is named. In the story his race is again named—and again and again. The headline may run something like this:

NEGRO ATTACKS WHITE WOMAN

or it may be only this:

NEGRO UP FOR CHICKEN-STEALING

The purpose of heads like these is, consciously or unconsciously, to justify and confirm the old tradition centering about the Aframerican. The Negro editor, a sensitively race-conscious being, is angered thereby, and watches for a chance to retaliate. If a propitious opportunity fails to tap at his door he goes out and drags one in. In consequence, readers of the Chicago *Defender* or the Boston *Guardian*, a week later, may see a headline like this:

WHITE BRUTE ATTACKS COLORED GIRL

or,

CRAPSHOOTERS HELD UP BY THUGS
Not a Negro Among Them

But these retaliations, of course, do not mark the limit of sensationalism in the Negro weeklies. The colored editor, believing that headlines eight columns wide and three inches deep sell more papers than modest ones, continues to seek matter to play up, and if he can detect in the week's crimes of the white brother no accomplishment worthy of consideration, he pins the badge on a member of his own race. So we have, from the Chicago *Whip*:

DORA COLT-DAY TRAPPED IN LOVE NEST

and, from the *Whip's* neighbor, the *Defender*, this social item:

MAN IS SLAIN IN GIRL'S ROOM

while the Pittsburgh *Courier* informs its readers somewhat more decorously that a

POPULAR MATRON SEEKS DIVORCE

Each of these heads, of course, represents a bit of legitimate news. It would be caviling to suggest that it does not. Printed somewhere on an inner page, in one column, each would be properly placed. But in every case I have cited it occupies eight columns, and, save in the *Courier*, it is printed in red ink.

There was a time when the ordinary colored American laughed at the suggestion that he read Negro newspapers. Even the maker of the suggestion usually smiled somewhat apologetically, for it *was* more or less a joke. But this indifference of the dark-skinned population to his feeble efforts was not the only difficulty the Negro editor had to overcome. Inadequate distribution was another. In those days no one dreamed of asking for black papers at white news-stands. The agents of the former, usually indigent high school students or intensely race-conscious elderly men, did not dream of asking white dealers to handle them. But of late a revolutionary change has taken place, and evidence of it is seen in the following full-page announcement in the Chicago *Defender*:

> So great is the demand for the Chicago *Defender* it became necessary to secure the best medium of distribution in New York City, Washington, Baltimore and other large cities. It was necessary to engage the services of national distributors. Our distributor, the Interborough News Company, of New York City, alone covers 6700 news-stands in Greater New York. Distributors in other cities are covering all news-stands and places of business.

* * *

II

From a pile of 220 Aframerican weeklies one may drop 197 as little more than waste paper. Of the remaining twenty-three, ten are mediocrities, yet sufficiently well equipped to qualify for notice: they show an excess neither of vice nor of virtue, of intelligence nor of imbecility. With their editors, the paste pot and shears often substitute for original matter. The following are better: the Baltimore *Afro-American*, described by its slogan as "A Champion of Civic Welfare and the Square Deal," and coming in two sections of ten pages each; the Chicago *Defender*, "The World's Greatest Weekly," in two sections of twenty-two pages in all; the New York *Amsterdam News*, sloganless and in two sections of eight pages each; the Norfolk (Va.) *Journal and Guide*, "The South's Best Weekly," in two sections and fourteen pages; the St. Louis *Argus*, sixteen pages; the Philadelphia *Tribune*, "A Family Paper Fit for the Home," sixteen pages; the Savannah *Tribune* no slogan, but carrying twelve pages; the Washington (DC) *Tribune*, "First in Advertising and Circulation," sixteen pages; the New York *Age*, "The National Negro Weekly," ten pages; the Kansas City *Call* (of which I happen to have no copy at hand); the Chicago *Whip*," A Paper with a Policy," twelve pages; and the Chicago *Bee*, "The Race's Greatest Newspaper," fourteen pages.

In size and makeup these papers greatly resemble their more yellow daily contemporaries. They have, like the dailies, tiers upon tiers of red, alternating with black headlines; conglomerations of photographs of "society" folk, cutthroats, footpads,[8] pugilists, bootleggers, preachers, schoolteachers, poets, politicians, and actresses; comic strips, cartoons, and patent medicine advertisements; and women's, children's, sports, theatrical, and radio pages. In addition they have "race" syndicate features of every variety for every shade of taste. Aframerican journalism, indeed, is violently race-conscious.

III

The Negro press takes its politics most seriously. There will be found in all Aframerica no paper which is not soul and body the slave of the Republican party, yet the observer will notice an almost universal discontent with the Coolidge régime. "Before election Mr. Coolidge was as eloquent as Mr. [William Jennings] Bryan," the Chicago *Defender* reminds its cliéntèle, "He knew what the people wanted—and he would give it to them. Since his election he has forgotten more completely than any person who preceded him into the White House." On the other hand, "We have no doubt as to the desire of the President to do something," consoles the Pittsburgh *Courier*, recalling Mr. Coolidge's latest message to Congress. The *Courier* gave itself unstintedly to the cause during the last campaign. It trounced the party's foes, interpreted the Coolidge idealism, and published a series of articles showing why colored folk should vote the Republican ticket forever. Its editor was frequently mentioned as the next Register of the Treasury.

The *Defender* suggests unreservedly "the appointment of a

member of the race to the President's Cabinet," but Prof. Kelly Miller,[9] a syndicated columnist, observes that the "audacity of the proposition startles us with a sudden shock," adding that "we have seen the Jew and the Catholic invited to sit around the Cabinet table as members of the President's official family, but the suggestion of a Negro's being invited seems ridiculous even to the Negro himself." Lest he be misunderstood, Prof. Miller expands this statement:

> The suggestion of the *Defender* is considered absurd only because the Negro plays no controlling rôle in the political drama. The great bulk of the race is effectively disfranchised and is given no more political consideration than a babe in the cradle. When the race actually voted, and was able to effect political results, such a proposition was not considered unfeasible.

Reverting to the Presidential message: "It is impossible," says the Washington *Eagle*, "for any colored man to understand what the President is trying to say about the Negro—if he has said anything." From a political standpoint," the Baltimore *Afro-American* believes, "our greatest possibilities come in closely contested years." The *Afro-American* insists that "we must grasp the fact that we can become important factors only in combinations and alignments. But, "it adds disgustedly and truthfully, "of course our pie-counter politicians will not mediate much on this situation when the G. O. P. gives the word." In the politics of their home towns the Aframerican news-sheets are occasionally potent factors, but more often they are of negligible account. Long and religious adherence to one party has made them ineffectual allies.

The Negro press, of late, has become brazenly irreligious. Utterances which a decade ago would have cost an editor his livelihood are accepted today even by the church folk. It is the church's patent failure, says the colored editor, to reconcile religious, racial and class differences that is responsible for the gradual drifting toward indifference of an important element of Negro journalism. The Boston *Chronicle* opines that the "world suffers now from an excess of religious fervor," adding that although the Puritans sought religious freedom in this country, yet, in the name of religion "they were inhuman brutes," while a contributor to the *Courier* adds that "the profession of Christianity by the Negro for all these years hasn't stopped him from being lynched, insulted and proscribed like a leper or a criminal." "Even the headhunters of African fame and the cannibals of Borneo were never more inhuman or barbaric than Christianized white men," is the conviction of the St. Louis *Argus*, and William Pickens,[10] writing for the Associated Negro Press, maintains that the white man is responsible for the Aframerican's gradual turning from Christianity, the Church, and religion in general. It is the view of Mr. Pickens that "white Protestant churches have largely fallen under suspicion of being Klux hotbeds," and that "if the Negro's suspicion is permitted to grow ere long he will have no confidence in any praying white man, and when the white preacher offers him heaven from one hand he will be suspected of holding hell in the other."

The Negro newspapers complain chiefly about the Christian's "hypocrisy." Christianity as a principle of conduct most of them believe to be good, but they criticize the agencies carrying out its programme as unfit for their mission. This opinion appears in the Chicago *Defender's* complaint that "the Catholic Church saw no reason to speak out against the savage crimes of race hate," but has now "raised its voice in a plea for freer liquor laws." The *Defender* adds scoffingly: "And the reason it gives is that Prohibition is 'flatly opposed to Holy Scripture'! The Catholic Church has a man's-sized job on its hands to explain away that hypocrisy. A church that can sit by in silence while men and women are tortured with a fiendish cruelty that sets at defiance every word of scriptural injunction doesn't cut a very heroic figure when it pleads for booze in the name of the Holy Bible."

The Dallas (Tex.) *Express*, denying that it belongs to the "purely critical element," says that the Church's waning influence among Aframericans may be ascribed to a preponderance of illiterate, ignorant, and ease-loving preachers. But there is by no means a severance of relations between the surviving religionists and these scoffing papers. There are always church advertisements, stories of ministerial doings, and sermons sticky with milk and honey.

* * *

IV

The Aframerican press does not contribute to the aid and comfort of the criminal by suppressing intelligence of his misdeeds. Most of its papers display the dirt generously and in the open. Their reasons for doing so are as ingenuous and naïve as are their white contemporaries.' For example, they published the filth of the Rhinelander case,[11] word for word and detail for detail, because it was "important news." But the conditions which contribute to crime are also dragged into the daylight and sometimes they are very intelligently discussed. Discussion, of course, usually ends the matter. Work for social improvements among the Negroes has lacked organization and system. The *Age*, in its campaign for improved housing conditions; the *Amsterdam News*, in its fight to compel the employment of colored young men and women in Harlem stores; the Boston *Chronicle*, in its struggle in behalf of the benighted of the South End and Roxbury for adequate social centres; and the *Defender*, in its continuous battle with the sloven unwashed hosts from Southern plantations: these are examples of progressive papers and of the contributions they are making to the social betterment of their readers.

Withal, the Aframerican journalist remains stanchly conservative. A "radical" Negro press simply doesn't exist. Liberalism may—and, in fact, does—show its head now and then, but the Negro editor surely does not long for a soviet government. A Boston *Transcript* special writer once charged that a "press campaign, under the organization of Russian propagandists, to arouse racial hatred in America by means of articles in the Negro press," is one of "five phases of Negro propaganda work in America today." Branding the *Transcript* a "timid old lady with reactionary tendencies," the Boston *Chronicle* replied:

> This charge is often made, and always succeeds in starting our temper on a rampage. The Negro press of the United States conducts a campaign to stir up hatred against the whites, said campaign being paid for by money from some strong-box at Moscow. As far as the *Chronicle* is concerned, Moscow has overlooked us. This silly charge has been so constantly and persistently made that we are beginning to wonder whether or not some of our worthy contemporaries are keeping something from us.

There is only one Aframerican daily, the Washington (DC) *Daily American*. It would be more properly classified as a handbill. As a factor in Negro journalism it is insignificant. A step toward relieving the weeklies of the burden of news-gathering was taken in the organization, seven years ago, of the Associated Negro Press. Then papers comprised the original membership. Today there are 112, but only 87 are active. The remainder have been suspended or are in arears. That indifference toward an organization which might benefit them greatly has been one of the chief causes of stagnancy in the Negro press.

The difficulties under which the Associated Negro Press works may be sensed from the fact that it has only eight regular correspondents. In order to make the best of them, it has placed them at strategic points throughout the country's localities in which news of importance to a dark-skinned cliéntèle is most likely to break. These correspondents relay the news they gather to the central office at Chicago, whence it is distributed twice weekly by mail. When last minute intelligence is considered sufficiently important it is sent by wire to those papers which have agreed to bear the expense of telegrams. The A. N. P. has an agreement with its members whereby each must send in its own news to the central office for redistribution. Here again only a few papers cooperate for the common good.

News dispatches distributed by this organization are easily recognized. Conspicuous for their conciseness, the correctness of their grammar, and the observance generally of good literary and journalistic usages, these items are written by men of more than fair education and newspaper training. The ordinary colored news-writer's besetting sin is his constant and studied abuse of a few words. The most outrageously treated is the word "race." Some of the papers—the Chicago *Defender* is a notorious example—go so far as to elevate the word "colored" to the honor and dignity of a proper noun.

Not many of the colored editors, indeed, show much journalistic skill. Take, for example, William Monroe Trotter, of the Boston *Guardian*. This nationally known agitator undoubtedly has done some splendid things for his people, but if he lives to twice his present fifty-odd years he will never be a newspaper man. Trotter was born in Boston and got from Harvard both the A. B. and the A. M. But there is nothing in the eight pages of the *Guardian* to indicate the fact. It is one of the most poorly-written Negro sheets in America.

Another editor who bears a reputation independently of his paper is Ben Jeff Davis,[12] of Atlanta. Davis is typically Georgian. He is fearless, but hopelessly a politician. As Republican national committeeman from Georgia, he is heir to the trappings of the lately deceased Henry Lincoln Johnson.[13] Jealous contemporaries whisper that the square-jawed Atlantan's feet rattle like dry bone in Linc Johnson's shoes, but in his Atlanta *Independent* Davis brands this a base lie. As a man he is all right. When he has something to say he knows how to say it. He is a better writer than Trotter, even though his degrees are mostly of the secret order brand. Many a white Georgian has been made to writhe under his cutting lash.

There is no doubt that the Chicago *Defender* is a remarkable phenomenon in American journalism, without reference to color or class. Its founder is one of those persons who may look to the casual observer like a nondescript nobody, and yet be a man of brains and accomplishment. He is Robert S. Abbott.[14] Essentially a newspaper man, he has made of the Windy City sheet a paper which so closely resembles in certain particulars Hearst's well-known rags that his zealous contemporaries still hint that Hearst is its real owner. That Abbott never denies the rumor is proof of his self-assurance. He has built in ten years a newspaper with a weekly circulation of more than 250,000. He gives his editors and reporters salaries comparable to those paid by the biggest dailies. When he sees in the *Herald and Examiner* a feature he likes he confiscates the idea under it and makes it a part of the *Defender*. Hence "The Week." When he sees in the *Tribune* something he thinks would look well in the *Defender* he copies it. Hence "The *Defender's* Platform for America" and Dr. A. Wilberforce Williams'[15] column. In consequence of these methods, Abbott has become the outstanding newspaper man of Aframerica. He rose from the ground, drawing himself to his present eminence by means of the well-known shoe-string, now grown into a dependable hawser.[16]

The *Defender's* rival is the Baltimore *Afro-American*, in some particulars the Chicago paper's superior. But the two sheets so closely resemble each other that one is often bought for the other.

The characters of the two editors, however are as dissimilar as are the circumstances of their early lives. Abbott had to struggle all the way, and, at manhood, strike out on a makeshift education. He knew nothing about newspaper education. He knew nothing about newspaper making previous to a decade ago, when he began publishing. He was even then well above thirty. But Carl Murphy[17] grew up with the *Afro-American*. When his father, old John Murphy, died not long since, Carl came, fresh from college and a year's travel in Germany, to carry on. A studious, cultured man of thirty-six with horn-rim glasses shielding unusually large and brilliant eyes, Murphy, too, is essentially the newspaper man. He is ingenious in his methods of exploitation and an excellent editorial writer.

The New York *Age* is the ancient harridan of black newspaperdom, and Fred R. Moore is her old man. He has lived with and been faithful to her for nineteen years. She is a fine brain in a somewhat passé body. Moore has seen sixty-nine years and a few sad disappointments. Taft appointed him minister to Liberia, and the appointment was confirmed, but he has not yet got to Africa. He was the first colored man to be nominated for the New York Assembly, and also the first to fail of election. Perhaps disappointments have had some influence on his editorship. At any rate, he continues to give the colored press one of its most trenchant pages of editorials. The drubbing he has rained upon the bootleggers of Harlem makes him widely respected.

There is no way of avoiding mention of Marcus Garvey among the conspicuous heads of Negro newspapers in America. At present Mr. Garvey is in that small section of Aframerica bounded by the walls of the Federal prison at Atlanta. Using the mails to defraud was the charge that sent him there. As Mr. Hearst directs the policies of his news-sheets from a hacienda in California, so does Mr. Garvey steer the course of the *Negro World* from his Southern retreat.[18] The *Negro World* is a jumble of "back to Africa" rubbish. There is no news save such as bears upon his beloved hobby. Yet the man himself is a remarkable personality. He has inspired in his followers a hatred of all but the full-blooded Negro gentry. He has held audience with the Grand Goblin of the Ku Klux Klan himself. He has elevated himself to the supreme dictatorship of an African empire. He has created hundreds of colored knights and ladies, and so done almost as much for plebian America as the exalted head of the Klan. He publishes a "newspaper," but I fear that, in so far as the real business of being a newspaper editor is concerned, he remains as deeply in the dark as a full-blooded Zulu in a deserted coal mine at midnight.

"The Opportunity Dinner: An Impression"
Opportunity (JULY 1927): 208–9

In March 1924, Charles S. Johnson, the editor of *Opportunity*, provided a dinner in honor of the publication of Jessie Fauset's novel *There Is Confusion*. This dinner, held at the Civic Club on West 12th Street in Manhattan, is often marked as the beginning of the Harlem Renaissance/ New Negro Movement. The gathering brought together both Black and white literary and cultural luminaries. The meeting would help occasion the publication of the *Survey Graphic* magazine (March 1, 1925) and subsequent anthology *The New Negro*, edited by Alain Locke, landmarks in African American literature. The success of the 1924 dinner led Johnson to continue hosting annual soirees, where important prizes were given in literary contests.

Gordon had first attended one of the *Opportunity* dinners in 1926 as leader of the Saturday Evening Quill Club. In 1927, he was awarded a prize for his short story "Game." His presence at the gathering shows his deep involvement in the literary and social happenings at the time. He was able to meet other talented figures and to make important connections.

The Opportunity Dinner
An Impression

When we arrived at the Fifth Avenue Restaurant, the scene of Opportunity's third annual dinner, we found the doors already open, and a number of persons scattered throughout the expansive white and gold and mirrored dining room, Mrs. Charles S. Johnson, petite, serious-faced and luminous eyed, stood near the door; she welcomed us, and I felt a thrill of pleasure that she remembered me from last year. We checked our coats and hats in the cloak room, then went out to see whether we knew anyone among the early arrivals. The first acquaintances we met from home were the Misses Alvira Hazard[19] and Florence Harmon, members of the Saturday Evening Quill Club, of Boston, who stood somewhat hesitantly near a table set for ten, and which bore in the center a white card with a red border and the inscription, "Reserved for the Quill Club."

Even at this early hour there is noticeable an air of tenseness, of suppressed expectancy. The Misses Hazard and Harmon are making their first visit, and I suspect that there are many others similarly experiencing a new emotion. The observant can almost unmistakably pick out the contributors from the mere visitors. Here stands a good-looking young woman from out-of-town; she is trying to carry on a lively conversation with another young woman and a man. Her quick, bright-eyed glances all about her, her tense clutching of the cords of her handbag, her brightened color, her concert of erratic movements—these all betray a nervousness which for weeks must have been growing upon her. At a table, agitatedly fingering the silverware, sits a small group which laughs and talks immoderately, in order to conceal its deeper feeling; individually they make inane or foolishly flippant remarks, quirking their heads about to observe the newcomers; remark repeatedly on the slowness with which the dinner is getting under way; finger their silverware.

But the tables are gradually being filled. Foreign-looking waiters fill the glasses with water and drop at each plate a chunk of bread—a crusted, brown roll. Then the waiters disappear for a moment behind mirrored columns or pots of tropic palms; presently they return with plates of soup. Repressed excitement begins to pain, for one knows now that the event for which all these persons have waited since February 28, the final date for accepting manuscripts, will soon reach its climax. Now, one by one and two by two, the long table at the end of the room begins to fill.

These are the judges: Harry Hansen, book review editor of the Morning World,[20] slides into his place. Over there in the corner is Charles S. Johnson. Then there is Professor John Dewey, the list of whose degrees and of the books that he has written overawes, and L. Hollingsworth Wood, head of the National Urban League; and Mrs. Edith R. Isaacs, editor of the *Theatre Arts Magazine*; and Paul Green, who has just received a big prize for the play, *In Abraham's Bosom*.[21] Mrs. Green, admiration for her handsome young husband reflected in her eyes, sits beside him. John Macy,[22] author of *The Story of the World's Literature*, and last year's chairman at the awards dinner, sits near Mr. and Mrs. Green. I wish I knew the names of the others, but I don't, and have no way of finding out. I observe also that scores of notable persons are seated with friends here and there all over the dining room.

Someone beside me touches my arm and whispers: "Say, who's that?" I've seen his pictures somewhere. Now, who . . ."

"Carl Van Vechten,"[23] I reply. "I've never met him, but once you see his picture you know him. Remember that interview in the *Boston Herald* in which he—"

"Who's that rather nice looking young fellow at the same table? I mean the fellow that's lost his necktie—and collar. He's wearing a blue shirt—"

"I can tell you who *he* is. That's Richard Bruce.[24] Didn't you read the first installment of his novel in *Fire?* Say . . ."

The soup plates have disappeared and the table is bare, except for the chunks of bread. I take up mine and write on its hard-shellacked surface: "Souvenir. Opportunity Awards Dinner, 1927. Quill Club." Everybody at the table is chattering that the idea is good. It is original. I take up my wife's silken-beaded bag and force the chunk of bread into it: wondering whether I am observed, and, if so, what my observer thinks.

Noah D. Thompson[25] comes and takes me to meet a Mr. [Charles] Barnett, who represents the Associated Press. With Mr. Barnett is a Japanese young man, publisher of a Japanese newspaper. His name, thrice repeated, is still elusive. Mr. Johnson introduces me to Wilbur Daniel Steele,[26] whose stories appear almost monthly in *Harper's*, and who persistently wins the annual O. Henry Memorial Award prize. I take Mr. Steele to my table and introduce the Quill Club to him. He is a tall, rugged man, with graying hair and a pleasant smile. He replies to a query that he was born in a theological seminary, and that by adoption and training he is a New England yankee.

Dinner has long since started, but only now are the last of the stragglers being seated. As these come to their places the anxiety on the faces of friends who have been craning in all directions for an hour, disappears. There is much loud laughter everywhere, most of it designed to conceal nervousness, much cheerful and loud chatter, much playful raillery; much teasing speculation.

James Weldon Johnson is bending over Carl Van Vechten and whispering; they are looking toward our table. Now they approach and touch Aaron Douglas' arm. Douglas and Van Vechten shake hands. Johnson and Van Vechten saunter off. Someone suggests in a whisper that Mr. Johnson has been telling Van Vechten about Douglas' drawings in *God's Trombone*.[27]

Another course is placed on the table. It is a full plate of half a broiled spring chicken, peas, and mashed potato. That passes, and then comes the dessert and coffee. In the meantime the judges at the long table are heading this way and that in earnest conversation with one another. I know that everyone is wondering what they are talking about. The buzzing of voices is now a smooth plane of sound; it is broken here and there only by tense laughter. The voices are less raucous than a few minutes ago. The climax . . .

A waiter in the rear of the dining room drops a plate, and its shattering pieces reverberate like a harsh gong; fire engines screech and roar in 24th street. . . . Our waiter places a saucer on the table and clinks a 50-cent piece into it.

"Bait!" someone laughs, and tosses in a dime. "No need to try to bait me; I've got to get back to Boston."

There follows a brief period of drinking sounds. Someone lays a dollar bill upon the small mound of coins and takes up three quarters. The roar of the fire engines outside has now become as the roar of presses in the bowels of a newspaper plant, or that of engines in an ocean liner. We strain our eyes toward the long table: we should like to know what those numberless sheafs of paper contain. Mr. Johnson seems to be distributing them to the chairmen of the various committees. When we look again at our own table it has been cleared. The white card with its inscription and its red border remain, and I pass it around for signatures. We shall frame this and hang it up somewhere. When *are* they going to start? . . .

Even while we wonder there comes a concerted rush and a roar as, everyone grabbling his chair, we stampede toward the long table. Now we are packed in close; there are row on row of chairs. Some of those who sat with us at the table are left behind. We look back and exchange smiles of sympathy. We are all near enough to see. So in our new position we look about for celebrities we could not see before. There is Mrs. James Weldon Johnson, a lady of stately carriage and queenly graces. Jessie Fauset, with pensive brown face and sad eyes, is sitting not far away. And there, someone really worth seeing, is the expatriate Mississippian, Maxwell Bodenheim, whose *Ninth Avenue*[28] dates even more than *Nigger Heaven*. Then there is Alain Locke, editor of *The New Negro*, and Eric Walrond of the *Tropic Death*[29] accomplishment, and Alice Dunbar Nelson, whose beautiful poems . . .

Charles S. Johnson is speaking. It is clear that his talk is extemporaneous, for he reiterates as he goes along . . . er . . . er . . . er . . ." He is wholly unconscious of it, and, becoming more and more interested, I, too, am unconscious of it. He has introduced John Dewey. Mr. Dewey introduces the chairmen of the various divisions of the contest. I cannot remember the order of the speakers, and I cannot hear very well what they are saying. It seems that I have been satiated with excitement through fulfilled hopes. Sights, sounds, the pressure of those nearest me, the pall of light descending from the lamps above—these are a crazy quilt of impressions in which I am completely wrapped. I know that Paul Green has just said something about knowing the colored people, mentioning his Pulitzer Prize play in passing; that John Macy, chairman of the awards dinner last year, has emphasized the point that color and hair texture have nothing to do with the producing of art; that there has just been some fine singing from the balcony over on the right and somewhat to the rear, close up under the ceiling; that a former Governor of Colorado named Sweet[30] has said something about how he kept segregation out of the State capital because the good people of Colorado could get along without it, and how, out of the goodness of his expansive heart, he approved the building of a colored Y. M. C. A. at the staggering cost of $85,000; that everything is over now except the shaking of hands, the uttering of platitudes to those who won and to those who did not, and the rushing for coats and hats.... Outside on 24th street some of the crowd stop to watch the fire engines. It is nearly 11 by the Metropolitan tower clock.[31] We move toward Fifth avenue and the Harlem buses.

"The Negro's Inhibitions"
American Mercury (FEBRUARY 1928): 159–64

Gordon's second article for the *American Mercury* stirred controversy among many Black readers. Here he asserts that some Blacks are so riddled with fear of being mocked by whites that they have "become sensitive, secretive and hypocritical, and full of inhibitions." They are especially bedeviled by a color complex in which light-complexioned individuals receive preferential treatment over darker ones. Some Black reviewers of the article did not see its humor or get Gordon's point that Blacks should ignore the gaze of whites and rid themselves of their anxiety-provoking "inhibitions." Instead, they thought he was writing to play into stereotypical white views of Blacks by revealing supposed racial secrets. An anonymous reviewer for the *Chicago Defender* (February 4, 1928), for example, calls the article "an unfortunate piece of literature—especially for the writer." However, in some ways, Gordon is not much different than Langston Hughes and other New Negroes who felt that Blacks should not be preoccupied with the views of whites.

The Negro's Inhibitions

Most of the Aframerican's native attributes—the inclinations, talents, tastes, preferences, prejudices and predilections that an All-wise Creator implanted in him—are fast oozing out of him. Standing in the glare of Caucasian ridicule, he has become sensitive, secretive and hypocritical, and full of inhibitions—in fact, a sad Freudian case. He is afraid to be seen eating a pork chop, or even a wing of fried chicken. The sight of a watermelon sets him to blushing. When he sings his spirituals, it is in an affected and "artistic" manner: the old innocent gusto is gone. When he needs a razor he sends a white agent to buy it for him. He is ashamed to be caught drinking gin. He forbids his wife to wear gaudy colors. He is ashamed of his kinky hair, and tries to get rid of its kinks. He spends many thousands annually on quack decoctions guaranteed to bleach his skin.

Let us come to cases. Boston nurtures an Aframerican organization called the Bachmars—*bach* from "bachelor" and *mar* from "married." Comprising the *crème de la crème* of the gayer section of the dark Four Hundred, the society's membership includes policemen, postmen, automobile mechanics, chauffeurs, postal clerks, caterers, and red caps from the South Station. They are all undoubtedly nice, respectable young men, even if they are somewhat light intellectually, and their social station is made securer through their ownership of Fords, Buicks, Essexes[32] and Chryslers, and their undoubted ease in hired "tuxes." Some of the swankiest events of the season among the Boston Negroes have their genesis in the Bachmar Club. Every New Year's Eve, for instance, it holds what it calls a "formal." On this occasion the keenest discrimination is displayed in the quality of those who are sent invitations. Except for the few wives of members, all the guests are unmarried girls.

Well, quality in these guests is determined by whether or not they are "light" or "dark" and have "good" or "bad" hair! Unless they can easily "pass," there is no place for them at a Bachmar breakdown. If, inadvertently, a genuine Negro girl were admitted to a New Year's party, she would feel as much at home as a Zulu expatriate among the igloos. It does not matter much about the fair one's position. She may not even have any worthy the name. What weighs heaviest, first and last, is that she is fair. At one such affair I once remarked on the conspicuous beauty of a girl who resembled an Italian madonna.

"She *is* pretty," conceded my dance companion, "but she's nobody."

"No? How's that? Why's she in here, then?"

"Why is she in here? Don't be funny! You know they'd never leave out a girl as light as that—so long as she wanted to come."

I learned that the girl was Polly Pepsin, "the notorious Polly Pepsin," as I sat out the next dance with my companion. Polly's mother was white, and her father would have been white, too, anywhere else than in the United States. Polly had left her husband to live with another man, and, with his cooperation, had contributed to the Hub's population. Later, she had left the other man (who incidentally, was a Bachmar), and was now with a third.

The women, true to the tradition, of their sex, scorned her, but the gallants literally danced attendance upon her. Not only was she early booked for every dance of the evening, but she could have extended her dancing to the middle of next Summer. Having learned the identity of the madonna, I begged a dance of a dark brown girl who had entered with a fairer friend, and had been completely ignored by her hosts. I learned that she was a senior at one of New England's best colleges, the holder of a Phi Beta Kappa key, and a charming lady. But mine was the only dance she got that evening!

The white man, no doubt, has placed an excessive valuation upon his white skin and "good" hair, but the middle-class Aframerican is generally willing to sacrifice his staunchest black friend to possess either. If he lacks these badges of superiority, he resorts to the quackeries of barber-shop and drug-store to obtain them. And if he chances to be one who personally does not care to possess any such trade marks of the redeemed, he will, nevertheless, demand them in the girl he woos and weds. Only the fairest find favor in the eyes of the typical Aframerican beau. The black girl—even the famed high brown—unless she has an established popularity through recognized personal attainments of family position, is a misfit and a pariah.

I overheard late Summer one fair-skinned young woman say to another, following the Bachmar's annual bungalow frolic: "It was simply grand! It was really superb! Why, every girl there could easily pass for white."

II

I cite the Bachmars as typical. In any social gathering in these colored United States the young man of genuinely African color and features must be thrice the superior of his lighter-skinned competitor, else he will lose. This is true whether the prize be a lady's hand or simply her smile. If the black boy with chinchilla hair drives a car, is fairly intelligent, and a fool with his money, he may perhaps capture even the fairest lady—but only provided a fair-skinned gallant, with similar qualifications, does not press his suit simultaneously. Unless, however, the black youth has these appurtenances, he is hopelessly done for. Even the blackest sister will accept him only as a final and desperate resort to escape spinsterhood and a lifetime of domestic drudgery. The fair one will have none of him.

But if the road of life for the black boy is rough with pebbles, the way of the black maid is strewn with boulders. The only way for a black girl in Aframerica to command acceptance of herself is for her to gain acceptance at the hands of influential whites. To the overwhelming majority of colored folk abroad in the land the white man is still the arbiter. He may be a simpleton and a fool, but that does not matter. Like their gentlemen friends, most cream-colored Aframerican ladies are intellectual featherweights. They know it and defend it. To be "light" is to be beautiful, and since pulchritude brings its own reward, why fritter away time in the study of the arts and sciences?

I know a splendid brown girl who will go through life with a cantankerous grievance against light-skinned ladies generally and one in particular. According to a story she often repeats, she met her fair friend downtown one day, but the fair one, being then in the company of a white girl, ignored her dusky playmate. Meeting again, later, the near-Nordic was amazed that her Negroid chum should feel aggrieved.

"Why," she demanded, when she understood, "should I offend my white friends just to please you?" Her tone bristled with indignation. "What can *you* give me if I lost them?" she asked.

"*Offend* your white friends? How?"

"Now you're playing dumb. You know how white people are. They don't like to be seen with anybody who is all the time speaking to a lot of Negroes."

I submit that there are many whites who are more liberal on this question than most Negroes are. There come instantly to mind numbers of them, men and women, who would sacrifice their friendships with their own people rather than be accused of such scurvy treatment of their black friends. But the Ku Klux psychology permeates the colored brother's and sister's systems. There are numerous recorded instances of Negroes being refused courtesies by their own kind because some Caucasian has withheld courtesies. There is nowhere a tyrant more oppressive than the Aframerican lackey at the door of a Jim-crow theatre, eating place, or apartment house. Such men often employ a huskier brand of force and a bitterer spleen, when ejecting their blood brothers, than any whites would exhibit. Vicariously, these peculiar folk, in such a situation, enjoy all the thrills of Klansmen at a Mississippi human barbeque.

Most Aframericans hesitate, lest they err, to accept their own men of accomplishment until the Nordic approves them and pronounces them sound. Take Charles Gilpin. For years he played almost unnoticed in Harlem. He was, to his indifferent audiences, only a fairly good ham actor, and a black one, at that. Then came his opportunity to play in "Abraham Lincoln," followed by the enthusiastic acclaim of the white metropolitan critics. Thereafter he was "The greatest actor the colored race has ever produced" to ninety-nine and forty-four percent, of these colored United States. They had forgotten for years that Romeo Dougherty of the *Amsterdam News*, and Lester Walton, of the New York *Age*, had been shouting that very thing, or, at least, words and music to that effect. After his "Emperor Jones" success Gilpin was fallen upon by some of the most noted of the Aframerican intelligentsia. Both cheeks were kissed, and he got the Spingarn medal[33] for gallantry in action, or something. At any rate, he was finally recognized by the very swells who had formerly ignored him, and this despite the fact that he was no whit better now than when he played at the Lafayette.[34]

The case of Roland Hayes is similar. For years, in Boston, he worked at odd jobs of elevator-running and window-washing, while schooling himself. On occasion he sang in a church to a few plebs like himself. Even when he was able finally to hire Symphony Hall, his audience was composed largely of his lowdown friends. These, with a few whites, believed in him, and it was their support that enabled him to go abroad. It was not until he returned from his European tour, his triumphs at Buckingham Palace and elsewhere having preceded him, that staid and cautious Aframerican patricians felt safe to applaud. These now, of course, are in the vanguard of the claquers.[35] "Oh, yes! Competent white critics say that Hayes is good!" Now they fall upon him, as they fell upon Gilpin.

It is eminently proper, always, to do what the best white folks do. If you do not, you seem different, and that is criminal. Your average Aframerican would rather be proper, and unhappy, than naturally himself, and in Paradise. If he is improper the white man will ridicule him. And ridicule hurts.

III

Clifton Wharton, secretary of the America legation at Monrovia, Liberia, resembles a Caucasian sufficiently to enable him to sleep above a Grand Goblin[36] in a Virginia Pullman. He lived for years in Boston. At the Boston University Law School he was popular with his classmates, and in colored society, with everybody. He was particularly attentive, everyone noticed, to a charming but decidedly Negroid maiden. "Of course, he's merely kidding her," the cream-colored feminine Bostonians told one another. "Boston's going to see a heart-broken brown baby when Clif drops her and takes one of us for his wife." But Clif married the brown lady. Together they went to Liberia, taking with them a brown baby, Clifton Wharton I.

Since that memorable marriage the fair sisters of Boston have been explaining how it happened. In the last analysis, every explanation comes back upon itself in the plaintive wail: "What *did* he see in her?" More than a little horror is felt over Wharton's having a brown son. The kid may even be black some day. "Poor innocent infant!" they moan.

This fear of producing black babies is an incubus[37] upon the hosts of fair-skinned Aframerican matrons. They run the risk, of course, when they occasionally wed black men, but they run still greater risks to forestall the tragedy. Consequently, the birthrate among them is amazingly low.

Lest the white man suspect them of studiedly segregating themselves, and thereupon conclude that they prefer segregation, Aframericans tacitly agree, among themselves, especially in New England, where race proscription is rare, to live in widely scattered areas. Often, the natural desire to live near relatives or friends is rigidly inhibited in order that no colony of blacks may grow up. The same tacit understanding obtains[38] in theatres and other public places. It is exceeding bad form for a Negro to gravitate toward another in such a place. If he dies opponents of the practice explain, it is likely that the next one who enters will do likewise, and the next; and the next. Then what have we? Why, a colony of blacks, conspicuous because black. And the management, naturally concluding that black folk desire the companionship of black folk, will itself graciously see to it thereafter that they sit together.

A brief outline of history is imperative at this point. In the dear dead days still mourned by ex-Confederates, neither love nor money could purchase edible delectables for the blacks. All the choicer viands belonged to the masters, and the serfs were generally discovered, following hog-killing, holding the bag. The bag, upon being opened, was found to contain such discarded offal as the head, the feet, the tail, and the entrails of the martyred swine. And since the white folk had grabbed the best (as they fondly thought), nothing remained for the blacks but to make the best of what they had.

Out of this and similar situations emerged certain notable Aframerican dishes. Always a good cook, from his remotest days on this continent, the Negro's culinary inventiveness under slavery made of hog's head and feet that appetizing delicacy known today as hog's head cheese.[39] Common pig's entrails became, through an application of gustatory acme and imagination, chitlings. Today, pigs' feet and chitlings are irrevocably intertwined with the American tradition about the colored man. They are admittedly *his* dishes. Pork chops, too, they say, are his, and fried chicken, but pork chops and chicken, in slavery days, seldom strayed so far from the Big-House as the slaves' quarters. Human nature, however, is the same the world over—and thus nothing would satisfy the chattels save pork chops and chicken. These victuals, then, were stolen. When the white folk discovered the depredations upon their smokehouses and henroosts they spread the news that the Afro was a hound for pork chop and barn yard fowl. The belief persists.

So much for a brief history of the case. Now for a few typical taboos and inhibitions. The average normal and rational person will readily concede the right of free-born Americans to eat whatever their money pays for. Nor is the average man given to criticism of his neighbors' tastes. He grants that it is only natural that a man at times may wish to treat his palate to a bowl of boiled chitlings soused in vinegar and plentifully sprinkled with salt and red pepper. Nevertheless, despite all these grants, the average Aframerican will shy stubbornly from the mere vicinity of a chitling or pigs' feet stand. If the place be located in the heart of Harlem, or in Boston's South End, where there is little likelihood of his being discovered by the leering gaze of the Nordic, he enters willingly enough, gorges himself, and is foolishly happy. But if the place be located on the fringe of the so-called Black Belt, he will avoid it by blocks.

So with the average Aframerican housewife. When she desires a chicken, she either orders it by telephone, or perhaps wheedles one of her fair-skinned neighbors to do the dirty work. Sometimes, if she knows the marketman to be a stolid, indifferent, unimaginative foreigner, she will not hesitate. But even so, she buries the fowl at the bottom of her shopping-bag and slinks home by way of dark alleys.

On such occasions as Aframericans entertain their Caucasian friends at dinner, the pale-faces will look in vain for any trace of chicken. The only time there is any is when the housewife is satisfied that the visitors discount the hoary tradition. Perhaps the guests' reaction at not seeing the fowl may be one of keen disappointment. But it is quite likely not to be so keen as the hostess' disappointment that an insurmountable inhibition forbade her serving chicken.

An amusing incident took place on Boston Common three or four years ago. Massachusetts had but recently granted the colored ex-service men a battalion in the National Guard and given them a colored major. He was a bright, clean-looking young chap, formerly a sergeant in the Twenty-fifth Infantry. Later, he was a captain of a machine-gun company over-seas, and later still (at the time of this incident) a student at Harvard. All the men were proud of him. Whenever they met him on the street, aboard the subway train, or in church, they snapped immediately to attention and saluted. The major liked it, and so did the boys. Then there was buck private named Fleetfoot. He worked at a downtown market—a deliveryman. Private Fleetfoot was one of the major's most loyal boosters. He was an idol-worshipper.

One day the major, in uniform and looking very handsome, was returning from a meeting of officers at the State House. He was bound for the subway at the other side of the Common. Coming toward the major, going to make a delivery on Beacon Hill, was Private Fleetfoot. He had two live chickens, one linked under each arm. Midway in the Common the major and the private met, and, in wild consternation, the commanding officer sensed the impending tragedy. Private Fleetfoot clicked his heels, snapped his right hand in salute, dropped the left smartly to his side, and . . .

For ten minutes thereafter private and major chased a hen. Perhaps had both men been white the incident would have been simply ludicrous, but, as it was . . . .

I have been told that the major has not eaten chicken since, even in the fastness of the armory kitchen.

IV

As most of us will agree, a woman is a woman, be she white or otherwise. And a woman, I am assured loves color in her clothes. This craving for color seems to be a common heritage. I think we are agreed, also, that it is responsible for the enhanced beauty of the passing scene: the red and green and blue hats, bobbing up and down on a Spring day, suggest a flower garden disturbed by a breeze. The point is that color in women's clothes not only is demanded, but is desirable.

Nevertheless, colored hats—and red, especially,—among Aframerican middle-class respectable women, are taboo. As a matter of fact, bright colors in any part of the clothing are shunned. The reason is that to wear colors may strengthen the white man's belief that the Negro is a childish race, and silly about flashy colors. As a consequence, the average gathering of dark ladies is a most solemnly drab and funereal affair. Only the fairer of the sex dare defy the taboo and wear what pleases their feminine fancies. The inhibition, I daresay, sprang from the tradition that Africans were often captured for the slave trader's exhibiting bright red cloth to the tribal chiefs.

Negro newspapers, books by and about Negroes, with this fact clearly evident on the covers, and Negro magazines are seldom read by respectable colored folk on street cars, or elsewhere in public. To read them may cause the whites to think the readers strange and different, and lead to ridicule. But to read the most slimy tabloid sheet is permissible, of course. Among the middle-class it is better to be a moron, like your white neighbor, than an intelligent, curiously minded individuality. It is the boast of some of the country's most socially prominent Aframerican ladies that they never read Negro newspapers. "I'd be mortified to death if I were seen reading one," they explain. As a result, an amazingly large number are wholly uninformed, save by stray bits gleaned from the white press, about themselves. In their zeal to belong, they lose the common touch.

Scores of Aframerican girls from time to time have lamented the taboo placed upon them by Negro business and professional men. The cry arises continually that a colored girl of intelligence and skill is without honor among her own kind. This charge is often true. I personally know of several offices in which white girls serve Negro professional men. To the colored girl who has spent years training for such work the situation is one of heartburning. Some of these girls are now finding employment in white offices, but the number is small. A Negro girl must possess extraordinary recommendations to edge out a Caucasian cousin seeking the same job.

The colored business and professional men retort to the charge of discrimination by a counter charge of incompetency. But this is not an incompetency involving inability to perform the tasks given; it is one involving social and business ethics. For the colored stenographer, being commonly high in the ranks of Aframerican society, is said to be prone to discuss an attorney's or a physician's confidential affairs with the persons most concerned. Coming all from the same social level, employée and employer outside office hours meet as common friends. This sort of contact is unavoidable, but that fact makes it none the less bad for office discipline. To maintain discipline, the Aframerican man of affairs employs girls whom he is not likely to see outside the office.

It is only among the plebs, on the one hand, and the intellectually emancipated, on the other, that the epithets "darkey," "coon," "nigger," and "blackamoor" get tolerated. Throughout the length and breadth of middle-class colored America every one of these words is still a signal for fisticuffs, or worse. This is especially true if the offender be Caucasian. Unless he be supported front, rear and flanks by his gang, he is fortunate to escape with a whole skin.

But to the lowdown Negro these are but play words. He bandies them among his friends, nor thinks aught of it. He is the same indifferent but happy and uninhabited soul who eats his pork-chop sandwich on the trolley car or in the park, poses for the World-Wide photographer with his shiny black face buried in a watermelon, and drapes the sable frames of his women in all the glorious colors of the spectrum. He is the exception, along with a few intellectuals, to all that has been said. Thus Charles S. Johnson, editor of *Opportunity*, comments upon the matter:

> There is much sensitiveness to the word "nigger" as a term of contempt, a sensitiveness varying in intensity according to geography and according to degrees of sophistication. It is, perhaps, weakest

in the most emancipated Negro circles of the East, and, at the same time, paradoxically enough, among the least emancipated Negroes of the South. It is strong, generally, throughout the West . . . . The cause of resentment is obvious, of course. But it seems that an unnecessary burden is assumed by the Negroes whose tastes and education remove them from the classes in question, *i.e.* mammy and darkey. It is needless sensitiveness that denies that they are, or, rather, were, Negro "mammies." They were contentedly loyal servants and midwives in the households of white Southerners of the slavery regime, and filled a definite position in the household. Only a few remain, and panicky protests invite suspicion. . . . Because "nigger" is a corruption intended most commonly as an expression of contempt, it is effective only when it makes Negroes *feel* inferior. The truly emancipated ones, who are certain of their status, refuse to feel a sting in the word.

V

I should be interested to know how fares Mr. Johnson's personal inhibition against the razor and the watermelon. The black man's predilection for the razor as a social appurtenance has been widely publicized. Probably more jokes, witty and inane, center about the razor than about anything else, unless it be the watermelon and crap shooting. Just as the white man's levity irritated the black man's sensitiveness about his kinky hair and gay colors, it also caused a stern taboo to be placed upon the old-fashioned razor. A colored gentleman of pride and self-respect nowadays avoids the old-time razor as scorched infants are supposed to avoid fires. Granted that he may be more adept at shaving himself with the old tool, granted that he has an abiding dislike of new-fangled notions, and granted that it is a great deal more expensive, yet he will refrain from purchasing any except a safety razor. To buy the other kind is likely to cause the dealer to speculate whether the instrument is wanted for toilet or social use.

The razor myth comes from the time when that tool was the black man's only offensive and defensive weapon. It grew in popularity for a number of reasons. It could easily be concealed on the person. It was more easily procurable than a firearm. It did rather a messy job, but an effective one. And it made no noise. But now it is taboo.

The watermelon question has developed into a more momentous one. Liberal, intellectually-emancipated editorial writers, poets, and publicists of Aframerica pass by the succulent, appetizing fruit, lest the white man's ribald conviction be substantiated. It does not matter that the Caucasian himself buries his pale face to the Adam's apple in the watery rind; the colored brother, if he eats it at all, must do so in the privacy of his home, or stand shamed before his race.

When an Aframerican housewife's craving for a watermelon compels her to yield, she is quite likely to order the fruit from a black tradesman, by telephone, insisting that it be concealed in a black bag, and delivered on a moonless night by a black delivery boy. Only by following such precautions is she assured both of defying her stubborn inhibitions and satisfying a craving that at times borders upon mania.

Perhaps middle-class Aframericans would release these unnatural inhibitions against watermelon and chicken if more of them had the common sense and the statistical turn of mind of a Baltimore *Afro-American* editorial writer. He observes sagely:

> The only difference we see between white and colored folk on the fowl and watermelon question is that these comestibles form a part of the Sunday menu for colored folk, while they are the everyday dish for the whites.
>
> United States government reports who $561,000,000 worth of poultry raised in the United States last year. July 1 there were 50,059,000 pounds of frozen poultry in cold storage.
>
> Last year, the Southern States shipped 50,000,000 watermelons. The Agricultural Department estimates that 199,360 acres of watermelons are under cultivation for commercial purposes.
>
> These figures indicate that these two products annually cost the people of the United States nearly three quarters of a billion dollars, which is just about one-third of the amount earned by all the colored people in the United States.

Thus, one by one, at the conscious and unconscious behest of the white man, the old traditions hooked up with the colored man's peculiar appetites are booted on to the bunk heap. His natural human inclinations, talents, tastes, preferences, prejudices and predilections, along with the bunk, are ground under the flat foot of Aframerican inhibition. Chicken, watermelon, spirituals, chitlings, pigs' feet, bright colors, black faces, kinky hair, friendly congregating, the old-fashioned razor, pork chops,—all are now in the Index Expurgatorius of Aframerica. The Caucasian may snigger at all this as a new joke, but the "better class" colored folk will not. 'Tis undignified to laugh, you know; the white man may think you boisterous!

"A Word in Closing"
Saturday Evening Quill (JUNE 1928): 72

Once ensconced in Boston, Gordon soon immersed himself in its fledgling cultural movement, organizing the Saturday Evening Quill Club in 1925; the club would often assemble at Gordon's home in Cambridge, and he edited annual anthologies of the members' work in 1928, 1929, 1930. The purpose of the journal was "originally conceived as an experiment, . . . containing essays, articles, poems, short stories, and plays by Negro writers, and drawings by Negro artists, [all] . . . members of the Club for distribution among themselves and a few interested friends."[40] Gordon also said that the writers did not intend to start "a revolution." In fact, the journal was fairly conservative both in its politics and in its literary style, unlike more radical literary journals such as Wallace Thurman's *Fire!*. Gordon also stressed an American tone. As editor, and in his own writings, there was no return to Africa, either literally as Marcus Garvey proposed it or culturally like those such as Alain Locke advocated. Instead, Gordon "considered the Afro-American to be as American as apple pie. . . . Gordon realized that black writers had some rich sources unavailable to whites, but he asserted that they must use the 'same method' and 'the same medium,' or language available to white authors.'"[41]

A Word in Closing
On Uncritical Criticism

From time to time colored American writers charge that their work is appraised by white critics not as the product of Americans, but as that of negroes—as that of alien blacks who know little of the fundamentally American things. This is a serious charge, and I regret that investigation shows it to be generally true. Investigation reveals that most white critics, upon learning that a writer is colored, almost unconsciously assume an attitude of tolerant, condescension; an attitude suggesting, "Well, let's see what *this Negro* has done," or "This isn't so bad for a darkey," or "Why don't these Negro writers be original, instead of aping the whites?"

Now, I can not comprehend how so stupid a fellow got his job as a critic. It is undeniably, stupidity in a person which prevents his realizing that so-called Negroes do not write *as such* (and how *should* a Negro write?), but as Americans of African antecedent; that at times the fact of African descent *may* influence what they write, and at other times may not. There is no reason under heaven why an Aframerican, whose ancestors came here more than three centuries ago, should be swayed by jungle influences; yet, many white critics, some of them decent and kindly, too, accept that fantastic fiction as fact. For example, there was the editorial writer of the New York *Herald-Tribune*, who, commenting on the prize-contest awards dinner given by *Opportunity: A Journal of Negro Life* in 1925, said:

> The young people ... were not trying to, imitate the white man nor repeating the white story-teller's dreary stencils of the "darkey." They were expressing their own feeling, frankly and unabashed even if it took them back to the jungle. When rain threshes on the roofs of their Harlem flats, they do not try to imagine what Wordsworth would have said about it. They stuff their fingers in their ears to shut out the sudden maddening memory of the sound of rain on banana leaves, of dances in the moonlight, and the tom-tom throbbing through the breathless tropical night!

We may pass over that nonsense about people listening to the sound of rain on an apartment-house roof and *remembering*(!) jungle sounds that neither they, nor their parents, nor their grandparents, have ever actually heard, but we may not *ignore* that writer's good intention. And if critics who are impartially inclined toward colored writers utter such rot, what shall we expect of a throw-back such as, say, this superb critic of American life, Roark Bradford?[42]

Such piffle as that is considered in some quarters as adequate criticism of modern Negro writers. On the contrary, it is neither adequate nor criticism. It is, however, fully as worthy of consideration as the statement that colored writers "imitate" the white.

This statement indicates a peculiar attitude of mind. It is an attitude which expects every so called racial group in America, save the Negro writer, to be influenced by the American environment. The colored artist is trained in the same schools that train the white artist, and at the hands of the same instructors. He gets the same stereotyped formulas of technique and style. He stands to the rendering of the Star Spangled Banner, and even, at times, tries to sing it. He salutes the flag throughout the farthest reaches of the land; eats baked beans and brown bread on Saturday night in Boston, sneers, in New York, at the "provinces"; falls in line to shake the President's hand at New Year's, in the District of Columbia; laughs at the comic strip; and he worships wealth and caste in true American fashion; yet, when he comes to write of the experiences which beat his life into conformity with his environment, he is called imitative of the white man and cautioned to "remember" Africa!

It is true that there is available to colored writers much material that is unavailable to most white writers. But to expect colored writers to transmute this material into a form the like of which has never been seen, is to expect the impossible. It *will* never be done because it *can* never be done. The American colored writer must express himself by the same method and through the same medium as the white, and for the reason that he has no other method and medium. And it is thoughtless, and childish of critics to expect him to act and speak differently. There is not one earthly reason why he should, but there is one excellent reason why he should not: his heritage, with all the accumulations appertaining thereto, is wholly American.

There is no adequate standard to apply to the Negro writer save the standard that is applied to other American writers.

Excerpt "Christianity and the Negro"
The Lantern (MARCH 1929): 14–18

Gordon published this piece in the short-lived Boston-based periodical *The Lantern*, which focused "upon facism [*sic*] and other dark disorders of the present day" (editorial statement). The antireligious statements expressed in the article provide an early example of Gordon's rejection of more mainstream views of religion and his shift toward communism. Other early antireligious views are expressed in poems, fiction, and essays published in the *Quill*.[43] In the *Lantern* essay, Gordon states that "for three centuries Christianity has been a plague upon the Negro in America." Christianity's teachings have left Blacks morally, politically, and financially bankrupt, teaching them not self-reliance, but to trust in "a vaporous and unsubstantial god." This tone would be consistent throughout all his later writings. Gordon maintains that Christianity does not prepare Blacks for "the dirty, rough work of a matter-of-fact world." However, he maintains that Blacks do need some doctrine to lead them if it is not Christianity, but it needs to be more assertive and less passive. Although he is not yet ready to posit communism as that alternative, he was well on his way to such a belief.

Christianity and the Negro

I

For three centuries Christianity has been a plague upon the Negro in America. During slavery, its enervating influence made him the patient, long-suffering creature typified in *Uncle Tom*. It taught him humility and meekness, it is true, but these negative virtues became his positive vices. For why should a serf desire more humility and meekness than are already imposed by kick and cuff? It implanted in him moral and physical cowardice. As an emasculator of his manhood, it was as potent as slavery itself. The American Indian is frequently referred to as the black man's superior because the red man died rather than yield to bondage. Real reason for the contrast lay in the Indian's refusal to be Christianized. So long as he was a pagan he was free. If he could have been subdued long enough to be inoculated with the Christian virus, he would have turned *his* other cheek.

Instead of teaching the Negro reliance upon self, Christianity taught absolute reliance upon a vaporous and unsubstantial god. He was advised to place his trust in some complex and mysterious triumvirate—a sort of spiritual Three Musketeers. All he had to do when he needed help was to pray to *one* or all of this Trinity, and *maybe* one of them would dash to the rescue.

II

If Christianity was slavery's ally in devitalizing blacks of the past, then Christianity is ally of the Negro church in holding them in moral, intellectual, spiritual, and economic thrall today.

Devout black women wear their knuckles out washing "the white folks' clo's"; they deprive themselves and their children not only of comforts but of necessities; and for what? In order to feed this Moloch[44] they call Christianity.

In the meantime the pastors egg them on. A goodly portion of each service is devoted to emphasizing the necessity of more lavish giving. They are merciless in their demands, declining nothing. "I want you people to send me to that ministerial conference in Washington," the Rev. Mr. Pompous will announce. Posing beside the bible stand, he allows his eyes to roam over the comely sisters nearest him. They flush and blush—and give their last nickle [*sic*].

• • •

It is my belief that in those findings too much virtue is granted the Negro church. True, it has supported schools and so-called colleges, and its social activity has been noticeable. But the educational program of the Negro church, as of necessity it must be of any church, is permeated with religiousness. Inherent in it is the fault to be found in all Christian institutions: insufficient emphasis upon methods of accomplishing the dirty, rough work of a matter-of-fact world.

Graduates of sectarian colleges are usually well read in holy literature. They face the world fit only for priestcraft or Y. M. C. A. secretaryship. And while each is meat for him who prefers it, everybody can not be a preacher or a Y secretary. Somebody must *work*. Somebody must build homes for the swelling ranks of smelly hordes from Dixie. Somebody must help add to the available food and fuel and clothing supply. Preacher[s] and Y. M. C. A. secretaries are seldom interested beyond their personal wants. They are more concerned about the quality of the gold cobblestones in Elysian boulevards. For that reason, if for no other, I should dispar[a]ge the value of educational work done by Negro churches.

Nor can I see any "strength" in the church's function as "a forum of discussion." Now and then church buildings are opened to such forums, but the users pay dearly for the privilege. The church itself stands apart and aloof. Such questions as those involving housing, better jobs, higher salaries, cleaner streets, neater front yards, and more sanitary back yards, are outside its province. Why should such discussions be held in Church? *This* is the house of God! And so it remains.

Exceptions always come to mind, and they are due acknowledgment. For example, the Brotherhood of Sleeping Car Porters has received cheering support from rostrum and pew. Many ministers have refused to accept one cent for the use of their churches for rallies. That is splendid. It is commendable. The ministers themselves admit that it exemplifies the Christ-like spirit. Perhaps it does. I do not know that. However, I do know this: those churches which are most friendly and in whom is most evident the spirit of the Lowly One, confess that their congregations number many Pullman porters. Sometimes the deacon answers to the name of "George."[45] Unless the flock is very lavish, the shepherd himself may be a porter. The point is that when Negro churches become forums of discussion, there are other reasons than that they desire to promote social betterment.

* * *

III

"That is all destructive criticism," someone objects. "If you take away the Negro's religion and the Negro's God and the Negro's church, what do you leave in their stead?"

I wish this criticism were far more destructive than it actually is. Nor have I ever been able to reconcile myself to the view that another gewgaw[46] must be given in exchange for a toy taken away. However, at the risk of being considered facetious (although I have never been more serious), I insist that the American Negro needs not only a new religion, i.e. a religion designed for his peculiar status, but a new, a wholly different, conception of God. It is unfortunate that any new religion must center about a god, but there is no avoiding a deity in the development of any people. If there be no god, the people will create one. Witness the cases of Gautama and Confucius. Neither of these sages visioned in his religion any place for a god. But what happened? Gautama, dead, because Buddha, of whom millions of images are worshipped. Confucius became the god of the Confucianists. Having no desire to be deified, I propose a god around which to build this Afro-American religion.

I propose such a being as guided the Hebrews' destinies in Moses's day. The God of modern Christians, if we accept the word of His chief earthly spokesman, Dr. S. Parkes Cadman,[47] is no wise the god of Moses. Jehovah was a jealous god. He occasionally got angry. He was vengeful and cruel, but only to the enemies of the Hebrews. He was a god of battle. Modern theology has denuded him of his magnificent original attributes. He is today as restricted by inhibitions as the average middle-class Negro society matron. He no longer waxes angry. He derives no pleasure from hurling thunder-bolts of vengeance. Long since, he ceased being amused at seeing sinners barbecued in hell. He is merciful, tender, forgiving—effete.

Aframericans need no conception of such [a] doddering, faltering, apologetic god. What they need is the conception as suggested in the earliest scribblings of the Hebrews: a smoking, flame-belching fire-eating, vengeful, angry, jealous, spiteful, war-like god. The Negro's situation, especially in Dixie, closely enough approximates that of the early Hebrews' to make such a champion desirable. Perhaps, following such a god, the water in the Negro's veins might metamorphose into red blood and militancy replace submissiveness. If Negroes of the Southland felt impelled by religion to live and die like men, fewer would have to die. The god of this new religion, therefore, would enjoin them to "Smite those that smite you."

Of course such militancy would result in attempts to annihilate the blacks. But that would not matter. Such attempts would be made only a few times. Besides, those who died would be religious martyrs, and religious martyrs invariably become saints. Thus, there would be something to aspire to. And after a few murderous retaliations on their chronic oppressor, the blacks would no longer be molested. Respect for them would replace hatred of them. Before long it would be a commonplace to see descendants of Uncle Tom sipping mint juleps with ex-confederate generals.

There remain countless details yet to be considered, and perhaps at some future time we may discuss them. For the present I am content to leave with the reader (1) my views on the bankruptcy of Christianity as a religion for the Negro, (2) evidence of the incompetency of the Negro preacher and the failure of the Negro church, and (3) a suggestion for a change. As to *how* the change might best me made—that would call for another discussion far more exhaustive than the present one. If the Negro's conception of God is changed, his religion, too, as a matter of course, will undergo a change; a change so subtle yet drastic as to give it the aspects of a New Religion.

"The Negro Grows Up"
Plain Talk (JULY 1929): 81–86

Plain Talk was a journal edited by Geoffrey Dell Eaton, a newspaperman and author of the now obscure novel *Backfurrow* (1925). In this essay, Gordon takes a more favorable view of Black writers than he did in "Negro Fictionists in America," written only three months earlier. Whereas in the former essay he takes the authors to task for being too sensitive to the views of whites, here he feels the writers are unafraid to present "unbiased and unflattering criticism of [Blacks]." The writer Gordon presents as initiating this change is Jean Toomer, author of *Cane* (1923). Toomer was unafraid to present Blacks truthfully, with their flaws, which was upsetting to many intellectuals. Others such as Wallace Thurman and Langston Hughes followed Toomer's lead. Gordon is also pleased that Blacks have begun to criticize "Christianity, the Negro church and the Nego Preacher," heretofore untouchable paragons. He is pleased to see that many Black leaders no longer see all whites as the enemy but acknowledge some as friends. Surprisingly, Gordon praises organizations such as the National Association for the Advancement of Colored People and the National Urban League, two groups he would soon criticize as being too conservative in their treatment of African American issues.

The Negro Grows Up

Whereas the American Negro used to whimper when hurt, he now sets his jaws. In those circumstances in which he once was pathetically childish he now is sophisticated and cynical. He used to smart under the mildest criticism, but now he critically dissects himself. In short, the American Negro has come of age.

There are involved at least six factors that tend to prove the truth of my assertion. The first is that the American Negro has become critical of himself and thereby tolerant of outside criticism. Second, he is less credulous of and also somewhat cynical toward what his preachers tell him about heaven and hell. Third, he has fewer inhibitions than formerly. Fourth, he is beginning to chafe under the patronage of paternalistic whites and to show evidence of desiring to propel his own craft. Fifth, he has begun a serious but enthusiastic study of Negro history. And, sixth, he is less distrustful of and bears less prejudice toward whites than was once the case. The Negro's unbiased and unflattering criticism of himself had its genesis in Jean Toomer. When this brilliant young Negro wrote *Cane* he shocked a great many staid and respectable colored folk. So impersonally objective yet so intimately understanding was it that scores of readers at first suspected its author of being a southern cracker.[48] Never before had any American Negro dared tell so much about his folk.

His readers were uncomfortably sensitive. Here was a Negro writer exposing his race's most shameful weaknesses to the supercilious stare of the whites. He talked of black prostitutes and white men, and of white prostitutes and black men. While everybody admitted that what he said was true, they insisted that since nobody had discussed it before there seemed no reason for discussing it now. The subject was absolutely taboo.

The great mass of colored folk could not appreciate Toomer. The great mass still can not appreciate him. As a matter of fact, the great mass of colored folk can not now bear to be criticized, despite the continuous stream of criticism that is released upon them by their more intelligent leaders. Perhaps I should add here that it is not to the masses I refer in the discussion of this subject. It is, indeed, to the increasing number of educated colored folk, especially the intellectuals. The masses had been taught for years that pride of race consisted primarily in maintaining silence regarding their human weaknesses. For some unexplainable reason they looked upon human frailty as Negro frailty, and the black man who exposed these frailties was considered a traitor. Thus, they came to suffer with chronic nicenastiness and were perpetually miserable.

Rudolph Fisher followed Toomer. Among other things he exposed the Harlem "rent party."[49] I have seen many a nice Boston colored girl blush with humiliation at the thought that whites would learn the dreadful truth that some colored folk gave "rent parties." One in particular, I recall, lost her appetite when, reading *The Promised Land*[50] while she ate, she came across the detailed description of such a party. At the same time other young Negro writers were bandying such racial phrases as "high yaller," "high brown," "chocolate brown" and "stovepipe black."[51]

Once the white man learned of these intimate pet designations, we were told, he would possess a most vital weapon of ridicule. But that was not all. These same writers told shamelessly how black boys and girls, under the natural urge of protective coloration in order to prevent their extinction, bleached their skin and straightened their hair. "What will the white people think?" wailed the staid and respectable. "Why give them all our most precious secrets? Aren't we supposed to keep any of our weaknesses to ourselves?"

They did not remember of course while protesting that whites in increasing numbers already knew more about these secrets than many colored folk knew. Many of the Negroes did not know even that it was the whites who manufactured, and advertised for sale, devices and decoctions for untangling kinky hair, bleaching dark skin, thinning thick lips and elevating flat noses, and that, therefore, black folk were not actually *giving* white folk "race" secrets. So the staid and respectable colored folk were self-conscious and terribly mortified.

Later writers, among them Wallace Thurman and Langston Hughes, turned other tricks out of the black bag. Thurman discussed the Harlemite's home life, his social life and his church. Hughes in an article in *The Nation* ridiculed the "nice" people of Washington because they professed disgust of Toomer.[52] In other places Hughes told of the American Negro's preferences in food, music, and entertainment, and dilated in his "blues" upon the dark brother's merits as a lover. Harlem was taken up, turned inside out, and shaken vigorously. The denizens thereof were studied like strange microscopic cultures. Nothing was omitted in the reports resulting from this study. Thus, a mysterious unknown black group came to be best-known of all the folk groups among us. Harlem, after all, was an excellent specimen.

Presently there came *Opportunity: Journal of Negro Life*, and *The Crisis: Record of the Darker Races*, offering prizes for poems, short stories, plays, essays and sketches about colored folk. There followed, naturally, more delving, scalpel-wielding, and probing; so that finally all who read at all knew the American Negro precisely for what he was. He no longer harbored dark secrets, from either the Caucasian or himself. At last the literate whites knew almost as much about the blacks as the literate and illiterate blacks knew about the whites— which was a great deal. For it is significant that Negro readers of the daily press have been for years better-informed of the Caucasians' secrets than the Caucasians have been about the Negroes. All the whites needed to do, even before colored folk began to expose themselves, was to peruse the Negro press.

This literary movement,[53] I say, was the beginning of the colored man's criticism of himself. When the first shock of the exposé diminished, Negro newspapers became bolder in the same direction. They criticized black folk for errors that previously had been condoned or overlooked. The Negro press had existed until now solely to propagandize the whites in the blacks' favor. Its news generally reflected to the discredit of the whites and to the credit of the colored folk. The black man was represented as a godly, long-suffering martyr. He had no fault, no blemish, no weakness—at least none that the white man was supposed to know about. Only the whites were vile.

This biased attitude was defended as necessary to combat the white man's cruelty and prejudice. It was said to foster race pride in colored folk. This it did, too, to an extent, but it also fostered silly prejudices.

Such was the old Negro press.

The colored writers already referred to with some not yet mentioned, caused the change. It was not long, following the appearance of these writers, until editorials in the Negro press catechized black folk on their sins. Negro "leaders" were stood up in the glare of the press spotlight and scrutinized until they squirmed. Colored feature, editorial and special writers, men like J. A. Rogers,[54] George S. Schuyler, A. Philip Randolph, Chandler Owen, and Theophilus Lewis[55] of the *Messenger*; William Kelley and Edgar M. Grey of the *Amsterdam News*; and W. P. Dabney,[56] editor of the Cincinnati *Union*, were characteristic of the newer order. Cold, passionless, objective in their point of view, impartial in their criticism of American life, these excellent writers discussed black men and white men alike. Very soon all who read at all were accustomed to the method. They no longer sweated in embarrassment when white writers mentioned unpleasant facts, for black writers had already mentioned them. And now we approach a situation in which facts cease altogether to be unpleasant.

But the Negro's self-criticism has not ended with his person. It has included Christianity, the Negro church and the Negro preacher. It is only recently that the American Negro church and its minister have been held less than sacrosanct. Hitherto both have been hedged about by a picket fence of taboos. The colored minister, like a few colored editors, has exercised unlimited license to attack whom he would, but he himself has been inviolate. Well, that day has passed. There is now seldom a gathering of intelligent colored folk in which soon or later there is not wholesome and exhaustive discussion of religion, church and ministry. The newspapers themselves are often scornful in their attitude toward brothers of the cloth and are generous with space in publishing their falls from grace They criticize the parson's illiteracy, his ignorance of human impulses, his inefficiency as a leader, his ineptitude as a businessman, and his monkeyshines in the pulpit. On the other hand, those preachers who deserve credit are not overlooked.

But if the newspapers are generous with criticism, the youth of the race are prodigal. Especially is this true of college youth, who go beyond questioning the church and its ministry.

They let it be known that they accept nothing without first subjecting it to close and careful scrutiny. It must meet their standard, which is to say the standard of modern civilization.

The most conspicuous movement is the middle-class Negro's disposition to lay aside color prejudices within the race. Criticism of this inhibition by his own writers has helped the black man to see the folly of it. Thus, its almost total collapse has been brought about by the colored Americans themselves. There are black men and women in the group who are a living refutation of the fiction that only mixed bloods are worthy. And although this prejudice is not totally dissipated, there are signs of its approaching dissipation.

One of the most significant of the phases indicating full growth is the black man's desire to help himself. "Not alms but opportunity!"[57] he cries, and he means it. College young men and women of colored America are more bitter today because of lack of opportunity than for any other reason. "Only give me a chance to show what I can do," they cry, "and you won't have to speculate whether to retain my service; you will retain it, if you like good work."

It was not many years ago that the Negro "leader" trembled with dread lest he actually be called upon to lead. Take Howard University, for instance. Founded more than a half-century ago, it was not until the last year or so past that Negroes favored a black president. Why?

"Really, the black man isn't yet ready to head an institution like Howard."

"Why not?"

"Well, because he couldn't command the respect of the student body. You see, the students have been used to seeing a white man over them, and we fear that the change might work to the detriment of discipline. Besides, a white man has more influence with Congress and with philanthropists. Howard needs money; how could a Negro, lacking influence, get it?"

Despite these objections, the younger element of the Howard alumni won. And although the man to whom they gave the presidency is a clergyman, with the colored clergyman's characteristic weaknesses in his position, he is far superior to the lot of white ministers who formerly headed the institution.[58] Certainly, he has vindicated those who insisted that he could not be worse than former white heads of Howard University.

The Kansas City *Call* published recently an excellent editorial titled "Still Carrying the Tin Cup." It candidly deplored the average Negro's willingness to accept gratuities from white men and women for Negro institutions, causes and enterprises, while the black folk themselves spent recklessly for their own pleasure. The editorial said in part:

> Of course, 60 years is a short time in which to rid ourselves of the tin-cup habit, but, even so, some little progress has been made, and the begging should decrease in proportion to the progress. By no means is the race self-sustaining, nor is it wealthy, but stages of independence have been reached and we should now be looking about our business.

As evidence that this sort of scolding is becoming general I might cite the fact that the *Call*'s editorial was republished generally throughout the Negro press. A similar attitude is illustrated by the National Association for the Advancement of Colored People and the National Urban League. These excellent organizations have both white and colored officials and members, but the masses of the membership are Negroes. And the masses of the membership support these organizations with their own hard-earned money.

The National Negro Business League, with headquarters at Tuskegee Institute, wages a continuous campaign among colored folk to support their own enterprises rather than those of the whites. While, taken by and large, this doctrine is not wholly sound, yet it is giving the black folk keener appreciation of their own efforts.

Edgar P. Benjamin is a colored lawyer of Boston. Not long since he gave his people $10,000 toward establishing Resthaven, a home for aged men and women of both races. A year or so ago, Mrs. Aaron

Malone, head of Poro College,[59] a business enterprise in St. Louis, gave $20,000 to Howard University. Casper Holstein[60] of New York was the colored man who made possible the literary contests that have been held by *Opportunity: Journal of Negro Life*. The *Crisis* contests also have been financed chiefly by Negro business men.

These contributions have all been comparatively small but have indicated nevertheless the colored man's determination to help himself.

What is perhaps the most significant of these indications of adulthood is the Negro's increasing pride in his own history. Led by Dr. Carter G. Woodson, director of the Association for the Study of Negro Life and History, of Washington, DC, Negro newspapers, magazines, fraternal bodies, sororities, and women's clubs annually hold "Negro History Week." During this period the newspapers and magazines publish little-known facts about great men of the race, and organizations hold essay contests and public symposiums, inviting noted Negroes to address them.

Dr. Woodson's association has done more than any other body to make Negro history popular. It has been instrumental in getting authentic histories of Negro achievement into high schools and colleges, while lately it has begun a "Home Study Department," which gives colored folk (or any other persons) a correspondence course in Negro history. The instruction staff, all Negroes, includes some of the best-educated men in the country.

Some of the country's best libraries now keep files of Negro newspapers and magazines. In these publications is set down the very essence of the Negro's pride in himself. It is unmistakably evident even to the most casual reader. And the very consciousness of the fact that white patrons of college and public libraries read his history strengthens the black man's self-esteem. However, long before the white man began curiously to delve into the black man's printed records of himself the Negro was lifting his chest with pride.

Finally—incontrovertible evidence of approaching maturity—the colored American is casting out fear and distrust of the white American. Among the masses of colored folk even today, "I ain't got no use for no white man" is a common-place expression. Why?

Because "you can't trust none of them"; because "all white folks are mean, ornery, hypocritical, and unjust."

The civilized reader will readily comprehend the reason for this attitude. It is not necessary to remind him that the "meanness," "oneryness" [*sic*], hypocrisy and injustice long practised against blacks by large numbers of whites are the causes. But the civilized minority of Negroes, in this instance as in others, is leading the masses of blacks out of the morass. Men like W. P. Dabney and George S. Schuyler are too intelligent to accept the white man as more than an ordinary human being like themselves. On the other hand, they are wearied of the asinine chatter about the "untrustworthiness" of all whites.

"We condemn this wholesale damning of the masses for the faults of the few," Mr. Dabney declares editorially in his newspaper, the *Union*. "We see the injustice of a similar attitude on the part of many white people toward us . . . We gain nothing by being unjust simply because we are, and have been, victims of injustice."

Mr. Dabney further points out that "among the teeming millions of this country there are many of the opposite race who are friendly toward us." He adds: "Were this not so, America would be a hell."

"Dabney is perfectly right," Schuyler applauds, and goes on:

> For some years it has been apparent to me the Aframericans whoop entirely too much about black this and black that, while singing a hymn of hate against all people, who happen to be of the group that is conveniently termed white. Some of our editors particularly are offenders in this direction. Take the words Negro and black out of the conversations and writings of some of our folks and substitute the words white and Caucasian, and their expressions would sound like the bellowing from some member of the Ku Klux Klan . . . In our endeavor to get away from the sickening attitude of the Uncle-Tom Negro, who slavishly eulogizes and trusts white people indiscriminately, some of us are going to the other extreme.

But white faces, most colored folk have long believed, are masks behind which lurk cruelty, hatred, and deceit. They forget that white men freed them, helped them to educate themselves, passed laws to protect their political rights, an even today give lavishly of their wealth to Negro needs. Of course this does not include *all* whites, but it includes a sufficiently large number to show men like Dabney and Schuyler that indiscriminate hurling of bricks into the ranks of the whites is certain eventually to strike and injure friends.

Yes, the American Negro has just about grown up. Naturally, he will continue to develop for some time, for he has not yet reached full growth. We are proud, however, to present him in all the promise of his fresh young manhood: a vigorous, stalwart, broad-shouldered, carefree and somewhat arrogant youth, yet one who soberly realizes the significance of a man's responsibilities.

Excerpt "Negro Society"
Scribner's Magazine (AUGUST 1930): 134–42

From its inception in 1887 to its demise in 1939, *Scribner's Magazine* was a highly popular and prestigious publication with a roster of well-known contributors such as Edith Wharton, Ernest Hemingway, and Theodore Roosevelt. As in "The Negro's Inhibitions," in this article Gordon is writing sarcastically about Black behavior for a largely white audience, often infuriating race leaders.[61] Gordon's displeasure with distinctions between classes based largely on wealth and color is evident. The pretentiousness and snobbery that go along with these distinctions is especially evident in Washington, DC, but as Gordon states, "as goes Washington so goes the rest of it." While one might wonder how Gordon could shift from writing sarcastic articles for a mainstream white publication to soon thereafter writing for communist publications, the shift is not as extreme as it might appear. His criticism of the class structure inherent within capitalism is a foreshadowing of the wholesale condemnation of the system he would soon unleash in communist venues.

Negro Society

Last summer a friend of mine who is in the real estate business gave his charming daughter, teacher in a Boston graded school, in marriage to a youth who held a Phi Beta Kappa key and an A.B. from Dartmouth and a diploma from the Harvard Medical School. The wedding took place one evening in a beautifully furnished cottagelike house near Boston, and everybody concerned owed allegiance to Afro-America. I noticed among the hundred or more guests lawyers of large and prosperous clienteles, physicians and surgeons whose fees support these gentlemen in affluence, a waiter from the Parker House,[62] a brilliant young pianist, two commercial artists, a chauffeur for a white business man; students and graduates of Harvard, Wellesley, Tufts, Radcliffe, Dartmouth, Fisk, Howard, and Simmons; a red cap from the South Station, a Pullman porter and his dowager wife, two stenographers, several girls of flapper type[63] employed in the civil service, an ex-policeman's wife, a cook for a family of North Shore Nordics, a half-dozen school-teachers, two officers of the National Guard, a newspaper editor, a banker, and a miscellany of post-office workers. Everyone was dressed, of course, strictly à la mode. The conversation was appropriate to the occasion. And the presents, which filled a small room up-stairs, were typical of those usually given newlyweds. In short, the scene was a representative one in to-day's Afro-American society. More important, it was representative too of scenes rapidly ceasing to exist. Negro society is becoming more discriminating of those who compose it.

Like the whites' the colored man's society is grounded in family and occupation. Unlike the whites the greater number of colored folk are unable to boast of family tradition. Some of them can—and do. The descendants of free Negroes who held slaves have as much to brag about as most of their white compatriots. These will be found in many sections of Virginia, Maryland, South Carolina, and one or two other Southern states. But the masses of colored folk have no such boast. The portion of their family trees that they esteem sprouted since the Civil War. If a black man's grandfather was senator or a congressman during the Reconstruction, he naturally has more to boast of than the man whose grandfather was a slave, whose father was an illiterate tenant-farmer, and whose mother was a cook in the big house. He, himself, in the third generation since the Civil War, may be a graduate of Harvard, a $60,000-a-year lawyer, an Odd Fellow, an Elk, and an Episcopalian, but he remains non-communicative on matters anent[64] family trees.

There being few who can adorn family trees with pretty tales, the colored folk have had to employ the white man's secondary measurement of social eminence, occupation. There are a few Negro bankers scattered across the country, and some are members of consequence in American affairs. There are also the insurance heads, newspaper editors and publishers, writers, musicians, college professors, school-teachers, civil-service workers, and menials (including domestic services). There being but few Afro-Americans of the type that would automatically become one with the highest stratum of Caucasian society, if a miracle wrought such a merger, the black blue-bloods find themselves incapable of outdistancing the climbers.

The observation is frequently made that in Negro society one may find the barber seated beside the bank-president. This is true, but the reason is obvious and near at hand. The most exalted men and women in these colored United States represent individual achievement. His father was not a banker but a butler, while his mother scrubbed to help out. That is why, in any large gathering of Afro-American élite, the sheep are found rubbing noses with the goats.[65] The reason the goats are there is that they could not be separated from the sheep. The goat just happens to be the big ram's father or brother or some other close relative.

II

But the situation is rapidly changing. Class distinctions within the race are multiplying and are being recognized by those affected. Not only that, but class distinctions within the race are being taken as a matter of course.

I have a room in a studio building in Copley Square, Boston. There I go occasionally to conduct a class in English composition. Descending in the elevator one evening, I was conscious of the frank stare of the only other passenger, white. He stepped out ahead of me, and the black elevator-boy touched my arm.

"Wait a minute, Mr. Gordon," he said. "I want to tell you something."

When the other man was beyond hearing, the boy said indignantly: "See that white fellow that rode down just now?"

"Yes."

"Well, what do you think he asked me up-stairs?"

"Don't know. What?"

"Well, he was lookin' for the freight-elevator man, and he seen you go in the studio, and he started after you. See! And I says to him, I says, 'Say, mister, wait a minute,' I says. 'That ain't the man you want,' I tells him. He stops and looks at me, and he says: 'Isn't that Jimmy?' 'I says: 'No, that's not Jimmy.' And he says: 'Well, it doesn't matter; he'll do.'" He wanted somebody to bring out a box of books and put 'em on the freight-elevator, you know. Now, can you imagine that!"

"What did you say?" I asked.

At the memory of it he spluttered with anger. "What I said? Y' ought to of heard me. I says to him, I says, 'Just because a man's colored he don't have to be nobody's servant,' I says to him. 'That man,' I says, 'is a teacher just like you.' You talk about a dumbfounded white man! Why, just because we're colored they think we got to be equals. Believe me, every time I gets a chance I tells 'em . . ."

Then, there was a washerwoman. One day she was occupied with something in our apartment. In some way the talk veered to the inevitable topic of black-and-white relationship.

"An' this woman says to me, Mrs. Gordon, she says, 'Martha, I didn't know colored people was so clean and intelligent,' she says to me. 'Are all colored people intelligent and clean like you,' she says. What do you think of that for ignorance, Mrs. Gordon? And I says to her, I says, 'Mrs. Goodblood, you'd ought to see some of our best colored people,' I says. 'Why,' I says, 'I'm real illiterate aside of some of them. Do you know what?' I says, 'Why, I know some people who wouldn't any more have me to sit down to eat with them,' I says, 'than you would.' What do you know about such ignorance, Mrs. Gordon? Just because we're colored they think we're all on the same level, don't they? Takes me to set 'em straight, it does."

The elevator-boy and the laundress are typical. These men and women look with prideful complaisance upon an AfroAmerican who can equal the Caucasian at his own game of snobbery.

Not long ago there was current among certain Nordics a fable to the general purport that the most rarefied of black society would joyfully and without question accept any white woman who condescended to present herself. If ever it was true, it is true no longer. A white face without character or accomplishment to recommend it is without a chance in the best black circles.

In spite of all these evidences of tendencies toward class separatism in Afro-America, many whites as well as a considerable number of blacks refuse to recognize the distinctions. So advanced a woman as Marcet Haldeman-Julius[66] wrote the following in the Kansas City *Call*, a colored news-sheet:

"Personally, I have had a great deal to do with Negroes. When I was a child I had a Negro nurse—a real mammy type she was. Her husband tended our yard and furnace.... Both of them lived with us until they died, and Mammy Gooch's death was my first real sorrow. I had a colored woman as nurse for my youngest child, Henry. She was from Alabama and could neither read nor write. My cook at this moment is her antithesis—a well-educated, capable, executive-type of woman, and a local leader among her race."

There is no disputing that Mrs. Haldeman-Julius is better informed of the personal qualities of her cook than I am, yet I challenge her allegation that her cook is "a well-educated, capable, executive-type of woman, and a local leader of her race." I agree that the woman may have capability—alone. I admit that she may be well educated. And I grant her executive ability—alone. But I refuse to accept her *in toto* as presented by her mistress.

Such a women would without doubt be a leader. She would probably be more than merely "a local leader among her race." But she would not be Mrs. Haldeman-Julius's cook. Instead, she would be a luminary in Kansas City's colored society. She would probably be, with her education and executive ability, head of a hair-straightening manufactory or some like enterprise. And she would *hire* a cook instead of being hired. Of course the reason Mrs. Haldeman-Julius, the man in the studio building, and laundrywoman's employer entertained their point of view lies in their lack of real acquaintanceship with Negro life.

There are some colored folk with a similar point of view. They know the truth but refuse to accept it. In the first place, they insist, there is no such thing as colored society. Who ever heard of such nonsense? they demand. In the second place, even if there were, what of it? The non-conforming black man will not retreat from the position he is as good as any other black man alive. Being black, he declares, places them all on the same level. He despises blacks who "think they're white" and "imitate" white society. In Boston recently a colored house-girl refused to accept employment in the home of William H. Lewis, formerly Assistant Attorney-General of the United States, when she learned that he was colored. "I'm just as good as he is," she maintained, demanding return of her fee by the employment bureau.

There are a few of this persisting type, but only a few. The greater number are accepting class separatism as an inevitable corollary of our present social order. And strange, too, the conformists are not illiterates, but of the type of Mrs. Haldeman-Julius' cook.

III

But, if there be discrimination between the menials and the "leaders," there is little enough discrimination between the various grades of those who compose the leadership. Here the progress of class distinction has been retarded. And the reason is apparent. A line must be drawn somewhere; so it may as well be drawn between the menials, as of the top of the lowest stratum, and the clerks, postmen, and other such workers, as of the bottom of the highest stratum. Thus do the postmen, policemen, clerks, stenographers, school-teachers, college professors, college presidents, heads of business concerns, bankers, writers, publishers, and professional men compose society. The upper layers of the crust have begun to withdraw into themselves, so that soon there will be several strata instead of, as now, only two. That time will come when the number of wealthy will have increased and when, after several generations more, family trees in Afro-America will be sturdier than now.

The accusation that Negro society is patterned upon the white, in imitation of the latter, is only partially true. The average black man of wealth and education has as extensive a background of American civilization as the average white man of wealth and education. Neither knows any other civilization or culture. Both being schooled in American institutions, there is nothing for either to do but conform. There remains for the black man, as for the white, nothing but to assimilate the American culture and to be assimilated into the general scheme. This being true, accusing the Negro of imitation seems to be overlooking important circumstances. Perhaps they will explain how an indigenous growth can be imitative of its own soil. The same sets of circumstances that produce white Babbits[67] and Ku-Kluxers and Odd fellows produce also their own black antitypes; if not actually, then in spirit.

* * *

IV

Where, if anywhere, is the social capital of these colored United States? Harlem claims the honor; Washington challenges the claim. Chicago presents some stalwart arguments, and so do Pittsburgh and Philadelphia. Boston does not say very much. Washington's challenge is thrust into the face of Harlem by the social arbiter of Howard University, Professor Kelly Miller:

"Washington is the social capital of the Negro race. Social celebrities from all over the country find fulfilment of their highest ambition to shine at some great function in the national capital. Every four years a President of the United States is inaugurated. The occasion is usually featured by an inaugural ball. Although the Negroes may have little cause for jubilation over the incoming administration, they usually have two or three inaugural balls, whereas the whites are satisfied with one . . . . The capital city furnishes the best opportunity and facilities for the expression of the Negro's innate gaiety of soul.

Washington is still the Negro's heaven, and it will be many a moon before Harlem will be able to take away the sceptre."

Harlem refuses to argue the question at length, for there is no community in the world more self-satisfied, more self-sufficient, more self-sustaining. And no challenger knows this better than Washington.

Harlem is letting her actions speak for her. And they *do* speak—eloquently. Visit a fashion show at Rockland Palace,[68] or drop in on one of the dinner-parties given by the daughter and heiress of the late Madame Walker, of hair grower fame,[69] or get invited to James Weldon Johnson's flat and sit on the floor in the midst of weighty intellects, or—Washington, Harlem, Chicago, Pittsburgh, Atlanta; Hop Toad, Texas; Norfolk; Assbray, Ga., and Braggadocio, S.C.,[70] have each a social circle which each thinks supreme.

V

The chief difference, as pointed out already, between the whites' and the blacks' society of the upper reaches lies in the omnium-gatherum composition of the blacks.' Effort is being made from the top, and observed with tolerant unconcern from the bottom, to make lines between social classes more sharply distinct. But the consummation of this effort, aimless and wavering as it is, is afar off. The occupational diversions of Afro-America are too conglomerate, reaching from the sewer to the cathedral spire, as they do, and being connected by blood-ties, as they are, to permit of indiscriminate discrimination. Thus, at an exclusive dinner-party, it often happens that the roster of guests represents an olla podrida[71] of Afro-Americana. Beside a bishop of the African Methodist Episcopal Church sits a lady whose delicate hands daily manipulate the kink-remover pliers. The good bishop may have an opinion about such promiscuity, but he is both a gentleman and a man of sense. He says not a word. There being no social register, it is left to the hostess's intuition and rather doubtful sense of values to determine who shall and who shall not grace her board. No one with so much as three thousand dollars in cash, regardless as to how this fabulous sum was accumulated, may be ignored. In a case of this sort there is no alternative. And some manipulators of the hair-iron are ladies of wealth and power. Besides, you've got to let *somebody* in. It is all right, perhaps, to exclude the truckdriver, if you want to be nastily snobbish, and the ashman, and the offal-cart attendant; but, good Lord, use discretion. Besides, the hair-dresser's son may be a professor at Howard, her daughter a graduate of Radcliffe, with a Ph.D. from the Sorbonne, and her husband an editor of an influential journal. Not only has she three thousand dollars in her own right, but she has achieved spiritually—if you get the meaning; and achievement, no matter how futile it may seem to the complacent Caucasian, is fittingly esteemed in these colored United States. Granting Washington to be typical of the best, let us consider her.

In Washington the top cream of colored society—as in most other places—is a thick layer of doctors and lawyers, with a somewhat thinner layer of Howard University officials, a still thinner and less important layer of teachers in the public schools, and a somewhat watery sediment of government workers. The top of the cream is tacitly acknowledged to be the doctors and the lawyers. No one ever disputes that. If any one did he would be suspected of all kinds of depravity. Some of the social notes printed in the *Tribune* and the *Eagle* of that fair city read like rosters from medical and law school reviews.

The houses these aristocrats occupy are well built and imposing, but old. Inside, examination would reveal most of them to be overrun with cockroaches and mice. Not one of this gentry owns a house built for his own use. They are content merely to chase out the harassed Nordic and to grab what he leaves. Some of the most moneyed of these folk are becoming more so through real-estate operations. Many lawyers and some doctors are turning realtors, but they are not losing caste thereby. They purchase the deserted mansions lately occupied by Klansmen's families and sell them for double and treble their worth to such of their own race as will pay the prices.

Most of the matrons of the Washington set are ludicrously snobbish—but so are the men. A majority of the women too possess Caucasian exteriors. To be able to "pass" is almost a requisite. It is an invaluable asset in a town where rests the centre of government of all the people, and where the congressmen and the senators spend their overtime thinking up new ways to humiliate the uppish darkies.

So the matron of the smart colored set, with her fair skin and her invariably beautiful face, sits beside the gentleman from Arkansas in Keith's or dines opposite him at the Mayflower,[72] or even relieves him of his seat in a trolley, since these gentlemen will not under any circumstances see a "white" woman stand in a public conveyance. The experiences encountered thus by the Afro-American élite serve as morsel for gossip at many a five-hundred party, or bridge game, or informal luncheon.

Some of the most conspicuous of the male members of society are conspicuous because of the contrast they make beside their fair-skinned ladies. It is not nearly so important that the man be "passable" as that the woman be so. A black man, as a rule, if he be anybody at all, may climb to the very top of the social ladder; this is seldom true with respect to the woman. The woman in every racial group, apparently, is socially more ambitious than the man. In this country the dominating group has set a standard of beauty, and it is the steadfast conviction of every woman, be she white or non-white, that she must conform to it. And that accounts for the almost pathetic attempt of the darker women to bleach the skin and to straighten the hair. Submerged in a group of a hundred million, the colored woman feels that her salvation lies in being as nearly as possible like the women for whom fashions are designed and beauty cults maintained. It is a question of survival, not one of simple imitation; as a matter of fact, it is not imitation at all, but conformity with the customs of their country.

An important ingredient of the Afro-American social mélange in Washington is the coterie of lawyers holding public office. In former years these have included the Register of the Treasury; to-day they are the recorder of deeds[73] of the District of Columbia, a judge of the municipal court, and an assistant to the attorney-general. The acknowledged leaders of colored society in Washington now are Congressman and Mrs. Oscar De Priest, of Chicago.[74]

It might be supposed that the Haitian minister to the United States would be a ringleader in Washington colored society; most emphatically he is not. Not that he would not be welcomed; society has more than once made invitatory gestures in his direction. But, being observant of the situation that obtains between black and white in the Land of the Free, the Haitian minister knows that if he ever crossed the social line into Afro-America he would find difficulty in returning. This is so, despite the ugly truth that the cultural level of Washington's colored society is flush with that to which the Haitian minister and his family are accredited. Therefore, that gentleman steers clear, accepting invitations from colored Washington only when the occasion is publicly in the open, like the inauguration, for example, of Howard University's colored president. The Haitian minister was present at that event; but so were the Secretary of War and the Secretary of the Interior.

About twelve years ago Maurice Menos, son of the dark-skinned Solon Menos, at that time minister from Haiti, eloped to Baltimore and was married to the daughter of a socially ambitious white family from Virginia. Colored Washington gasped; clasped its hands and waited to see what would happen. Nothing happened beyond the usual when a member of the diplomatic corps takes an American wife. The couple got the usual amount of newspaper space, and the young woman got into the "Social Register." The point is that colored Washington considered it a sort of personal triumph; but, of course, it was nothing of the sort. If young Menos bore toward colored Washington anything other than indifference, no one saw it.

Below the doctors and the lawyers come the school-teachers. Some of the most beautiful women of the country are undoubtedly to be found teaching in Washington's schools; and I refer to alleged Negro women. Of a lower social order, many of them graduate into the upper strata by getting married to doctors and lawyers. They make excellent matrons and dowagers, often completely eclipsing the pretty *dumm belles* whom the society gentlemen married because they *were* pretty.

The government workers and the menials are the mainstay of the upper crusts, the former, of course, being away out of sight above the latter. As for the washerwomen, the cart-drivers, the elevator operators, and the other essential but thoroughly snubbed multitudes, they go their way in sweet contentment. They have few if any complaints to make. Now and then their ire may be stirred by the supercilious behavior of an erstwhile associate who, being pretty, has captured a doctor or a lawyer. But they soon forgive her and rejoice in their good fortune. It means progress when even one succeeds in scaling the heights. It means that the "cullud fo'ks is gittin' mo' lak d w'ite fo'ks evha day," and that, I assure you, in a world where white is the badge of the redeemed and black that of the damned, where snobbery and class distinctions and tinsel riches are the new Baal[75] to be fearfully worshipped—that, I say, is something to aspire to! And as goes Washington so goes the rest of it.

"The Legion Takes Boston"
The Nation (OCTOBER 29, 1930): 469–71
Used by permission of *The Nation* magazine.

The Nation has a long-standing history as one of America's leading progressive magazines. It was founded in 1865 as a successor to William Lloyd Garrison's abolitionist paper *The Liberator*. Being published in *The Nation* established Gordon's status as one of the leading Black journalists in the country. Gordon's politics had been shifting leftward for several years, and publishing in *The Nation* provided a perfectly natural movement to the more radical publications that would soon follow.

    An article on the American Legion would seem to be fairly innocuous, but Gordon signals his ridicule of the group in the first sentence, describing its weeklong convention in Boston as "an occupation." Despite the legionnaires' lawless behavior, Mayor James Michael Curley, Harry J. Harriman, president of the Boston Chamber of Commerce, and the police commissioner all praised the group. But the legionnaires not only played childish pranks, such as dropping paper bags of water on those passing by; in addition, "automobiles were tipped over; bonfires were built in the streets and fed with waste paper and packing cases; crap games flourished on the Common and in the lobbies of hotels; bootleggers shouted their wares from positions on the streets." There were also "militaristic and imperialistic voice[s] which chanted about the 'next war.'" Meanwhile, the behavior of the legionnaires was tolerated. Why? Because the city brought in millions of dollars in revenue. Therefore, no criticism of their behavior could be brooked. Instead, while this behavior was going on in the name of capitalism, Congress was taking steps "to safeguard the national welfare by proper combative and remedial action in all cases of seditious activity [by communists] whether from within or without the boundaries of our country or its possessions." All in all, the article cleverly lambastes not only the American Legion but also the newspapers, merchants, hotel owners, police, and government officials who all profit from this lawless behavior done in the name of patriotism.

The Legion Takes Boston

As I write, Boston has just been released from the grip of an occupation that lasted almost a week, an occupation the like of which this old town had not previously seen. It was the twelfth annual convention of the American Legion. A substantial portion of the citizenry hopes that it will not see the like again. There are others who would not mind repeating the experience next year, with all its accompaniments of pomp and ceremony, noise and glitter, horseplay and drunkenness, childishness and arrogance, militarism and vulgarity.

Opinions expressed in Boston during the convention concerning the value of the American Legion's contribution to American culture and progress are hopelessly at variance. Let me cite a random few. We listen first to the retiring commander of the American Legion, O.L. Bodenhamer:

> In our Americanization work we must admit that a nation is just as great as are its men and its women. To make permanent American ideals, and to advance American institutions, it is necessary to look to the proper training of the boys and girls of today in the duties and responsibilities of American citizenship for tomorrow. The American Legion is a fine agency through which the spirit of education can be promoted.

Then there was General Pershing, who assured his former soldiers that "America will continue to move forward under the inspired leadership of her best citizens, in whose front ranks will ever be found the Legion of Veterans." (I report this speech as W. A. MacDonald wrote it for the *Transcript*.)

Across the Charles River in Cambridge the Harvard *Crimson*, when the occupation was ended and most of the army had departed, carried the following editorial:

> Two days ago in South Carolina President Hoover spoke of the purity and inherent rights of American institutions, but, surely, whatever the moral correctness of the institutions, no other country in the world would countenance the spectacle of the recent American Legion convention in Boston. The highest official of what other land would have lent his presence in what, in effect, is merely an excuse

for a wholesale brawl, exceeding in its disgusting completeness any similar spectacle the United States has to offer? Even Boston, with a police commissioner who has been astonishingly vigorous since he has been in power, has seen fit to allow a total relaxation of law and order during the stay in the Hub of the "buddies" of the Legion, those glorious Americans who fought, the slogan says, to make the world safe for democracy, and who have come back to raise hell annually so no one can forget it.

The *Crimson* does not wish to be misunderstood, and hastens to add:

> ... at Harvard at least there are few conscientious objectors of the Eighteenth Amendment, but the worst subway riot, the drunkest football crowd are piddling trifles in the way of disturbances compared to a Legion convention.

The *Crimson* adds graciously: "Detroit has been awarded the convention for next year; by God, we hope she's satisfied." Such heterodoxy would be expected to unstop the vials of wrath; it did. Local officials of the Legion attributed the point of view, charitably enough, to "an immature mind."

Both Major Paul Hines, who handled the publicity for the Legion, and Mayor Curley of Boston declared that there had been no evidence of drinking among any of the 70,000 marchers in the parade. But to some eyewitnesses, at least, there was overwhelming evidence of it. Some men drank as they marched, turning the flasks up to their lips. Others were supported over the route by their "buddies."

Secretary of the Navy Adams,[76] in the words of a reporter for a Boston paper, suggested:

> ... that the Legion had in its power the furtherance of the spirit of Washington and Lincoln, and he went on to epitomize the extraordinary development of the country, which had grown in riches and in population far beyond what the founders had imagined, and with that growth had come dangers also beyond imagination a few years ago.

Mr. Adams, having pointed out the bugaboo to the boys, cunningly played upon their immature sense of patriotism. "Can you be sure," he whispered, "your country will not again be involved in mighty combat?" No, they could not be sure; nevertheless, everybody cheered, stamped, and clapped. They could not be sure but Mr. Adams was. "In view of this great need of the development of the spirit of justice," he said, further befogging the issue for them, "and of the uncertainties, don't you think it may be well to maintain rather a strong navy so the voice of justice may have a hearing?" There was a great deal more applause, but no one thought of asking the Secretary of the Navy when battleships and cruisers had come to be the ear trumpets of justice.

Harry J. Harriman, president of the Boston Chamber of Commerce, was on the program with Mr. Adams. He referred to the Legion as a "potent force for good in the nation . . . ." But meanwhile the Reverend Raymond H. Palmer, minster of the Lynn Unitarian Church, was writing in the church magazines that "anyone looking on at the doings in Boston during the past week could hardly have escaped the conclusion that we do not live in a country which has yet reached a high stage of civilization," because he "saw more drunken men on the streets of Boston in a few hours than I have seen anywhere in the past five years," and because, also, "I have heard women insulted . . ." At the same time Police Commissioner Hultman was writing the following letter to the head of the American Legion:

> I should like to say to your organization before it leaves the city of Boston that our records show that while there have never been so many people in the city as during the week of your national convention, there has been little or no disorder.
>
> I am therefore taking the opportunity to congratulate you on the manner in which the members of your organization have conducted themselves while having what I hope has been a pleasant visit to our city.

The American Legion, according to its officials, is composed of more than 888,000 men and women. I don't know how many of these were in Boston, but the number in the parade has been estimated variously at 50,000, 70,000, and 75,000. There were perhaps thousands of members who for one reason or another did not parade. The "buddies" began to arrive in Boston several days before the convention was to open. Most of them were in uniforms of odd design and fantastic color combination. The reaction to war-time drabness was manifest. An American reporter recording such a spectacle in Haiti or Mexico would call it "gaudy"; in Egypt or Abyssinia, "barbaric"; but in twentieth-century, cultured Boston it was simply "colorful." I have never before seen such naïve and childish delight over color as the legionnaires and their women displayed. Silver-plated helmets, gold-plated helmets, and brass-plated helmets; red breeches, green breeches, black-and-white breeches, pantaloons that made their wearers look like clowns; blue smocks, red berets, berets of green, blue, black, and yellow; boots and shoes of every shape and color combination; Sam Browne belts[77] (which in the army are restricted to the use of officers) of white, black, tan, and scarlet; uniforms in imitation of those American doughboys used to sneer at when French soldiers wore them, uniforms in imitation of the Canadian Black Watch, uniforms in imitation of the Royal House Guards, of the Dragoon Guards, and of Hussars. So bedizened, they marched stolidly or hilariously, with soldierly attention or with uncertainty, depending on the temper or the mood or the physical condition of the marcher. Ahead of them marched brass bands or drum-and-bugle corps led by prancing or strutting drum majors. The "buddies" carried rifles with bayonets fixed; they lugged tiny cannon, which the irrepressible humorists of the "40 and 8" fired every so often. They bore the flag of the United States beside the Legion flag, and each flag bearer was flanked by two guards with rifles.

The women marched with the men, likewise bearing arms. They were dressed like so many clowning children at play, but they were marching to the still command of a militaristic and imperialistic voice which chanted about the "next war." It took the parade from ten in the morning until nearly eight at night to pass a given point, yet in that interminable procession I saw only two episodes which might, with excessive generosity, be interpreted as anti-militaristic. One of these was a float depicting the death of "Scotty," a local newsboy who enlisted and was killed overseas, and the other was a float made to resemble a cemetery studded with white crosses and covered with poppies.

On the evening following the parade Boston went through an experience somewhat similar to the police strike twelve years ago. Automobiles were tipped over; bonfires were built in the streets and fed with waste paper and packing cases; crap games flourished on the Common and in the lobbies of hotels; bootleggers shouted their wares from positions on the streets, naming the kind of stuff and the prices thereof. From the upper floors of the Statler Hotel,[78] where many Legion posts had headquarters, playful "buddies" dropped paper bags of water upon the heads of home-going passers-by and into open automobiles. It was great sport. There was no need of anyone's protesting. There was nobody to receive the protests. The police laughingly looked on, while the indignant sufferers swallowed their pride and cursed the day the saviors of the republic were born.

The city authorities issued a permit for block dancing in Copley Square, a great green triangle upon which face the Boston Public Library, the Copley Plaza Hotel, Trinity Church, and some of the best business blocks of Boston. Later this permit was canceled, lest outdoor dancing interfere with traffic. But the defenders of the nation, the upholders of the law, the future rules of the country, ignored the ban and went ahead with their program. As a consequence traffic died in its tracks.

Looking upon all that infantile display, yet sensing the potential dynamite under it, the thoughtful person can but entertain misgivings about the future. There are 880,000 of these legionnaires, according to official figures. Their type of mind may be gauged by the resolutions they passed. For instance, they "favor continued support of the American Legion marksmanship program, under a national director of marksmanship"; they recommend to Congress "a large defense organization, carrying with it provisions for organization throughout the country of rifle clubs, pistol clubs, and similar units; an army of 12,000 officers and 125,000 men, and a national guard of 210,000"; and, most characteristically, they resolve "that Congress be urged to establish a nonpartisan, non-political federal bureau of criminal investigation and research, comparable to the English Scotland Yard organization, whose duties will be to curtail all phases of criminal activity in the United States and possessions, and to safeguard the national welfare by proper combative and remedial action in all cases of seditional activity, whether from within or without the boundaries of our country or its possessions." This resolution, the newspapers admitted, was "aimed at Bolshevik activities in this country." The only resolution offered by a Negro legionnaire was killed; it was "aimed at" lynching in this country.

As I write the account of these events the men and women who created them are gone. Next year they will meet in Detroit. In the meantime Boston is wondering what she gained from their visit. Only the rank and file, however, are thus wondering. The police are satisfied that there was no disorder of any kind. The Governor sent the Police Commissioner a letter in which the head of the commonwealth expressed his "hearty commendation for the excellent service the department has performed." The newspapers are pleased; special Legion features were displayed day by day and circulation jumped. The department stores and shops are complacent and happy, having "garnered" according to one Boston news sheet, "at least $3,000,000." The hotels and restaurants, of course, are not complaining. Meanwhile the politicians have been going into a frothing rage at the least semblance of criticism of our noble visitors. The answer to all this conspiracy of denial is that legionnaires have money to spend, as have their various relatives; they have votes to cast; they have influence among hundreds of thousands of mob-minded men and women.

"The Negro's New Leadership"
New Masses (JULY 1931): 14–15

It has been shown how Gordon had begun attacking the capitalist system, often in a sarcastic tone and frequently in mainstream publications. In this article, he moves to the logical next step, writing in communist publications. His first foray into this territory is in the *New Masses*. Soon he would not only be writing for the publication but editing it as well. The magazine included editors such as Mike Gold and Max Eastman, both on the board of the earlier radical magazine the *Masses* (1911–17). Its contributors were a who's who of American literature including William Carlos Williams, Theodore Dreiser, Upton Sinclair, Richard Wright, Langston Hughes, Eugene O'Neill, and Ernest Hemingway. Gordon was now in truly auspicious company.

In his earlier writings, Gordon would hint about unity between the races. In "The Negro's New Leadership," this would be a muscular plea, one that would dominate the remainder of his writings and indeed his life. He goes into a history of Black leadership. The first "leaders" inevitably came from the clergy and were often "cunning, shrewd, and crooked." Often, they would do the bidding of the white ruling class. Over time, it led to class divisions where the working class was exploited by the petty bourgeoisie, who enabled criminal factions for their own benefit.

When Blacks began to look for secular leaders, they turned first to the so-called leaders of the race such as "Negro physicians, lawyers, politicians, hair-straighteners, newspapers editors, and feature-story writers," who don't give a damn about them. In desperation, they turned to groups like the NAACP ("the Nicest Association for the Advantage of Certain Persons"), who simply proposed "a compromise" with and eventual surrender to the ruling class.

Finally, "the Negro masses have of late been stirred to enthusiasm by the action of the International Labor Defense (ILD), the League of Struggle for Negro Rights, and the Communist party of America [who go] to the very stench hole of American capitalist class hatred and [challenge] the thugs and lynchers on their own ground." After seeing how communists help all workers, regardless of color, Gordon feels Blacks will understand that "such leadership is the only leadership for the man who works, whether he be white or black."

The Negro's New Leadership

Until today it has been axiomatic with the Aframerican since his socalled [*sic*] emancipation that no white man lives whom black men may trust as one trusts a comrade. "You can't trust no white man no time," the Negro worker said. They taught their children to say it. "It don't make no difference how much of a friend a white man makes out he is," they said; "soon's he gets what he's after he's all through with you." Thus [the] white man in the United States, boss or worker, has been looked upon by the black worker as a double-crosser, a hypocrite, and a liar. The Negro's own duplicity when dealing with whites was excused on the grounds of justifiable retaliation. "Never give a white man no quarter," they said, "because he won't give *you* none—'ceptin' to get a stronger hold on your throat."

This doctrine of justifiable retaliation has been widely disseminated and closely adhered to. It has been bolstered up by the ruling class both of the North and of the South. The ruling class's ideology of Nordic supremacy has engendered in the white workers distrust of the Negro; in the Negro worker it has built up complexes of inferiority and defeatism. Shut out of unions affiliated with the American Federation of Labor, the black workers have been driven back upon themselves. You who have seen cattle herded into a small corral know how they swirl concentrically upon themselves until the center is a maelstrom of locked horns and legs. There seems to be no way out; there seems to be no way of disentangling themselves. The state of the Negro worker was similar to that of the cattle. There was leadership for them neither within among the blacks nor without among the whites. Even if the whites had proffered them a leadership the blacks would doubtless have scorned it.

Negro leadership immediately following the civil war was almost completely in the hands of illiterate and ignorant gospel shouters. Black ministers who dominate that field today are fully as ignorant, if somewhat more literate. Previously to his "emancipation" the black man had had a leadership of equally illiterate and ignorant white preachers. Perched in the lofts of the white master's church, the black slave listened to sermons concocted as a virus to deaden his desire for freedom, to give him delusions of grandeur concerning the white masters, and to stupefy him with complacency and self-satisfaction. "Obey your masters," they were told, "and great will be your reward in heaven." They learned that as black slaves they were destined forever to create wealth not for themselves but for men and women who held work to be a special device of the gods to degrade the blacks and keep them in their place.

In those days of white-preacher leadership there were "conservative" Negroes who, like their descendants today, yelped madly when the "radicals" among them grumbled about their degradation and hailed the day when the black worker would get the benefit of his toil. These "conservatives" damned the irresponsible young radicals as a menace to the peaceful relations and the fine sense of understanding that existed between master and slave. They threatened to expose the soreheads who did not know when they were well off. There was no lynching in those days, and for the reason that a black man was property. To kill a black worker who belonged to a neighbor was to destroy private property, and to destroy private property was then as now a crime. Thus the black worker was safe from the lyncher. It was not until he became a free man that the black worker's life was endangered by the rope and torch of the plantation owners. Perhaps the Robert Russa Motons[79] and Kelly Millers were shrewd enough to vision the problems emancipation would create so they exhorted the slaves to be content and loyal. Just as Robert Russa Morton and Kelly Miller are content with the *status quo* today. But "freedom" came, in spite of them, and with it a new leadership arose. It came from the churches and its purpose was to show the direction, to furnish guidance, to encourage.

It did all three. Most Negro preachers of that day were like most of them now—cunning, shrewd, and crooked. Their cunningness, shrewdness, and crookedness seemed to increase in direct ratio to their literacy. Among them were counselors and unconscious, willing and unwilling, tools of the masters, and they executed the orders their masters issued. It was a venal leadership. The direction it pointed was lost in a maze of "spiritual" superstition and capitalistic ideology; the guidance it afforded was a check upon and a preventive of revolutionary thinking and acting; the encouragement was all to the effect that the black man would continue to be an inferior until he could become a parasite like his master.

When the leadership was not immediately dictated by the white ruling class, it nevertheless reflected the ideology of that class. To work with the hands was the degradation god almighty stamped upon the slave. The well born—the gentlemen and their ladies—did not work. Therefore, every "po' white" and every ambitious black who hoped some day to attain the class of the well born, to be a gentleman or a lady, shied away from working with the hands and studied like hell to "better" themselves: they became doctors, lawyers, school teachers, preachers, politicians, editors, and small business men. Their ideal was wealth and idleness, with illiterate blacks to wait on them. "Better your condition," the leadership advised; which implied: "Rise above these common blacks so you can have someone to look down on. The Negro can't have a higher class if there isn't a lower class." The leadership encouraged individualism of a roughshod and ruthless kind: scheme, connive, double-cross, crush. Climb to the top on the thick skulls of these stupid blacks who worship you because they see in you a reflection of their white masters.

This ideology was not confined to the "spiritual" leadership. It pervaded the atmosphere breathed by the professional man, business man, and politician. It stimulated the growth of the petty bourgeoisie which today is as close to the working class that supports them, in aims and in sympathy, as Seventh avenue is to Lenox.[80] A chasm lies between the two classes, and those at the top are frenziedly digging to make the chasm wider. They have come to boast of the purity of their society, diluting upon the necessity of cleansing it of all traces of actual workers. One New York Negro newspaper may be cited as typical of the black capitalist attitude toward the common man and woman. The New York *Amsterdam News* carries this box at the head of its society column:

> "The more exclusive the society, the more possessed its members should be of good character and integrity—worthwhile endeavor and achievement.
>
> The careful host or hostess excludes from social functions persons of disreputable character, menials, and those possessed of ill-gotten gains."

Anyone who knows anything about Negro "society" is aware that if all those who possess "ill gotten gains,"—i.e., numbers kings, gamblers, small stock market manipulators, lawyers, politicians, preachers, to suggest just a few,—were kicked out, there would be no "society." There would be so few left that it would die of its own inertia.

The leadership to which the masses of black workers has had to look has been weak, vacillating, hypocritical, ignorant, venal, and self-seeking. It is all these things in its very nature. It could not be anything else and exist as a part of the capitalist system and a defender of that system. Take Harlem again. The Negro physicians, lawyers, politicians, hair-straighteners, newspaper editors, and feature-story writers don't give a damn for the groping black hundreds of thousands who live from five to ten in a single room, who walk the streets in search of work, whose garbage is left to decay in the hallways and the dumbwaiter shafts, whose children are underfed and ill, and who squirm under the heel of the rapacious landlord. If they cared would they run from them as if from pestilence, seeking always to "better" themselves while leaving these others to make out as best they can—or not make out at all? Would they have grabbed possession of the Dunbar apartments,[81] which were said originally to be intended for workers? Would they be today the prostitutes who sell all they have—the Harlem which they protest so much to love?—to every degenerate parasite who comes seeking a thrill? This leadership is the kind that the Negro has been afflicted with. But he is beginning at last to open his eyes. He is beginning to see that these "big" Negroes are not concerned about him and his future. He is beginning to see that some white men may honestly wish to help him. He is discovering, to his dazed bewilderment, that a new leadership is beckoning to him.

When the National Association for the Advancement of Colored People was founded and it announced its program of fighting for the rights of the under-privileged, the black masses of the country thought they had at last discovered a leadership they could follow with absolute trust. But, although these workers did not know it, the NAACP was, after all, a ditch-straddling body which depended for sustenance on the whims of rich and doty liberals. The organization was no freer, therefore, to condemn the system upon which its capitalist supporters battered than the Negro preacher out of slavery was to fly in the face of conditions which kept the "freedmen" peons. The system which in both cases brutalized the workers also fed, pampered, petted, and flattered the men it picked to mislead the workers. In its early days the NAACP frequently did things which were almost daring; but its most daring performance was simply a compromise. However, a compromise, Negro leaders in the South tell us, is better than a surrender, and the NAACP has finally admitted surrendering completely. It is no longer the National Association for the Advancement of Colored People, but the Nicest Association for the Advantage of Certain Persons. It has as much to do with the black masses of workers and share-croppers as any similar group of scented, spatted, caned, and belly-filled white parasites have to do with the white masses. It is ultra-nice, ultra-respectable, and ultra-fastidious. It has a reputation to preserve, so it cannot afford to be seen in company with dirty reds or other radicals, no matter what the common end is supposed to be.

This dainty withdrawing from an organization because it is composed of common workers has done more than any other one tendency of the NAACP to reveal its true character to the Negro masses. Observing its aloof and grudging "help," the Negro worker recalls suddenly that there has never before been a body of men who, white and black, actually *fought* for the most degraded black man in the country. The Negro masses have of late been stirred to enthusiasm by the action of the International Labor Defense, the League of Struggle for Negro Rights, and the Communist Party of America in going to the very stench-hole of American capitalist class hatred and challenging the thugs and lynchers on their own ground. Seeing all this, the black workers remember the incident of the NAACP secretary in Texas, some year ago who, caught pussyfooting by thugs hired by Texas bosses to get him out of the state, was beaten and chased to the railroad station. They remember the letter of resignation this NAACP official wrote, in which he asserted that he saw no hope of securing the Negro's rights through the means his organizations was [*sic*] pursuing. They remember their feeling of despair when they read his wail of defeat; a wail which implied that if others wished to risk their hides for the sake of "common niggers," let them; he certainly didn't intend to do so any more.

Then Negro workers think of the countless times Communists have been beaten insensible for defending the Negro workers, yet have gone from the hospital right into the fight again. They remember the white men who were tried and convicted in the USSR, and remember the trial in New York of a white worker who was tried and humiliated for his jim crow attitude toward black workers. They look at the most daring experiment in American journalism, the actual printing of a Communist newspaper[82] in Chattanooga, the heart of the lynching desert, and they are thrilled! They hear of members of the LSRN [League of Struggle for Negro Rights], white and black, going to eat in an "exclusive" Washington restaurant and wrecking the place when the Negroes in the party are refused service. They see the ILD [International Labor Defense] and the LSRN, supported by the Communist Party, rushing defense to the nine Negro youths at Scottsboro long before any other organization in the country has condescended to glance superciliously in their direction, and they see the loyalty and the staunchness of the men and women who are giving their time and energy and money and talent—everything they have—to save these boys. Seeing and hearing all these things, the Negro worker in the United States would be a fool not to recognize the leadership that he has been waiting for since his "freedom." And the masses of blacks being *no* fools, they *have* recognized it and they have begun to accept it. The Negro workers are beginning to understand that such leadership is the only leadership for the man who works, whether he be white or black.

"Scottsboro—and the Nice People"
Labor Defender (AUGUST 1931): 157

On March 25, 1931, nine young Black men in Paint Rock, Alabama, were accused of raping two white women, Ruby Bates and Victoria Price. Despite the flimsiness of the case, in early April 1931, four separate all-white juries in courts in Scottsboro, Alabama, found eight of the defendants guilty. The case quickly became a cause célèbre, spotlighting Southern racial injustice. The Communists, spearheaded by white but especially African American members, rose to the defense of the accused. Two of the party's race auxiliaries, the League of Struggle for Negro Rights and the ILD (International Labor Defense), took the lead.[83] Gordon spoke at a Communist benefit for the Scottsboro Boys on May 15, 1931,[84] and wrote two articles on the Scottsboro Boys in the *Labor Defender* (August 1931 and June 1932). The *Labor Defender* was the organ of the ILD, led by the Workers Party of America. Gordon's article, "Scottsboro—and the Nice People," skewers both the NAACP (the Nice People) and the organization's field secretary, William Pickens, for their inaction. The nine Black boys in Scottsboro, Alabama, had been accused of rape and eight of them were scheduled to be executed on June 24, 1932. The fierce resistance to the planned killing helped prevent this outcome, although the boys were still not released.

Scottsboro—and the Nice People

Now that the N. A. A. C. P. has discovered that there is a "Scottsboro case," the black and the white workers of the country may get ready for some amusing moments. They may even prepare for some good belly laughs, if they can find the courage to laugh in the face of starvation, evictions and persecutions in general. But the N. A. A. C. P., and its cohorts are laughing, and if *they* can do it, why shouldn't the workers laugh, too? Of course, the members of the Nice Association are laughing at the Scottsboro case: really, it is the funniest thing they have ever heard of. Let Mr. William Pickens, the Association's field secretary, tell you the story, if you don't believe it's funny.

The Boston branch of the Nice Association held a meeting the other night, having chosen for its rendezvous what the daily papers referred to the next day as "the fashionable Mount Vernon Congressional Church at Massachusetts Avenue and Beacon Street." The Mount Vernon Congressional Church is at least a mile and a half away from the nearest Negro church in the South End.

The pastor of the Church, the Rev. Mr. Sidney Lovett, spoke telling how glad he was to open his doors in behalf of justice. We are all children of the same Father, you know, and "we are coming to realize that God is no respecter of persons." He said also that "obedience to law is liberty," and his audience of High Colored Society clapped its manicured hands with cultivated studiedness. Advising his hearers not to judge Alabama and the South "too harshly," because "we have been known to have lynchings even in the North," the Rev. Mr. Lovett walked sanctimoniously to the rear of the church and sat down.

Then came Mr. William Pickens, and the audience forgot where it was and guffawed. Pickens has that effect on one, it seems. He appeared to like it. Launching immediately into an account of his visit at Scottsboro, he described the case with all the noted Pickensian humor. The audience was now in a festive frame of mind. Those who had sat slumped in their seats, evidently expecting to hear sordid details of an unpleasant story, perked up and smacked their lips. It was as if having been bored by tenth-rate stunts at a vaudeville show, their favorite comedian had suddenly came up on the stage. The chief laughing point of the speaker's talk was his description of the difficulties the nine boys would have encountered trying to rape two white p[r]ostitutes atop a sandpile on a flat car. Every time he alluded to that point the audience forgot its surroundings, its culture, its apings, and laughed aloud. It was a great show.

The Rev. Samuel Weems, of the North Cambridge Congregational Church, the only Negro minister in Greater Boston who has shown himself to be one of the workers, leading in the fight constantly night after night and Sunday after Sunday, rose and demanded to be heard. The fashionable audience was dumbfounded. Mr. Wilson stood poised like a frightened gray squir[r]el. The Rev. Mr. Sidney Lovett stood looking perplexedly around to the rear of the church. A sergeant of police and two patrolmen swaggered into the pews. Shouts rose all over the house: "We demand to be heard!" "We demand that the audience be told the truth about the Scottsboro frame-up!" "We demand the right to ask questions!"

In the vestry Mr. Wilson apologized for this unseemly conduct, addressing Mr. Lovett. The crowd flowed around the walls and waited for something to happen. Mr. Wilson backed against the wall and flanked by two brutish policemen, said that Mr. Pickens would be glad to answer any question seeking information about the case.

"Mr. Pickens," someone shouted, "is it not true that at the beginning of the Scottsboro case you said you did not know why the N. A. A. C. P. was not doing anything, and is it not true that you contributed to the I.L.D. to help defend these boys? Why are you attacking the I.L.D. now, Mr. Pickens?" Stumped for a moment, the noted N. A. A. C. P. end man cleared his throat and said: "Yes, I did say that, not knowing that the N. A. A. C. P. was silently working on the case while I was away out there in Oklahoma. And as for my helping, I would help the devil if I thought he would save these boys."

"I'll tell you a little story," he offered. But one of the workers shouted, "We're here to hear you answer questions, not tell little stories." This uppercut made Dean Pickens mad, and he shouted that he would answer questions in any way he saw fit. He started again. Someone in the rear again called him to order. The ex-attorney-general, pale as his handkerchief, suggested to Mr. Wilson that the church had been let to them only until ten, and since it was now ten minutes after, they should adjourn. Mr. Wilson grasped at this straw and declared the meeting adjourned.

"Negro Novelists and the Negro Masses"
New Masses (JULY 1933): 16–20

Gordon had given a harsh description of Black writers earlier in "Negro Fictionists in America" in the *Saturday Evening Quill* (April 1929). In this article from the *New Masses*, he goes much further. He traces the origin of Black literature back to its history of slavery and Jim Crow. African Americans were "a suppressed nation" with no outlet of expression. This created "an unhealthy national culture which was reflected in the national psychology in the forms of a peculiar national psychosis." This illness was reflected in the writings of early Black authors such as Chesnutt, Dunbar, and Du Bois. The latter writer, according to Gordon, also manifested a "personal psychosis." Those who presented a more working-class agenda, such as Frank J. Webb and William Wells Brown, were "unreadable." Later writers, including Wallace Thurman, Countee Cullen, and Rudolph Fisher, were simply presenting stereotypes of Blacks that were demanded by white upper-class readers and publishers.[85] Langston Hughes's *Not Without Laughter* (1930) "is the only novel in which the Negro worker is pictured as seeing the way out through the class struggle." Others who had fared better in Gordon's earlier critique are not deemed sufficiently class conscious. Gradually, however, Gordon maintains that a group of working-class writers will emerge and lead the masses "toward a healthy consideration of their own interests."

Negro Novelists and the Negro Masses

As a national minority, the Negro people in the United States had their origin in the agricultural South. The institution of slavery in this country, being confined principally in the southern section as a matter of economic necessity, was the second stage in their development from a heterogeneous medley of tribal remnants into homogeneous people. They were heterogeneous to begin with because so-called Negroes came neither all from Africa nor (when they did come from Africa) from any one section of that continent. They were brought here not only from the West Coast, the Southeastern Coast, and the Upper Niger, but also from the Sahara Desert region, from Senegal, from the Lake Chad region, and from the Zambesi Delta. Captives included people so alien to the African black as Moors from the southeastern Mediterranean coast, Malays from Madagascar, and natives of East India. This diversity in their origins accounted for the early diversity in the "racial" characteristics of the plantation "blacks" even before inter-mixture between them and the whites had taken place. On the same plantations, moreover, there were also slaves who possessed not only different physical characteristics, but customs so different as to indicate sharp differences in social and economic development. There is no telling how long this physical and social disharmony would have persisted, if circumstances had not brought an end to the first stage of development of these aliens into a nation and begun the second stage.

The second stage marked off the end of their status as indentured servants; it indicated the beginning of their status as slaves. I must go somewhat into detail at this point. Negroes were not brought to the American colonies originally as slaves but, as many of the poor whites who were coming in at that time, as indentured servants. The status of the blacks was identical with that of the white servants. This servitude to which both the poor whites and the stolen blacks were subjected was (according to the International Encyclopedia) "a legalized status of Indian, white, and Negro servants preceding slavery," and was common throughout the English colonies. This system originated in 17th century England, when, driven to desperation by debts, men indentured (or bound by contracts) themselves into servitude to pay their passage to this promised land of America. "The transition from servitude to slavery was effected in the case of the black man," explains the *Negro Year Book*, "when the custom established itself of holding Negroes 'servants for life.'"

It was a natural sequence of the system that those who enjoyed its benefits should come in time to lengthen the terms of their servants from an indefinite period to life. It was a logical consequence of the system that the black servants rather than the white should be those whose status became that of private property. Being an alien race, and feared because they were an alien race, the Africans were forced deeper and deeper into the morass of servitude in perpetuity. The changed status was so gradual and occurred over so long a period of time as to be almost unnoticed. It was a change that grew naturally out of the objective conditions of society: increasing necessity for cheap labor; increase in the number of laws restricting movements of slaves (as fear of them deepened); change in the sentiment of the master class from regarding the blacks as servants to regarding them as slaves. In general terms, the reason for the change of status from servant to slave was that as slaves these black aliens, whom the master class did not understand (and made no effort to understand), were more readily controlled as slaves than as servants. Before the heterogenous mass of blacks was conscious of what was happening, generations had passed. It was already taken as a matter of course that the child should inherit the status of the mother (a system, incidentally, which was partly responsible for the beginning of the freed Negro class, since children born of white servant women and black slave men were not slaves). Children born in slavery thus were slaves; the institution of slavery was thus firmly established.

The birth and death of generations of blacks, who passed from the status of indentured servants to the status of slaves effected profound changes in the mass psychology of the blacks.

The factors of slavery had already so welded together these diverse peoples that long before 1863 they had been *forced* into the category of an incipient nation. Differences in physical characteristics were less sharply apparent; a common tongue (English) had been developed; they all lived compactly together under the enveloping aegis of slavery. Here lay a condition fallow for the birth of a national psychology; here lay a promising of a peculiar national culture.

If the upper classes were unconscious of what they had created when they altered the Negro's status from one of servitude to one of slavery in perpetuity, subsequent events made them aware of it. Certainly the 25 or more insurrections of slaves, — even before the revolution against England! — was irrefutable testimony that the black had suppressed all ethnic, tribal and cultural differences among themselves and had grown to recognize the slave-holders as their common enemy. It was directly a result of the common national understanding among the slaves that plantation owners, in gradually mounting waves of terror, began to restrict the free movement of the Negroes, that they abrogated the right of slaves to assemble even for Christian service, and that they decreed it a major crime for blacks to seek an education. In Maryland, for instance, the blacks were "forbidden" to assemble or attend meetings for religious purposes which were not conducted by white licensed clergymen or by some "respectable white of the neighborhood authorized by the clergyman." The slave-owners were learning already that the church was a sword that cut both ways: toward power through organization, in the hands of the slaves; toward suppressing the slaves by anesthetizing them, in the lands of the masters. Thus, real slavery heightened the second stage of the Negro's development into a homogeneous people; gave this development an impetus that ordinary servitude could never have given.

This artificially created nation, of necessity, gave birth to an unhealthy culture. Of necessity, there arose from this culture an unhealthy psychology. Developing as a nation, the Negroes were, nevertheless, a suppressed nation, more, they were a slave nation. Natural vents to national aspirations were clogged up so that a national phychosis [*sic*] resulted. National aspirations could find no outlet except in futile protests; prayers and hymns to the white "God" of the master class; uprising[s] which, betrayed by the Christians among the slaves, were turned into abortive gestures; a fierce hatred which included all whites, but a hatred which in various slaves manifested itself in various forms, — hypocritically, as loyalty or love; as cunning or deceit; in actual physical violence against any white who crossed their path. The psychology of the slave nation was, therefore, as malodorous as the culture from which it grew. The gradual transition from indentured servant into slave-in-perpetuity, the status extending to unborn generations; the ruthlessness with which tendencies toward the most innocuous social organizations were crushed; the savagery with which uprisings were put down;—these factors, bearing upon the developing national culture, created in most slaves a fatalist outlook on life, in spite of their white God. They would get what was decreed for them (having a suspicious feeling that God was a sort of puppet, anyway, manipulated by the master class). It was as inevitable that this unhealthy psychology should stamp the slaves with a sense of inferiority as it was that the psychology developed in the white servants should operate in the opposite direction. The black slave, on the one hand, had "learned" that he was an inferior being; the poor white, on the other hand, forced out of his position by the black slave, nevertheless felt a superiority over all blacks. The master class wrote "scientific" and religious treatises and books to prove that both the black slave and the poor white had the correct outlook on life.

The Civil War crystallized this geographic-economic-political situation into a peculiar national situation, and from this peculiar national situation there emerged an unhealthy national culture; an unhealthy national culture which was reflected in the national psychology in the forms of a peculiar national psychosis. Cursed with this phychosis (which was a result of repressed desires for national and individual actions), the developing Negro fiction writers inevitably epitomized in their characters and situations the "virtues" that slavery had taught them most passionately to desire: in general, all those things which to the slave seemed to make life on earth worthy the struggle,—wealth, and all it signified, including especially leisure, education, a sophisticated culture, and a freedom of action comparable to that of the former master. Of course there were individual writers who approached the matter of interpreting their people according to their individual outlooks on life and their individual comprehensions of the Negro's problem.

For instance, the preacher who turned novelist did not immediately abandon the churchly for a materialist approach to life. In the case of the Rev. Lorenzo D. Blackson,[86] to cite a specific instance, religion was the force which eventually would free the blacks; he tried to prove it in *The Rise and Progress of the Kingdoms of Light and Darkness; or, The Reigns of King Alpha and Adabon*, a fantasmagoria based upon an illiterate preacher's understanding of *Paradise Lost* (published in 1867). Blackson's "novel" is significant only in that it marks the beginning of imaginative expression in prose among the ex-slaves. Those who followed him, however, were of hardly more value to the masses of Negroes who were crying desperately for leadership. Blackson, the preacher, thought religion would open the way out. Charles W. Chestnut [*sic*], the first Negro novelist to attract the attention of the white upper class, thought an Olympian detachment was essential to an interpretation of "primitive" Negro psychology; he wrote simple folk tales after the fashion of Joel Chandler Harris and Thomas Nelson Page.

Maintaining his Olympian balance so well that, as a recent critic said of Chestnutt's *The Conjure Woman*, "There is nothing—to indicate that the author was colored." Chestnutt's novels and short stories of the black masses of the South were such innocuous but sentimental portrayals as the whites of the North demanded. The fact that many of these works appeared in the *Atlantic Monthly* (from 1887 to 1905) is not only suggestive of their content but is also evidence of their author's upper class alignment. Being as white in appearance as any "Nordic," Mr. Chestnutt held himself physically aloof (as he had a right to do, of course), from the masses of blacks, and when he wrote of them in *The Colonel's Dream, The Conjure Woman*, and *The House Behind the Cedars*, he wrote as a liberal who sympathized with their plight and wished them well in their struggles before the law," but who felt no common bond between them and himself. Psychologically he reflected his class, which was the class of those who, reading the Atlantic, looked upon the ex-slaves as quaint "darkies" belonging to another world. Their only contact with these Negroes came through the sentimental "interpretations" of Harris, Page and Chestnutt. Bostonians desired no other contact. Chestnutt was their contact man, bringing the flavors and the odors of the Old South vicariously to the quivering nostrils of the Beacon Hill bourgeoisie.

Early Negro fiction writers assumed varied attitudes in their approach to the black masses, these attitudes representing in each of them his own psychological reactions to the objective conditions of his life. There are two reasons why the Negro proletariat, during the decade following emancipation, produced no writers of fiction. One reason was their depressing ignorance, a natural heritage of slavery; another reason was that they had no leisure even to try to express themselves in imaginative prose. This was a period also of the rising Negro bourgeosie [sic], a class which chafed fretfully under the oppression of the white upper class; a Negro bourgeoisie which, stunted in its historical development, was forced by necessity to express its resentment through the best means at its command. This means was fiction, and those who employed it most successfully for their class were Charles W. Chestnutt and William E. Burghardt DuBois [sic]. Both these men belonged to the Negro upper class, and they both, therefore, dreamed of the day when the "racial" barriers separating the white bourgeoisie from the black would be demolished and destroyed. But Chestnutt's approach to the Negro masses as a novelist was purely in the tradition of the Olympians, while that of DuBois was more the approach of a sociologist than a novelist. As a creator of "pure" art, Chestnutt did not share the pangs of those whom he made suffer; he was psychologically the aristocrat. DuBois, on the other hand, although by training and temperament an aristocrat, nevertheless suffered intensely with the characters whom he created. The reason for this difference in approach of two upper-class Negro novelists lay almost wholly in their environments. Chestnutt's was a "normal" American environment; DuBois, while still very young, came face to face with what he describes as "the veil" of color. He himself describes the shock of realizing suddenly one day that he was "different" from his white playmates when a little girl called him "nigger." Here was the beginning of a new and personal psychosis. This unhealthiness has shown itself in everything that he has written. His [sic] has resentment against white peoples in general, because, he feels, they are responsible for the ignominy of the colored bourgeoisie. His two novels, *The Quest of the Silver Fleece* and *The Dark Princess*, although purportedly both to be concerned with the problems of the

Negro masses, are actually concerned with the problems of the colored upper class. His interest in the Negro masses is obviously theoretical.

Paul Laurence Dunbar belonged to the Negro proletariat, but his aspirations as he acquired friends among both the white and the Negro bourgeoise, were toward the upper class. That is why his earlier poems expressed faithfully the aspirations of the Negro worker, while both his later poems and his novels reflect his desire to be with the class which had adopted him. Dunbar's three novels, *The Uncalled, The Love of Landry*, and *The Fanatics*, deal in a most artificial manner with the trivializations of parasitic whites. In the first two there are no Negroes at all, and in his third book black workers are used only to create "atmosphere."

There were two Negro novelists of this period whose propaganda works aimed to place the Negro masses favorably before the "reading public"; but there was no such public, because the stuff was unreadable. These men were Frank J. Webb[87] and William Wells Brown.[88] Up to 1920 the Negro workers had not produced a writer of fiction with a proletarian-revolutionary approach to the Negro's problems.

It is significant that the present group of Negro novelists numbering fewer than twelve, appeared at the very moment when the bourgeoisie, having reached its apogee immediately following the World War and started upon its plunge into decay, demanded a new kind of amusement, a new kind of story, a new form of entertainment. The moment bourgeois culture in the United States began to crack and crumble, the moment the sated and blasé bourgeoisie began to realize that it need look no longer for new appetizers among the dregs of the old order, they turned to the Negro. Here lying at their very back door was a vast and unexplored dark continent, they thought, and began to investigate it at his edges. The first hardy pioneer to venture into this unknown black wilderness came later to be known as the white-haired boy of Harlem Colored society. Carl Van Vechten came to the colored bourgeoisie as the final fruition of its despairing hopes, as the answer, at last, to its fervent prayers: the white aristocracy was taking notice of the colored aristocracy. Mr. Van Vechten was treated with the deference and honor due an emissary from one great people to another great people. Nothing was too good for him, whether it was their kitchen-sink gin or their women. Van Vechten tarried, for this experience among an exotic people was exhilarating. He wrote. The offspring of this strange cohabitation was named *Nigger Heaven,* and the bastard made its old man rich. Van Vechten tarried yet a little longer to thrill at the genuflections while the book was being extolled, but when the hosannas died down he began to long for home, and he took the long journey back to Mt. Olympus, the long trek back to Greenwich Village. *Nigger Heaven* was an "interpretation" of the colored upper class: a vicarious distortion of the lives even of these fragile parasites. But it was what they loved, because it appealed to their childish class-vanity: they felt that now they had formed an unbreakable link with aristocracy, for, like members of the aristocracy they had been immortalized in a novel. They did not know that instead of being immortalized they had really been embalmed. Van Vechten set this pace which Negro novelists of New York tried immediately to follow.

The reaction to *Nigger Heaven* among the Negro bourgeoisie was ecstatic, because they had been belatedly discovered by a "white artist" and fittingly apostrophized; their reaction to Claude McKay's *Home to Harlem* was one of general nausea and pains in sections of the anatomy other than the neck. For McKay, a retired radical sojourning in the Montmartre [*sic*], wrote of the Negro worker. It did not matter to the colored aristocracy that McKay's workers were entitled to that designation only by literary courtesy; it despised those blacks of the "lower classes." What McKay really did, however, was to write an autobiographical sketch of himself, dilating upon his love life. For *Home to Harlem* was not the story of workers who worked; it was about "workers" who swaggered through Harlem's night life perfecting the art of love. It was not a novel of workers who live in hovels of tenements; who schemed to outwit the greedy landlord and his eviction agent. It was a novel of "workers" who lie concealed in the rat holes of Harlem by day, drinking until sodden, the women fighting like beasts for the possession of some man's body, the men perpetually on the verge of committing murder to possess the body of some woman.

A novel by a radical which does not touch upon the workers' struggle to survive in a capitalist society is so queer an anomaly as to be weird; that was *Home to Harlem*. But McKay was no longer active in the radical labor movement. He had served his apprenticeship under Max Eastman[89] on the Masses, had written an indignant poem[90] wholly lacking in working-class content, attacking lynching, had disappeared mysteriously to the Soviet Union,[91] and had retired exhausted to the sidewalk cafes of Montmartre. His treatment of a small group of Negroes, a few of whom had returned fashionably "disillusioned" from the World War, cannot in any sense be extended as adequate treatment either of Negro workers as such or of Negro soldiers. The returning soldier, disillusioned concerning wars in general, was rather a popular hero in fiction at that time; for that very reason, a radical ought to have handled the theme differently. For disillusionment alone—simple disgust and cynicism expressing themselves in physical debaucheries—is unfit as a theme for a working-class novel. If [a] novelist's workers must have illusions, then these workers, to have any value for us, must have also disillusionment evolving into sanity of mind and clarity of vision. If there be no class-consciousness action following this awakening into reality, there should be, at least, a forecast of it. Straying from this rule, fiction about workers has no validity for the working class. Certainly *Home to Harlem* has none. McKay's second novel *Banjo* differed in only unimportant details from *Home to Harlem*. The retired "radical" had grown fat, and ill, and indifferent in Paris.

Since Van Vechten captured upper-class Harlem there has been a small troop of Negro novelists, all viewing this subject from approximately the same level and the same angle. We shall consider first George S. Schuyler, who used to be called a radical, but whose enemies, even, would blush at pinning such a tag on him today. Possessed of considerable talent as a newspaper man, Schuyler is nevertheless uninterested in the working class and its struggles. The masses of black toilers are, to him, a doltish lot, and he would, perhaps, like to do something about bringing them "up" to his own rarified status as a sophisticated "intellectual"; but for the present, he believes imperialism is an excellent training course for nations like Haiti and Liberia, while, according to his pronouncement, "we cannot do away with the clergy in capitalist America or Communist Russia" because, he explains learnedly, "under any form of society the masses of people must believe, and it makes little difference whether it is in the miracles of Jesus Christ or the wizardry of Karl Marx." These quotations from Schuyler, who has never outgrown his adolescent cynicism, are typical of his writings, being designed to arouse a jeer from some Communist sympathizers (since the Communists themselves ignore him). To respond to such obvious bids for response would be out of place here, especially since they do not occur in his fiction but in a newspaper column; however, these quotations are indicative of Schuyler's methods, whatever he writes. The proletarians in his novel *Black No More*[92] are an inarticulate mass of fools with eyes set upon the conjury of pseudo-science, hoping thereby to cure their fundamental economic and political ills by changing themselves into white men. Like most other Negro writers of fiction, Schuyler believes the Negro masses to be oppressed under capitalism because of their superficial racial characteristics, and logically, Schuyler makes his workers voice Schuyler's profundities.

Four other Negro writers have dealt with the Negro worker in fiction, these being Wallace Thurman, Countee Cullen, Rudolph Fisher, and Langston Hughes, but none of them except Hughes has, evidently, heard of the class struggle. Thurman's dilettantism, revealed in his absorption in the "problems" of white and colored degenerates and common parasites; Cullen's snobbishness, betrayed in the speech and actions of his puppets,—their philosophical imbecilities; Fisher's carefree happy-go-luckies with their repartee suggestive of cheap vaudeville;—these men are obviously not to be considered for any proletarian-revolutionary treatment of the Negro worker. They are writing for the upper classes who demand the stereotype which fits most neatly into their conception of what the Negro ought to know.

Thus far, Langston Hughes, in *Not Without Laughter*,[93] has written the only novel in which the Negro worker is pictured as seeing the way out through the class struggle; it is the only novel by a Negro which is at the same time a critique of fiction. *Not Without Laughter* is lacking in many important elements, the reason being, chiefly, that Hughes at that time was lacking almost wholly in political development; but his political development since the novel was written indicates a fulfillment of the promise it contained.

The unhealthy national culture of the Negro people—reflected in the national psychology as a peculiar national psychosis,—is gradually evolving into a sound national culture, as works other than fiction proves. As working-class Negro novelists arise, however, and organize the experience of the Negro worker imaginatively and artistically, they will turn the black masses away from the poison of bourgeois propaganda toward a healthy consideration of their own interests.

"Blacks Turn Red," *Negro*
EDITED BY Nancy Cunard, Wishart & Co., 1934

Shipping line heiress Nancy Cunard was known for stirring up controversy as a result of her radical politics and her penchant for having relationships with men out of her race. When she decided to assemble *Negro*, an anthology of writings by and about Blacks from around the world, she did it in her usual flamboyant manner. The completed work was over 800 pages and included many notable authors, both Black and white, including Langston Hughes and Zora Neale Hurston. Gordon had attracted Cunard's attention with several of his articles. Although he was not paid for contributing, Gordon was drawn to Cunard's communist beliefs, and he knew that inclusion in such an anthology would add to his political and literary credentials.

He composed "Blacks Turn Red" quickly and was surprised when Cunard showed up at his doorstep in Boston to collect the manuscript. The article restates several of his themes: criticism of organized religion, conservative Black leadership, fascism, anti-intermarriage laws, denying workers' rights, and capitalism. He goes on to make the case for communism and lists the party platform advanced at the party convention in 1932.

Gordon wrote an entertaining and informative article on Cunard and his first meeting with her in "'The Green Hat' Comes to Chambers Street" in *Nancy Cunard: Brave Poet, Indomitable Rebel 1896–1965*, edited by Hugh Ford (Chilton Books, 1968): 133–40. For more on Cunard and *Negro* see Anne de Courcy *Five Love Affairs and a Friendship: The Paris Life of Nancy Cunard, Icon of the Jazz Age* (2022); Anne Chisholm *Nancy Cunard: A Biography* (1981), and Lois Gordon *Nancy Cunard: Heiress, Muse, Political Idealist* (2007).

Blacks Turn Red

Entrenched Negro leadership both secular and saintly is disturbed today as never before. Seeing prerogatives of generations slipping from its clasp, it is desperate. The leadership of Aframerica today is like a parent who awakes suddenly to the disturbing discovery that Percival has slipped the reins of parental restraint, defied parental authority, thumbed his nose at parental dogma, and shouted at parental dignity to chase itself down the alley. In its role of abused and outraged parenthood, entrenched Negro leadership is recounting reproachfully all the benefactions it has bestowed on, and all the suffering it has endured for, the ungrateful wretch, predicting calamitous mishaps to befall the miscreant unless he returns his footsteps to the gullied paths of tradition. The reason for Negro leadership's despair is that a shockingly large mass of patient, good-natured, long-suffering blacks have become surly towards the *status-quo*. They disregard the counsel of their hoary prophets and flitter after base and clay-footed gods. In short, masses of blacks formerly extolled for their ass-like docility are lingering rather long before the soapbox of the Red agitator. In fact, thousands have themselves become Red agitators. For the first time in American history whole masses of Negroes are contradicting the stencil that although they are gratuitously and regularly persecuted, they stand by loyally, appealing dumbly for a chance to spill their last drops of blood for their beloved oppressors.

And—most incomprehensible!—blacks who are guilty of this treason are not all "ignoramuses and illiterates," an influential metropolitan news-sheet to the contrary notwithstanding. Some of the best minds of Aframerica are among them. Yet he would have a ludicrous misconception of the Negro worker's changing psychology who supposed this turning of blacks to Reds to be a trick of colored intellectuals. For it is nothing less than mass metamorphosis springing from mass wretchedness and disillusionment.

Entrenched Negro leadership is that which presumes the right of paternalism over the black masses. It is both Caucasian and Negro.

When the snobbish Boston *Transcript* and the supercilious New York *Herald-Tribune* assume an attitude of condescending paternalism towards the black worker, advising him for his soul's good to flee from Communism, the *Transcript* and the *Herald-Tribune* manifest traits of entrenched Negro leadership. These and other newspapers frequently do so. That it is wiser to examine the thing they are warned to stay away from than to heed the advice and flee, is already axiomatic among Negro workers. No other people in the world is quite so chary of the Greeks who come bearing gifts.

Entrenched Negro leadership came to flower in the church in slavery days, and until today it has felt secure because it has seen the Negro perpetually in the role of a cringing, grateful dependent praying for white ruling-class benevolence. From the beginning white masters comprehended the value of Christianity as an opiate to induce sluggish content. So effectual was the narcotization of the blacks that, with one or two exceptions, recorded instances of slave rebellion make wearisome reading. Why? Because such revolts were usually but half-formed, sissified gestures. Christianity's mollycoddling had rotted the very fabric of their stamina.

This early leadership of the black masses did its work well. Complaint today among sable Men of God against Communism is chiefly that "them Reds is atheists; they don't b'lieve in no God." It is only now, after all these scores of years, that the black masses are struggling out from under the mountainous disabilities loaded upon their backs by the leadership of the pre-Lincoln era. It was a leadership that turned black feet into a maze of by-ways which until now have kept the Negro bewildered and uncertain. Having found his way out of the maze, the black worker's uncertainty gives way to a conviction and his bewilderment no longer exists.

Leadership following "emancipation" assumed a complexion slightly dark. Being the beginning of an era of struggle for an economic foothold, it was, dialectically, the beginning of Negro parasitism. This parasitical leadership was composed of two sections, the Negro ministry and the Negro editor-politician. Both ministers and editor-politicians dreamed of power and possessions; but the ministry hoped that the Men of God would form the black aristocracy, while the editor-politician could conceive of no élite which excluded him. Both agreed that the black worker was to be kept in his place. Thus the preacher exhorted the worker to support the church and to scorn materialism. Supporting the church, the black millions remained in poverty, being degraded to the status of a new slave system, while the rising aristocracy of the church accumulated vast material possessions.

Editor-politicians were less individualistic. They worked for a class of wealthy landowners and professional men; a class which, composed of editors, holders of political office, physicians, lawyers, and insurance heads, would be supported by the toiling masses. This was their dream of the black aristocracy. Both groups succeeded somewhat, but the aristocracy of the Holy Men apparently prospered beyond that of their materialistic brethren. Wealth tied up in Negro churches, from which the ministers derive direct benefit, greatly exceeds that owned by the professional aristocracy.

Off and on through this period of struggle for economic security the black masses sought a leadership which would be adequate in all ways. Now and then an individual leader arose, a Frederick Douglass or a Booker Washington; but his vision was invariably clouded by the miasma of opportunism. A petty political office or the condescending patronage of the ruling class usually turned his head so far aside that he could not see the miserable degradation of the black masses who prayed he would deliver them. If either Douglass or Washington, in his later and affluent days, saw the true plight of his Negro kinsmen, he did not concern himself about it. Douglass, turned petty Republican politician, vegetated like a contented country cabbage on the outskirts of Washington, DC, while millions of blacks all around him wallowed in ignorance and neglect. Booker T. Washington compromised readily with the vindictive white South, eschewing social and political equity for the masses while grabbing at even the shadow of it for himself.

Entrenched Negro leadership is today totally bankrupt, and the masses are hoarse with clamoring for a figure tall enough to be seen above their heads and a voice penetrating and steady enough to be heard above their own cries of wretchedness. Having chafed for generations under burdens laid upon their backs by these misleaders, the masses of blacks feel that they have a right to choose their leadership of the future. They have chosen it.

II

Present Negro leadership is dominated by the press. The Negro church exerts the next greatest influence. Following the church strut the politicians. Individual newspaper writers like Kelly Miller, William E. B. DuBois, George S. Schuyler, Gordon Hancock,[94] and William Pickens remain individual leaders. Each has a small following of thoughtless hero-worshippers. None of them could possibly rally an appreciable percentage of the workers, the reason being that none of them has anything basic to give. Kelly Miller is intellectually sterile because intellectually stranded; the swift current of events leaves him untouched. DuBois, who calls himself a socialist and tries valiantly to love the masses, is incurably snobbish. George S. Schuyler is an opportunist of a most odious sort. Gordon Hancock is Uncle Tom reincarnate. William Pickens is not dependable, having shown that he will retract if his owners order him to do so. Nor are the well-written and well-edited editorial pages of the Norfolk *Journal and Guide*, the Chicago *Defender*, the New York *Amsterdam News*, the Chicago *Whip*, and the Pittsburgh *Courier*, each constantly dominated by the influence of the Republican or Democratic party, nearly so powerful as they used to be. Having played for years on one tuneless string, their weary song of race-solidarity, loyalty to the Republican party, loyalty to the Democratic party, and unswerving patriotism to our great country, is no longer heard. The noise is there but it penetrates no one's consciousness.

The Negro church is still influential in places. The reason for this unfortunate condition is that millions of black workers are forced to continue in ignorance. But the power of the ministry is waning. Enlightened Negroes long since turned from the ministry as a field for leadership. If one now and then enters it today he does it for the same reason that a boy enters West Point or the Naval Academy. It will offer a soft job with a lot of graft. Church membership falls off gradually from year to year, as United States Census Bureau statistics show. In short, the Negro church, still influential to some degree among a few of the peasant blacks of the South, is a pitiable joke to most of the offspring even of these saintly souls. When young folks come to make ribald allusions to Yahveh it is time to junk him. The automobile, the newspaper, the radio, and the motion picture have carried knowledge to the backwoods, and the church, with its mumbo-jumbo superstitions, has retreated, mouthing curses.

As for the black politicians, they do not pretend more than a periodic and selfish interest in black voters. If the casual observer wonder perplexedly how year after year these sleek and engaging scoundrels control the Negro vote, the voter himself is completely befuddled. Steeped for generations in the nonsense of "race pride" and "race consciousness," he doubts whether to trust the suave Negro politician who "proves" that a colored gentleman in office reflects a golden glory upon the lowliest black worker, in whatever hovel he may sleep or from whatever garbage can he may filch his meal. The bewildered black voter tries to recall one instance of *his* wages being raised, or *his* rent being reduced, because he obeyed instructions of a colored political boss and voted the boss's boss into the mayor's seat. Yet, because he *has* had race pride and has been race conscious, he obeys orders. "We Negroes must stand together and put our own kind into office," the black worker is told. But once in office the Assistant United States District Attorney, or the Assistant Corporation Counsel, or the Assistant Clerk of the Juvenile Court, moves so far beyond smelling distance of the black workers' slums that he has to buy a powerful straight-eight[95] to reach his office on time. The black worker is thinking about all these things now. He is thinking of them both as worker and as voter. One of the results of his thinking has been the swelling Communist vote in Negro neighborhoods. His thinking about these things has not led him to vote Communist in a vindictive or reformist spirit. He knows that a rotten vegetable cannot be reformed into a sound one, or that a decaying carcass cannot be rejuvenated into a frisky animal. He votes differently to indicate that he wants a radical change. Moreover, he feels sure that voting for this change is simply a gesture and that radical changes are not brought about simply by thumbing the nose.

I must make a parenthetical mention of organisational leadership here. This leadership has done its share of confusing the masses, but the majority of Negro workers are now aware that any organisation—such as the National Association for the Advancement of Colored People and the National Urban League, to name two—is impotent when it depends for its very existence upon the class which oppresses those it purports to lead. The workers see clearly that these organisations are tools manipulated by puppets at the hands of those who give the money.

The black masses today stand searching the horizon for leadership: one which will not exploit them; which will endeavor to keep its promises to them; which will be of them; which will so understand them and share their lives that, if called upon to do so, will either die with them or for them; whose program, however, is for richer, happier living on earth, excluding all consideration of a hereafter. They have never found such a leadership in all the 300 years they have been here. They have doubted that such a leadership was to be found. And now the eye of the Negro worker has caught the eye of the Communist; and the eyes of these two hold each other in mutual understanding.

III

Entrenched Negro leadership is naturally terrified at what it sees in the eyes of the black worker. His old worshipful attitude, that old look of awe, his respectful deference, his cringing self-effacement, his doglike loyalty to an indifferent master, his blind and dumb patriotism—these attributes of the old Negro are vanishing. There is a smirk of cynicism; there is an arrogant self-assurance; there is forceful assertiveness. These are characteristics of the transition period. Later there comes the self-assurance without arrogance; there is no longer a cynical smirk, for the worker knows that a whole new world lies ahead of him. The roundly developed adult is too intelligent to be cynical. The white boss and the black errand boys are so many parasites; he catalogues them as such and ignores them except as they get in his way. Entrenched Negro leadership thereupon decides frantically that this strange new creature will bear watching. Learned Negro editors discuss him weightily in *The Crisis*, using this alien word "communism" as if it were an obscenity or a sacrilege. It is evident that few of the discarded leaders know what to make of it. The editor of the Norfolk *Journal and Guide*, for instance, marvels that "The Communists in America have commendably contended for and have practised equality of all races"; but he shakes his head doubtfully, muttering that the Communists have also "aroused such charged feelings in many sections" that it is "difficult for the best of both races to get together and study and correct problems in an orderly way." The kindly editor is perhaps too bewildered to recollect that "the best of both races" have been getting together for decades, that very fact being one of the reasons for the revolt of the masses today.

That there is still a strong inclination on the parts of "the best of both races to get together and study and correct problems in an orderly way" seems to be well established in the utterances of at least two men. One of them is Bruce Reynolds, white, compiler of a volume of anti-communist protestations; the other is the Negro editor of the Atlanta *World*.[96] The white man (who loves Negroes and wishes to see them kept in their place) and the black man (who loves Negroes and wishes to keep his place) arrive at some amazingly similar conclusions.

Reynolds says:

> The true American Negro is . . . perfectly satisfied with his present status in Society. . . . In fact, he has contempt for the white person who fawns upon him and offers him equality and intimacy. He knows that this is hypocrisy and deceit. But the Communist agitator from Moscow has figured out that there are enough of the bad, unintelligent element among the Negroes from which to draw adherents to Communism through picturing to them this "Heaven-on-Earth," when all barriers will be smashed and the Negro will be a first citizen, enjoying full and equal rank and privilege with the whites. . . . The day of race prejudice in America is past. . . . There is a place in American society for every man, no matter what his color, creed, or religion.

The editor of the Negro Atlanta *World* avers that he knows personally of blacks who joined the Communist Party only so they could dance with white women. He is uncompromisingly opposed to social equality of this kind. Not only that, this editor says, but "Small groups of Negroes in the South going Red have harmed themselves and others in the community. Violence and bloodshed have resulted," he declares; and he blames the militancy of the black share-croppers of Camp Hill, SC,[97] for the murder of some of their number when, in a meeting to form a union for common protection, they defended themselves with rifles against white landowners who militantly objected.

Agreeing further with this representative of the master class, the Negro editor says:

> This race is slow to change. It would prefer keeping its present status, no matter how low, then fly to a system, no matter what its worth, that is constantly lambasted by press and radio.

But he is given the lie by one of his fellow craftsmen, the editor of the Philadelphia *Tribune*,[98] remarking that although it is "paradoxical that Negroes must seek protection under some flag other than the Stars and Stripes, the flag for which they have fought to keep flying in the cause of justice and human liberty," nevertheless, "thousands of converts have sought solace and comfort within the folds of the deep-pink banner of the party of Lenin and Stalin." Why, he exclaims "I am told that there are more dark-skinned than white Communists in Philadelphia"; and he adds: "If numbers mean success, then the drive for Negro numbers succeeded." It is unmistakably clear that the editor of a Negro paper in Philadelphia is more likely to be honest about these facts than his brethren in Atlanta. Therefore I think we may accept the *Tribune*'s estimate as being more honest than that of the *World*.

There are various other discussions by gentlemen of the capitalist Negro press, most of them revealing that these men are forced to admit the seeping spread of Communism among Negroes. They admit it grudgingly, as if to do so breaks their very hearts. Thus the Houston *Defender* laments that, "Being an exploited, maltreated and disadvantaged minority group, there is grave danger that Negroes will embrace any doctrine which offers them relief from certain oppressive, repressive, and depressive conditions under which they live and eke out an existence"; while the Houston *Informer* points out reproachfully that the whites may expect Negroes to go on "grabbing at straws," being "lured by Communism and every other name that holds out to them bright hopes of relief from their burdens." The New York *Amsterdam News* does not wonder that "the Negro is beginning, at least, to think along Communist lines, but that he did not embrace the doctrine *en masse* long ago."

Most of these editors of the Negro press discuss the black Red weightily and fearfully, but it is patent that few of them have learned from an original source what Communism is. To one it is something to "sell," like a headache powder; another refers to it mistily as being similar to Christianity. One scholarly scribe speaks of the radical changes in the Soviet Union as "reforms," and another, equally erudite, tells us that Communism is the big "plan" we have been hearing about. Only two of these learned gentlemen see what the masses of black workers saw long since: that Communism is no longer mere *promise* of better days and things, but a working program, in operation every day of the week, towards bringing about the changes promised. The most farseeing of these men is the editor of the Baltimore *Afro-American*,[99] who says briefly that the Communist appears to be the only party "going our way."

Thus entrenched Negro leadership, white and black, contemplates this new menace to its waning authority; this new menace to a social system which has given it wealth and power. Indeed, the word "contemplates" is far too mild, for there is a defining counter-struggle going on against this rising leadership of the Negro masses. The politicians, utilizing Oscar DePriest as their spokesman, warn Congress that *they* will not be responsible if, through Congressional indifference and neglect, black voters turn Red. The preachers shout to the masses that Communism is an illegitimate child of Satan. The professional class begs the workers to realise that only through creating a strong middle class can the race "find" itself.

Meanwhile news dispatches tell of workers throughout the country who, imbued with what the capitalist detractors sneeringly refer to as "the Communist religion," evince such fortitude in the face of persecution as "the good old-time religion" has never inspired. Thus we see a black worker organising the unemployed in Wellsville, Ohio, while the police arrest and beat him again and again. Thus we read of the black miner in the Kentucky coal fields who ignored bribes to get out, and continued organising whites and blacks until beaten to a pulp and thrown into jail. Thus we hear of black men and women in Chicago, Camp Hill, Pittsburgh, Cleveland, Boston, and New York fighting with such zeal and suffering with such fortitude as the black worker has never before been known to possess. We shall continue to encounter such dispatches, for the Negro's recognition of his new inspiration is just beginning. While a discarded leadership fumes impotently at what it considers the "treachery" of the black worker, the Communist Party issues a release and the Negro masses read:

> With the demand for equal rights for the Negro people and self-determination for the Black Belt[100] as one of its major political planks, the Communist Party of the United States issued through its Central Committee a call for a nominating convention to be held in Chicago May 28 and 29 [1932].
>
> In this convention [announces the call][101] all workers and farmers, Negro and white, and their organizations, all persons and workers' organizations prepared to support a militant workers' platform and candidates, are invited to participate.
>
> The convention call lists six major points in the platform of the Party, on the basis of which it will ask support of the workers and poor farmers. These points are:
>
> 1. Unemployment and social insurance at the expense of the state and employers.
> 2. Against Hoover's wage-cutting policy.
> 3. Emergency relief, without restrictions by the government and banks, for the poor farmers from taxes, and from forced collection of debts.
> 4. Equal rights for the Negroes and self-determination for the Black Belt.
> 5. Against capitalist terror; against all forms of suppression of the political rights of the workers.
> 6. Against imperialist war; for the defence of the Chinese people and of the Soviet Union.

Reading these six election planks, the black worker seizes upon those which most directly apply to him. He asks: "What is the exact meaning of the demand in your program of 'equal rights for Negroes'?"

Here is the answer he gets:

> By equal rights for Negroes we mean complete equality in every sphere of life. Political equality includes the right to vote, to hold office, to sit on juries, to enter into political and other organizations, to take part in the whole political life of the community. This demand includes those so-called democratic rights supposedly granted to everyone, but in reality denied workers and especially Negroes—certain court rights, for example, denied to Negroes, especially in the South.
>
> The Communist Party fights against jim-crow restriction in the daily life of the Negro workers—residential segregation, jim-crow in restaurants and theatres, transportation lines and schools. We demand the abolition of the anti-intermarriage laws which exist in 29 states at the present time.

Blacks Turn Red 311

> On the economic field we struggle against the special discrimination to which Negro workers are subject in their efforts to make a living. We are pledged to determined struggle for equal wages for Negro workers, for the right to work at every trade, against discrimination practised openly or in a hidden manner in the job agencies and relief stations.
> Our program holds good for every section of the country, including the South.

Having read this declaration, the Negro worker entertains no doubts of which party he will vote for hereafter. He realises clearly two facts. One is that campaign promises have been made by other parties in other days and forgotten. The other is that the Communist Party is the only one which works at its program day after day throughout the year:—directing the organisation of Negro share-croppers at Camp Hill; leading black workers in demonstrations against evictions in Chicago, Cleveland, New York, and scores of other cities; defending a homeless and friendless Negro worker in the courts of Maryland and preventing a legal lynching; forcing the courts of Alabama to delay execution of eight Negro youths[102] whose guilt has been questioned the world over; forcing the management of an "exclusive" Brookline, Mass., hotel to admit Negro high-school graduates to a class dance with their white friends; punishing white Americans in the Soviet Union for assaulting a Negro worker; protesting against the massacre of black workers in the Belgian Congo who revolted against labor conditions in commercial enterprises; constantly fighting against capitalist imperialism; organising agriculture workers among black peoples of American, French, British, Belgian, Dutch, Portuguese, Spanish, and Italian imperialism. And the Negro ceases looking for that leadership he has sought for generations. He knows that he has found it and that it has found him, at last.

Having vainly entreated Yahveh to reveal the secret of changing Red blacks into the ordinary, simple-minded blacks they originally were entrenched, Negro leadership gloomily bows its head, mournfully rolls its eyes, and mutters resignedly: "Brethren, only one course is open to us, and that is the course this leadership has pursued since emancipation. We must continue to pursue it to the bitter end. Brethren, while there remains an opportunity for us to do so, let us *prey*."

Excerpt "The Borden Case: The Struggle for Negro Rights in Boston"
League of Struggle for Equal Rights (AUGUST 13, 1934)

Another important case in which Gordon became involved was that of George Borden, a Black porter, who lived in Roxbury. Borden had only had a couple of minor traffic violations on his record when on July 8, 1934, two city workers (Everett Gardner, motor vehicles inspector, and William Harmon, a police officer, wearing civilian clothing) entered his home while he was eating dinner with his family. They said they had a warrant for his arrest for "driving without a license." Having heard frightful stories of the police, Borden attempted to escape. In the ensuing melee, Borden was shot by Gardner and died from his wounds on July 14. Police claimed Gardner was justified in killing Borden. As Zebulon Miletsky states, Borden's killing may not have been noticed without the attention Gordon drew to it. By this time, Gordon had already begun to be a well-respected member of the community, and "using the power of the pen, Gordon marshaled his considerable intellectual weight to spread the word about injustice for Borden and other Black Bostonians."[103] In this piece, Gordon clearly posits the communist belief that class consciousness must be more important than race consciousness.

The Borden Case
The Struggle for Negro Rights in Boston

INTRODUCTION

George H. Borden, a young Negro worker, was surprised at dinner in his cellar apartment with his family and a friend by two swaggering white men in civilian clothes. They were both armed, and they both gave the impression that they might be thugs; one said he was Motor Vehicles Inspector Everett Gardner, and that the man with him was a policeman. They had come to arrest Borden for driving without a license.

Borden, frightened by the appearance and the actions of the men, asked permission to go to an upstairs apartment to telephone a friend. He knew someone who might bail him out. The policeman, William Harmon, followed the janitor upstairs his hand on his pistol. Finding nobody in the apartment, Borden was suddenly stricken with terror. He was without influential friends; he had been arrested once before, for violating a minor traffic law and held for three days like a desperate criminal, incommunicado. He knew something of the workings of Law and Order, and he was afraid. Suddenly panicky, he made a dash for the back stairs and freedom.

Harmon fired. Borden ran to the basement, the policeman shouting and shooting. Gardner, who had waited downstairs, ran out into the yard to head off the harassed and frightened man. It was while Borden was in the act of lifting himself upward out of the basement window that Gardner shot him four times. These events took place Sunday, July 8, 1934.

There was one organization in Boston which was supposed to look after the interests of persons like Borden, that is, friendless persons who find themselves all at once overwhelmed by the brutal forces of society. That organization was the National Association for the Advancement of

Colored People, headed by the colored lawyer, Butler R. Wilson. There was a very weak branch of the League of Struggle for Negro Rights and a Branch of the International Labor Defense.

The League, weak as it was, acted immediately. Members went to see Borden's wife; they attempted to get a warrant for the arrest of the police assailants. They interviewed witnesses. The head of the International Labor Defense was absent from the city. The National Association for the Advancement of Colored People assumed the usual attitude of "watchful waiting," presumably to decide whether the case justified the Association's entering it.

A mass meeting, called jointly by the League of Struggle for Negro Rights and the International Labor Defense, was held on the following Friday evening in Roxbury, where the police tried to intimidate the gathering by massing at the entrance and turning off the lights. At the very moment a speaker was denouncing these characteristic police tactics to the mass meeting of Negro and white citizens, word came that Borden was dead. That was Friday evening, July 13th.

From this mass meeting there was organized a new branch of the League of Struggle for Negro rights—a Roxbury branch, which was named George Borden, for the murdered man. It was this newly organized branch of the L.S.N.R. which, with the I.L.D., took charge of the funeral arrangements, assuming all responsibility for expenses. These organizations prepared for and conducted the largest public funeral of an ordinary worker that Boston had ever seen. It made a profound impression not only upon the Negro and white citizens, but upon the police also. This pamphlet is made up of the speeches which were delivered at the funeral exercises and of a paper answering attacks of Buster R. Wilson, N.A.A.C.P. head, on the L.S.N.R. and the I.L.D.

Boston, August 13, 1934.

Funeral Services
Introductory Remarks
By EUGENE GORDON, Pres. George Borden Branch, L.S.N.R.

Sunday's papers quoted one of our substantial and respectable colored citizens, Mr. Butler R. Wilson, as being deeply concerned about the activities of the "reds" in behalf of the common janitor,

George Borden, and in behalf of George Borden's family. With his delicate and aristocratic hands uplifted in righteous horror, Mr. Wilson protested that he saw no reason why the body of this man should receive the kind of consideration that those whom he spoke of contemptuously as "reds" were giving it. The action of Borden's friends, common working men and women like himself, might stir up "race feeling," was the excuse given by Mr. Wilson for his objection.

Is this an occasion for answering or launching attacks, or is this an occasion for mourning? Before us there lies the murdered body of a Negro worker—murdered both because, being a Negro, he had no rights, and because, being a common janitor, an ordinary worker, he was without pull or prestige, or friends whose influence come from political parties or wealth. We who honor him here and now were unable to prevent the assassin's attack; we are able and shall fight to prevent attacks upon his character, upon the character of his family, and upon the character of the only friends his destitute wife and infant children have. These friends are the persons whom Butler Wilson sneers at as "reds": everybody is a "red" who actually organizes for a determined struggle for our most elementary human and citizenship rights. We are here to bid farewell to a worker from the ranks of those who, confused by the turmoil and the hardships of this life-long day to day battle even for the right to live, batter their poor heads against the stone wall of ruling-class oppression. Thus we are not here to mourn the death of George Borden; we are here to honor him, who, as one of us, must needs die in order to arouse us to action against this thing, which threatens us all. We are met, therefore, as fighters rather than as mourners. George Borden's murder at the hands of our enemies shall not go unavenged! We declared it at the instant of his death last Friday night; we repeat it now with the vigor and assurance that organized strength gives us. This is an occasion both to answer attacks and to launch counter attacks; it is an occasion for taking the counter offensive against our enemies—the police and the whole brutal system of oppression and terror of which the police are a part and of which they are sworn and paid defenders.

We do not resent being called "reds" because we have begun a militant offensive against the forces that killed George Borden. Only a little while ago every Negro was without question disdainfully and scornfully labeled "nigger" and automatically classified as "inoffensive" or "loyal" or "good"—in short, as [a] direct descendant of a meek and long suffering Uncle Tom—if he did not show resentment when the white bully spat in his face. He who labels and classifies us in that manner is a liar. Indeed, that sort of labeling and classifying is ceasing, even in the South where oppression and suppression of masses of Negroes are most ruthless and brutal. Among the great masses of Negro workers there is developing a new kind of Negro: class consciousness rather than "race" conscious, he sees and understands the common bond between him and the white worker. Being class conscious, he sees and understands the true friendships, genuine loyalties, unshakeable solidarity, can be effected only among those who belong to a common class in society, owing to the fact that they take part in a common struggle against poverty and oppression.

This new kind of Negro, in short, identifies his interests with all other people who are degraded and oppressed, regardless of what their so-called "race" may be. That is why you see Negroes and whites side by side among class-conscious workers. That is why there have sprung up among these Negro and white workers a spirit of sympathy so keen and a sense of understanding so profound that neither police terror nor appeals to the ancient superstitions or "race" differences—superstitions which the class Butler Wilson worships strives desperately to keep alive—can drive them apart. As a matter of fact, these forces let loose upon us by the arrogant and domineering rich and powerful only weld us more firmly together. Thus, instead of honoring a murdered worker, our action completely undermines the foundation of and destroys "race feeling." Race hatred, being an artificial and man-made device to trick us with, disappears like a cube of ice in a July sun in the atmosphere of common working class solidarity that prevails among us.

But people who believe as we do and fight the common enemy together as we do—Negroes who have determined that they will no longer bend their backs like slaves and kiss the bloody hands that beat them—we Negroes are called "reds" by Butler Wilson and the police and their rich and powerful masters. Thus we learn the definition of the word "red"; thus we learn the definition of the term a "dangerous" or a "bad" Negro. A "red" is anybody who does not agree that it is patriotic and American to starve, to go naked, and to sleep in parks and doorways, when food is molding in storage or is being destroyed, when clothes are rotting in the stock rooms, and when great hotels and apartment houses are empty of tenants yet locked against the homeless. The man who merely speaks about these crimes against the masses of people is a "red."

A "dangerous" or "bad" Negro is one who will not submit to seeing his wife and daughters abused by men of influence and pull, and who avenges his fellow Negroes through organized, militant action. If these actions be characteristic of "reds" or "bad" Negroes, let us be so classified. To Butler Wilson we readily accede the title of Gentlemen's Waiting Man, Uncle Tom, or Professional Kisser of Ruling Class Feet, a title for which he has persistently fought and of which he is justifiably proud.

Butler Wilson admits that the sole reason his organization entered the case was to check the influence of the "reds" among the Negro people; not for the welfare of the surviving family, not for the interest of those fatherless children, not for the life and death interests of the Negro people, not for one blow against the vile and putrid system which makes George Borden, Scottsboro, Herndon,[104] and Mooney[105] cases possible—inevitable. Oh, no! But against the "reds," whose very reason for existence is to fight against and destroy these things. Out of his mouth has he condemned himself!

So these ceremonies over the body of George Borden are the preliminaries of battle. They are not the muted tones of stricken mourners who will slink in silence to the wretched holes to which this society has consigned them. They are the actions against race but of an oppressed race, and of an oppressed class, against the bloody-handed oppressors of the masses of working men and women and children, both white and black.

"The Position of Negro Women" (Gordon with Cyril Briggs)
Workers Library Publishers, 1935

One of the major pieces Gordon wrote was a pamphlet "The Position of Negro Women," which he coauthored with Cyril Briggs in 1935. Briggs, a committed Communist, founded the radical African Blood Brotherhood, which advocated the need for Black self-defense. The Workers Library Publishers was the Workers Party of America's New York City–based publishing house for pamphlets.

Gordon had long held an interest in the struggles of women going back to his time editing the *Saturday Evening Quill*. In addition, he wrote several articles pointing out women's oppression under the capitalist system. This pamphlet is his manifesto on the subject. Observing chauvinism in the workplace, Gordon and Briggs tried to address the problem as they point out "to be both a woman worker and a Negro is to suffer a double handicap." Often, they receive the lowest pay, are assigned the most onerous tasks, and have the least job security. Gordon and Briggs advocated for unity between Black and white workers and that white women workers needed to take the lead in improving conditions for Black workers.[106] Since the two men saw capitalism as a major obstacle for women to gain equality, they advocated following the lead of the Soviet Union: "The victorious workers and peasants of the Soviet Union point the revolutionary way out of the morass of capitalist race hatred and national oppression, chronic mass unemployment and suffering, fascist reaction and imperialist war."

The Position of Negro Women

In a society based on production for profit, to be both a woman worker and a Negro is to suffer a double handicap.

The Negro woman worker is doubly victimized. She suffers both from the general discriminations against women workers and from her identity as a member of a nationality singled out by the ruling class for special plundering, persecution and oppression.

As a woman worker she feels the general inequalities—lower wages, longer hours, bad working conditions, etc., imposed upon women in a society based on private ownership of public wealth and resources, private control of the social means of production.

As a Negro, she is paid even less than her exploited sister, made to work under even harder conditions, longer hours, etc., and is systemically excluded from all but the heaviest and dirtiest jobs. She is barred from promotion, as a rule. On her lower wages, she must meet the discriminative higher rentals extracted from Negro workers by piratical landlords, both Negro and white, in the segregated ghettoes into which she and her family are forced to live by Jim-Crow laws or practices. Thus the dirty deal that falls to all working women in capitalist society falls heaviest upon the Negro woman worker.

For 300 years, under both chattel slavery and wage slavery, Negro women had worked on the plantations as laborers and in upper class households as domestics and personal servants. They were almost solely limited to these occupations up to 1910. From that year, however, the reports of the U.S, Department of Labor show that Negro women have been following the general shift from the farm into the industrial centers.

The entry of Negro women into industry was facilitated by the World War. In the early days of that bloody conflict when American participation was limited to furnishing loans and war material to the Allies, the expansion of the war industries and allied industries created a demand for extra labor. Immigration being at a low ebb because of the war, the northern industrialists turned to the Southern plantations for Negro labor. Recruiting agents scoured the South, offering the Negro share-croppers and peons "work and freedom" in the North. The economic base was thus afforded for a mighty mass migration of Negroes from the South. Hundreds of thousands came North, seeking political freedom, decent wages and working and living conditions, and educational facilities for their children; eager to escape the terror-ridden South with its new slavery of peonage and share-cropping.

In 1917, when the rulers of the United States demanded the conversion of white and Negro workers into cannon fodder to protect the loans of the House of Morgan[107] to the Allies, women were used to replace men, either wholly or partly, in many industries. White women so employed were paid less than the men had been getting, while Negro women received still lower wages. In addition, the Negro women were assigned to the heaviest and most hazardous jobs in the war industries, and to the more menial and grueling work in other lines, such as textiles and clothing factories, food industry, wood-product manufacture, etc.

"The census of 1920, taken immediately after the war period, showed that Negro women in the manufacturing and mechanical industries had increased by over one half," a Labor Department bulletin reports.

Negro women, tormented by the memory of the drudgery and humiliation of farm and domestic service, happily imagined themselves firmly planted in the industries, with their relatively better conditions. Then came the end of the World War, the collapse of war-time "prosperity" which, because of the correspondingly high cost of living, was confined mainly to the munition barons and other war profiteers and 100 per cent "patriots." The crisis of 1921[108] led to wholesale firing of workers, with the women, and particularly the Negro women workers, the first to be discharged. Hand in hand with the mass firing went the slashing of wages for those still employed, and the replacement of women workers with the demobilized men at greater speed-up and a resultant increase of profits for the employers.

Only in the laundry industry, notorious for its high speed-up, low pay, and terrible working conditions, and in certain departments of textiles, etc, with similarly bad reputations, were the Negro women able to hold their own. In these low-pay, unskilled industries, the employers can employ workers new to industry and therefore lacking in the traditions of organized labor. The Negro women fitted this bill. In addition to their inexperience in labor organizations, the bosses find it possible to isolate them from the white workers in the plants by the chauvinist poison of race hatred and prejudice which is carefully instilled into the minds of the white workers by the capitalist press, schools and other institutions, both governmental and private.

FOUGHT FOR BETTER CONDITIONS

But the Negro women workers were not slow to protest against conditions. In some instances they even forced a betterment of the conditions in the industries. The history of labor struggles in the last two decades affords abundant proof that Negro women and men workers are among the best fighters for the interests of the working class and against capitalist oppression. Negro women participated in many strike struggles, and in several instances (Chicago and St. Louis nut-pickers' strikes) carried out militant strikes in factories where mostly Negro women were employed.

> "In clothing and food manufacture, there had been a great increase of Negro women by 1930," a bulletin issued by the Women's Bureau of the U.S. Department of Labor reports, "very much larger—particularly in clothing—than the proportional additions to the American-born white women employed in these industries."

In food manufacture in 1930, the latest date for which we have Department of Labor figures, there was one Negro woman to every eight American-born white women. In the same year, nearly every fourth woman working in cigar factories was a Negro. Meantime "there had been a decline for Negro and some gain for white women" in textiles.

The highest weekly wages of Negro women in any branch of textiles in the fifteen states studied was $8.95 in bag making, while as low as $4.25 was paid those workers handling wastes. The N.R.A.[109] codes, with their legalization of wage differentials for Southern white workers, and a still lower wage differential for Southern Negro workers, have made very little difference to the Negro women workers in textiles.

N.R.A. "BLESSINGS"

The N.R.A. codes, which have been used to cut wages under the pretext of establishing a minimum wage (which in many industries has become the maximum wage), operated particularly sharply against the Negro working woman. In many cases employers paying even below the N.R.A. minimum have fired their Negro employees rather than increase their wages. In most instances, however, the employers have found the N.R.A. authorities willing to co-operate in continuing wage discriminations against Negroes.

The Southland Manufacturing Company, for instance, a cotton shirt making concern of Alabama, employs mostly Negro women (95 per cent). The N.R.A. code for cotton-making industries calls for a weekly wage of $12 in the South. The company appealed for, and obtained, exemption on the pretext that its Negro women workers were "incompetent" and "deserved" only $9 a week at the most. This wealthy company, a subsidiary of the Reliance Manufacturing Company, was staunchly supported in its wage discrimination and slander of Negro women workers by Dr. Robert Russa Moton, principal of Tuskegee, and Dr. G. Lake Imes, secretary of the institution.

The N.R.A. ruling in this case is typical of the wage differentials permitted under the N.R.A. against Negro workers, and Southern workers generally. For instance, the cotton code allows a $12 a week wage in the South, as against a $14 wage in the North. As shown above, the $12 Southern wage is further cut in the case of Negro workers.

The number of dressmakers and seamstresses not in factories declined among both white and Negro women between 1920 and 1930, owing to increased demand for cheaper factory-made clothes. So although there were nearly 27,000 Negro women in the field in 1920 by 1930 the number had dropped to slightly more than 20,000.

Today, there are more than 18,000 Negro women employed at some form of tobacco manufacture. Their work is generally confined to "the more menial, the lower paid, the heavier and more hazardous" jobs.

LARGEST GROUP IN DOMESTIC SERVICE

The largest group of Negro women workers are still to be found in domestic and personal service. In 1930, there were considerably more than 600,000 of the nearly 2,000,000 Negro women workers reported for that year, in domestic and personal service. Of these, the domestic servants—cooks, chambermaids, house-hold maids, etc.—and the day workers are probably the worst exploited. Wages of these workers are as low as ten dollars a month. Wages paid day workers—women hired by the day to clean and do the washing, etc.—are as low as fifty cents a day in New York City, and probably lower in most other communities. As a rule they are given only one meal by their employers and must provide their breakfast before reporting for work, and their supper, after their day's work. All out of 50 cents, from which they must also pay rent, buy clothes, etc. In addition, many report robbery of their pitifully small wages by racketeering employers. Their employment is highly irregular.

In 1930, Negro women workers had also made some slight gains in industrial employment, before the crisis which began in 1919 had resulted in a general breakdown of capitalist production, with unparalleled mass unemployment and suffering for millions of working class families and small tradespeople.

The figures of the Women's Bureau show that slightly more than 50,000 were in steam laundries and cleaning and dyeing establishments in 1930. During the same year, about 18,000 Negro women were working as housekeepers and stewards, with perhaps a like number of waitresses. Nearly 16,000 worked as untrained nurses and midwives, while considerably over 12,000 served as hairdressers, manicurists and barbers. Charwomen and cleaners numbered more than 11,000; elevator operators slightly exceeded 4,000.

FIGURES CONCEAL TERRIFIC EXPLOITATION

Dry as these bare figures are, and concealing the terrific exploitation and unhealthy working conditions to which Negro women workers are subjected in the steam laundry and other industries, they are significant and important. They show that Negro working women, battling against tremendous odds, have made inroads into fields from which they were formerly barred. The conditions imposed upon women workers, and in particular upon the Negro working women, are barely hinted at in a bulletin, "Women At Work," issued by the Women's Bureau of the Department of Labor:

> "While women workers in general have been restricted by lack of opportunities for employment, by long hours, low wages, and harmful working conditions, there are groups—the latest comers into industry—upon whom these hardships have fallen with doubled severity. As members of a new and inexperienced race arrive at the doors of industry the jobs that open up to them ordinarily are those vacated by an earlier stratum of workers who move on to more highly paid occupations. Negro women constitute such a new and inexperienced group among women workers."

This picture of progressive advancement, of older workers moving on to higher paid occupations is deliberately false. It is a hypocritical justification by a governmental agency for job and wage discrimination against Negroes generally, and Negro women in particular. To expose its falsity we have only to remember that the same policy of studied discrimination operates against the employment of Negroes as clerks in the big stores, as conductors on street cars and subway and railroad systems, and in other unskilled categories. The Southern white ruling class frankly explains this policy as aimed to keep Negroes "in their place," that is, at the bottom of capitalist society.

Confining Negro workers to "the more menial, the lower paid, heavier and more hazardous jobs," not only enables the bosses to subject them to greater exploitation, but to use them to depress the wages of all workers. All the tricks at the disposal of the white ruling class are used to force the Negro into a lower position, to create antagonism and hatred between Negro workers and white workers, and thus to hamper united effort for better conditions.

UNITY OF WHITE AND NEGRO WORKERS ESSENTIAL

Only where discrimination against Negroes is vigorously combatted and the unity of all workers forged in joint struggles can the working class better its conditions. It is up to the white women workers, themselves the victims of wage and other discriminations, to realize the necessity to struggle for, and with the Negro women workers, for equal rights, equal pay for equal work, and an end to intolerable working conditions. The white working women, in their own interests, must stand at the head of the struggle for improved conditions for

Negro working women. The same is true of the white men workers whose own interests demand that they conduct the sharpest fight against all practices of sex and racial discrimination. They, too, must demand equal pay for equal work and the right to all categories of jobs for women, white and Negro, and the youth, which also suffers special discrimination at the hands of the exploiters of labor.

Simply to recount the abstract figures of gains and losses for the Negro working women in various industries does not tell enough. How about the kind of work they do? "Food manufacture" sounds impressive. What kind of work do Negro women do under this head? We quote from "Negro Women in Industry in 15 States," U.S. Department of Labor, Women's Bureau Bulletin No. 70:

> "This industry, in which many of the occupations are disagreeable in the extreme, forms a good example of the placing of newcomers in the most undesirable of its tasks, since in many cases it was in the most unpleasant of these that Negro women, a group recently come into the industry, were engaged. For 60 per cent of all the women included, occupations were reported. About one-third worked with casings and chitterlings. The latter are the intestines of hogs; the former, coverings for sausage, prepared from intestines and other internal membranes of cattle, sheep, and hogs. The earliest processes of removing the contents, turning wrong side out, scraping, brushing, and trimming, are often *done in rooms with cement and brick floors that sometimes are covered with so much standing or running water that the workers find it necessary to wear rubber boots.* [Our emphasis—E.G. and C.B.]

> "While work in these departments is usually performed by men, some Negro women were found in casing and offal departments and on the killing floor. They turned, cleaned, scraped, and washed casings; washed fat; pulled fat from casings; and trimmed fat. A few singed off hair, and additional occupations in this department were cleaning racks, slitting weasands,[110] braining heads, taking out hogs' eyes, ripping guts, measuring bladders, shaving ears, plucking lungs, and skinning sheep tongues. Casings are again handled in the sausage department, where it is more usual to find Negro women than in the earlier processes. In the making of wet (fresh) sausage they were washing casings, pulling fat from chitterlings, tying and linking sausage, and one was a scaler (weigher). In the preparing of dry sausage they were turning, brushing, scraping, salting, trimming, cutting, matching, and sewing casings."

OPPRESSION OF NEGROES DUE TO CAPITALISM

"Ford Manufacturers" thus affords an example of the kind of jobs to which Negro women are relegated, *as a matter of capitalist policy*, where they find it possible to find employment. Wages paid these women "compare favorably," we are told, with those of white women. "Compare favorably" and "are identical" have different meanings, just as "democracy" and "self-determination" have different meanings when uttered by representatives of different classes of capitalist society. Under capitalist democracy, which is in reality the dictatorship of an exploiting minority against the vast toiling majority of the population, Negro workers and working women are expected to get along on less pay. A favorite argument of the bosses is that the Negroes' standard of living is "lower" than that of the white workers.

To force Negro workers to exist on a lower standard of living and then use their impoverished conditions to justify lower wages and job-discrimination is typical of capitalism, which is based on the exploitation of the majority by a minority of capitalists and rich landlords, plus the special plundering and violent suppression of the Negro people as an oppressed nationality. The exact opposite obtains in the Soviet Union, where the victorious October Revolution[111] which overthrew capitalism swept out at the same time all the garbage of race hatred, national oppression and sex discrimination by which capitalism maintains its murderous rule. Today, under the guidance of the Communist Party and its leader, Joseph Stalin, the women workers of the nationalities formerly oppressed under tsarism are equal partners with all sections of the Russian toilers in the triumphant construction of Socialist industry and agriculture. The October Revolution ended the age-long oppression of women throughout the length and breadth of Russia. This is no accident. We find the same process in the Soviet districts of China, and wherever the Soviet flag has been raised by the revolutionary working class. Only through the Soviet Revolution can the oppressed working women, white and Negro, of the capitalist countries, achieve emancipation.

Earlier in this pamphlet we referred to the mass migrations of Negroes from the South in search of decent economic and living conditions and political freedom. Even a brief and incomplete survey such as this, of the condition of the Negro working woman, affords dramatic proof that the half-slave conditions in the Southern Black Belt continue to set the pattern for the economic and social oppression of the Negroes in the North as well. The stifling lynch atmosphere of the South hangs like a cloud over the whole country. It is thus clear that the struggle for better conditions in the North must be directed against Negro oppression in the Black Belt, as well, for governmental and administrative control and authority over the Black Belt territory by the Negro majority in that territory, with full rights for the toiling white minority.

DISCRIMINATION AGAINST NEGRO WHITE-COLLAR WORKERS

So far we have considered only the conditions of Negro women in industry and domestic service. What of the Negro women professionals and white collar workers? Is their lot any better?

It is especially in the "respectable" professional and white collar jobs that the ruling class draws a sharp line between what it marks off as "Negro jobs" and "white jobs." Most of the big department and chain stores, mercantile establishments, etc., refuse to employ Negroes in any capacity other than porters and charwomen. Like Negro jurors in Southern states and many northern centers, Negro stenographers, typists, file clerks, business executives, etc., are "curiosities" not to be encouraged.

Regardless of her training and capabilities, the Negro professional woman worker finds it almost impossible to secure a job. The employers themselves put up the barriers, usually resorting to the alibi either that "the customers won't stand for it," or that the white workers won't. The fallacy of both arguments has been proven by experience where Negro professionals have been given employment. In many cases, white workers have been won to supporting the demands raised by the Communist Party, Young Communist League, the League of Struggle for Negro Rights and other organizations, for employment of Negroes as clerks, store managers, etc., without any firing of workers already employed.

COLOR LINE AMONG TEACHERS

School teachers comprise the largest professional group among Negroes, and here women predominate. Confined almost wholly to segregated sections of big cities, or to rural Southern schools, Negro teachers are forced into a position of economic and social inferiority to white teachers. In the North, the pay of white and Negro teachers is usually identical, but in the South a teacher is paid according to her color. If she is black she gets much less. For example, in Louisiana elementary school teachers receive an average of $292 a year, as against $1,107 for white elementary school teachers. Negro high school teachers receive $661, while white high school teachers are paid $1,419. In Arkansas, Negro teachers in the elementary schools are paid $434, white teachers $634; Negro high school teachers $696, white high school teachers, $1,236. Behind these figures is a deliberate attempt to limit the education of Negro children, with shorter school terms, etc. In Alabama and other Southern states, most of the Negro schools have been shut down during the past two years on the pretext of shortage of funds.

The crisis, which has dealt hammer blows to the smaller businesses, in particular, has had a tremendous adverse effect on the development of enterprises owned by Negroes. But even at its best, Negro business has been able to afford jobs for only a relatively small number in any Negro community, and usually at wages even lower than those paid Negroes by white enterprises.

Few Negro stores employ more than one clerk in addition to the proprietor, while in many cases the proprietor and his family do all the work in the store. Negro newspapers, theatres, real estate offices, etc., have provided jobs for a number of Negro professionals, but nothing in proportion to the number turned out by business schools and colleges each year.

Among the Negro physicians, lawyers, dentists, etc., the picture is somewhat different, but still discouraging on the admission of reformist leaders themselves. However, because of the enforced segregation of the Negro masses and discrimination at the hands of white physicians, and others, the Negro physicians, lawyers and dentists usually get the business in their communities. The impoverished conditions of the Negro masses are, however, reflected in the small earnings of the Negro doctors, lawyers and others. Negro women in these professions are relatively few.

It is evident that Negro business does not come within a thousand miles of providing jobs, not to mention decent wages and working conditions, for any significant proportion of the toiling Negro population. Nor is it true, as some reformist leaders maintain, that Negro unemployment can be solved simply by forcing white stores in Negro neighborhoods to employ Negroes. The fight for jobs for Negroes, and against all discriminatory practices, must be broadened out to include the big factories, department stores, etc., which are outside of the Negro ghettoes. This fight, to be successful, must be based on a united front promoted by the Communist Party, the League of Struggle for Negro Rights, and other militant organizations. It must raise at the same time the demand for unemployment and social insurance, without discrimination. It must support the mass fight to force the U.S. Congress to pass the Workers' Unemployment Insurance Bill, H.R. 2827.[112] This bill is the only one which provides for decent relief, and guards against discrimination against Negro and foreign-born workers.

EFFECTS OF UNEMPLOYMENT

Negro women workers, the most exploited in industry, are also the worst sufferers from unemployment. The situation of the jobless Negro woman worker is described by the Women's Bureau of the Department of Labor as "extremely serious and upsetting to the economic welfare of the country." Official Labor Department statistics for the whole country for the past five years are lacking, but the special unemployment census taken in 21 selected areas in January, 1931, prove that the Negro working woman gets the dirtiest deal at *all* times. It must be remembered, too, that these figures represent 1931, and that conditions for all workers, Negro and white, men and women, have worsened considerably since then. We quote from the Women's bureau bulletin "The Employment and Unemployment of Negro Women":

> "Of the 18 cities and three boroughs of New York City each of eight cities and ten boroughs gave normal employment to 10,000 Negro women or more. In these areas taken together 42 per cent of the Negro women workers were out of work as compared with 18 percent of the American-born white woman and 13 (12.8) per cent of

the foreign-born white woman. The proportion of Negro women unemployed ranges from 29 per cent in Brooklyn and Manhattan Boroughs of New York City to 75 per cent in Detroit. Over 40 per cent of the Negro women normally employed were jobless in Detroit, Chicago, Cleveland, St. Louis, Houston and Philadelphia. Of the nine cities, Philadelphia, with 22 per cent of the American-born white women workers unemployed, had the worst record for this class. In every case very much smaller proportions of whites, both American and foreign-born, than of Negro women were jobless."

The opposition of the employers and their governmental agencies, and of the A.F. of L. bureaucrats, to real unemployment and social insurance operates especially severely against the unemployed Negro woman worker. Inadequate relief, humiliating treatment, and often callous denial of any relief whatever, is even more often her lot than of the jobless white woman. As a rule, she is given smaller food and rent checks where she has been placed on the relief roles. And she is the first to be dropped in the periodical attempts of the relief agencies to curtail relief to the barest minimum with which they can get away.

Even more than unemployed white families, Negro unemployed families have been forced to double up in homes, with resultant overcrowding and menace to health. This has led to a similar increase in Negro infant mortality, disease and death rates.

WHAT IS TO BE DONE?

Even the meager relief grudgingly given to the unemployed was won only after the sharpest struggles. Unemployed and employed, Negro and white, welded together under the leadership of the Communist Party, forced this concession from the bosses and their government. Similar joint struggles in various parts of the country have wrested additional concessions from the relief agencies from time to time. These joint struggles of Negro and white workers against unemployment and hunger, and the unity of the working class which is being forged in these united actions, were given great impetus by the world-wide fight organized and led by the Communist Party and the International Labor Defense against the Scottsboro lynch verdicts and for the lives and freedom of the nine innocent, framed-up Scottsboro lads.

White and Negro workers, uniting in struggle against Negro oppression, have forced a halt to discrimination in relief in many instances, have blocked evictions of unemployed Negro families (Chicago, Cleveland, New York, etc.); have forced the hiring of Negro workers in a number of instances (Empire Cafeteria,[113] New York, etc.).

These struggles must be intensified and broadened. Larger masses of white workers must be drawn into the fight against Negro oppression, against racial and sex discriminations, for full economic, political, and social equality for the Negro people, and for the right of self-determination for the Black Belt. The Communist Party's position that the white workers can be won for this struggle has been confirmed in countless joint actions of white and Negro workers during the past six years. It received dramatic confirmation in the world-wide mobilization of millions of white workers in defense of the Scottsboro boys and the oppressed Negro people. Under the guidance of the Communist Party, increasing sections of the white toilers are beginning to realize that their own emancipation is inextricably linked up with the liberation of the Negro people. Neither the Negro masses nor the white workers can achieve real freedom unless they achieve an unbreakable unity in the fight against their immediate and common enemy—the white capitalists.

The Soviet Union offers the shining example of the correctness of the Communist program of unity of white and Negro workers, and of all sections of the toiling population. In the Soviet Union, women have been emancipated. Nationalities and races who, under the old Tsarist regime, suffered oppression equal to that of the Negroes of the United States, are now, under the new Soviet government of the workers and farmers, enjoying complete freedom, equality and the right of self-determination. There the workers and farmers of the varied nationalities have united in fraternal and harmonious union in the work of building up a Socialist society. They have abolished race hatred and national oppression as well as unemployment and mass misery. The economic and cultural standards of the whole toiling population are being constantly raised as a result of fresh victories in the triumphant building of Socialist industry and agriculture.

The victorious workers and peasants of the Soviet Union point the revolutionary way out of the morass of capitalist race hatred and national oppression, chronic mass unemployment and suffering, fascist reaction and imperialist war.

"From 'Uncle Tom's Cabin' to 'Stevedore'"

New Theatre (JULY 1935): 21–23

The New Theatre League was organized in 1935. It was a left-wing group that included little theaters and amateur theatrical groups that produced plays dealing with the political issues in the 1930s and '40s. *New Theatre* was one of the group's organs. The July 1935 issue containing Gordon's "From 'Uncle Tom's Cabin' to 'Stevedore'" is a special one on Negro theater in America.

Gordon's essay is a sketch on the history of Black theater in America. He starts with the stereotype of Uncle Tom based on Harriet Beecher Stowe's novel and transformed into a play by Charles Townsend in 1889. Gordon maintains that the image of Tom was "a being psychologically doomed to slavery forever." It reinforces the mentality of the ruling class on slavery. However, to Gordon the image presented was no more realistic than the minstrel plays that preceded and coincided with it. Plays of Black life by white authors such as Eugene O'Neill, Paul Green, and Du Bose Heywood also present the inferiority of the Negro demanded by white audiences. Radical drama such as George Sklar and Paul Peters's *Stevedore* (1934) succeeds except when it deviates from truthfully depicting Negro life. A play such as *Stevedore*, despite its failings, is, for Gordon, a great advance over the earlier minstrel plays. It and other like-minded drama can be "effective weapons against those innumerable economic weapons against those innumerable economic and cultural differences which will persist for the black man until we destroy the last vestige of slavery."

From "Uncle Tom's Cabin" to "Stevedore"

Ever since the night Uncle Tom first shuffled upon the stage, American drama has emphasized the ruling class concept of the Negro's place in this social order. It makes no difference that Uncle Tom and other "Negroes" often were whites smirking under burnt cork and groveling under kinky wigs; the idea of the Negro's place was so emphatically implied that succeeding generations of colored actors have naturally assumed the stereotype.

The ruling class decreed the Negro's place to be down below, in the spheres both of economics and of art, and permitted none but white men to personate the ruling class concept of the black man. Society cut the pattern for black-white relationships, slave-plantation mode of production, plotting the outline with blacks on the lowest level. Since men habituate themselves in all relationships according to their peculiar roles, enacting their parts automatically, the roles of master and slave bore a constant relation to each other.

Uncle Tom's Cabin reflected ruling class opinion of the Negro's place in bourgeois American life, although neither Harriet Beecher Stowe, who wrote the novel, nor Charles Townsend, who adapted the play, purposed it. The points of view of the South and the North were fundamentally identical: the Negro was definitely a being *psychologically* doomed to slavery forever. *Uncle Tom's Cabin* reflected this viewpoint. For instance:

> ELIZA: You, down the river where they work you to death. Uncle Tom, I'm going to run away and take Harry with me. Won't you come too? You have a pass to come and go at any time.
> TOM: No, no—I can't leave Mars Shelby dat way. But I won't say no to you're [*sic*] goin.' But if sellin' me can get mas'r outer trouble, why den let me be sold. I s'pose I can bar it as well as any one. Mas'r always found me on the spot . . . he always will. I never have

> broken trust, and never will. It's better for me to go alone, than to break up the place and sell all. Mas'r ain't to blame, and he'll take care of my wife and little 'uns!

Harriet Beecher Stowe's plan of attack on slavery was gradually to destroy it so that the ensuing hardships to the master would not be too great: reduce his property by removing a slave here and there, now and then, until all are freed. Uncle Tom falls in with the plan: better for him to go alone "than to break up the place and sell all." "Mas'r aint to blame," so be tender with him. It is the fault of the system. Mas'r is, in a way, as much a slave as Uncle Tom. This sentiment is implicit in that one passage. The whole play implies more.

Loyalty and devotion in general are the essence of nobility: a slave is noble if loyal and devoted. This is the lesson of Christianity. It is ruling class ideology; it is the message of *Uncle Tom's Cabin*. The author commends Uncle Tom for remaining with Mar's Shelby. Speaking through the playwright, the ruling class commends all Negroes who are loyal and devoted to the white master class.

Tom was neither loyal nor devoted to his last owner, Legree. Why? Because Legree was not of the master class. He was an upstart, villainous poor white, deserving and receiving contempt. Slaves were taught loyalty and devotion to those God ordained to rule; this doctrine implied scorn for those hired to rule.

Uncle Tom's Cabin reflects ruling class ideology from another angle. Tom's second owner, St. Clare, is speaking to Maria, St. Clare's wife: "I've brought you a coachman, at last, to order. I tell you he is a regular hearse for blackness and sobriety," and so on. The audience has already met George Harris and Eliza. Harris is a "pretty good-looking chap," for he is "kind of tall," has "brown hair" and "dark eyes"; in other words, George Harris is an octoroon. His wife, Eliza, is also "as white as you are," Shelby tells Haley, the slave trader.

Does all this detail about the physical appearance of Tom, Harris, and Eliza serve no purpose than to heighten dramatic interest? Hardly; but dramatic interest is heightened not only by showing that slavery's leprous hands often fell on "whites," but that "white" Negroes were given less than blacks to mumbling nonsense about loyalty and devotion. The "fullblooded" Negro, implies the author, is inferior to the Negro with "white" blood. Mixed bloods are portrayed as impatient of restraint as if slave psychology is foreign to them alone.

Uncle Tom's Cabin was the artistic expression of the industrial bourgeoisie on slavery. It was also the expression of the ruling class as a whole: roughly, the capitalists in the North and slave-holders in the South. It was the conviction of this class that it had a god-ordained right to be. The fundamental "right," therefore, of one class to rule another was not the question at issue. The question was how to reconcile differences between the non-slaveholders and the slaveholders so as to unite the ruling class. Was Uncle Tom more effectively exploited by the wage slavery of the North or by the chattel slavery of the South? That was the question reconciliators must consider. The author of *Uncle Tom's Cabin*, however, was as unaware of her role of reconciliator as Paul Green or Eugene O'Neill is unaware today of assuming a traditional attitude toward, and repeating traditional slurs about, the Negro. The man who dramatized her novel similarly played his role.

Uncle Tom's Cabin was one of the first instances "where an attempt is made to present to the American public in a realistic manner the authentic life of the Negro," asserts Montgomery Gregory[114] in his introduction to the plays in *The New Negro*. The other drama, he says, was Dion Boucicault's *Octoroon*.[115] Gregory thinks these plays "served to rationalize somewhat the stage conception of the Negro," which, until now, had been the 'darkey' of minstrelsy, "and accustomed the theatregoing public to the experience of seeing a number of Negro characters in other than the conventional 'darkey' roles."

Gregory's saying that *Uncle Tom's Cabin* "served to rationalize somewhat the stage conception of the Negro" is correct. It *was* "somewhat," in a most limited sense. *Uncle Tom's Cabin* and *Octoroon* no more presented "in a realistic manner the authentic life of the Negro" than the earlier minstrels had done. In minstrelsy, the slave was an irresponsible happy-go-lucky; in "serious" drama, he was a saint who had only to die to join the "authentic" angels. To the playwright whose interest lay with the South, the black man belonged forever in slavery; to the playwright whose interests were one with the rising bourgeoisie, the Negro was capable of development as a free man. These playwrights agreed that in neither case should the black man be a member of the ruling class.

"The minstrel tradition continued until the middle nineties, when John W. Isham[116] organized a musical show, *The Octoroons*," declares Gregory. There followed a succession of musical comedies, the casts of which were completely Negro. The minstrel tradition did not end with the Negro's writing and producing musical comedy, but continued in a more refined form. When the Negro produced for the first time in his own theatre he recognized and adhered to the stereotype—with trifling variations—that the ruling class tradition had cast on the psychology of Americans.

The dialectical development of American drama dealing with the Negro reveals itself clearly. *Uncle Tom's Cabin*, despite its capitalist bias, *was* anti-slave. To that extent it was an advance over all earlier plays concerning the Negro. Bringing the Negro on the stage with whites in *Uncle Tom's Cabin* and *Octoroon* was part of the general sympathetic treatment Negroes were to expect from liberals.

We can appraise these various plays correctly only by taking each of them in relation both to its period and to American drama as a whole. When we look at American drama in this way we discover the significant position the Negro has held in it.

Used from the first as the cheapest labor and, later, after emancipation, as a threat to white labor whenever it rebelled against exploitation, the Negro, with his peculiar racial characteristics, has been a godsend to the ruling class. His racial characteristics are the identifying marks by which the "inferior" is distinguished from the "superior." Therefore, they must be preserved. Jim Crow laws, laws forbidding intermarriage, slums to which Negro workers are confined, separate Christian churches—these are some of the means of preserving the Negro's identifying marks. The theatre is an especially valuable art form to the ruling class, due to the drama's power to illustrate graphically the differences between whites and blacks,

The tradition of Negro inferiority penetrates even such recent "realistic" plays as Ridgeley Torrence's[117] *Granny Maumee, The Rider of Dreams*, and *Simon, the Cyrenian*, Eugene O'Neill's *The Emperor Jones* and *All God's Chillun Got Wings*, Paul Green's *In Abraham's Bosom, The No 'Count Boy*, and *Roll, Sweet Chariot*, Du Bose Heywood's *Porgy*, and Ernest Howard Culbertson's[118] *Goat Alley*.

Negro workers who know the "stark realism" of say O'Neill's, Green's and Heywood's plays look upon it not as the kind of realism the black man actually encounters, but as just another and a more "civilized" method of attack. It is only the upper class Negroes who accept the false fatalism of *All God's Chillun Got Wings, Roll, Sweet Chariot*, and *The Emperor Jones* as true to Negro life. These people do not accept it because they believe it is "authentic," but because, accepting the present social order as defender and preserver of their prerogatives of helping to exploit the black workers they must defend the capitalist culture.

O'Neill's, Green's, and all other "liberal" writers' plays about the Negro serve the capitalist class better than the old minstrels, while the older dramas—for instance, Thomas Dixon's *The Clansman* (from which the film, *The Birth of a Nation* was made)—with their uncompromising depiction of the Negro as sub-human, were crude in their elemental hatred beside the plays of today's "friendly" playwrights. The very openness of *The Clansman's* assault blunted its point, but the subtle calumny in *All God's Chillun Got Wings*, and others in this category makes these plays the more dangerous since their deadly influence is often fatal before it is observed. In *All God's Chillun Got Wings*, O'Neill rears the white girl, Ella, and the Negro boy, Jim, together through childhood, rather honestly portraying their reactions to a hostile environment. They finally get married, but, instead of showing how a black man and his white wife may fight and win, the author prefers to show them in defeat. He even shows the Negro failing in his law examinations—as if seeking further to prove his "natural" inferiority.

O'Neill must make Ella insane in order to keep her Jim's wife, and O'Neill must add, when the white wife kisses her black husband's hand (his *hand*, mind you!) "as a child might, tenderly and gratefully." Why should she not kiss him as a woman might, possessively and with passion? Because the Negro's place is that of an inferior, especially in social relations, most emphatically inferior when a Negro *man* and white *woman* are socially involved. Even so, Ella must be made crazy before she kisses her man, so that the audience will realize her ignorance of what she is doing. *All God's Chillun Got Wings, The Emperor Jones, Roll, Sweet Chariot, Porgy*,—all these "serious" plays of Negro life succeed in doing what Gregory praised *Uncle Tom's Cabin* and *Octoroon* for doing: "rationalize somewhat the stage conception of the Negro" and accustom "the theatre-going public to the experience of seeing a number of Negro characters in other than the conventional 'darkey' roles," but they do not change the basic attitude toward the Negro.

Ruling class conception of the Negro worker is a "darkey," regardless of his playing the minstrel Jim Crow or the tragic Emperor Jones. Although *In Abraham's Bosom* is sympathetic, in *Roll, Sweet Chariot*, Paul Green refurbishes the *Uncle Tom's Cabin* theme. John Henry, being black, cannot find "redemption" except through suffering on the chain gang. Happiness comes in Heaven: it is reached only by way of the grave.

O'Neill's treatment of the Negro is no better than Green's, although O'Neill is a better artist. Ruling class tradition has so warped both their judgments that what they are doing is a sort of automatic writing, the hoary shade of Uncle Tom being the spirit which guides their hands. Brutus Jones achieves "great" heights, yet his pinnacle but touches the soles of Smither[s]'s muddy and broken shoes.[119] At the crest of Jones' glory he is still inferior, at least in the social scale, to the cockney outcast. Look at the last lines of *The Emperor Jones*:

> LEM: (calmy) Dey come bring him now. (*The soldiers come out of the forest, carrying Jones' limp body. He is dead. They carry him to Lem, who examines his body with great satisfaction*).
>
> SMITHERS: (*leans over his shoulder—in a tone of frightened awe*). Well, they did for yer right enough, Jonesey, me lad! Dead as a 'erring! (*Mockingly*) Where's yer 'igh an' mighty airs now, yer bloomi' Majesty.? (*Then with a grin*) Silver bullet! Gawd blimey, but yer died in the 'eight o' style, any'ow!

Radical drama comes closest to being a dialectical representation of life because it shows the relation of black workers to the means of production, to class-conscious white workers, to the ruling class, to the upper class of their own race, and to all the other elements of society. John Wexley's[120] *They Shall Not Die* and Paul Peters' and George Sklar's *Stevedore*[121] are the first clean breaks from tradition. These authors bring the Negro upon the stage as a genuine human being, showing him in his actual relation both to the productive forces and to the whites of his class. Their portrayals mark the difference between distortion gleaned from without and perception gained from within.

Alliances once unthinkable, alliances between white workers and black workers, have evolved from the changed relationships as shown in these plays. The dramas fall short of "socialist realism"[122] to the extent they fail to integrate these various relationships. Both *They Shall Not Die* and *Stevedore* are less than first rate plays simply because they do not truthfully show the interplay of all the elements these dramas represent. *They Shall Not Die*, for instance, is untruthful in slurring over the potency of mass pressure upon the courts of so-called justice. The defence lawyer becomes the "hero," whereas the real "hero" is nothing less than the international proletariat, with its weapon of organized mass pressure.

Stevedore is better than *They Shall Not Die* because it is dialectically better constructed. It is truer to the life of workers today, when whites and blacks are coming to recognize their common interests, when they are seeing that they all are oppressed by the identical forces of capitalist society in decay and that the oppressors—the various agencies of decaying capitalism—are the common enemy of black and white workers.

Stevedore's conspicuous departure from "socialist realism" occurs in the staging of Scene I, Act III. Negroes do not sing hymns around their dead at a wake. One feels that this scene is meant to catch the fancy of the upper class, which "adores" the Negro's spirituals. It seems like another form of bowing to tradition; another way of linking the Negro actor of today with the Uncle Tom tradition.

The interval between *Uncle Tom's Cabin* and *Stevedore* marks the difference between a Negro who servilely bowed himself into his place *beneath* the whites and the one who militantly takes his place beside his white fellow worker. Plays like *They Shall Not Die* and *Stevedore* are effective weapons against those innumerable economic weapons against those innumerable economic and cultural differences which will persist for the black man until we destroy the last vestige of slavery.

"How Prostitution Has Been Fought and Almost Completely Eliminated in the USSR"

Moscow Daily News (APRIL 14, 1937): 6[123]

Gordon had long wanted to visit the Soviet Union. He had a chance when he took a leave from his position at the *Boston Post* and went to Russia from 1935 to 1937, acting as a correspondent for the English-language newspaper the *Moscow Daily News*.

Prostitution in Russia has long been a social problem, with various methods being used to try to deal with it, from severe penalties to decriminalization. From 1843, prostitution was legal, and women were issued "yellow tickets" indicating their profession. The growth of prostitution after the Russian Revolution was an embarrassment to the Soviet regime. Years of civil war and political and economic instability led to the displacement and other unemployment of women, always a vulnerable part of the workforce. Women were seen to be victims of an exploitative capitalist system with communism as the only solution.

The Communist method for dealing with prostitution was to treat women in a prophylactorium and train them so they could join the workforce. They would also provide the women with a sense of worth and community that most were lacking. Gordon reports that the program showed remarkable success in decreasing venereal disease and prostitution. He states, "Once a woman begins working at the prophylactorium, she is no longer referred to as a prostitute. Here the past is dead. She is a worker and proud of it." The prophylactoriums seem to have improved the situation through the 1930s, but it is hard to determine by how much since the state tightly controlled reporting on subjects such as prostitution and venereal disease. What does seem clear, as Frances Lee Bernstein suggests, is that over time, this benevolent treatment of prostitution often gave way to repressive state control of women.[124] Gordon wrote a second article on prostitution, "Former Prostitutes Tell How They Have Become Useful Members of Society" (*Moscow Daily News*, April 22, 1937). For more on prostitution in the Soviet Union during this period, see Marcelline Hutton *Resilient Russian Women in the 1920s & 1930s* (2015).

How Prostitution Has Been Fought and Almost Completely Eliminated in the USSR

Twenty thousand prostitutes walked the streets and boulevards of Moscow in 1913. In 1931, only 700 such women were found in Moscow; in 1932 there were 470. The Women's Curative-Labor Prophylactorium of Moscow, an institution for combatting prostitution and rehabilitating former women of the street, reports that its last records (for August, 1936) showed the number of prostitutes to be about 100.

What became of the others—where are they today? How was the number reduced to 100? Who are these 100, and why have they persisted? We may answer the last question immediately: the others require extended treatment.

"Most of the 100 are remnants of the bezprizorny,[125] waifs made homeless by the Civil War," says Dr. Mark Semyonovich Danishevsky, director of the prophylactorium. "They are women who have not learned how to organize their lives. Most of them are illiterate or mentally backward.... It is the function of the prophylactorium to help them."

The story of the Soviet Union's struggle against prostitution has been recorded by Dr. Danishevsky for a forthcoming book. And it is from a copy of his manuscript that most of these facts have been taken.

In an interview Dr. Danishevsky stated, "In 1928 there were 40 prophylactoriums in the USSR. Since 1931, four have been closed in Moscow and 12 in other parts of the country. There now remain only six in the whole USSR, quite enough to take care of the few remaining homeless women."

THE TSARIST HERITAGE

To appreciate fully what Soviet [word illegible. Ed.] has had to combat, we must know what it inherited from tsarism. After a visit to the great annual fair at Nizhny Novgorod.[126] Alexander Dumas, the playwright, referred to the old town as "the city of prostitutes." One would like to know what he would have said had he realized that, in addition to the 1,000 women he saw in the daily "parade of prostitutes," there were several thousand who dared not parade because they were not registered.

Nizhny Novgorod, despite its reputation, was only fourth among Russian cities in number of prostitutes, St. Petersburg, Moscow, and Warsaw leading, in that order. We learn, moreover, directly from tsarist authorities, whence the women came.

Dr. P. E. Oboznenko, member of the tsarist committee for supervising prostitution, wrote that 83.5 per cent of 4,000 in St. Petersburg "started from sheer economic need—nowhere to live and no work."

Dr. N. A. Torsuyeva, another authority, showed that a majority of the women tried to avoid the final step; two-thirds had been wage-earners but had lost their jobs. Statistics covering the period 1897–1903 show that earnings of men increased 12 per cent. while women's wages remained at about eight rubles monthly. Food prices, however, shot up 25 per cent.

A majority of all street women from the working class had formerly been employed in the needle trades. Factory workers gave the profession only 5 per cent of its victims. "The reason for this difference," says Dr. Danishevsky, "was that the factory worker, in spite of difficulties, resisted. She was in an atmosphere of workers' class consciousness. Needle workers were not factory workers. They toiled long hours at low wages in small shops, under direct supervision of a boss who not infrequently was a procurer." The housemaid in a bourgeois household, usually a peasant girl, he said, "was doomed from the start."

With its poor and neglected peasantry, the Russian village was the chief source of supply of streetwalkers to the cities. Dr. Torsuyeva records that 77.4 per cent of all prostitutes had formerly been simple peasants.

Inheriting both prostitution and tsarist laws against the woman victim, the young Soviet state attacked under the slogan "Fight Prostitution, Not the Prostitute." The revolutionary content of this idea is lost unless one realizes that it has had no precedent in history. The campaign planned in 1922 by the People's Commissariat of Health, jointly with the Commissariat of Labor and the trade unions, envisaged simultaneous struggle on two fronts: to attack the causes of prostitution while attacking the remnants of the old order.

For the first part of the campaign—to prevent prostitution—the fundamental regulation was laid down that no enterprise should discharge women employees who were without economic resources, single girls without parents, pregnant women, or women with children.

[First line of paragraph illegible. Ed.] prostitution—the campaign was to proceed along three main lines: first, the militia, to exercise extraordinary supervision over railroad stations, hotels, workers' dormitories, ports and public bathhouses; second, the state to conduct a stern legal fight against all agents and agencies of prostitution; third, the state to establish free dispensaries for treating venereal diseases. The regulations detailed the rights of the women involved. In arresting a streetwalker, the militiamen "must exercise the utmost consideration; he must not act brutally either in word or deed." He must remember that the woman's material and economic condition brought her to prostitution.

DECREASE IN VENEREAL DISEASES

The militia throughout the country in 1924 and 1925 uncovered and abolished 2,228 establishments. The People's Commissariat of Health and associated organizations opened dispensaries for gathering statistics, treating the infected, helping the militia to ferret out houses of prostitution, and through personal contact, assisting the former woman of the street to a socially useful life. From 1914 to 1928 the number of persons affected by venereal diseases decreased by more than half.

Tsarist laws had ignored the man in the case, but neither in the general campaign of propaganda and education nor as an actual culprit was he overlooked by the Soviet power. The man, when apprehended, was written up in the wall newspaper[127] of his organization, if he was a worker. If he was director of a plant, or held some other responsible post, he was written up both in the wall newspaper and in the regular press. The guilty man, in other words, was an exploiter of women and was treated as such.

Late in 1929, the Government issued a decree outlining ways of hastening abolition of prostitution. The decree recommended the further raising of women's qualifications for industry; urged against discharging women from jobs; called for intensification of anti-prostitution propaganda; demanded punishment of persons guilty of debauching young girls; suggested establishing two farms near Moscow for reclaimed women who needed outside work; explained how the work of the 40 prophylactoriums of the country could become more effective; and, finally, outlined plans for founding an institute of labor education for younger girls.

The Women's Curative Labor Prophylactorium was established in 1924 for the purpose of returning former prostitutes to profitable Socialist labor. Its main task was to attract homeless and unemployed women who might be forced into the streets by bad economic conditions. Prior to 1930, 17 per cent of the women of the institution were prostitutes.

NEW PRINCIPLES

Beginning without precedent, the prophylactorium had to work out its own principles. How should the women be treated: Should this be a "home"[128] reminiscent of the one which the wife of Emperor Justinian founded on the Bosphorus for 500 women, some of whom jumped into the sea to escape? Should it be a "corrective" institution? It was decided, first, that the women must enter voluntarily and that the severest punishment allowed would be expulsion.

The second principle was that absolutely no funds would be acceptable from private sources. Thirdly, all doctors' services, all care and attention to the patients, and all medicines, must be given without cost, the state paying the bills. Finally, a woman was required to remain at the prophylactorium for an average of two years, to be discharged when the institution had found her a job and room outside.

The first stage in rehabilitating a former streetwalker is to cure her illness, treatment being started and greatly advanced at the main prophylactorium. Later she goes to the affiliate prophylactorium in another locality. Here there are factories and shops, clinics and elementary schools, living quarters and a meeting hall.

TAUGHT TO WORK

Each shop maintains a school for women who have never before worked. The average wage is about 250 rubles a month, of which 100 rubles cover expenses—four meals a day, housecleaning, bed linen, towels. Theater and concert tickets are free. Stakhanovites[129] among the women—and there are many—earn as much as 400 rubles monthly.

When a woman leaves to work and lives outside, the institution continues to watch over her for a given period. Dr. Danishevsky says that 2,500 women, comprising workers of the Stalin Auto Plant, the Kaganovich Ball Bearing Plant, the Kuibyshev Electrocombinat, and the Second Watch Factory, have been sent out by the prophylactorium. Thirty-two per cent have been rewarded several times. Seventeen per cent are students in technical schools and institutes. Sixty-five per cent have been married, and 34 per cent are now mothers.

Dr. Danishevsky emphasized one point. Some of these women had more than the past of prostitutes to overcome, for hundreds were thieves and robbers and scores were drunkards and drug addicts. "Our records show that 10,000 women have been saved from possible destruction by the prophylactoriums of Moscow. Among them are women who have become physicians, aviators, singers, actresses, musicians, engineers, members of the Young Communist League and members of the Communist Party."

Once a woman begins working at the prophylactorium, she is no longer referred to as a prostitute. Her past is dead. She is a worker and proud of it.

"Alabama Authorities Ignore White Gang's Rape of Negro Mother"

Daily Worker (NOVEMBER 19, 1944): 10

The tragic story of Recy Taylor, a Black woman brutally raped in Abbeville, Alabama, in 1944 by six white youths, was first reported in the *Pittsburgh Courier* (October 28, 1944). Gordon would be the first to report on it in a white periodical, the Communist *Daily Worker*. Gordon was vehement in his anger at Southern editors who ignored the rape of a Black woman yet insisted that Black rapists of white women must be "burned to death in Florida's electric chair." Gordon did not stop with the one article. He wrote another piece, "Alabama Officials Feel People's Pressure in Mrs. Taylor's case" (*Daily Worker*, December 12, 1944), which talked about how public outcry forced Alabama Governor Chauncey Sparks reluctantly to launch an investigation of the case. Although no one was ever indicted, many feel the Recy Taylor case helped build the movement culminating in the Montgomery bus boycott. The Alabama legislature finally issued an apology to Taylor in 2011. For more, see Danielle L. McGuire, *At the Dark End of the Street: Black Women, Rape, and Resistance—a New History of the Civil Rights Movement from Rosa Parks to the Rise of Black Power* (2010). A documentary was also made by Nancy Buiriski, *The Rape of Recy Taylor* (2017).

Alabama Authorities Ignore White Gang's Rape of Negro Mother

Mrs. Recy Taylor, 22-year-old Negro woman, wife of a soldier and mother of a two-year-old-daughter, was kidnapped, stripped of her clothing, and raped near Abbeville, Ala. on the night of Sept. 3. Alabama justice to date has been blind, deaf, and mute. Mrs. Taylor was on her way from church in company with two friends, Mrs. Fanny Daniels, 61, and West Daniels, 18. It was between 11 and 12 p.m. when an auto load of white youths stopped beside the three. Somebody shouted, "Halt!"

The gang surrounded the two women and the boy and, brandishing knives and guns, grabbed Mrs. Taylor. One of them said:

"This girl is wanted by Sheriff Gamble for cutting a white boy in Clopton this evening. Sheriff Gamble doesn't know her, but we do, by the clothes she's wearing, and he has us out looking for her. You are the one, and we must take you, dead or alive."

She was shoved into the car and driven in the direction of Abbeville. It turned off the road, however, at Three Points, heading toward the old Columbia Highway.

HUNT ATTACKERS

Mrs. Daniels and West went to the home of a white man named Cook. Hearing their story, he asked her to stay with his sick wife. He and a man named Bennie Corbitt and Mrs. Taylor's father sought High Sheriff George Gamble and not finding him, got Deputy Sheriff Louis Corbitt. They hunted for the hoodlums.

Mrs. Taylor, the next day, staggered home, naked, dazed, and bleeding. She said the gang had driven her out of the Old Columbia Highway, while she pleaded with them for her baby's and her husband's sake, not to kill her. Stripping her, they forced her, at the point of a gun, to submit to one after the other of the six or seven members of the gang.

Early in the morning, she was blindfolded and driven back to Abbeville. They dumped her out at Charlie Norton's Corner, ordering her not to remove the blindfold until they were gone. Deputy Sheriff Corbitt was with the father when she staggered in.

Corbitt, with her detailed description of the car, found it and its driver, Hugo Wilson. He arrested Wilson, who named Penute Hasting (or Hasty), Skipper Reeves, Dillard York, Luther Lee, and two or three others, as accomplices. Mrs. Taylor confirmed these identifications.

ALL EXONERATED

Deputy Sheriff Corbitt, High Sheriff Gamble, a solicitor, and Mrs. Taylor drove to the scene of the crime. They admitted that all evidence tended to prove her charges. Yet, when the Grand Jury met on Oct. 9 and listened to her, Mrs. Daniels', and West Daniels' story, every member of the gang was exonerated.

What have Alabama authorities done since then as protectors of its citizens' rights? Alabama, typical of the South in general, boasts of its concern for its womanhood.

The answer is found in reply to a telegram send by John McCune, editor of the *Birmingham Age-Herald* to the *Daily Worker*. He wired that his paper had never heard of the case.

It is clear that if the state had taken action, it would have been known to the press of the whole South. Every Southern newspaper played up the "rape" of the unnamed wife of a white soldier in Florida. They had a grand time also when the alleged rapists, the youngest of whom was 16, was burned to death in Florida's electric chair.

Alabama has done nothing about Mrs. Taylor.

The Daily Worker is the only newspaper, aside from the Negro press, which has mentioned this case.

The whole country must be aroused to action against this and other similar outrages against the Negro womanhood.

"Cult of the White Woman," 1944
Unpublished, Eugene Gordon Papers[130]

In this unpublished piece, Gordon compares the rape case of Recy Taylor in 1944 with that of an unnamed white Florida woman. Gordon is probably referring to the execution of three Blacks, James Davis (16), Freddie Lane (18), and James Williams (25) on October 9, 1944 for raping a white woman in Florida.

Gordon makes several comparisons between the two cases in this essay. First, Taylor's name was made public, and she had to suffer the humiliation of knowing everyone in her community was aware of what had happened to her. The white woman's identity was protected. Second, the punishment for the crimes was vastly different. Whereas Taylor's rapists were never tried, even though they were well-known in the community, the fate of the Black boys was much different.

Gordon uses this article to speak of the differing treatments of women of different races in the South. Black men are killed by whites over the defense of a white woman's honor. Yet Black women receive none of this protection. As a result, they can be raped at will by whites. Gordon feels that all women, white and Black, must be emancipated. This would provide "the solution of the South's most stubborn problem 'the Negro problem.'" Written on such an explosive topic, it is not surprising that this powerful essay was never published in Gordon's lifetime.

Cult of the White Woman

An unnamed woman—unnamed because unknown except to a select few—was allegedly raped on a lonely road near Quincy, Florida, sometime near the end of July, last. She was said to be about 22 years old and the wife of a United States soldier. The soldier, too, was unnamed and unknown.

As soon as the rumor of her alleged attack reached law officials three young men—the youngest a mere child, being, in fact, 16 years old—were picked up by highway patrolmen out looking for the alleged assailants; they were beaten, arrested, and forced to sign a "confession." This "confession," the prisoners later swore, was not theirs; it had previously been prepared. It had not been read to them. One of the prisoners, at least, was illiterate, so he himself could hardly have read it.

The three were forced, nevertheless, to sign their names to, or make their marks on, this document, thus dooming themselves. For the prisoners, on the basis of this "confession," were given an eighty-minute "trial." They were found guilty, convicted, and sentenced to death. A week or so later they were electrocuted. The prosecution's theme song, reiterated in the newspapers of that region, was "Protection of Southern Womanhood." Indications that this previous womanhood had been protected by an incident in the death chamber. The last of the three youths having been killed, the father of the alleged victim (or—should I say?—the alleged father of the alleged victim) grasped and shook the hand of the executioner. Newspapers made much of that incident.

During preparations for the executions, while there still was time for contemplating the nature of this peculiar case and of the so-called evidence presented in it, appeals from all parts of the country reached Governor Spessard L. Holland[132] to grant the prisoners a *real*, a *genuine*, trial. The following facts were cited as justifying retrial: The "confessions" were frauds; the hour and twenty minute "trial" had voided any chance of the court-appointed defense counsel's consulting adequately with the prisoners; the alleged victim of the alleged rape had not been put on the witness stand; all witnesses friendly to the boys, including relatives, had been barred from the court; a mob of several thousands had hung about the courtroom chanting for the prisoners' lives; photographs of the prisoners had been hawked among the crowds; the governor's broad hint in the press that the prisoners surely would die at the hands of the state—this to placate the mob—had prejudiced the populace.

The foregoing facts formed the basis of appeals to the state supreme court, too. Both the governor and the court turned them down. The court said the facts were "frivolous"! The governor and his attorney general maintained that the "trial" had been fair and that the main issue had been and still was the protection of "our" women from rapists.

I suggest that these main outlines of the case be kept in mind while we examine a parallel one.

Even while the unnamed and unknown woman's *alleged* attackers were being tried, found guilty, and sentenced, in 80 minutes, to death in Florida's electric chair, there was being enacted, at Abbeville, Alabama, relatively a short distance away, a tragic drama in futility and heartbreak. Mrs. Recy Taylor—note that her name *is* known—was abducted at the point of guns and knives, driven by car into the woods off a wagon trail not far from Abbeville, stripped of her clothing, and raped by at least six young men. (Note that I not only say she *allegedly* was raped, but raped. Evidence in the hands of the sheriff and his deputy, evidence which has since been heard and mulled over by the Henry County grand jury, proves that Mrs. Taylor *was raped as stated.*) This breach of the Code for the Protection of Southern Womanhood occurred on the night of September 3, last [1944]. Up to four months later that breach still stood, unrepaired.

Mrs. Taylor also is a young woman, being 24. She is the wife of a young farmer, Willie Guy Taylor, and mother of a two-year-old daughter. Willie Guy Taylor was called up in the draft but was rejected. He was at home minding little Joyce Lee while his wife, the child's mother, was, unknown to him, being obscenely debased by young fellows who were not afraid to call one another's name in her presence, an eloquently significant fact.

One can see from what I have told of the Abbeville rape case that we know a great deal about the principals. We know nothing, however, which is not known also to Sheriff George Gamble and Deputy Sheriff Louis Corbitt, of Henry County, Alabama, and, by now, to every person of that region. Governor Chauncy Sparks and Attorney General William N. McQueen have been given these facts repeatedly in resolutions and letters requesting action. It was months after Mrs. Taylor, according to the South's known standards, was brutally outraged, before Alabama hinted, even, at moving toward her aid; this despite the fact that the state had her name, her address, her history, and the names, the addresses and the histories of her rapists, as well as the time and the place of the rape. Until recently but one item concerning the outrage had appeared, that was in a weekly newspaper published in Chicago.[133] This item, bearing a small head of its own, was buried in a column under the general title of "National Roundup."

Here, in Mrs. Taylor's own words and exactly as she wrote—except for such changes necessary to render her writing legible—is a letter in answer to my request for a complete story of what happened to her on the night of September 3:

"I and Mrs. Fannie Daniels and West Daniels was coming from the church. When we got this side of . . . (*illegible*)[134] . . . we see this car past [*sic*] by and come back by and then back up and five boys got out and halted us three times."

"Mrs. Fannie said, 'Halt for what?'"

"He said, 'Don't you move. You the one that cut a boy in Clopton this evening.'"

"I said I did not. I was down at Mrs. Fannie's all evening.

"We got to carry you to the sheriff. If you ain't the one, we will bring you right back here.'

"I couldn't get away.

"If you don't get in the car I will kill you. I will shoot your damn head off. We got to carry you back, dead or alive. Get in the car.'

One said, 'Kill her if she don't get in.' I said, 'I ain't been to town.' They said, 'Town, hell! Get in the car!'

"I got in the car, and when I see they never went to Abbeville, I said, 'Please don't carry me way from home. I thought you all was carrying me to the sheriff. I have to ask you, please don't kill me.'

All six raped me about 15 minutes apiece . . . One of them blindfolded me and they put me out the car and said, 'Don't you move until we get away from here.'

"Let me tell you all they ain't doing anything about it and they ain't saying anything about it. *I* can't do anything about it. You do all you can . . ."

You must realize by now what I purposely have refrained from telling—that the unnamed and unknown woman was white and that Mrs. Recy Taylor is black; that the unnamed and unknown woman's *alleged* rapists were black and that Mrs. Taylor's *known* rapists are white.

Now, what, I ask, have we here?

II

We have here a typical case in a 300-year series of manifestations of the Negro woman's deliberate, calculated degradation by certain white men. We have here a problem to solve, a task to accomplish. But let us, looking at this problem and contemplating this task, ask ourselves how, in the first place, the Negro woman got into such a fix; and let us then ask ourselves, if it is now time to get her out of it for the good of all our souls, how to proceed to do it.

The Negro woman attained her inferior social status through precisely the same route as the Negro man; or, perhaps it would be better to say that this burden of social inferiority was thrust upon the Negro woman precisely as it was thrust upon her man. That was through economic degradation during slavery. The Negro did not enter America first as a chattel slave; he entered as an indentured servant.[135] He entered, at Jamestown, in 1619, with the same status as most white workers who entered during that period. The Negro woman for more than two generations after that date, was not treated worse by the gentlemen and ladies of Virginia than the servant, or working-class, white woman was treated. The Negro woman's treatment became worse as her value increased as a mother of slave laborers.

The custom grew rather slowly, but it grew steadily, of giving the child the same status as the mother's. That custom became fixed in law when the white masters realized that a body of black labor could never be built up as long as black indentured servants could, at the end of a six-or seven-year indenture, go free, disappear into the general humanity of citizens, and live on a basis of complete equality with any white person. That custom must end if the quantity of cheap, or slave, labor was not to diminish to the point of disappearance. The best way to end the custom was to hold a servant in that status for life. The best way to insure a servant's being held for life was to declare his or her status to be the same as the mother's. New generations were thus born as servants for life—or as slaves.

The Negro woman as a slave-breeder could not, *must* not, be treated as a woman. She must be degraded to subhuman status. For a free woman could not be both free and a breeder of slaves. The Negro woman must not, therefore, be free even to act like a woman. Any white man, consequently, could cohabit with any Negro woman, in accordance with or against her wishes. The penalty sometimes was public whipping. But cohabitation, naturally, went on—to such an extent, indeed, that efforts were made no longer, after a while, to prevent white men from possessing black women, *so long as their relations were master to slave* or so long as they were, at any rate, as superior to inferior. It was forbidden absolutely that the relationship be as man to wife. For *that* kind of relationship would lift the female black to the status of a *woman*. And that would ruin her function as a slave-breeder, concubine, or unpaid house servant.

The degradation of Negro women was a logical by-product of chattel slavery; its persistence today in the South, with reflections throughout the country, is a hangover, economically, socially and psychologically, from the slave era.

Hangovers from the slave era are, one after another, being removed during the process of our removing the most efficient preservatives of these hangovers, fascism. Fascism, with all its recrudescences of the most bestial barbarism, uses these slave hangovers for its purposes. The attack on Mrs. Taylor was an act of fascist-like barbarism. Her treatment at the hands of young men brought up in an environment of white-supremacist thinking was similar to treatment accorded women in territory conquered by Nazi troops. Her treatment by the law officials of the town is similar to what would be expected if these officials wore the Nazi brassard.[136] The time is here, in the height of our military successes against fascism, to destroy this slave hangover—the degradation of Negro women—as a means of lessening the chances of fascism's getting rooted in our soil. The South's bland and contemptuous disregard of the Negro woman's rights provides fertility to the soil in which fascism might grow.

Mrs. Taylor's is not an isolated case. What happened to her is so commonplace that a national organization with a reputation for fighting for Negro rights declined to touch it.[137] It is a fact that a Negro porter in an Abbeville, Alabama, bank was warned by Henry County police recently to leave town or be lynched: the story had got around that the boy was "going with" a white woman! It did not matter that the woman was "going with" white men whose black mistresses were known to everybody in town. The boy left Abbeville that night. A white man—I learned these facts when I personally investigated on December 7, last—has lived for years with a Negro woman just outside Abbeville.

"Sure, everybody knows it," I was told. "Don't everybody see 'em go round together?"

The difference between this white man's black mistress and the black Mrs. Recy Taylor is that the mistress perhaps did not fight against what finally overtook her. Or, perhaps, she did not fight very hard. The approach of the man in the case, certainly, was different from that of the six, who, for 15 minutes apiece, possessed Mrs. Taylor. He probably "propositioned" her and she accepted. That sort of thing happens throughout civilized society. It is only in a society whose members are partly civilized—who recognize groupings on the basis of inferior and superior races or nationalities—that it is accepted or condoned by the "superior" while being tolerated with bitter resentment by the suppressed. For it is not that the black man objects, *per se*, to a black woman living with a white man. What burns up the black man is the white man assuming to possess the black woman as *the white man's right*, while forbidding a similar right to the black man and the white woman.

The evil lies deeper still than that. As the white-supremacists rebel at giving any Negro full manhood status, no matter how "white" he may look, lest it stimulate ambition in other Negroes and thus threaten the white jim crow system, so does white-supremacist psychology prevail against full womanhood status for the black woman, lest it threaten the base of her economic, social, and physical exploitation. Thus the struggle for complete emancipation of the Negro woman is inseparable from the struggle for complete emancipation of the Negro people.

The Negro woman is not fully freed until her husband or her brother or her father or her sweetheart has authority and legal means to protect her. That is another way of saying that Negro men must be able to protect Negro women in Alabama and in Maine, in Georgia and in New York, in Florida and in Massachusetts, else neither Negro women nor Negro men are free anywhere in the United States. The Negro man today in the South possesses neither the authority nor the legal means to protect his wife, sister, daughter, sweetheart, or mother from any white man who would attack her or take her as his concubine.

III

This shocking truth was dramatized by a story I overheard in a Birmingham barbershop. The story proved also that a Negro woman who became a white man's mistress may sometimes have been forced by circumstance to yield. I was on my way to Abbeville on the Taylor case when my barber, pausing in the process of lathering my face, said of somebody passing the window: "There's the fellow that had his wife stolen from him." Everybody, naturally, was curious, so the barber told this story.

This man and his wife, John and Jane Simpson—no, I am not giving their right names—lived about 10 miles outside Anniston. Deciding to move to town and set up a little business, John sent Jane ahead to prepare things. She was as competent as she was pretty. "Pretty as that gal Lena Horne in the moving pictures," the barber said. There was the usual understanding between John and Jane, of course, that she would write as soon as she arrived in Anniston. But she didn't. Not then nor for a month afterward. His letters were not returned, so he felt sure they were being received. Disturbed, he hastened to Anniston and to the house he and Jane were buying.

He asked neighbors whether they had seen June Simpson. They were reluctant to talk. One man did go so far as to advise John not to fool round here. "I wouldn't, if I was you," the man said, "unless I wanted to get killed." John rang. He knocked. He unlocked the door and went in.

It was as he entered his wife's bedroom that the side of his head was nearly bashed in. He was grabbed from behind and his arms pinned against his sides. A man beat him until he dropped unconscious. During all this he managed to get one glimpse of his wife's agonized face and to hear her pleading. It was not until he was recovering in the hospital that he learned the meaning of that attack, though he must have guessed it.

Jane Simpson had simply been appropriated by an influential white man the moment he had seen her. That had been a few days after she had entered Anniston. She had yielded, under death threats to herself and her husband, to the pressure he had put upon her and to the pressure. of an environment which decreed that white man's act to be legal and proper. The white man had appropriated her letters as he had appropriated her body. He and a trusted friend had attended to the husband. When the husband, recovered, complained discreetly to friends of his helplessness, he was discreetly advised to keep his tongue or lose his life.

Husband and wife managed to get away to the relatively safer environment of Birmingham.

I have referred to Mrs. Taylor's case as a tragic drama in futility and heartbreak. Imagine a family in which the pretty young wife is known to the whole town to have been raped by six men who swagger before the populace daily in defiance of everybody and everything. Imagine the husband and father in this situation. What does he think? How does he feel? The Negro man in the South, I reiterate, is *unable* to protect his woman. Tragically, *she* realizes it as well as he. Their child realizes it. Her despoilers realize it.

"How do you feel about it?" I asked Willie Guy Taylor.

He thought for a moment, his broad black face tightening in perplexity how best to answer. Rain poured on the roof and swirled in white sheets beyond the open back door and across broad, black fields. I was glad it was raining, for the car which had brought us from Dothan, the driver dozing at the wheel, would be less likely noticed by curious Abbevilleians. I watched Taylor struggling for the answer. In Recy's own words: "Oh they just ast me if I knowed any of 'em an' if I was sure these was the right ones. I said I knowed 'em by they names. I been hearin' they names all my life round here. I said sure these was the right ones. They took me round to show 'em the place in the woods where they—where they rape me . . ."

"What did the grand jury say or do after that?"

"Said they'd sen' for me."

That had been more than three months ago. They had not sent.

"Why?" I asked Governor Sparks and Attorney General McQueen, in Montgomery, next day. "Why hasn't the state acted? It acted swiftly enough in the Scottsboro case to protect its womanhood. Florida, a few months ago, acted quickly enough to protect *her* womanhood."

The Governor and his attorney general had heard of the Abbeville case "by rumor" just that day! They had begun a "complete and thorough investigation," with investigators, McQueen added "working out of my office." They would take such measures as the finding warranted. They wanted no publicity, in the meantime, *please*, for any news about the investigation might hamper it. That was interesting, for, as I knew, they would not have heard the "rumor" had it not been for publicity engineered by the newly formed Committee for Equal Justice for Mrs. Recy Taylor. The sudden decision to investigate, after three months of ignoring the case, was undoubtedly a result of pressure generated by publicity from the committee's office at 112 East 19th Street, New York.

The governor and his attorney general found "Northern interference" equally distasteful. It was clear, however, that these gentlemen did not resent *Northern* "interference" so much as "interference." That fact was emphasized by their rejecting the Southern Conference for Human Welfare's application to see the attorney general on the case. The reason why the governor of no Southern state wants "interference" with the South's treatment of the Negro is that such "interference" in time may undermine the state's right to perpetuate a system of inequality between black and white citizens of the United States. The reason why there are Willie Guy[s] and Recy Taylors and John and Jane Simpsons throughout the South is that the Negro *is* the white man's inferior, according to the South's standards.

Americans outside the South but loving the whole of their county organized the Taylor committee *in cooperation with* the Southern Conference for Human Welfare and Southern trade unions. Local 206, Transport Workers Union of America, CIO, is as Southern as the New Orleans through which it distributed, weeks ago, more than 10,000 petitions to Governor Sparks on the Taylor case. Branches of the committee in Alabama, Florida, Maryland, North Carolina, Oklahoma, and Texas are sponsored by men and women native to the South. No. It is not the South's resentment of "interference" by the North so much as awareness that *the South itself*—which means the white and the black portions of it—is coming more and more to "interfere" in matters affecting its own welfare. It is the Southern political machine which actually fears "interference" and not so much the rank-and-file white citizenship. This machine does not operate solely to dominate and persecute the Negro—and the Negro is learning this fact very rapidly: it is a machine essentially designed to perpetuate its manipulators in power.

The fight for the Negro woman's full freedom is essentially a fight to abolish jimcrow; the fight to abolish jimcrow is a continuous struggle for [the] economic, social and political equality of white and black citizens. The Negro man will be in a position, when that equality has been attained, to protect his woman. But when that equality has been attained the Negro man will have discovered that his woman no longer needs *special* protection; for, black and white citizens being equal, there will be no "superior" white man to impose his will and himself on the black woman. Being the white woman's equal, economically and socially, the black woman will be in a position which is every American woman's birthright: *the right to demand that the law protect her even to the extent of forcing the man who has taken advantage of her sexually to marry her.* She is not free until she has *that* right in the South.

The struggle, therefore, for complete emancipation of the Negro woman is a part of the anti-jimcrow front; yet it must be also a conscious, planned, purposeful struggle in its own right, possessing its own platform of principles and its own definite program. It must be organically a part of the fight for women's emancipation in general. For it is a fact that when the Negro woman has become in actuality the white woman's equal through abolition of economic, social and political differences, she still will be inferior, socially, economically, and politically, to men in general. The struggle to free the Negro woman is, for that reason, a struggle to free *all* women. *All* women, for their own good, must participate.

Every woman's organization, and every individual woman with a reputation of being a fighter for women's rights, ought, it seems to me, enlist in this campaign for justice for the South's Recy Taylors and Jane Simpsons. The winning of justice for Mrs. Taylor is the extending of the fight for justice for Mrs. Taylor's counterparts. The Cult of the White Woman, an exaggerated and hypocritical obeisance behind which the reactionary South justifies lynching black men while raping black women, is being rejected by white women, as having no place in a progressive civilization.

Protect Southern womanhood? Yes! *All* womanhood! That is what, in the opinion of most Negroes, this antifascist war is being fought for. They have been strengthened in this opinion by what, in the deep South, even, they have seen all around them. They know that it was not just chance which made 20 odd white college professors and instructors, preachers, schoolteachers, lawyers, physicians and newspaper editors, early in 1944, publicly condemn South Carolina's "white supremacy" resolution as put across in the legislature. It did not just happen, in the opinion of Negroes of the South, that 150 leading white citizens of Georgia, in a letter to the *Atlanta Journal* on the Sunday preceding the primary elections last year, called shame upon those who would bar the Negro from the polls. Negroes whom I met in tours of the South were almost unanimous in their conviction that forces organized by our antifascist war must be thanked for the growing interest of white persons, individually and in organizations, in the Negro's welfare. The progressive trade union movement was named as [the] first of such forces. For whatever industrialization has occurred in the South, there a body of progressive persons had come into being. For the trade union movement there has transformed its workers as industry has transformed communities and regions.

Hundreds of thousands of black persons and white persons in the South see in *this* profound fact the solution of the South's most stubborn problem, the "Negro problem." The solution of that problem will put an end to the Cult of the White Woman.

Excerpt "Black Women's Long, Tough Course: From 'Dat Gal' Carline to This Woman Angela," 1972

Unpublished, Eugene Gordon Papers[138]

Gordon wrote this unpublished essay, his last major piece, after reading Frederick Law Olmsted's three volumes on slavery, *A Journey in the Seaboard States* (1856), *A Journey Through Texas* (1857), and *A Journey in the Back Country* (1860). The three volumes were later reissued as a two-volume work titled *The Cotton Kingdom: A Traveller's Observations on Cotton and Slavery in the American Slaves States* (1862). In Olmsted's work, Gordon was drawn to the story of a brave enslaved girl, Carline, who reminded him of Angela Davis, who had been involved in an attempt to free three prisoners, the Soledad Brothers, accused of murdering a prison guard at a California penitentiary. Davis was put on the FBI's ten-most-wanted list on August 18, 1970. She was arrested on October 13 and was incarcerated for sixteen months before being acquitted in 1972. Gordon admired Davis's strength and courage, and his defense of her was consistent with his advocacy for the rights of women and of the oppressed overall.

Black Women's Long, Tough Course
From "Dat Gal" Carline to This Woman Angela

Most United States working people are afraid of and bar their homes against kidnappers, murderers, and persons who conspire to kidnap or murder: working people have confidence in schoolteachers and the teaching profession: these being *simple* facts, a *profound* fact is that Aframericans historically are both among the most illiterate and the most eager of the whole population to become educated and cultured. They believe that by such means people get jobs and respectability. They look up to the black woman or man who, mentally competing with whites in whites' own schools, colleges, and universities, equal[s] or surpass[es] whites. If some whites wonder what's more thrilling than a football game, most blacks think it's the competitive game of living—when the white side "plays fair," as they've been credited as doing, say, in the Girl Scouts.

So comes along this black girl, Angela from Birmingham. Yes. Alabama again—in Birmingham with a streetcar line that actually *required* blacks to occupy seats in front of whites (because most lines' numerous head on collisions killed more whites than niggers). Her father, B. Frank Davis, now "in business for himself"—a service station—has been a public schoolteacher. Her mother Salle—notice that even plain Sally takes on style—has been a public schoolteacher. Angela's sister, Mrs. Fania Davis Jordon, graduate of Swa[r]rthmore, was now a graduate student at the University of California (San Diego). Her brother Benjamin, a professional football player (Cleveland Browns), is a graduate of Defiance (Ohio) College. Her younger brother, Reginald, was a student at Defiance.

And Angela herself? Most Aframericans were shocked and confused when having long since heard of the Board of Regents' and Governor Reagan's moves to rid the U.C.L.A. faculty of this twenty-six year old "avowed Communist," they now were being told that Angela Davis, "assistant philosophy instructor," was listed by the F.B.I. among its TEN MOST WANTED. Charges, said the broadcasts, "Kidnapping, murder, and conspiracy to commit murder."

To be, successfully, merely a *suspected* Communist, as we near 21st U.S.A., your area of responsibility being in the Respectable Category, is probably to feel as secure as a roller skater on the sloping icy fringe of a precipice; but to be an *avowed*, Communist and black, in a state governed by Ronald Reagan and at a university with psychologist Arthur Robert Jensen[139] (University of California, Berkeley) may not be much worse than declaring your head a target for rifle practice and, to accommodate the rifleman, your painting a bullseye on your forehead.

If Angela Davis frankly, honestly, and openly avowed her belief in Communism as the best way of life, and proved her belief by frankly, openly, and honestly beginning to organize people's *thinking* that what *she* did was what *they* too should do, observing and commending what she did, mere observers might become doers. What did she do that people she did it for loved her? And this woman Angela—who is she?

That child Angela! Sunday school; young people's church discussion group; winner of Badge and Certificate, Girl Scouts of America; player of piano, clarinet, and saxophone.

That girl Angela! Parker High School of Birmingham, and a picket protesting jimcrow housing; Honor Graduate, Elizabeth Irwin High School, New York; graduate Phi Beta Kappa (majoring in French Literature) magna cum laude. Brandeis University, Waltham, Mass., student, French Literature and philosophy, Sorbonne, Paris.

This woman Angela! Graduate student, philosophy, University of California, San Diego; Acting Assistant Professor of Philosophy U.C.L.A.; dressed like a bum—old slacks, run-down shoes—tall, beautiful, solemn, walking beside taller, handsome bodyguard Jonathan Jackson in a picket line, her banner reading SAVE THE SOLEDAD BROTHERS FROM LEGAL LYNCHING![140]

That beautiful trio: Angela, George, and Jonathan. The youngest, Jonathan, who undoubtedly suggested to Angela that he be her bodyguard, she being repeatedly threatened now because of her extracurricular studies of that side of society which rots and stinks on the sidewalks, alleys and the gutters; in slum houses that cripple minds and bodies in prisons that, crippling some, and, in spite of itself, revise, upraise, and exalt, others: for example, George Jackson, Jonathan Jackson's older brother.

Jonathan wanted to protect Angela against the enveloping, unseen presence of death. She bought what he told her he needed for her protection. He was the keeper of the defensive arsenal. He was, in the biblical sense, Angela's keeper, too. "Don't *you* worry; let *me* handle things. I'll tell you what I need; you just buy them, that's all . . ." That was Jonathan Jackson.

And, all the time, he's been planning his fantastic adventure. How often did Jonathan see his brother, George? Did George speak, on such occasions, as he wrote in a letter (June 27, 1970) to "Dear G?" . . . "To be denied or rejected means less to this man, but never nothing. And if he is still healthy of mind, he knows he can't be practical: he can't afford practicality. His have-nothing status, the absence of the all-important controls, predispose him to impracticality. He can never relax. He is or becomes the desperate man. And desperate men do desperate things, take desperate positions; when revolutions come he is the first to join it. If it doesn't come, he makes it."

That's how Jonathan, too, reasoned.

* * *

Jonathan died in what he seemed to believe was prelude to revolution. I've associated with (on the English-language *Moscow News* and on New York's *Daily Worker*), communists enough to *know* that they traditionally have opposed—and most strenuously—such terrorist acts as Jonathan's and his companions'. From Marx's time through Lenin's to the present their opposition to such acts in favor of organized mass people's action is expressed in their literature, among latest expressions being *The Meaning of San Rafael*, a 21-page pamphlet by Harry Winston, the US Communist Party's black national Chairman. Winston, who talked with Miss Davis when she was in a New York house of detention for women, writes, criticizing the heroic young blacks: "Revolutionary coups can be brought off by conspiracists, but not social revolutions. Coups are manipulations at the top. Social revolution is basic transformation of society, basic change in economic, political and social relationships. More, *socialist* revolution represents a transition in which not a tiny minority of exploiters but the overwhelming majority—the working class and all working people become the rulers. So profound a transformation cannot be made by coup or conspiracy . . ."

"Now Professor Davis is a prisoner of that society that should have welcomed her talents, her honesty, and the contribution she was making toward understanding and resolving the most critical problem of that society—the division between its oppressors and its oppressed": a beautiful but unrealized sentiment: that, by twenty-nine of her former U.C.L.A.-specialist associates in the introduction to their excellent pamphlet *Lectures on Liberalism,* by Angela Davis (24 pp. 50 cents/ New York Committee to Free Angela Davis, 150 Fifth Avenue, New York, NY 10011). Nobody better understands "the most critical problem of that society "than its manipulators; and it is *they* who, considering Miss Davis an important element of "the most critical problem," took imprisoning her for conspiracy to commit murder, kidnapping, and murder, as one excellent means of resolving *their* problem.

Canvassers for the weekly *Muhammad Speaks*,[141] writes Joe Walker, New York editor, "walked the streets of Harlem and asked black people—men and women from a wide variety of occupations as well as students and unemployed—what they would ask Miss Davis if they could, or what troubled them about her case." This question (they being "listed in order of frequency, the postmarked question first, etc.)" headed the list:

"WHY ARE YOU A COMMUNIST?"

"Before anything else, I am a black *woman* . . ."

* * *

Society's division during slavery into the owning and the hiring classes, these developing under the impact of machine manufacture into definitely opposing classes, there evolved in our society that which Henrietta Buckmaster,[142] condemning the outcome of the Recy Taylor case (no indictment; no trial of her rapists) called this country's *white-woman cult.* We have seen the artificial simulation of that cult by white men of the master class: we have witnessed its artificial but rampant growth. Implying all white women's superiority to all black women, this white-man created cult did not imply white women's equality with men. Thus, this cult of the white woman, says Miss Buckmaster, unless destroyed, will continue degrading both black women and white women.

A prior cult was, of course, that of the white man, who, subjectively, ego-wise, both South and North, became a racist owing to his dominance of a society ruled by whites subsisting on the labor of enslaved blacks. Angela Davis being both black and a brilliant political opponent is *naturally* to be hated and, if possible, destroyed; but what of black women who support and try to improve those white man's social institutions? What, for instance, of Mrs. Patricia Roberts Harris,[143] temporary chairwoman of the 1972 National Convention's Credentials Committee?

Owing to the slave-born cult of the white woman, then Angela Davis, an Associate Professor of Philosophy, U.C.L.A.; a U.S. Representative Shirley Chisholm; a Temporary Chairwoman for the coming Democratic Convention. Mrs. Patrica Roberts Harris, and the armies of Aframericans—and ethnic Mexican and Indigene and of Puerto Rican migrant worker women—all according to this standard, are equally inferior and expendable.

Miss Davis being for the moment symbolic of black women's *thralldom*, she is the immediate object of our concern; and, as she responds to the question why she is a communist that "First, I am a black *woman*," it is well that we black men remember *Roget's International Thesaurus* linking *thralldom*, *nigger* and *slavery* as synonymous, we being privately known as *niggers*, nor forgetting, either, that Angela Davis' final words in her answer were that "even if I am eventually allowed to leave the dungeon, I will not consider myself free . . . until all black people are free."

What, meantime, is "freedom" to most of us? It is
An illusion,
Comparable in substance to
Strands of gold in sunbeams
Or diamonds in drops of dew
Clutch them, and there's—*nothing!*

Notes

INTRODUCTION

1. Quoted in Robin D. G. Kelley, *Hammer and Hoe: Alabama Communists During the Great Depression* (University of North Carolina Press, 1990), 92.
2. A person who can change shape and appearance to adapt to any situation. The term was made famous in Woody Allen's film of the same name in 1983.
3. Daniel Candee, "A Pair Against Oppression: June Croll, Eugene Gordon, Communism and the Forging of American Anti-Racism" (MA thesis, University of Chicago, Social Sciences, 2022), 4.
4. See, for example, the collection of essays in Richard Crossman, ed., *The God That Failed* (Harper & Brothers, 1949), particularly Richard Wright's essay on pages 103–46, which first appeared under the title "I Tried to Be a Communist," *Atlantic* (August/September 1944).
5. These pseudonyms include Egor Don, Frank Lynn, and Clark Hall.
6. Only in recent years have scholars such as Verner Mitchell, Cynthia Davis, Lorraine Elena Roses, Alan Wald, Zebulon Vance Miletsky, Brian Dolinar, and Daniel Candee begun to give his work the attention it deserves.
7. Candee, "A Pair Against Oppression," 11–12.
8. See Central Florida Railroad Depots, University of Central Florida, richesmi.cah.ucf.edu.
9. Quoted in Paul Ortiz, *Emancipation Betrayed: The Hidden History of Black Resistance and White Violence in Florida from Reconstruction to the Bloody Election of 1920* (University of California Press, 2005), 71.
10. Candee, "A Pair Against Oppression," 13.
11. The Ponderosa Stomp Foundation, "South Rampart Street, a Closer Walk, NOLA," a closerwalknola.com.
12. Candee, "A Pair Against Oppression," 13.
13. William Ivy Hair, *Carnival of Fury: Robert Charles and the New Orleans Race Riot of 1900* (Louisiana State University Press, 1976), 73.
14. Quoted in Hair, *Carnival of Fury*, 91.
15. Many of Gordon's autobiographical works seem to involve some elements of his imagination. A note by Andre Elizee, processor of the Gordon papers, wrote in 2006 that "Much of Gordon's Autobiographical works are presumed to be fictionalized narratives, as his brother Buddy (handwritten note in the collection) did not recognize them as factual." Guide to the Eugene Gordon Papers," Autobiographical Writings, Box 2, Folder 13. The Gordon papers are located at the Schomburg Center for Research in Black Culture, New York Public Library, SC MG-117. Thanks to Chiwe Gordon for allowing permission to cite and publish Gordon's papers.
16. Census of Population and Housing, Census.gov.
17. Gordon said that this incident was the source of his first published piece in the Atlanta *Constitution*. Autobiographical Notes, Eugene Gordon Papers, Box 1, Folder 2.

18 Lorraine Elena Roses, *Black Bostonians and the Politics of Culture 1920-1940* (University of Massachusetts Press, 2017), 103-4.
19 Candee, "A Pair Against Oppression," 18.
20 Eugene Gordon Papers, Box 1, Folder 2.
21 Eugene Gordon Papers, Box 2, Folder 16.
22 "Eugene Gordon to Visit Soviets," *Negro Liberator* (May 15, 1935), 5.
23 Lawrence P. Jackson, *The Indignant Generation: A Narrative History of African American Writers and Critics, 1934-1960* (Princeton University Press, 2011), 45.
24 Lorraine Elena Roses, ed. and intro., *Selected Works of Edythe Mae Gordon: African-American Women Writers, 1910-1940* (G. K. Hall & Co., 1996), xviii-xx.
25 W. N. Colson and A. B. Nutt, "The Failure of the 92nd Division," *Messenger* (September 1919), 22.
26 Roses, *Black Bostonians*, 104.
27 Verner Mitchell and Cynthia Davis, *Literary Sisters: Dorothy West and Her Circle, a Biography of the Harlem Renaissance* (Rutgers University Press, 2012), 170, n. 61.
28 Candee, "A Pair Against Oppression," 31.
29 Roses, *Black Bostonians*, 105. Gordon's later disenchantment with the military and with its treatment of Black veterans is recorded in his essays, "Negroes in the World War" (*Chicago Defender* September 15, 1934) and "Negro Soldier—Pawn of the Ruling Class" (*Fight* January 1934). He also wrote an editorial "Jimcrow Can't Inspire Men of the 92nd" in the *Daily Worker* (March 17, 1945), stating that present army conditions had not improved for Black soldiers. For more on Gordon's unit, see Emmitt J. Scott, *Scott's Official History of the American Negro in the World War* (Homewood Press, 1919).
30 Cynthia Davis and Verner Mitchell, "Eugene Gordon, Dorothy West, and the Saturday Evening Quill Club," *CLA Journal* 52 (June 2009), 194. "These United States: Massachusetts," *Messenger*, June 1925.
31 James Oliver Horton and Lois Horton *Black Bostonians: Family Life and Community Struggles in the Antebellum North*, rev. ed. (Holmes and Meier Publishers, 2000), 2.
32 See Violet Showers Johnson, *The Other Black Bostonians: West Indians in Boston, 1900-1950* (Indiana University Press, 2006).
33 Horton and Horton, *Black Bostonians*, 2-3.
34 Zebulon Vance Miletsky, *Before Busing: A History of Boston's Long Black Freedom Struggle* (University of North Carolina Press, 2022), 65.
35 Thomas O'Connor, qtd. in Miletsky *Before Busing*, 65.
36 Davis and Mitchell, "Eugene Gordon, Dorothy West," 396; Candee "A Pair Against Oppression," 3-40.
37 Davis and Mitchell, "Eugene Gordon, Dorothy West," 396.
38 Candee, *A Pair Against Oppression*, 39-40.
39 "A Statement to the Reader," *Saturday Evening Quill* (June 1930): 2.
40 Abby Johnson and Ronald Marbery Johnson, *Propaganda and Aesthetics: The Literary Politics of Afro-American Magazines in the Twentieth Century* (University of Massachusetts Press, 1979), 93.
41 Roses, *Black Bostonians*, 109. Gordon and members of the Quill club would

probably have been shocked to learn that they had already garnered the attention of the FBI (Mitchell and Davis, *Literary Sisters*), 93.
42 For more on the *Quill* contributors, see Roses *Black Bostonians*, 100–128, and Mitchell and Davis, *Literary Sisters*, 68–95.
43 Mitchell and Davis, *Literary Sisters*, 86.
44 Resume, Eugene Gordon Papers, Box 1, Folder 1.
45 Author Alice Dunbar Nelson, for example, praised the *Quill*, deeming the publication "seventy-two pages of very excellent material." W. E. B. Du Bois stated, "Of the booklets issued by young Negro writers in New York, Philadelphia and elsewhere, this collection from Boston is by far the most interesting and the best.... It is well presented and readable and maintains a high mark of literary excellence." Charles S. Johnson, editor of *Opportunity* magazine, reiterated on the quality of the journal: "Here we have what seems to me the best evidence of a substantial deposit after the feverish activity of the last few years." Quoted from the inside front cover *Saturday Evening Quill*, June 1930.
46 *Saturday Evening Quill*, June 1928.
47 Autobiographical Notes, Eugene Gordon Papers, Box 1, Folder 2.
48 Mary Hellen Washington, *The Other Blacklist: The African American Literary and Cultural Left of the 1950s* (Columbia University Press, 2014), 15.
49 Washington, *The Other Black List*, 13.
50 Edythe also published two stories about marital problems, "Subversion" (June 1928) and "If Wishes Were Horses" (April 1929), in the *Quill*.
51 "Contest Spotlight," *Opportunity* (July 1927): 2.
52 Mitchell and Davis, *Literary Sisters*, 88.
53 Eugene Gordon Papers, Box 9.
54 In another article called "Liberals in Boston" (*Plain Talk*, April 1930), Gordon kept whittling down the number of real "liberals" in the city. He starts with an estimate of as many as thirty-five hundred, but of these, "not very many are really Liberals." By the end of the article, he concludes there are "50 or so who are actually liberals."
55 Quoted in Theodore Draper, *American Communism and Soviet Russia* (Viking Press, 1960), 316.
56 Philip Foner, *American Socialism and Black Americans: From the Age of Jackson to World War II* (Greenwood Press, 1977), 319.
57 Barbara Foley, *Radical Representations: Politics and Form in US Proletarian Fiction, 1929–1941* (Duke University Press, 1993), 87.
58 W. E. B. Du Bois, "Socialism and the Negro Problem," *New Review* (February 1, 1913), 138–41.
59 Walter T. Howard, ed. and intro., *Black Communists Speak on Scottsboro: A Documentary History* (Temple University Press, 2008), 6–7.
60 Quoted in Candee, "A Pair Against Oppression," 59.
61 See "Understanding the Negro Question," *Daily Worker* July 28, 1948.
62 Hakim Adi, *Africanism and Communism* (Africa World Press, 2013), 65.
63 Mark Solomon, *The Cry Was Unity: Communists and African-Americans, 1917–1936* (University Press of Mississippi, 1998), 85–90.
64 Solomon, *The Cry Was Unity*, 129–43.
65 Candee, "A Pair Against Oppression," 70.

66 Nathaniel Mills, "Black Cultural (Inter)nationalism: Communism and African American Writing in the Great Depression," in *African American Literature in Transition, 1930-1940*, ed. Eve Dunbar and Ayesha K. Hardison (Cambridge University Press, 2022), 329.

67 Jackson, *The Indignant Generation*, 46. Gordon was a member of the League of American Writers and gave this talk at a conference held in New York City on April 26-28, 1935. Entitled "Social and Political Problems of the Negro Writer," the article was published in Henry Hart, ed., *American Writers' Congress* (International Publishers, 1935), 141-45. For more on this conference see Alan Wald, *Exiles from a Future Time: The Forging of the Mid-Twentieth Century Literary Left* (University of North Carolina Press, 2002), 264, and Mark Naison, *Communists in Harlem During the Depression* (University of Illinois Press, 1983), 201-6. Lawrence Jackson maintains that Gordon's insistence on a separate Black nation in the Black Belt "Split the Renaissance in half." "'The Aftermath': The Reputation of the Harlem Renaissance Twenty Years Later," in *The Cambridge Companion to the Harlem Renaissance*, ed. George Hutchinson (Cambridge University Press, 2007), 245-46. Much of what appears in this piece was first published earlier in his essay, "Negro Novelists and the Negro Masses," *New Masses* 1933, included in this anthology.

68 Howard, *Black Communists*, 9.

69 Washington, *The Other Black List*, 5-6.

70 Candee, "A Pair Against Oppression," 52-56

71 Kelley, *Hammer and Hoe*, 93.

72 William J. Maxwell, *New Negro, Old Left: African American Writing and Communism between the Wars* (Columbia University Press, 1999), 1.

73 Solomon, *The Cry Was Unity*, 277.

74 Anthony Dawahare, *Nationalism, Marxism, and African American Literature Between the Wars: A New Pandora's Box* (University Press of Mississippi, 2002), 87.

75 Brian Dolinar, *The Black Cultural Front: Black Writers and Artists of the Depression Generation* (University Press of Mississippi Press, 2002), 25. For more on the John Reed Clubs and literature, see Eric Homberger, "Proletarian Literature and the John Reed Clubs 1929-1935," *Journal of American Studies* 13 (August 1979): 221-44.

76 Mills, "Black Cultural (Inter)nationalism)," 337-38.

77 Wald, *Exiles from a Future Time*, 84.

78 Solomon, *The Cry Was Unity*, 278.

79 Roses, *Edythe Mae Gordon*, xxii. Edythe gives her own version of the breakup to the FBI in 1954. See Mitchell and Davis, *Literary Sisters*, 93-94.

80 Candee, "A Pair Against Oppression," 40-41.

81 Eugene Gordon, FBI file October 6, 1944. Gordon's FBI files are numbered 100-14692 and 100-14710. I have given the date of the letters in the hope of making them easier to locate in the files. When I reached out to the FBI offices requesting the files (FOIPA Request No. 1412816-000) on November 8, 2018, I was informed that "Records which may have been responsive to your request were destroyed on October 20, 2004. . . . Therefore your request

is being administratively closed." Fortunately, Verner Mitchell had a copy of the files and was kind enough to send me a copy of them.
82 Eugene Gordon FBI file May 7, 1942; *New York Times*, August 6, 1960.
83 Gordon had one child, a son, Eugene, who had a daughter, Chiwe.
84 Dolinar, *The Black Cultural Front*, 31.
85 Dolinar, *The Black Cultural Front*, 26–27.
86 For more on Scottsboro, see James R. Acker, *Scottsboro and Its Legacy: The Cases That Challenged American Legal and Social Justice* (Praeger, 2007); Dan Carter, *Scottsboro: A Tragedy of the American South* (Louisiana State University Press, 1979); James Haskins *The Scottsboro Boys* (Henry Holt and Company, 1994); James A. Miller *Remembering Scottsboro: The Legacy of an Infamous Trial* (Princeton University Press, 2009). For a discussion of its cultural legacy, see Maxwell, *New Negro, Old Left*, 125–51.
87 Eben Simmons Miller, "'A New Day Is Here': The Shooting of George Borden and 1930s Civil Rights Activism in Boston," *New England Quarterly* 73 (March 2000): 4–5.
88 Kate A. Baldwin, *Beyond the Color Line and the Iron Curtain: Reading Encounters Between Black and Red, 1922–1963* (Duke University Press, 2022), 14–22.
89 "To Study Soviet Russia," *Chicago Defender* (April 27, 1935): 3.
90 Some of these writings are contained in the Eugene Gordon Papers, Box 6, Folder 10.
91 Candee, "A Pair Against Oppression," 76–77.
92 "Genuine vs Bogus Democracy," Eugene Gordon Papers, Box 6, Folder 5. Gordon attempted to publish the piece in the *New Republic* on March 2, 1938, but it was rejected.
93 "Eugene Gordon Back from 3 Year Stay in Russia, Lauds Soviets," *New York Age* (February 5, 1938): 3.
94 He was considered by agents to be a "key figure" of the party (Eugene Gordon FBI File, September 22, 1943), a "brainy Negro" (Eugene Gordon FBI file July 20, 1942), and "one of the smartest Communists in the country" (Eugene Gordon FBI file August 20, 1942).
95 Eugene Gordon FBI file, September 23, 1944.
96 Mitchell and Davis, *Literary Sisters*, 88.
97 Gordon also wrote a pamphlet on the case with Earl Conrad in 1945, "Equal Justice Under Law." See also Danielle L. McGuire, *At the Dark End of the Street: Black Women, Rape, and Resistance—a New History of the Civil Rights Movement from Rosa Parks to the Rise of Black Power* (Vintage, 2010), 20, 30. A documentary film was made of the case in 2017, https://www.therapeofrecytaylor.com/the-film/. Gordon's notes on the case may be found in the Eugene Gordon Papers, Box 7, Folder 9.
98 *Gainesville Sun*, October 8, 1944.
99 Dolinar, *The Black Cultural Front*, 53.
100 Gordon wrote many notes and drafts of his article on the Bandung Conference. See the Eugene Gordon Papers, Box 8, Folders 1–6. See especially his draft "Before—and Seven Years After—Bandung," Box 8, Folder 5. Aronson's letter to Gordon and his response are located in the Eugene Gordon Papers, Box 8, Folder 72.

101 Robbie Lieberman "'Another Side of the Story': African American Intellectuals Speak out for Peace and Freedom During the Early Cold War Years," in *Anticommunism and the African America Freedom Movement: Another Side of the Story*, ed. Robbie Lieberman and Clarence Lang (Springer, 2009), 28–31. Articles from "Another Side of the Story" are located in the Eugene Gordon Papers, Box 5, Folders 7–8.
102 Eugene Gordon Papers, Box 2, Folder 2.
103 Nell Irvin Painter, *The Narrative of Hosea Hudson: The Life and Times of a Black Radical* (W.W. Norton, 1994), 32–33.
104 See letter to Elliott Schryver, October 3, 1940, Eugene Gordon Papers, Box 5, Folder 4.
105 Letter to Angus Cameron, October 19, 1960, Eugene Gordon Papers, Box 1, Folder 14.
106 Letter to Angus Cameron, October 19, 1960, Eugene Gordon Papers, Box 1, Folder 14.
107 Letter to Schryver, Eugene Gordon Papers, Box 5, Folder 4.
108 Eugene Gordon FBI Files January 19, 1954 (1009966122). The TOPLEV program was an FBI initiative to get potentially disaffected high-level Communist Party members to turn evidence against other members. Clearly, Eugene still did not fit this description.
109 "Moscow Through Brown Eyes," blog March 23, 2008. No longer available without permission.
110 "'The Green Hat' Comes to Chambers Street," in *Nancy Cunard: Brave Poet, Indomitable Rebel 1896-1965*, ed. Hugh Ford (Chilton Books, 1968), 133–40. There is a letter from Cunard to Gordon in the Eugene Gordon Papers, Box 1, Folder 17.
111 Lieberman, *Anticommunism*, 17.
112 Eugene Gordon Papers, Box 7, Folder 6; Box 5, Folders 10–12.
113 Eugene Gordon Papers, Resume, Box 1, Folder 2.
114 Davis and Mitchell, "Eugene Gordon, Dorothy West," 404.
115 Eugene Gordon Papers, Box 1, Folders 10–11.
116 Eugene Gordon Papers, Box 1, Folder 11.
117 Eugene Gordon Papers, Box 1, Folder 11.
118 Eugene Gordon Papers, Obituary, Box 1, Folder 1.

AUTOBIOGRAPHICAL WRITINGS

1 Cynthia Davis and Verner Mitchell, "Eugene Gordon, Dorothy West and the Saturday Evening Quill Club," *CLA Journal* 52 (June 2009): 194.
2 Judas betrayed Jesus to the Romans by kissing him. Matthew 26:47–50.
3 A rural county in central Georgia. Hawkinsville is the county seat.
4 J. Pope Brown made an unsuccessful bid for the governorship in 1912.
5 Derogatory term for whites, especially from rural areas of the South.
6 To cauterize.
7 A type of necklace that often has uniform oval links.
8 Brogans are heavy, ankle-high leather shoes.

9 Box 2, Folders 14–15.
10 Some elements of the autobiography seem fictitious. How, for example, could Gordon recall events when he was a toddler? Other parts may be embellished. Later in life, Gordon tried to publish some of these pieces, such as the Robert Charles episode, as short stories. In a note in the Eugene Gordon papers, his brother Buddy indicates that he does not recall some of the events described.
11 Eugene's younger brother, Ernest.
12 Gordon attempted to publish this section separately under the title ("Snakes and Men." Eugene Gordon Papers).
13 The through street in New Orleans closest to the Mississippi River.
14 An embankment for buttressing the base of a levee and forming a berm, a mound of dirt.
15 Algiers is the 15th ward in New Orleans. It is a historic neighborhood located on the lower Mississippi River.
16 A hoecake is a Southern cornmeal pancake. Also known as johnnycake.
17 Box 1, Folder 2.
18 A cart or truck used to carry heavy loads.
19 A small gift given to a customer by a merchant.
20 A canopy and its supports over a bed.
21 A natural fiber fabric net woven in such a way to literally bar mosquitos from entry.
22 In Florida.
23 The route of the St. Charles Street car line; the uptown area was known for its wealthy mansions.
24 In the book of Psalms, King David pleads with God: "Purge me with hyssop [a shrub used to make medicine], and I shall be clean; wash me, and I shall be whiter than snow." 51:7.
25 Box 3, Folders 5, 11. Published under the pseudonym Clark Hall.
26 William Ivy Hair, *Carnival of Fury: Robert Charles and the New Orleans Race Riot of 1900* (Louisiana University Press, 1976), 12.
27 Hair, *Carnival of Fury*, 169–74.
28 Daniel Candee, "A Pair Against Oppression: June Croll, Eugene Gordon, Communism and the Forging of American Anti-Racism" (MA thesis, University of Chicago, Social Sciences, 2022), 14.
29 Henry McNeal Turner (1834–1915) was a radical preacher who was an advocate for migration to Liberia. He published two newspapers, *The Voice of Missions* (1893–1900) and *The Voice of the People* (1901–04). Although Eugene was not an advocate of Black migration to Africa, he undoubtedly admired Turner's courage.
30 Box 2, Folder 21.
31 A boot with hobnails (nails inserted into the soles of the boots).
32 *Tageblatt* was a German language daily newspaper published in Berlin from 1872 to 1939.
33 A German, usually referring to a soldier.

FICTION

1. A witty thought or remark.
2. A device that can transmit sounds such as a phonograph.
3. A diapason is a type of pipes often called principals.
4. Eugene Gordon Papers, Box 3, Folder 5.
5. Flournoy Eakin Miller and Aubrey Lyles were an African American comedy team who composed many songs and plays, including "Shuffle Along" (1921).
6. Eyes that are misaligned.
7. The Boston *Evening Transcript* (1830–1941) was a daily afternoon newspaper.
8. Rudolph Valentino (1895–1926) was an Italian-born silent film star billed as the "Latin Lover." He was in such classics as *The Sheik* (1921) and *Blood and Sand* (1922).
9. A lying-in hospital was the name for a hospital where the patient would be confined for a period before or after birth.
10. An adhesive such as glue.
11. An inferior or illegally obtained alcoholic beverage.
12. A breechloader is a firearm in which the ammunition is inserted in the rear (breech) end of the barrel.
13. A short drum roll, perhaps five or six seconds.
14. A musical instrument of bells.
15. Built in 1868, the Franklin Square House was once an elegant hotel. It closed in 1888 and became a women's dormitory for the New England Conservatory. In 1904, it served as a residential hotel for young working women.
16. A rustling or rushing sound in trees or the ocean.
17. Lorraine Elena Roses, *Black Bostonians and the Politics of Culture, 1920–1940* (University of Massachusetts Press, 2017), 113.
18. Roses, *Black Bostonians*, 114.
19. Kilmer's poem "Trees" was published in 1914.
20. Let's get back to what we were talking about.
21. King Tut's tomb was discovered in 1922 by archaeologist Howard Carter. The discovery set off a frenzy of interest in Egyptology.
22. The Western Deffufa was a large adobe temple in Kerma, in present-day Sudan.
23. Meroë was a city on the east bank of the Nile River (about 300 BCE to AD 400). It is located in present-day Sudan.
24. The Huksos Period was the Fifteenth Dynasty, which flourished c. 1650–1550 BCE.
25. The Twelfth Dynasty lasted from 1991 to 1802 BCE. It was a relatively stable period marked by territorial expansion.
26. His name is the same as the protagonist in "Rootbound."
27. Lothrop Stoddard (1883–1950) was a white supremacist whose ideas were embraced by the Nazis as well as US President Warren Harding. Stoddard was a member of the Ku Klux Klan, the American Birth Control Society, and the American Eugenics League and is best known for his book, *The Rising Tide of Color Against White World Superiority* (Charles Scribner's Sons, 1920).

28 To move or twist one's mouth or eyebrow suddenly.
29 Gordon is recalling his own wartime experience.
30 A four-in-hand necktie is a popular knot used because of its simplicity.
31 Eugene Gordon Papers, Box 3, Folder 4.
32 Eugene Gordon Papers, Box 3, Folder 4.

NONFICTION

1 *Freedom's Journal* (1827-29) was founded by Reverend John Wilk and other free Blacks in New York.
2 *Rights of All* (1829-30) was an abolitionist paper founded by Samuel Cornish.
3 *The National Reformer* (1838) was founded by William Whipper and was the organ of the American Moral Reform Society.
4 *The Palladium of Liberty* (1843-44) was formed by David Jenkins and other Black Ohioans to support African American rights in their state.
5 *The Herald of Freedom* (1851-55) was established by African American abolitionist Peter H. Clark in Wilmington, Ohio.
6 The *Christian Recorder* is the oldest continuously published Black newspaper in the United States. It is the official newspaper of the African Methodist Episcopalian Church.
7 Journalism based on sensationalism. The term derived in the 1890s to apply especially to the *New York World*, owned by Joseph Pulitzer, and the *New York Journal*, operated by William Randolph Hurst.
8 Footpads were highwaymen who robbed on foot.
9 Kelly Miller (1863-1939) was a scientist, author, and academic. He was dean of arts and sciences at Howard University from 1907 to 1919. Miller was a well-known intellectual and was positioned between Booker T. Washington and W. E. B. Du Bois in his political and social beliefs. He was the father of Harlem Renaissance author May Miller.
10 William Pickens (1881-1954) was an author and educator. He was affiliated with the NAACP for over twenty years. Although he was opposed to communism, he supported some leftist causes.
11 The marriage in 1924 of Leonard "Kip" Rhinelander, son of a millionaire, and Alice Jones, a mixed-race immigrant, became a hot topic of society gossip. When rumor got out that Jones was Black, the Rhinelander family took her to court in 1925, where Jones was forced to expose parts of her body before a judge and jury to determine her race. They decided she was "colored," but would not grant an annulment. In 1929, Jones agreed to a divorce, and the marriage was annulled. Jones was given a settlement of $32,500 and $3,600 a year for life.
12 Benjamin Jefferson Davis (1903-1964) was a communist and a lawyer. He was elected as city councilperson from Harlem in 1943. In 1949, he was sent to prison for five years for violating the Smith Act, prohibiting violent revolution against the United States government.

13 Henry Lincoln Johnson (1870–1925) was an Atlanta lawyer. A prominent Republican, he was appointed by President William Howard Taft as recorder of deeds for the District of Columbia. He was the husband of writer Georgia Douglas Johnson.
14 Robet Sengstacke Abbott (1870–1940) was founder and editor of the *Chicago Defender*, which had the highest circulation of any Black-owned newspaper in the country.
15 Williams (1865–1940) was a doctor and a journalist.
16 A hawser is a thick rope often used to moor a ship.
17 The *AFRO* began publication in 1892, founded by John H. Murphy. When he died in 1932, his son, Carl, became editor.
18 In 1923, Garvey was sentenced to five years in prison on charges of mail fraud. After his appeals failed, Garvey was sent to Atlanta Federal Penitentiary in 1925. His sentence was commuted by President Calvin Coolidge with the stipulation that Garvey be deported from the United States.
19 Alvira Hazzard was a teacher, short story writer, and playwright. Florence Marion Harmon was a short story writer.
20 Gordon intends the New York *World*. Hansen was the book review editor beginning in 1926 and remaining in the position even after the paper was sold and renamed the New York *World-Telegram* in 1931.
21 *In Abraham's Bosom* opened on December 30, 1926. It received the Pulitzer Prize in Drama for 1927.
22 *The Story of the World's Literature* was published in 1925. Macy, a Harvard professor and a socialist, was married to Anne Sullivan, the teacher of Helen Keller.
23 White American author who wrote the controversial novel *Nigger Heaven* (1926).
24 Richard Bruce Nugent (1906–87) was a gay poet and writer who was part of the Harlem Renaissance. He illustrated Gordon's short story "Game" in *Opportunity* (1927). The novel referred to is the avant-garde short story "Smoke, Lillies and Jade."
25 Noah Davis Thompson was a journalist and activist. He was married to writer Eloise Bibb Thompson.
26 A once highly regarded writer of drama and fiction now best remembered for his short stories. Steel was one of the judges of the *Opportunity* fiction contest that awarded Gordon's "Game" a prize. Eugene Gordon Papers, Box 3, Folder 5.
27 A book of poems patterned after sermons and published in 1927.
28 *Ninth Avenue* (1926) was set in the West Village area of Manhattan where Bodenheim lived.
29 A collection of short stories published in 1926.
30 William Ellery Sweet (1869–1942) was governor of Colorado from 1923 to 1925. He was a strong opponent of the Ku Klux Klan, which may be a reason why he lost reelection.
31 The Metropolitan Life Insurance Tower is located on Madison Avenue and 24th Street in the Flatiron District of Manhattan.
32 The Essex was a moderately priced automobile designed by the Essex Motor

NOTES TO PAGES 229-252   379

Company in 1918-1922 and the Hudson Motor Car Company between 1922 and 1933.
33 Begun in 1914 and awarded annually by the NAACP for a notable achievement by an African American. Joel Elias Spingarn was a white writer and activist who was chairman of the board of the NAACP.
34 The Lafayette Theatre was located at 132nd Street and 7th Avenue and operated from 1912 to 1951.
35 *Claquers* were professional clappers in French theaters.
36 An organizational level of the Ku Klux Klan. A province (equivalent to a country) was ruled by a Grand Giant, who was assisted by four goblins.
37 A demon intent on having sexual intercourse with women while they are asleep.
38 To exist or to prevail.
39 Hog's head cheese is generally made from boiling a pig's head (minus the brains and eyes) and forming it into a jelly. It could include pig's feet, tongue, and heart.
40 "A Statement to the Reader," *Saturday Evening Quill*, June 1930.
41 Abby Johnson and Ronald Marbery Johnson, *Propaganda and Aesthetics: The Literary Politics of Afro-American Magazines in the Twentieth Century* (University of Massachusetts Press, 1979), 93.
42 Roark Bradford (1896-1948) was a white popular journalist and fiction writer from Arkansas. He often dealt with African American life in a stereotypical manner. His book of short stories *Ol' Man Adam an' His Chillun* was the source for Marc Conelly's Pulitzer Prize-winning play *Green Pastures* (1930).
43 Lorraine Elena Roses, *Black Bostonians and the Politics of Culture 1920-1940* (University of Massachusetts Press, 2017), 112-13.
44 Moloch appears several times in the Hebrew Bible, particularly in the book of Leviticus. He is associated with sinful practices such as child sacrifice.
45 George was the generic name for a Negro Pullman porter, after the Chicago businessman George M. Pullman, who designed and manufactured the train cars.
46 An object that is showy but worthless.
47 Doctor S. Parkes Cadman (1864-1936) was an English-born American liberal Protestant minister who opposed antisemitism and racial prejudice.
48 Derogatory term for whites, particularly the poor from the rural South.
49 Parties often held in Harlem in the 1920s in an attempt to raise money for rent.
50 "The Promised Land" was a short story by Rudolph Fisher published in *The Atlantic* in 1927.
51 Gordon is probably thinking of Claude McKay, whose *Home to Harlem* (1928) contains these and other descriptions of color.
52 Gordon is referencing Hughes's article "The Negro Artist and the Racial Mountain," published in *The Nation* (June 23, 1926).
53 Gordon is referring to the Harlem Renaissance or the New Negro Movement.
54 J. A. Rogers was a Jamaican American journalist and author of several books on Black history.
55 Theophilus Lewis was perhaps the best-known reviewer and critic of the

Harlem Renaissance. Most of his writing appeared in the *Messenger* and later in the Catholic periodical *America*.
56 Wendell Phillips Dabney was an author, musician, editor, and civil rights activist.
57 The credo of *Opportunity* magazine.
58 Mordecai Wyatt Johnson was president of Howard University from 1926 to 1960.
59 Poro College was founded as a cosmetics school by Annie Turnbo Malone in St. Louis. It was named after the Poro society—a secret organization in West Africa that exemplified physicality and spirituality. Hair product entrepreneur Madame C. J. Walker received training at the school.
60 Casper Holstein (1876–1944) was a numbers banker from the Danish (now US. Virgin Islands who funded the Opportunity Prize awards.
61 Verner Mitchell and Cynthia Davis, *Literary Sisters: Dorothy West and Her Circle, a Biography of the Harlem Renaissance* (Rutgers University Press, 1996), 88.
62 The Parker House is a storied hotel founded in 1855. It has been at its Beacon Hill location since 1927 and has had numerous literary and political figures as guests.
63 Flappers were rebellious young American women who bobbed their hair, wore short skirts, admired avant-garde art, and listened to jazz music.
64 "Anent" means concerning or about.
65 Matthew 25:31–46 tells the parable of Christ separating the sheep from the goats.
66 Marcet Haldeman-Julius (1887–1941) was an American feminist actress, civil rights activist, and playwright.
67 Babbitts are conformist and materialistic middle-class businessmen. The name is taken from Sinclair Lewis's novel *Babbitt* (1930).
68 The Rockland Palace was located at 280 West 155th Street and 8th Avenue. It was originally called the Manhattan Casino. The Palace held the Hamilton Lodge drag balls that would attract over eight thousand partiers in the 1920s.
69 A'Lelia Walker was heiress to her mother's beauty fortune and a prominent social figure.
70 Hop Toad, Assbray, and Braggadocio are obviously made-up, humorous names.
71 An olla podrida is a mixture of miscellaneous things, a stew.
72 The Mayflower was one of the most luxurious hotels in Washington, DC. It was opened in 1925. That same year, it hosted President-Elect Herbert Hoover's Inaugural Ball and hosted an inaugural ball every four years after until 1981. The hotel filed for bankruptcy in 1933. It has had several owners since then.
73 In Washington, DC, the position largely recorded deeds, mortgages, and other documents relating to real estate. The position traditionally went to African Americans since the appointment of Frederick Douglass in 1881.
74 Oscar De Priest (1871–1951) was the first African American to be elected to Congress in the twentieth century. He was elected on April 15, 1929, and represented Chicago's South Side.

75 Baal is a fertility god that was worshipped by many ancient Middle Eastern communities, especially the Canaanites.
76 John Francis Adams III (1866–1954) was a lawyer and politician who was secretary of the navy from 1929 to 1933.
77 Sam Browne belts are named for their inventor, General Samuel Browne (1824–1901). The leather belt has a supporting strap that passes over the right shoulder. It is especially popular with the military and the police.
78 The Statler Hotel was opened on March 10, 1927. It was built by hotelier E. M. Statler. It is now called the Boston Park Plaza.
79 Robert Russa Moton and Kelly Miller were two conservative Black leaders. Moton (1867–1940) served as president of Tuskegee Institute after Booker T. Washington's death in 1915.
80 Lenox Avenue (now Malcolm X Boulevard) and 7th Avenue (now Adam Clayton Powell, Jr. Boulevard) run parallel to one another.
81 The Dunbar Apartments, a complex of buildings located on West 149th and West 150th Streets, were built by John D. Rockefeller, Jr. between 1926 and 1928. They are named for poet Paul Laurence Dunbar. The buildings became the gold standard in Harlem, with famed residents such as Matthew Henson, Paul Robeson, Countee Cullen, A. Philip Randolph, and W. E. B. Du Bois.
82 The *Southern Worker* began publishing in 1930 and ended in 1937.
83 Walter T. Howard, ed. and intro., *Black Communists Speak on Scottsboro: A Documentary History* (Temple University Press, 2008).
84 Mark Naison, *Communists in Harlem During the Depression* (University of Illinois Press, 1983), 70.
85 Mark Solomon, *The Cry Was Unity: Communists and African-Americans, 1917–1936* (University Press of Mississippi, 1998), 277.
86 Lorenzo Dow Blackmon wrote *The Rise and Progress of the Kingdoms of Light and Darkness: Or, The Reign of Kings Alpha and Abadon* (1867), modeled after John Bunyan's *Pilgrim's Progress* and John Milton's *Paradise Lost*.
87 Frank J. Webb wrote the novel *The Garies and Their Friends* (1857).
88 William Wells Brown was an abolitionist, novelist, and playwright perhaps best known for *Clotel: Or, The President's Daughter; A Narrative of Slave Life in the United States*, in 1853.
89 Max Eastman (1883–1969) was a poet and editor of the socialist magazines *The Masses* and *The Liberator*.
90 Gordon is probably intending McKay's militant poem "If We Must Die."
91 McKay was in the Soviet Union in 1922–23.
92 *Black No More* is a satiric roman à clef (1931). Schuyler was a frequent butt of Gordon's ire. See, for example, "Who Is George S. Schuyler?" *Worker* (January 6, 1946): 8. Gordon recognized Schuyler's abilities and was frustrated by what he saw as wasted talent.
93 Hughes' semiautobiographical novel *Not Without Laughter* was written in 1930 and concerns a Black family in small-town Kansas.
94 Gordon Hancock (1884–1970) was a pastor in Richmond and a professor at Virginia Union University.
95 A straight-eight is an eight-cylinder internal combustion engine, often used in luxury automobiles.

96 Established in 1928, the *Atlanta World* is Georgia's oldest Black newspaper. William Alexander Scott II was the editor at the time Gordon was writing. Bruce Reynolds wrote an anti-communist volume *The Communist Shakes His Fist! He Would Fight the Battles of Moscow on the Streets of New York* (George Sully and Co., NY (1931).
97 Camp Hill is located near Spartanburg, South Carolina. A group of Black farmers refused to leave their land when threatened by powerful landowners. Gordon writes about the incident in "Camp Hill," *Daily Worker*, July 28, 1931.
98 Eugene Washington Rhodes was editor from 1922-1970.
99 Carl J. Murphy, who edited the paper from 1922 until his death in 1967.
100 Places in the American South with a large Black population living in an area with rich black soil, such as the Mississippi Delta. The Communist Party of the United States in a controversial plan pressed for Black autonomy in these regions.
101 Brackets are in the original here and above.
102 The Scottsboro Boys.
103 Zebulon Vance Miletsky, *Before Busing: A History of Boston's Long Black Freedom Struggle* (University of North Carolina Press), 70.
104 Angelo Herndon (1913-97) was a Black labor organizer who was arrested and convicted for trying to organize Black and white workers in Atlanta in 1932. He was found guilty largely on the basis of Communist materials found in his room. The Supreme Court ultimately ruled Georgia's insurrection law unconstitutional and he was freed. Thomas Mooney (1882-1942) was a white political activist and labor leader convicted of a bombing in San Francisco in 1916. Despite evidence proving his innocence, Mooney served twenty-two years in prison before being pardoned in 1939.
105 Daniel Candee, "A Pair Against Oppression: June Croll, Eugene Gordon, Communism and the Forging of American Anti-Racism" (MA thesis, University of Chicago, Social Sciences, 2022), 4.
106 The banking firm started by John Pierpont Morgan Sr. (1837-1913).
107 A deep deflationary recession lasted from January 1920 until July 1921.
108 The National Recovery Act established by President Franklin D. Roosevelt in 1933. Its goal was to establish fair business practices and to end cut-throat competition.
109 Throats.
110 The October Revolution November 6-7 or (October 24-25 in the Julian Calendar) was also known as the Bolshevik Revolution. Vladimir Lenin led an almost bloodless coup to control the government.
111 Also known as the Ernest Lundeen Bill. Initially authored by the Communist Party in 1930, the popular bill was introduced in Congress several times before passing in 1936. It essentially provided unemployment insurance and aid for the sick and elderly and allowed paid maternity leave.
112 A cafeteria in Harlem that was boycotted because it did not hire Black workers.
113 Thomas Montgomery Gregory (1887-1971) was a dramatist and educator who taught in the Drama Department at Howard University.
114 Dion Boucicault's popular play was first performed in 1859. It was con-

troversial because of its sympathetic treatment of enslaved people in the South. It has been adapted numerous times, including a social satire by Branden Jacobs-Jenkins in 2014.
115 John William Isham (1866–1902) was a vaudevillian known for his octoroons, based in part on traditional minstrel shows and featuring attractive Black chorus girls.
116 Frederick Ridgely Torrence (1874–1950) was a white poet and editor. His plays, although initially performed by white casts, later used Black actors. The plays listed premiered in *Three Plays for a Negro Theater* (1917).
117 *Goat Alley: A Tragedy of Negro Life* opened in 1921.
118 Smithers is a white trader in Eugene O'Neill's play *The Emperor Jones* (1920).
119 *They Shall Not Die*, based on the Scottsboro case, was first performed in 1934.
120 *Stevedore*, in which an innocent Black man is accused of rape, was first performed in 1934.
121 A Marxist aesthetic theory using literature, art, and music to help develop social consciousness. It depicts communist values in a positive light.
122 Eugene Gordon Papers Box 6, Folder, 7.
123 *Negro Liberator*, May 15, 1935, 5.
124 Frances Lee Bernstein, *The Dictatorship of Sex: Lifestyle Advice for the Soviet Masses* (Northern Illinois University Press, 2007), 34–35.
125 *Besprizorny* were homeless children. There were thousands of such children in the Stalinist era, and the party attempted to blunt this image by establishing youth groups such as the Young Pioneers (ages 9–14) and Komsomol (ages 14–18) to provide activities for children and young adults.
126 A large city on the Volga founded in the thirteenth century.
127 A placard designed to be displayed indoors or outdoors.
128 Theodora, a former prostitute, established a home for prostitutes after becoming empress in 527 CE.
129 Those who are exceptionally hard workers.
130 Taylor was twenty-two at the time.
131 Box 6, Folder 2.
132 Spessard L. Holland was governor of Florida from 1941 to 1945 and a senator from Florida from 1946 to 1971.
133 *Chicago Defender*.
134 "Illegible" was written in the original text.
135 An indentured servant was under contract to work without a salary for a set period of time to repay an indenture or loan.
136 A brassard is a piece of cloth or other material worn around the upper arm.
137 The NAACP.
138 Material on Angela Davis in Box 5, folders 9–11.
139 Arthur Robert Jensen was a psychology professor at the University of California, Berkeley, who maintained the controversial position that disparities in IQ scores between whites and Blacks were based on genetic and racial differences.
140 The Soledad Brothers were three inmates falsely charged with the murder of a prison guard, John Vincent Mills, at California's Soledad Prison on

January 16, 1970. The three men were George Jackson, Fleeta Drumgo, and John Cluchett.

141 A Black Muslim newspaper. It was the official paper of the Nation of Islam from 1960 to 1975.

142 Henrietta Delancey Henkle (1909–1983), is better known by her pen name Henrietta Buckmaster. She is best known for writing historical studies and novels and for being active in the civil rights movement.

143 Patricia Roberts Harris (1924–85) was an American politician and diplomat. She served as the US secretary of Housing and Urban Development from 1977 to 1979 and as the US secretary of Health and Human Services from 1979 to 1981.

Index

Note: References following "n" refer notes.

Abbott, Robert S., 207, 215–16, 381n76
Adams, Charles F., 272–23
Adams, John Francis, III, 381n76
Adi, Hakim, 371n62
African Americans. *See also* Negro
African Blood Brotherhood, 318
African Methodist Episcopal Church, 265, 377n6
AFRO, 378n17
Afro-American (Baltimore), 209–11, 215–16, 236, 309
Age (New York), 210, 216, 229
Allen, Woody, 369n2
All God's Chillun Got Wings (play), 336, 337
American Communist Party (CPUSA), 16–19
American Federation of Labor, 277
American Legion, 270–75; annual convention in Boston, 271–75; anti-lynching resolution, rejection of, 275; composition of, 273; criticism and press responses, 270–72; membership and parade, 273–74; militarism and patriotism rhetoric, 271–73
American Mercury, 1, 14, 206, 224
American Negro. *See* Negro
American Negro Labor Congress, 16
American Writers' Congress, 17
Amsterdam News, 12, 209, 213, 228, 252, 280, 304, 308
"Anent," 380n64
The Annals of the American Academy of Political and Social Science, 206
Another Side of the Story, 26
Argus, 212
Arnold, Bobby, 71–72
Arnold, Dicky, 71–72
Aronson, James, 25
Associated Negro Press, 212
Atlanta, 177, 216

Atlanta Federal Penitentiary, 378n18
Atlanta Independent, 215
Atlanta Journal, 361
Attucks, Crispus, 9

Baal, 381n75
Babbitt (Lewis), 380n67
Bachmars, 225, 227
Backfurrow (Eaton), 248
Bandung Conference, 373n100
Banjo (McKay), 297
Besprizorny, 383n125
Birmingham Age-Herald, 348
The Birth of a Nation (film), 337
Black Belt, 327, 331
Black Communists: racial solidarity challenges, 176–91; *vs.* white allies, 178–80
Black identity. *See* Negro identity
Black masses, 294–98; leadership and, 302–3, 306; right of paternalism over, 301
Black Muslim, 384n141
Black No More, 381n92
Black press. *See* Negro press
Blackson, Lorenzo D., 293
Black theater in America, 332–39; liberal playwrights, 336–38; Negro representation, 333–39; New Theatre League, 332; radical theater, 338–39; slavery and race in, 333–35; *Stevedore*, 332, 338–39; tradition of Negro inferiority, 336; *Uncle Tom's Cabin*, 333–38, 339
Black Worker in the Deep South (Hudson), 26
Black youth: crime and, 213; curfew restrictions, 192–93; police harassment of, 193–99
Blood and Sand (film), 376n8
Bloor, Ella (Mother), 21
Bodenhamer, O. L., 271

385

Bodenheim, Maxwell, 222
Borden, George H., 312–17; death and police shooting, 312–13; funeral, 314; public mobilization, 314; racism, 313–17
Borodin, Mikhail, 23
Boston, 9–12; American Legion of, 270–75; Black population, 9–10; Gordon's move to, 9–10; racism, 9–10; Saturday Evening Quill Club, 10–12
Boston Herald, 12, 220
Boston Meat Market, 129–32
Boston Post, 1, 8–9, 19, 23, 24, 104, 340
Boucicault, Dion, 335, 382n114
Bradford, Roark, 379n42
brassard, 383n136
breechloader, 376n12
Briggs, Cyril, 24, 318
Brotherhood of Sleeping Car Porters, 12, 245
Brown, J. P., 39, 374n4
Brown, William Wells, 288, 295, 381n88
Browne, Samuel, 381n77
Bruce, Richard, 220
Burghardt, William E., 294
Burke, Lillian, 3

Cadman, S. Parkes, 246, 379n47
Call, 254
Camp Hill, 382n97
Candee, Daniel, 1, 7, 82
Cane (Toomer), 248–249
capitalism, 27, 270–71, 318, 337; wages and job-discrimination, 326–27
Carter, Howard, 376n21
Catholic Church, 212
Catlett, Elizabeth, 25
cause of women, 24–25
Chapman, Edythe Mae, 7–8
Charles, Robert, 4–6, 34, 37–39; death of, 94; influence on Gordon, 82, 95; police confrontation, 82; portrayal in press, 89; reputation among Black community, 89–90
Chestnutt, Charles W., 288, 293–294
childhood, 34–49; early years in South, 34–35; Georgia Christmas morning, 42–46; interracial childhood friendships, 39–42; Negro preacher, 46–49; Robert Charles incident, 34, 37–39
Christianity, 212, 242–47, 302; bankruptcy of, 247; hypocrisy in, 244–45; slavery and, 243; teachings, 242. *See also* Negro church
Christian Recorder, 207, 377n6
Chronicle, 211, 213
Civil War, 260, 292
The Clansman (play), 337
class: black professors' exclusion from, 167, 169; differences, 200–3; domestic aspirations and limitations of, 114–16; economic struggles, 59, 68; self-worth linked to, 114–16; social hierarchy, 71–72, 128, 132, 136; tensions of mobility and status, 117–18; white and Black working conditions, 59–60; working-class Black laborers, 59–61; working-class families, 69–71, 83–85, 88–90; working-class whites, 84–85, 200–3
class-consciousness, 288, 297, 316; communist belief and, 312; white workers, 338; workers, 49
class struggle: intersection with racism, 176, 178–80; sharecropper organizing, 178–79
Cluchett, John, 384n140
Coleman, Ralf, 11
The Colonel's Dream (Chestnutt), 293
colored girl(s): appearance, 226–28; Boston, 250; discrimination, 227–28
colorism, 73, 225–28, 267; light skin preference, 209–10; in marriage, 128–29, 133; self-perception, 132–33, 136
color line, 202–3; among teachers, 328–29
Colson, W. N., 8
Commonweal, 12
Communism, 15–17, 306, 364; black masses leadership and, 302; interracial labor solidarity, 277, 282–83; spread among Negroes, 308–9
Communist Party of the USA (CPUSA),

INDEX

1–2, 16–19, 282–83, 307, 310–11; interracial collaboration, 176–91; Southern organizing, 178–80
The Conjure Woman (Chestnutt), 293
Cooke, Marvel, 25
Coolidge, Calvin, 210, 378n18
Cornish, Samuel, 377n2
The Cotton Kingdom (Olmsted), 362
Courier (Pittsburgh), 208–9, 210, 212, 346
CPUSA. *See* Communist Party of the USA
crime: Negro youth, 213; press sensationalism, 208–9
Crimson, 271–72
The Crisis: Record of the Darker Race, 251, 306
criticism (literary): bias in toward Negro writers, 239–41; color line in, 239; jungle stereotype, 239–40
Croll, June, 1, 21, 26; death of, 28
Crowl, Sonia, 21
Culbertson, Ernest Howard, 336
Cullen, Countee, 288, 298, 381n81
Cunard, Nancy, 27, 300
Cuney, Waring, 11
Curley, James Michael, 10, 270, 272

Dabney, W. P., 252, 256, 380n56
Daily Worker, 1, 24–25, 346, 348–49
Daily World, 28
Daniels, Fanny, 347–48, 353
Daniels, West, 347–48, 353
Danishevsky, Mark Semyonovich, 341–42, 345
The Dark Princess (DuBois), 294
Davis, Angela, 27–28; background and education, 363–64; charges and imprisonment, 364–65; communist beliefs, 364–67; media and public reactions to, 366; relationship with Jonathan and Jackson, 365; symbol of resistance and Black womanhood, 365–67
Davis, Benjamin Jefferson, 215, 377n12
Davis, B. Frank, 363
Davis, Cynthia, 13
Davis, Fania, 363
Davis, James, 350

Davis, Salle, 363
Defender (Chicago), 210–14, 224, 304, 308; Abbott's leadership, 207, 215–16; circulation growth, 209; sensationalism, 207–8
Defender (Huston), 308
De Priest, Oscar, 267, 380n74
Dewey, John, 220, 222
discrimination, 327; denial of protection, 86; economic vulnerability caused by, 91–92; in employment, 225–27, 234; interracial play forbidden, 71–72; medical care disparities, 76–77; racial insults and threats, 83–86. *See also* inequality
Dixon, Thomas, 337
domestic domination: resistance and retaliation, 137–40; by wife, 128–29, 134–37
Douglas, Aaron, 221
Douglass, Frederick, 303
Dreiser, Theodore, 22, 276
Du Bois, W. E. B., 8, 288, 294–95, 304, 377n9, 381n81
Dunbar, Paul Laurence, 288, 295, 381n81
Dunbar Apartments, 381n81

Eagle, 266
Eastman, Max, 276, 381n89
Eaton, Geoffrey Dell, 248
Egyptology, 166–68, 171–74
Ellison, Ralph, 13
Emma Lazarus Federation of Jewish Women's Clubs, 28
The Emperor Jones (play), 336, 337–38, 383n118
Ernest Lundeen Bill, 382n111
Essex Motor Company, 378n32
Ethiopia, 167, 170–71
Evening Transcript, 132, 213, 271, 302, 376n7

The Fanatics (Dunbar), 295
Fauset, Jessie, 218
fear: of Black men, 155–58, 161–63; of isolation, 155–57, 161; of natural surroundings, 155–57, 161–62; of violence, 154–58, 161–63

Finnish Workers Club, 17
Fire! (Thurman), 11, 220, 238
Fisher, Rudolph, 250, 288, 298, 379n50
Flappers, 380n63
flood: anxieties about, 71, 79–81; house flooding during storm, 80–81
Florida, 2–3
Floyd, George, 29
footpads, 377n8
four- in- hand necktie, 377n30
Franklin Square House, 376n15
Freedom's Journal, 207, 377n1
friendship: childhood, 39–42; interracial, 201–2; segregation in, 82, 95

Gamble, George, 347–48, 353
Gardner, Everett, 313
Garrison, William Lloyd, 9
Garvey, Marcus, 3, 11, 216, 238, 378n18
gender: in marriage, role in, 114–16, 121–4; reform and obedience, 117–18, 121. *See also* domestic domination; Negro women
"Genuine vs Bogus Democracy," 373n92
Georgia: backwoods of, 40; Christmas morning incident in, 42–46
Gilpin, Charles, 228–29
Goat Alley (play), 336
God's Trombone, 221
Gold, Mike, 276
Gordon, Charles, 3, 39–42; "gentleman farmer," 39; intelligent Negro, 40; obeying, 41; physical appearance of, 39
Gordon, Elijah, 2–4; boarding house enterprise, 60–61; business ownership, 68–70; courage and belief, 6; migrated to Oviedo, Florida, 3; moved back to Hawkinsville, Georgia, 5; moved to New Orleans, 3–4; reaction to lynching story, 56; response to violence, 88–94; role as protector and provide, 51–54, 59; struggles with work on levee, 59–60
Gordon, Gussie: death and burial, 77–78; illness and treatment, 74–77
Gordon, Stella: 77, 84, 87, 98–99

Gordon, Mrs. (mother): attitude toward children, 62–64; fear of wild tree and house, 52–53; reaction to lynching story, 4, 37–38, 49, 56–57; response to violence, 83–87; teachings of, 6, 35–36, 42
Granny Maumee (play), 336
Great Depression, 17, 18
Green, Paul, 220, 222, 332, 335, 337
Green Pastures (Play), 379n42
Gregory, Thomas Montgomery, 335–36, 382n113
Grey, Edgar M., 252
Guardian (Boston), 208, 214–15

Haldeman-Julius, Marcet, 262–63, 380n66
Hall, Prince, 9
Hancock, Gordon, 304, 381n94
Hansen, Harry, 220
Harding, Warren, 376n27
Harlem, 264–65; conditions of poor Black residents, 280–81; night life, 296; upper-class, 297
Harlem Renaissance, 1, 12–13, 206, 218, 378n24, 379n53
Harmon, Florence, 219, 378n19
Harmon, William, 312
Harriman, Harry J., 270, 273
Harris, Joel Chandler, 293
Harris, Patricia Roberts, 384n143
Hawkinsville, Georgia, 5, 39, 42, 374n3
Hayden, Harriet, 9
Hayden, Lewis, 9
Hayes, Roland, 229
Hazard, Alvira, 219, 378n19
Hearsey, Henry, 4
Hemingway, Ernest, 258, 276
Henkle, Henrietta Delancey, 384n142
Henry Bradley Plant, 3
Henson, Matthew, 381n81
The Herald of Freedom, 377n5
Herald-Tribune, 239, 302
Herndon, Angelo, 22, 317, 382n104
Heywood, Du Bose, 332, 336–37
Hines, Paul, 272
Hiss, Alger, 26
Hitler-Stalin pact of 1939, 2
hoecake, 375n16

INDEX 389

Holland, Spessard L., 383n132
Holstein, Casper, 380n60
Home to Harlem (McKay), 296–97, 379n51
Hoover, Herbert, 272
Horton, James Oliver, 370n31
Horton, Lois, 370n31
The House Behind the Cedars (Chestnutt), 293
housing, 62–64; race and class in, 59, 62; racism in, 68–70; segregation in 132–33. *See also* domestic domination
Hudson, Hosea: *Black Worker in the Deep South*, 26
Hudson Motor Car Company, 378n32
Hughes, Langston, 12–13, 224, 248, 251, 276, 288, 298, 300
Huksos Period, 376n24
Hurston, Zora Neale, 300
Hutton, Marcelline, 340

ILD. *See* International Labor Defense
ILGWU. *See* International Ladies Garment Workers Union
Imes, G. Lake, 322
immigrant communities, 64
In Abraham's Bosom (play), 220, 336, 338, 378n21
The Indignant Generation (Jackson), 372n67
inequality: academic, 166–70; domestic, 128, 132–33, 136; economic, 82, 121, 125; in employment, 59–60, 129–30; gendered labor roles, 202–3; health care and poverty, 74–77; housing conditions, 68–70; press access and literacy, 212; racial access to services, 76–77; in social treatment, 132–33. *See also* discrimination
Informer (Houston), 308
innocence, childhood: challenged by racial norms, 200–3; interracial friendship, 201–3
intergenerational trauma, 57–58
International Labor Defense (ILD), 23, 314, 330; Black workers, supporting, 282–83; conflict with NAACP, 286;

involvement in Scottsboro case, 284; Scottsboro defendants, aid to, 282
International Ladies Garment Workers Union (ILGWU), 21
interracial solidarity: operational tensions, 178–80; political necessity, 176–78
Isaacs, Edith R., 220
Isham, John W., 336, 383n115

Jackson, E. G., 25
Jackson, George, 365, 384n140
Jackson, Jonathan, 364–66
Jacobs-Jenkins, Branden, 383n114
Jenkins, David, 377n4
Jensen, Arthur Robert, 383n139
Jim Crow laws, 359–61
johnnycake, 375n16
John Reed Club, 20 Johnson, Charles S., 218, 219, 220, 234–35
Johnson, Georgia Douglas, 378n13
Johnson, Helene, 1, 11
Johnson, Henry Lincoln, 378n13
Johnson, James Weldon, 221–22, 265
Johnson, Mordecai Wyatt, 380n58
Johnson, Ronald Marbery, 370n40
Jones, Alice, 377n11
Jones, Lois Mailou, 11, 24
Journal and Guide, 210, 304, 306
journalism, 20, 212, 214–15, 282; sensationalism, 145–46, 148–49; social hierarchy in, 145–46, 148; yellow, 207–9. *See also* Negro press
A Journey in the Back Country (Olmsted), 362
A Journey in the Seaboard States (Olmsted), 362
A Journey Through Texas (Olmsted), 362
justice system: failure in rape case, 347–49

Keller, Helen, 378n22
Kelley, William, 252
King Tut's tomb, 376n21
Komsomol, 383n125
Ku Klux Klan, 216–17, 228; anti-union violence, 176, 178; infiltration tactics against, 180–88

labor. *See* Negro workers
Labor Defender, 22, 284
Lafayette Theatre, 379n34
Lane, Freddie, 350
The Lantern, 242
League of American Writers, 372n67
League of Struggle for Negro Rights (LSRN), 23, 282, 284, 314
Leftward, 20
Lenin, Vladimir, 382n110
Lenox Avenue, 381n80
Lewis, Sinclair, 380n67
Lewis, Theophilus, 252, 379n55
The Liberator, 9, 270
Lieberman, Robbie, 374n101
Locke, Alain, 7, 11, 218, 238
The Love of Landry (Dunbar), 295
Lovett, Sidney, 285–86
LSRN. *See* League of Struggle for Negro Rights
Lyles, Aubrey, 376n5
lynching, 90, 94, 165, 178; of Black man at Indian River house, 56–58; implied threats, 188–90; racial violence norms, 164–65; symbolic violence, 143; tree, memories of, 56–58. *See also individual incidents of lynching*

Macy, John, 220, 222–23, 378n22
Malone, Aaron, 254–55
Malone, Annie Turnbo, 380n59
Manhattan Casino, 380n68
marginalization, violence through, 172–75
marital discord: alienation in marriage, 154–56, 160–61; duties and pressure, 155–56, 160; isolation and resentment of spouse, 155–56, 160–61
Marxism, 15, 17
masculinity, 146, 149–50; and identity crisis, 125–26; insecure, violence and, 118–25; in journalism, 145–46; linked to race and economic identity, 114–17; reassertion of control, 137–40; self-worth linked to, 114–16; working-class, 145–46, 150, 152
McCarthy, Joseph, 25, 26

McCune, John, 348
McKay, Claude, 13, 296–97, 379n51
McKay, Claude, 13, 296–97
McQueen, William N., 353, 359
Mencken, H. L., 14, 206
Menos, Maurice, 268
Meroë, 376n23
The Messenger, 1, 12, 14, 206, 252
Metropolitan Life Insurance Tower, 378n31
Miletsky, Zebulon, 312
Miller, Flournoy Eakin, 376n5
Miller, Kelly, 211, 264, 278, 304, 377n9
Miller, May, 377n9
Mills, Nathaniel, 372n66
Mississippi Delta, 382n100
Mitchell, Verner, 13
Mooney, Thomas, 317, 382n104
Moore, Fred R., 216
Morgan, John Pierpont, Sr., 382n106
Morning Bulletin, 144–45
Moscow Daily News, 1, 23, 340
Moton, Robert Russa, 278, 322, 381n79
Mount Vernon Congregational Church, 285
Mulon Farm, battle of, 105–13
Murphy, Carl J., 216, 382n99
Murphy, John H., 378n17
Muse, Clarence, 25

NAACP. *See* National Association for the Advancement of Colored People
Nathan, George Jean, 206
The Nation, 1, 14, 251, 270
National Association for the Advancement of Colored People (NAACP), 18–19, 254, 281–82, 284–86, 305, 313–14
National Committee for the Defense of Political Prisoners, 22
National Negro Business League, 254
National Negro Congress, 17
National Recovery Act, 382n108
The National Reformer, 377n3
National Urban League, 13, 18, 220, 248, 305
Negro: Christianity and, 242–47;

denial of cultural contribution, 167–71; family life, 68–70; Gordon's mother's teachings on, 35–36; language, 71, 73; museum representations of, 171–74; new leadership, 276–83; oppression, 35–49, 178–79; racial identity, 35–49, 71, 73, 154, 158, 163; racial pride, 255–56; Reveren' Stanley, 46–49; self-criticism, 248–52; social progress, 248–57; social status and segregation, 39–42; unhealthy national culture, 298–99. *See also specific subjects*

Negro (Cunard), 27

Negro church, 243–45; inefficacy, 252–53; influence of, 304–5; wealth tied up in, 303. *See also* Christianity

Negro identity: and ancient civilization, 167–72; challenged by white scholars, 167–71; internalized color hierarchy, 114–16, 118; masculinity and self-worth, 114–17, 121–25; vindication of, 173–74

Negro leadership, 276–83; Black middle class as exploiters, 279–81; black politicians, 305; dominated by press, 304–5; editor-politicians, 303; entrenched, 301–2, 306–11; history, 277–81; NAACP criticism, 281–82; Negro workers, praised by, 282–83; parasitical leadership, 302–3; radical alternatives emerging, 282–83; "spiritual" leadership, 279

Negro masses. *See* Black masses

Negro novelist/writers, 11, 19–20, 238, 250, 252; 288–99; artistic expression, 240–41; disconnect from working class, 289, 291, 295; fiction writers, 292, 294–95; New York, 296; political struggle, 291–95; preacher who turned, 292–93; response to criticism, 239–41; training and education, 240; upper-class, 294; white and Black women, portrayals of, 289–90; working-class, 288, 299. *See also individual novelists*

Negro parasitism, 302

Negro preacher, 46–49, 281; characteristics of, 279; incompetency of, 247; self- criticism, 252

Negro press, 14, 233, 251, 266; Associated Negro Press, 212; growth and criticism, 206, 208, 214; history of, 206–17; political bias, 210–11; quantity *vs.* quality, 206; Recy Taylor case, 346, 349; religious skepticism, 211–12; and self-censorship, 233–34; social activism, 213; yellow journalism, 207–9

Negro society, 258–69; class divisions, 258–69; colorism, 259–60, 264–65, 266–67; conformity to white norms, 259–63; intragroup prejudice, 259–66; masses, 294–98, 302–3, 306; teachers, 267–69; Washington, DC, 264–69; women professionals, 267–69

Negro women, 268; color line among teachers, 328–29; cult of inferiority, 366–67; degradation of, 355; discrimination against Negro white-collar workers, 327; emancipation of, 360; fight for freedom of, 360; fighting for better conditions, 321; figures conceal terrific exploitation, 323–24; girls, 226–28, 237; group in domestic service, 322–23; intellectual achievements, 363–64; legal protection, lack of, 347–49; N.R.A. codes, 322; oppression by capitalism, 326–27; political repression of, 366–67; position of, 318–31; sexual violence against, 346–49; as slave-breeder, 355; social roles and resistance, 362–67; social status of, 354; unemployment, effects of, 329–30; unity of white and Negro workers, 324–25

Negro women workers: abstract figures of gains and losses for, 325; discrimination against, 319, 324, 327; domestic workers, largest group of, 323; exclusion from skilled and white-collar jobs, 328–29; exploitation in industrial labor, 319–22; in food and textile industries, 321–22; standard of living of,

Negro women workkers (*continued*) 326; unemployment, effects of, 329–30; unionization and rights, lack of, 323–25; unity of white and, 324–25; wage inequality, 319–23

Negro workers, 59–61, 297, 302, 305; changing psychology, 301; Communist Party support, 19, 282–83, 310–11; confining, 324; dehumanization of, 155–58; exploitation of, 277–78; labor hierarchy, 129–30; masses of, 316; massacre in Belgian Congo, 311; N.R.A. against, 322; Southern, 321; "stark realism," 337; state of, 277; white workers' racism, 277; writer of fiction, produced, 295

Negro World, 216–17

Negro Year Book, 290

Nell, W. C., 9

Nelson, Alice Dunbar, 222

New England Conservatory, 376n15

Newman, Dr., 73

New Masses, 1, 18, 276, 288

The New Negro, 218, 222, 335

New Negro Movement, 218, 379n53

New Orleans, 3–5, 35–49, 59, 68–81

newspapers: *Afro-American* (Baltimore), 209–11, 215–16, 236, 309; *Age* (New York), 210, 216, 229; *Courier* (Pittsburgh), 208–10, 212; *Defender* (Chicago), 207–15, 224, 304; *Defender* (Huston), 308. See also Negro press

New Theatre, 332

New Theatre League, 332

Nice Association, 285

Nicest Association for the Advantage of Certain Persons, 281

Nigger Heaven (Van Vechten), 222, 296, 378n23

Ninth Avenue (Bodenheim), 222, 378n28

The No 'Count Boy (play), 336

Northern, 359

Not Without Laughter (Hughes), 288, 298, 381n93

N.R.A. codes, 322

Nugent, Richard Bruce, 378n24

Nutt, A. B., 8

Oboznenko, P. E., 342

O'Brien, Hugh, 10

October Revolution, 326, 382n110

Octoroon (play), 338

The Octoroons, 335, 336

Ol' Man Adam an' His Chillun (Bradford), 379n42

Olmsted, Frederick Law, 362

Oneal, James, 16

O'Neill, Eugene, 276, 332, 335–36, 338, 383n118

Opportunity, 1, 14, 20, 114, 128, 239, 251, 255; dinner, 12–13, 218–23; fiction contest, 176

oppression, 16, 294, 315–16; Blacks and whites unite against, 18, 331; courage against, 2; masses fighting against, 28; political and economic, 20; racial, 168–71; ruling-class, 315; violence and, 96; of women, 318, 321, 326–27

Ortiz, Paul, 369n9

Owen, Chandler, 12, 252

Page, Thomas Nelson, 293

The Palladium of Liberty, 377n4

Palmer, Raymond H., 273

Parker House, 380n62

Patterson, William, 26

Peters, Paul, 332, 338

Pickens, Dean, 286–87

Pickens, William, 212, 284–87, 304, 377n10

Pittsburgh Courier, 208–9, 210, 212, 346

Plain Talk, 14, 248

police, 92–93; Borden's death, role in, 312–13; confrontation with Robert Charles, 82; harassment of Black youth, 193–99; racial profiling, 195–98; third-degree tactics, 195–96

Ponderosa Stomp Foundation, 369n11

Porgy (play), 336

Poro College, 380n59

The Promised Land (Fisher), 250, 379n50

prostitution, 340–45; abolition of, 344; new principles, 344–45; prostitutes taught to work, 345; tsarist

INDEX 393

heritage, 342–43; venereal diseases, decrease in, 343–44; Women's Curative Labor Prophylactorium, 345
Pulitzer, Joseph, 377n7
Pullman, George M., 379n45

The Quest of the Silver Fleece (DuBois), 294

race-consciousness, 208–10, 305, 312, 316
race relations: childhood perceptions of, 201–3; press role in, 207–17; societal conditioning, 200
race(s): ambiguity and identity, 73; betrayal and suspicion between, 54, 64; bias in publishing, 239–41; children's understanding of, 72–73; class distinctions within, 260; in housing, 59, 62; in marriage and social standing, 114–17; Northern *vs.* Southern perceptions, 155–56, 161; race-based violence, 82–94; and sexual stereotypes, 154, 163–64; terror tactics, 188–90. *See also* colorism
racism: in Boston, 9–10; in cultural heritage interpretation, 171–73; in drama and media, 333–38; in Hawkinsville, 5; in healthcare, 76–77; in housing, 68–70; inequality in employment, 59–60; institutional, 82–83, 86–87, 156, 158, 163, 166–70; internalized, 154, 164, 208–10; interpersonal, 71–72, 82–95, 123–25; in journalism, 207–8; learned behavior, 200; lynching of Black man, 56–68; Northern urban manifestations, 192–99; Northern *vs.* Southern manifestations, 155–56, 161; in NYPD, 195–98; self-perception and relationships, 125–27; systemic, 82–95, 128, 132; urban *vs.* rural, 154, 158, 163; verbalized as abuse, 123–25

Randolph, A. P., 12, 252, 381n81
rape: Florida execution case (white victim), 351–53; media double standard, 346, 348–49; use in racial terror, 351–53, 359; white prostitutes, 286
Recy Taylor rape case, 24–5, 346–49, 366; abduction and assault, 346–48, 351–55; grand jury decision, 348–49, 359; hunting attackers, 347–48; lack of justice for, 348–49; media response, 349, 361; racial violence, 355–61; rapists, 350; support from Black press, 349, 359–61
Reeve, Karl Marx, 21
The Reigns of King Alpha and Adabon (Blackson), 293
Reliance Manufacturing Company, 322
religion: Christianity, 242–47; proposed new religion, 246–47
Resilient Russian Women in the 1920s & 1930s (Hutton), 340
Reynolds, Bruce, 307, 382n96
Rhinelander, Leonard "Kip," 377n11
Rhodes, Eugene Washington, 382n98
The Rider of Dreams (play), 336
Ridley, Florida Ruffin, 11
Rights of All, 377n2
The Rise and Progress of the Kingdoms of Light and Darkness (Blackson), 293
Robert Charles incident. *See* Charles, Robert
Robeson, Paul, 12, 381n81
Rockefeller, John D., Jr., 381n81
Rockland Palace, 380n68
Rogers, Joel Augustus (J. A. R.), 206, 252, 379n54
Roll, Sweet Chariot (play), 336–38
Roosevelt, Franklin D., 382n108
Roosevelt, Theodore, 258
Roses, Lorraine Elena, 10, 13

Sam Browne belts, 381n77
Saturday Evening Quill, 1, 19, 144, 154, 166, 288, 318
Saturday Night Quill Club, 1, 10–12, 218–19, 238
Schalk, Gertrude, 11
Schryver, E. W., 50

Schuyler, George S., 22, 252, 256–57, 298, 304
Scott, William Alexander, II, 382n96
Scottsboro Boys, 284
Scottsboro case, 282, 284–87, 317, 330
Scottsboro Unity Defense League, 22
Scribner's Magazine, 1, 14, 258
segregation: in class and housing, 132–33; in friendships, 82, 95; neighborhood divisions, 71–72; within political systems, 211; of public space, 84, 201; racial, 59, 62–64; residential separation, 150–52; in U.S. Army, 104–5. *See also* racism
self-criticism, 252
self-esteem, 128, 132–33, 136
self-help, 254-5
self-worth: class and masculinity, linked to, 114–16; crisis and emotional unraveling, 125–27; threatened by racial dynamics, 118–25
Seminole Indian tribe, 3
Simon, the Cyrenian (play), 336
Simpson, Jane, 357–59, 361
Simpson, John, 357–59
Sinclair, Upton, 276
skin tone hierarchy, 225–28
Sklar, George, 332, 338
slavery, 230–31, 243, 289–94, 319; children born in, 290; history of, 289–92; institution of, 289, 290
social hierarchy, 71–72, 128, 132, 136; in journalism, 145–46, 148
Socialism, 15–16
social isolation, 155–57
social mobility, 59–60
Soledad Brothers, 383n140
soldiers, 104–13
Southern Worker, 381n82
Southland Manufacturing Company, 322
Soviet Union, 297, 309, 311, 318, 340; Gordon's time in Moscow, 23–24; October Revolution, 326; unity of white and Negro workers, 331; views on race and labor, 23. *See also* prostitution
Sparks, Chauncey, 25, 346, 353, 359–60

Spingarn, Joel Elias, 379n33
Stalin, Joseph, 326
Stanley, Reverend, 46–49; description, 46; impact on Gordon, 49; lynching and burning, 48–49
Statler, E. M., 381n78
Statler Hotel, 381n78
Steele, Wilbur Daniel, 221
stereotypes: behavioral compliance with, 225–27, 230–37; fear of confirming, 225–26, 232, 236; of jungle heritage, 239–40; sexual, 154, 163–64. *See also* racism
Stevedore (drama), 332, 338–39, 383n120
Stewart, Maria, 9
Stoddard, Lothrop, 376n27
The Story of the World's Literature (Macy), 220, 378n22
Stowe, Harriet Beecher, 332–34
Strong, Anna Louise, 23
Sullivan, Anne, 378n22
Survey Graphic, 218
Sweet, William Ellery, 378n30

Taft, William Howard, 216, 378n13
Tageblatt, 375n32
Taylor, Recy. *See* Recy Taylor rape case
teaster, 70–71
theater. *See* Black theater in America
Theatre Arts Magazine, 220
There Is Confusion (Fauset), 218
They Shall Not Die (play), 338–39, 383n119
Thompson, Eloise Bibb, 378n25
Thompson, Noah D., 221, 378n25
Thurman, Wallace, 11, 238, 248, 251, 288, 298
Timucua, 3
Toomer, Jean, 248–50
TOPLEV program, 374n108
Torrence, Frederick Ridgely, 336, 383n116
Torsuyeva, N. A., 342
Townsend, Charles, 333
"Trees" (Kilmer), 376n19
Tribune, 210, 215, 266, 308
Tropic Death, 222
Trotter, William Monroe, 214–15

INDEX

Turner, Bishop, 88, 92
Turner, Dr., 73, 76–77
Turner, Henry McNeal, 375n29

The Uncalle (Dunbar), 295
Uncle Tom's Cabin (play), 333–36, 338–39
Union, 252, 256

Valentino, Rudolph, 376n8
Van Vechten, Carl, 220–21, 295–97
verbal abuse, 134–36
violence, 118–25, 176, 178; against African Americans, 88, 91–92; domestic, 123–24; fear of, 154–58, 161–63; and lynching, 35–49; race-based, 82–94; racial, 164–65; racial violence in Recy Taylor rape case, 355–61; resistance strategies, 180–88; sexualized, 154, 163, 346–49; symbolic, 143; through marginalization, 172–75; against white professor, 172
The Voice of Missions, 88, 92, 375n29
The Voice of the People, 375n29

Walker, David, 9
Walker, A'Lelia, 380n69
Walker, Madame C. J., 380n59
Washington, Booker T., 6, 303, 377n9
Washington, DC, 7–8
Washington, Fredi, 25
Washington, Mary Helen, 18
Webb, Frank J., 288, 295
Weems, Samuel, 286
West, Dorothy, 1, 11, 24
Western Deffufa, 376n22
Wexley, John, 338
Wharton, Clifton, 229–30
Wharton, Edith, 258
Wheatley, Phillis, 9
Whip (Chicago), 208, 304
Whipper, William, 377n3
white Communists, 178–80

white supremacy, 20, 355–57, 361; defense narratives, 164; regional variations, 155–56, 161
white women: cult of, 351–61; fear of Black men, 155–58, 161–63; as Northern outsiders in South, 155–65; racial privilege, 164; vulnerability narratives, 154, 163–64
Wilk, John, 377n1
Williams, A. Wilberforce, 215
Williams, James, 350
Williams, William Carlos, 276
Wilson, Butler R., 314–17
Wilson, Hugo, 347–48
Winston, Henry, 26, 28, 365
women, status of: in Black domestic life, 114–17; expectations vs. autonomy, 121–24; inequality: gendered labor role, 202–3; right to defend, 164; suppression of self-expression, 233–34. *See also* Negro women
Women's Curative Labor Prophylactorium, 344
Wood, L. Hollingsworth, 220
Woodson, Carter G., 255
workers. *See also* Negro women workers; Negro workers
Workers Library Publishers, 318
Workers' Unemployment Insurance Bill, H.R. 2827, 329
working-class masculinity, 145–46, 150, 152
workplace hierarchy, 145–49
World, 307–8
World-Telegram, 378n20
World War I: African American soldiers in, 104–13; German prisoners of war, 108, 112; No Man's Land, 105–6
Wright, Richard, 12–13, 276

Y. M. C. A., 244
Young Communist League, 327, 345
Young Pioneers, 383n125

LOUIS J. PARASCANDOLA, a native of Brooklyn, New York, has been a Professor of English at Long Island University, Brooklyn for over thirty years. He holds a PhD in english from the CUNY Graduate Center, an MLS in library science from Pratt University, and an MA in history from St. John's University. He has published articles in several scholarly journals and has edited seven books on African American and/or Afro-Caribbean authors as well as one on Coney Island.

www.ingramcontent.com/pod-product-compliance
Lightning Source LLC
Chambersburg PA
CBHW031411230426
43668CB00007B/275